LEADING
THE WAY

*THE TRUE GOSPEL AND
HOW TO SHARE IT*

AN INSTRUCTOR'S MANUAL
FOR GROUP STUDY

WITH THE WORKBOOK QUESTIONS
AND SUGGESTED ANSWERS

DONALD E. JONES, PHD

J & A BOOK PUBLISHERS
www.jabookpublishers.com

(C) 2017 Donald E. Jones, PhD

Printed in the United States of America

All rights reserved. No part of this book may be reproduced in any form without permission in writing from the author, except in the case of brief quotations embodied in critical articles or reviews.

All Scripture quotations are from the World English Bible. This version was selected because it is in the public domain and can be quoted without limit. A personal translation of a verse or passage will be designated with (DEJ).

ISBN-13: 978-1946368126
ISBN-10: 1946368121

DEDICATION

I dedicate this book to my Savior and Lord Jesus Christ. He has been with me every step of my journey upon the Earth, and I so look forward to being in His presence forever and ever.

CONTENTS
(WORKBOOK QUESTIONS FOLLOW EACH CHAPTER)

Introduction to the Instructor's Manual	1
Introduction to the Personal Study	12
Introduction to the Workbook	15
Chapter - 1. Know the Kingdom Plan (Study)	17
Chapter - 1. Know the Kingdom Plan (Wkbk)	39
Chapter - 2. Herald the Epic Message (Study)	49
Chapter - 2. Herald the Epic Message (Wkbk)	81
Chapter - 3. Accept the Divine Mandate (Study)	91
Chapter - 3. Accept the Divine Mandate (Wkbk)	137
Chapter - 4. Allow God to Be Sovereign (Study)	147
Chapter - 4. Allow God to Be Sovereign (Wkbk)	175
Chapter - 5. Allow Man to Be Challenged (Study)	185
Chapter - 5. Allow Man to Be Challenged (Wkbk)	207
Chapter - 6. Persist in Watchful Prayer (Study)	217
Chapter - 6. Persist in Watchful Prayer (Wkbk)	237
Chapter - 7. Proclaim the Proper Message (Study)	247
Chapter - 7. Proclaim the Proper Message (Wkbk)	297
Chapter - 8. Utilize Your Interests and Skills (Study)	307
Chapter - 8. Utilize Your Interests and Skills (Wkbk)	359

Chapter - 9. Welcome an Initial Response (Study)	369
Chapter - 9. Welcome an Initial Response (Wkbk)	401
Chapter - 10. Pursue a Saving Faith (Study)	411
Chapter - 10. Pursue a Saving Faith (Wkbk)	457
Chapter - 11. Expect a Dramatic Reaction (Study)	466
Chapter - 11. Expect a Dramatic Reaction (Wkbk)	485
Chapter - 12. Counter with a Loving Attitude (Study)	495
Chapter - 12. Counter with a Loving Attitude (Wkbk)	549
Chapter - 13. Disciple with a Serious Intent (Study)	559
Chapter - 13. Disciple with a Serious Intent (Wkbk)	611
Conclusion to the Personal Study	621
Conclusion to the Workbook	625
Conclusion to this Manual	627

ACKNOWLEDGMENTS

I want to thank my wonderful and gracious wife Carol who has supported me in this ministry with sacrifice, enthusiasm, encouragement, and accountability. Most of all, she has been a constant blessing because of her willingness to listen. I was always sharing with her the truths God had been teaching me as I studied His word and wrote this book. It consumed many hours. Thank you, Carol and I deeply love you.

I want to thank my son Gregory R. Jones for volunteering to be the primary editor of this important book. Without his time and effort in painstakingly and meticulously going over every word and every sentence checking and rechecking the sentence structure and grammar, I would not have been able to complete it. Thank you for your ministry to me. I love you my son.

I want to thank my other children, Krista, Matt, and Kara for their love for Christ and His Word and their willingness to live for Him. I love you all.

AN INSTRUCTOR'S MANUAL

Introduction to this Manual

The purpose of this instructor's manual is to help the group leader facilitate the study and discussion of the group books with the same title. Since you have been given such an important responsibility as leading a group of Christians in the study of the Bible, I would like to share with you some principles utilized by the apostle Paul in his teaching and preaching ministry. These will assist you in your time with the believers God has given to you to minister to. These are in no particular order, but all are important. The Lord does not expect us to be perfect in them, but to simply do the very best that we can. If we are willing to do our part, then He will do His part through His Spirit.

In 1 Corinthians 12:5-7, Paul explains, "There are various kinds of service, and the same Lord." Here Paul, the apostle, acknowledges that the saints can minister to one another in a variety of ways. Then he adds, "There are various kinds of workings, but the same God, who works all things in all." As each person ministers, they will have a different impact than others, but it is all the work of the Holy Spirit. Finally, he continues, "But to each one is given the manifestation of the Spirit for the profit of all." Your service in this ministry is coming from the giftedness which is a work of God's Spirit to benefit all. Do the best you can with these principles and let the Spirit do the rest.

1 Corinthians 12:5-7
There are various kinds of service, and the same Lord. There are various kinds of workings, but the same God, who works all things in all. But to each one is given the manifestation of the Spirit for the profit of all.

Your Unceasing Prayer

Paul prayed for the Christians that he served in God's Word. In Romans 1:9-10, he writes, For God is my witness, whom I serve in my spirit in the Good News of his Son, how unceasingly I make mention of you always in my prayers, requesting, if by any means now at last I may be prospered by the will of God to come to you." Paul depended on prayer and so should you. Pray for every person in your study by name and ask God to work powerfully through His Word as you share it in these materials.

Romans 1:9-10
For God is my witness, whom I serve in my spirit in the Good News of his Son, how unceasingly I make mention of you always in my prayers, requesting, if by any means now at last I may be prospered by the will of God to come to you.

Your Persistent Practice

As Paul taught the Scriptures, he always practiced what he preached. As you study the biblical principles in these books you should practice them yourself. The believers will look to you to see if you are attempting to apply the truths as they are. In Philippians 3:17, Paul asserted, "Brothers, be imitators together of me, and note those who walk this way, even as you have us for an example." He explained to the Philippians that not only were they to listen to what he said but watch how he practiced them. In the discussions, you should describe how you are applying the principles also.

Philippians 3:17
Brothers, be imitators together of me, and note those who walk this way, even as you have us for an example.

Your Sound Doctrine

These materials stand on their own in regard to the proper handling of God's Word. You merely have to be consistently staying within the bounds of this study. Often times, believers will desire to share opinions about what these Scriptures may mean based on personal feelings and preferences. Yet, the Bible is written by God and should be studied in light of what He meant the various Bible passages to say and how they might apply them. It is important that the discussion portion of the study remain within the limits of application rather than interpretation. I have spent many carefully interpreting the texts themselves and am confident that these are God's truths. In 1 Timothy 4:6-7, Paul writes to Timothy, his son in the faith now a pastor, "If you instruct the brothers of these things, you will be a good servant of Christ Jesus, nourished in the words of the faith, and of the good doctrine which you have followed. But refuse profane and old wives' fables.

1 Timothy 4:6-7
If you instruct the brothers of these things, you will be a good servant of Christ Jesus, nourished in the words of the faith, and of the good doctrine which you have followed. But refuse profane and old wives' fables. Exercise yourself toward godliness.

Exercise yourself toward godliness." The word translated "good" means "sound" and speaks of the solid truths and principles of the Scriptures rather than human opinions of what people may feel they mean to them.

Your Confidential Interaction

You should set up from the very beginning of the study that what is shared is confidential. There are times for public discussion for all to hear, but in small groups it is best to keep things private. In Acts 23:18-20, Paul had been arrested and his nephew had found out there was a plot to ambush and kill him. So, Paul has him taken to the commander. Luke records what happened next, "So he took him, and brought him to the commanding officer, and said, 'Paul, the prisoner, summoned me and asked me to bring this young man to you, who has something to tell you.'" Now, notice what the commander does, "The commanding officer took him by the hand, and going aside, asked him privately, 'What is it that you have to tell me?' He said, 'The Jews have agreed to ask you to bring Paul down to the council tomorrow, as though intending to inquire somewhat more accurately concerning him.'" Here, Paul's privacy is guarded for his protection. You should guard the privacy of the members of the group.

Acts 23:18-20
So, he took him [Paul], and brought him to the commanding officer, and said, "Paul...summoned me and asked me to bring this young man to you. He has something to tell you." The commanding officer took him by the hand, and going aside, asked him privately, "What is it that you have to tell me?" He said, "The Jews have agreed to ask you to bring Paul down to the council tomorrow, as though intending to inquire somewhat more accurately concerning him.

Paul also encouraged Pastor Timothy to exhort his flock not to become involved in any gossip (1 Timothy 3:11; 5:13). The sharing of difficulties outside the group can certainly lead to this grievous behavior. Please check with the laws in your land and the policies in your local church concerning when confidentially can and cannot be breached. Usually, this involves the harming of oneself or others.

1 Timothy 3:11
Their wives...be reverent, not slanderers, temperate, and faithful in all things.

1 Timothy 5:13
Besides, they also learn to be idle, going about from house to house. Not only idle, but...gossips and busybodies, saying things which they ought not.

Your Flexible Strategy

Sometimes you will not be able to stick directly to the materials because you will have a "teachable moment" occur. Please take advantage of these moments. These may involve a particular situation shared or even a difficulty occurring on the day or week of the study. It is perfectly fine to depart occasionally. It is best to not allow members of the group to dominate it due to frequent issues. If this occurs, team them up with others outside the group to assist them individually. In Acts 17:23, Paul entered Antioch and was struck by all of the statues of idols in the city.

Acts 17:23
For as I passed along and observed the objects of your worship, I also found an altar with this inscription: 'TO AN UNKNOWN GOD.' What therefore you worship in ignorance, I announce to you.

He found one identified as an "unknown god" and shifted his preaching strategy to begin with his proclamation of the "unknown god" as the God of the Universe. Luke records Paul's words to the leaders of that city, "For as I passed along, and observed the objects of your worship, I found also an altar with this inscription: 'TO AN UNKNOWN GOD.' What therefore you worship in ignorance, this I announce to you.'" He was flexible. His letters indicate that he geared them toward particular issues the churches were having rather than simple methodical instruction. We do know that he taught systematically, but his letters allow a real flexibility.

Your Loving Relationships

Christians are brothers and sisters in Christ and a study such as this can establish and develop these relationships as the saints interact with the Word, you, and each other. In 1 Thessalonians 3:12, Paul speaks of the love the Thessalonian believers had for one another and for him. He describes his prayer that they would grow in this, "And the Lord make you to increase and abound in love one toward another, and toward all men, even as we also do toward you." A group of believers in a small group centered on the Word of God is a great place to grow. The believers can also practice the "one anothers" so often spoken of in Paul's letters.

1 Thessalonians 3:12
May the Lord make you to increase and abound in love toward one another, and toward all men, even as we also do toward you.

Romans 12:10
In love of the brothers be tenderly affectionate to one another; in honor preferring one another.

Romans 14:19
So then, let's follow after things which make for peace, and things by which we may build one another up.

Romans 15:7
Therefore accept one another, even as Christ also accepted you, to the glory of God.

Galatians 6:2
Bear one another's burdens, and so fulfill the law of Christ.

Ephesians 4:32
And be kind to one another, tender hearted, forgiving each other, just as God also in Christ forgave you.

Your Troubles Shared

You should also be willing to share your difficulties in the areas you all are studying in the Scriptures. This should be done with common sense, so you do not undermine your own testimony as you are leading the group. It is important that members of your study group know that applying these principles are a battle and not something we simply decide to do. In 1 Corinthians 9:26-27, Paul speaks of the struggle he had with his own sin, "I therefore run like that, as not uncertainly. I fight like that, as not beating the air, but I beat my body and bring it into submission, lest by any means, after I have preached to others, I myself should be rejected." Here, he compares his struggle within himself as a boxing match between his spirit and his flesh. He was constantly fighting it to be holy and righteous.

1 Corinthians 9:26-27
I therefore run like that, not aimlessly. I fight like that, not beating the air, but I beat my body and bring it into submission, lest by any means, after I... preached to others, I myself should be rejected.

Your Intent Listening

As everyone shares make sure you listen intently to the other group members as they share the answers to the many questions in the workbook. Sometimes, teachers get so caught up in what they want to say that they do not listen to the group members. Listening provides an opportunity to share in the joys and sorrows of those involved in the group. In 1 Thessalonians 3:6, Paul explains to the church the news he had heard about them from Timothy, "But when Timothy came just now to us from you, and brought us glad news of your faith and love, and that you have good memories of us always, longing to see us, even as we also long to see you." These words convey Paul's desire to know how they were and what they were experiencing.

1 Thessalonians 3:6
But when Timothy came just now to us from you, and brought us glad news of your faith and love, and that you have good memories of us always, longing to see us, even as we also long to see you.

Your Safe Openness

Not all believers are at the same level in their spiritual maturity. It is important that each respect the other as they share. Paul explains this principle in 1 Corinthians 8:1. He writes, "Now concerning things sacrificed to idols: We know that we all have knowledge. Knowledge puffs up, but love builds up." Here, he is not saying we should not be knowledgeable in the Scriptures of course we should. The Bible is what helps us grow as Christians. He is describing believers who look down upon and are impatient with the biblical or spiritual immaturity of other saints. Instead, they should be building them up in their love. This means loving tolerance as they lovingly correct the mistakes in their knowledge and the patterns of behavior in their Christian lives which may not be mature. You will have to guide the members of your group in this area. If you have to, you can take some aside and explain that it is through love that one helps another become more like Christ. This does not mean we are not to correct believers who are in error or in sin.

1 Corinthians 8:1
Now concerning things sacrificed to idols: We know that we all have knowledge. Knowledge puffs up, but love builds up.

Your Gentle Correction

In any discussion there will be a wide variety of ideas and experiences that people draw upon that might be different than others. These should be embraced as the Holy Spirit leads. The only limitation on this should be when members say something that is in direct opposition to the Scriptures. These false notions and ideas should be corrected gently. If error is left without any comment, then some of the less mature members may believe them and have errors in their

Scriptural understanding. This is not very popular today as people are often allowed to share anything they desire, truth or error, without correction because they are entitled to their opinion. This is not God's way. The Lord's opinion is what matters most. In 2 Timothy 2:25, Paul explains to Timothy how to deal with error, "In gentleness correcting those who oppose him." The apostle Paul spoke of those who opposed the sound teaching of Timothy from the Word. It cannot be allowed to continue because error destroys. Then Paul adds, "Perhaps God may give them repentance leading to a full knowledge of the truth."

2 Timothy 2:25
In gentleness correcting those who oppose him: perhaps God may give them repentance leading to a full knowledge of the truth.

As you or members of the group gently correct people, the Lords will work and turn them from the error to the full knowledge of the truth. If you are not sure if someone said something that may not be correct, you will have to consult some resources to help you. Then when you are ready, you can gently bring up the topic at the beginning of a study and correct it. If it is concerning differences among churches, then you will have to take the position of the church sponsoring the group.

Your Limited Discussion

As you follow these study books, there may be those who may want to discuss controversial, philosophical, or political issues. You must gently, but firmly guide them back to the study. Why? What God says is what matters in the meeting. He speaks through his Holy Scriptures, and this must have priority. This would include questions that are off topic. In 1 Timothy 1:4, Paul asserts, "And not to pay attention to myths and endless genealogies, which cause disputes, rather than God's stewardship, which is in faith." Your stewardship is to deliver the Word of God to others, not become involved in endless discussions that go nowhere. To respond to such people you might say, "That's a good question or issue and let's talk about that after the meeting."

1 Timothy 1:4
And not to pay attention to myths and endless genealogies, which cause disputes, rather than God's stewardship, which is in faith.

Your Constant Encouragement

When people are deal with life-changing principles from God's Word, they will need much encouragement to keep trying to follow the Word. They must battle old habits and notions which may give them trouble. Your encouragement can go a long way in helping them continue trying to apply these supernatural principles. In Acts 15, the church had dealt with a major controversy over the salvation of Gentiles. When the decision was made, Paul and Barnabas were sent to share what had been decided. This encouraged the saints greatly. In verses 30-31, Luke records, "So, when they were sent off, they came to Antioch." This refers to the church in that location. Then he adds, "Having gathered the multitude together, they delivered the letter. When they had read it, they rejoiced over the encouragement."

Acts 15:30-31
So, when they were sent off, they came to Antioch. Having gathered the multitude together, they delivered the letter. When they had read it, they rejoiced over the encouragement.

In Ephesians 6, Paul calls the Christian life a battle against dark forces. The saints will need the encouragement to continue on in their growth in Christ in the areas they are studying.

Ephesians 6:11-12
Put on the whole armor of God, that you may be able to stand against the wiles of the devil. For our wrestling is not against flesh and blood, but against the principalities, against the powers, against the world's rulers of the darkness of this age, and against the spiritual forces of wickedness in the heavenly places.

Your Loving Nurture

This time in God's Word is a time of nurturing the faith of others. When Paul ministered to the Thessalonians and then left, he discovered that they had been growing immensely in Christ. When he wrote to them, he described the manner in which he served them. In 1 Thessalonians 2:7, he wrote, "But we were gentle among you, like a nursing mother cherishes her own children." He ministered to them with the purpose of nurturing them in the faith. His way was that of a loving mother nurturing her own children not a harsh father that is always disciplining them. We must lead in a nurturing and cherishing manner.

1 Thessalonians 2:7
But we were gentle among you, like a nursing mother cherishes her own children.

These are just a few of the numerous principles one could apply to their teaching ministry. I encourage you to gather some resources and continue this study of this subject on your own if needed. Carefully look over the format of the books and their accompanying workbooks. I have provided the basic answers to the questions, and you can add to them as you wish. I suggest as a format that each member of the group reads that chapter and fills out the questions in the workbook the week before. Then open with a short prayer and go through the questions one by one. If there is time, you can share prayer requests or have refreshments. I would focus on the study first, so you do not get sidetracked and use up the valuable time in God's Word.

Introduction to the Personal Study

In *A Tale of Two Cities*, Charles Dickens wrote, "It was the best of times, it was the worst of times, it was the age of wisdom, it was the age of foolishness, it was the epoch of belief, it was the epoch of incredulity, it was the season of Light, it was the season of Darkness, it was the spring of hope, it was the winter of despair, we had everything before us, we had nothing before us, we were all going direct to heaven, we were all going direct the other way-in short, the period was so far like the present period that some of its noisiest authorities insisted on its being received, for good or for evil, in the superlative degree of comparison only. The world is in chaos." Indeed, the world is in chaos but not as the author imagines. The world is in the chaos of unbelief.

This chaos has caused numerous problems for man both within and outside of himself. For some, the chaos affords opportunities for wisdom, belief, light, and hope in the good news of Jesus Christ; unfortunately, for most it becomes a time of foolishness, incredulity, darkness, and despair in this life and the life to come. For the problems of this life, man turns often to counselors, therapists, friends, physicians, and others for help, comfort, and guidance. These professionals and others may give some solace with some solutions for this life, but only true Christians utilizing the Word of God can provide real supernatural solutions with comfort for this life and the life to come.

One part of Dickens' statement was not true, "We were all going direct to heaven, we were all going direct the other way." Few are going direct to heaven, and many are going the other way. In Matthew 7:13-14, Jesus said that men were to enter in the narrow gate. The gate to destruction is wide and broad; but to life, it is narrow and restricted. Few enter by it. This verse demands that the good news must be the foundation upon which all other aspects of the relationships of believers with unbelievers must build. In Matthew 16:26, the Lord declares, "For what will it profit a man, if he gains the whole world, and forfeits his life [soul]? Or what will a man give in exchange for his life?" Jesus indicates that a man will profit nothing even if he gains everything the world can offer in this life but loses his life in eternity.

Christians cannot love someone into the kingdom of God; they must present the gospel. Christians may help, even give advice and money to those unsaved, but what have those unbelievers gained when they have lost their soul to hell for all eternity? The saints can definitely bless their city and its citizens by cleaning up the trash, rebuilding homes, finding shelter for the homeless, and providing food to the needy which are all good deeds. Yet, without the gospel presented and accepted, all unbelievers in the city will perish in their sins into an eternity of despair and darkness. Therefore, the first and most important blessing and aid churches can offer as they view the needy world is the gospel of Jesus Christ. This would be a truly compassionate response.

The Bible calls for believers to be courageous Christians involved in a lifetime of witness. There is a joy that comes from being used by God to bring someone to His Son. It is an experience I have had on many occasions, and the feeling of being involved in someone entering into eternal life can be unimaginable. This evangelism book provides the tools necessary to share the true message of the good news. This book is for Christians who desire a deeper understanding of evangelism: what it is and how to do it.

This book is a completely original work on sharing the gospel and evangelism. It is not based on other books that I have read and simply collated or edited. To produce this critical written work, I carefully read through the entire New Testament verse by verse. As I was reading, I identified and categorized every individual verse or passage dealing in some way with the gospel. As I studied, many categories were built from the individual passages, rather than some set of preconceived notions. These categories became the biblical principles found in each chapter of this book. All biblical passages cited were meticulously studied in their historical, grammatical, and scriptural contexts.

Once my interpretations were complete, I compared them to the interpretation of other commentators both past and present. Finally, I compared my interpretation of the biblical passages to the historical interpretation of the evangelical church. I attempted to stay away from the typical study cycle of some in Christianity. Often times, when Christians desire to study a topic, idea, or doctrine, they simply read a book already written about it. The book they read is usually based on a book or books that others wrote. This cycle may go on for several generations. This continues until all the information passed from book to book becomes extremely limited and incomplete. I have ventured away from this approach to broaden the...church's understanding of this important teaching.

One last thought. At the end of each chapter, I discuss an experience I have had sharing the gospel. Due to the desire for every situation to be fully confidential when it involved others, I have added or subtracted details so no one can be identified. Also, I have mixed together common elements I have seen, details from books and films, bits from my own life and the lives of people I have known, and thoughts from my imagination to create an evangelistic situation where biblical principles discussed in the chapters can fully be applied. I have seen every one of these principles used in real life situations to share the gospel and see people come to Christ. These blueprints of the Lord God described in the Scriptures are powerful, applicable, and will change lives through the Holy Spirit. Read the book. Study the Scriptures contained within it. Share the gospel. Be prepared to be used by God. Watch for the fruits of your labor. Trust in His Spirit to lead you (2 Timothy 2:7).

AN INSTRUCTOR'S MANUAL

Introduction to the Workbook

This workbook is designed to aid in the comprehension and application of the truths from the Scriptures which are found in the book of the same name. It has a question-and-answer format because asking questions was a powerful teaching method that the Lord used to reveal God's divine truth. Jesus asked over one hundred and thirty questions as He instructed the people of God and others. These are only the recorded ones. We can only speculate as to how many questions He might have actually asked. The Lord used His questioning techniques to prompt His listeners to focus, understand, analyze, evaluate, and apply the principles He was proclaiming to them. The same has been done in this workbook.

In John chapter six, through His healing ministry, the Lord Jesus had gathered a large crowd from the surrounding villages and towns who were following Him and fed over five thousand of them from a few loaves and fish in a boy's basket. The people were so astounded by the miracle that they thought they should take Jesus by force and make him king. As a result, Jesus left the crowd by Himself. The disciples took one of the boats and ventured across the Sea of Galilee at night. It was at this time Jesus walked in the water, was received into the boat, and it was immediately at the other side. When morning came the crowds found Him in the city of Capernaum having searched everywhere. John records their first question. In John 6:25, it says, "When they found him on the other side of the sea, they asked him, 'Rabbi, when did you come here?'"

Jesus knew what was in their hearts and acknowledged that they had come for more bread. He urged them to stop seeking the food for their bodies and instead the food for their souls which he could provide. They disregarded what Jesus declared and asked Him to bring bread out of heaven as the prophet Moses had done. They wanted their physical needs met, not their spiritual. When the Lord Jesus refused, they begged for the power to create their own physical bread.

Then, He claimed that they needed to believe in Him and receive eternal life. Utilizing the bread as an analogy, the Lord proclaimed that He was the "bread out of heaven" and they needed to eat His flesh and drink His blood (possess Him spiritually) to have eternal life. They thought they already possessed eternal life as Jews, why would they need to Him to be saved? They needed Him for a miracle. With this, some of his many followers (not the twelve) left.

Then, Jesus asks the first of two penetrating questions. In John 6:61, the apostle writes, "But Jesus knowing in himself that his disciples murmured at this, said to them, 'Does this cause you to stumble?'" He knew some had followed Him only for what they could receive from Him in this life (Judas is implied here also). Yet, this was not why He came. As many left, Jesus ask the next one to His disciples alone. In John 6:67-69, His question and their response are described, "Jesus said therefore to the twelve, 'You don't also want to go away, do you?' Simon Peter answered him, 'Lord, to whom would we go? You have the words of eternal life. We have come to believe and know that you are the Christ, the Son of the living God.'" Here, Peter shows they were true followers. They needed Him for His Words first.

Their confusion was not over the eating and drinking His blood but over eternal life coming only from Him. The Lord used questions to discover their belief. His questions helped them focus, understand, analyze, evaluate, and apply truth. May these do the same for you in this book.

AN INSTRUCTOR'S MANUAL

Chapter 1

Know the Kingdom Plan

This plan that redeems was ordained in eternity past and fully revealed to man over thousands of years in the Old and New Testaments. It is an amazing story.

A Typical Scenario

Have you ever been in a situation that was something like the following? Whenever you pull up in your driveway, you see your neighbor sitting out in front of his house. You are busy and you hardly notice him. Every once in a while, you think to yourself, "Maybe I should go over and talk to him about the Lord?" Once you shut the door and settle down in the house, the thought usually fades away. In this chapter, we will learn that your next-door neighbor was created to be in fellowship with the Triune God. Unfortunately, due to Adam's rebellion, your neighbor was born in sin. If the man received the Lord, he would be given all the blessings of heaven and experience what you have. After you learn these powerful truths, perhaps this same neighborhood experience could look quite different.

Now, you decide every day when you arrive at home, you will simply see him as lost in sin and yet created to be with God. You will ask the Lord Jesus Christ to give you great boldness to start a conversation with him. After a few days, you begin to wave to him before you go into the house. Then you shout, "How's it going?" Later, you strike up a conversation about his lawn. You might ask him how he gets his lawn so green. You continue to view him solely from the perspective that he was created to fellowship with God not spend his life in sin.

One evening, you notice he left his garage door open, so you decide to knock on his door to inform him. He looks at you and asks, "How come you are such a friendly neighbor?" Your moment comes and you casually respond that you are a Christian. You explain to him that you want to show your neighbors that Jesus is in your life as much as you can. Then, he inquires, "Who is Jesus Christ?" Now, you share the good news.

Though this is an imaginary scenario, it is very typical of the kinds of situations we find ourselves in where the gospel can be shared, but because we do not know or perhaps are not cognizant of the kingdom plan, we miss the opportunity to share the gospel. Man was created to become a kingdom for God's Son. When man fell, he lost all the benefits of that plan. Understanding this plan can motivate us to share this good news. Then God stepped in and redeemed man by the death of Jesus, His only Son, and man was given even more benefits as he chooses to believe in Him. This brings us to the first principle which involves knowing this plan.

A Scriptural Principle

For Christians to share the gospel they must know and understand the kingdom plan. Our first principle is "we must know the kingdom plan." This plan is the foundational understanding of the what, why, and how of the good news. It also provides the important motivation for moving out of our comfort zone, our busy lives, our self-focus, and helps in seeing the world for what it truly is. It is a world that is not following the purpose for which it was created. The people of Earth are not enjoying all the fruits, blessings, and benefits of being citizens of heaven. Though the world itself will not achieve this until the second coming, individuals can enjoy this by receiving Jesus Christ as their Savior and Lord. These individuals then become members with other individuals on the Earth who are also part of the kingdom of heaven. This group is known by numerous names: the Church (Matthew 16:18; 18:17; Acts 9:31), the Body of Christ (Romans 12:5; 1 Corinthians 12:12; Ephesians 1:22-23; Colossians 1:24), the Temple of God (1 Corinthians 3:16; Ephesians 2:19; 1 Peter 2:5), the Bride of Christ (2 Corinthians 11:2; Ephesians 5:22-25; Revelation 19:7), the Flock of God (John 10:22-25; Acts 20:28; 1 Peter 5:2), and the Vine and Branches (John 15:1-15).

Matthew 16:18
I also tell you that you are Peter, and on this rock I will build my assembly, and the gates of Hades will not prevail against it.

Matthew 18:17
If he refuses to listen to them, tell it to the assembly. If he refuses to hear the assembly also, let him be to you as a Gentile or a tax collector.

Acts 9:31
So the assemblies throughout all Judea, Galilee, and Samaria had peace, and were built up. They were multiplied, walking in the fear of the Lord and in the comfort of the Holy Spirit.

Romans 12:5
So we, who are many, are one body in Christ, and individually members of one another.

1 Corinthians 12:12
For as the body is one...has many members, and all the members of the body, being many, are one body; so also is Christ.

Ephesians 1:22-23
He put all things in subjection under his feet, and gave him to be head over all things for the assembly, which is his body, the fullness of him who fills all in all.

Colossians 1:24
Now I rejoice in my sufferings for your sake, and fill up on my part that which is lacking of the afflictions of Christ in my flesh for his body's sake...assembly.

LEADING THE WAY

1 Corinthians 3:16
Don't you know that you are a temple of God, and that God's Spirit lives in you?

Ephesians 2:19
So then you are no longer strangers and foreigners, but you are fellow citizens with the saints and of the household of God.

1 Peter 2:5
You also, as living stones, are built up as a spiritual house, to be a holy priesthood, to offer up spiritual sacrifices, acceptable to God through Jesus Christ.

2 Corinthians 11:2
For I am jealous over you with a godly jealousy. For I married you to one husband, that I might present you...a pure virgin to Christ.

Ephesians 5:22-25
Wives, be subject to your own husbands, as to the Lord. For the husband is the head of the wife, as Christ also is the head of the assembly, being himself the savior of the body. But as the assembly is subject to Christ, so let the wives also be to their own husbands in everything. Husbands, love your wives, even as Christ also loved the assembly, and gave himself up for it.

Revelation 19:7
Let's rejoice and be exceedingly glad, and let's give the glory to him. For the wedding of the Lamb has come, and his wife has made herself ready.

John 10:22-25
It was the Feast of the Dedication at Jerusalem. It was winter, and Jesus was walking in the temple, in Solomon's porch. The Jews therefore came around him and said to him, "How long will you hold us in suspense? If you are the Christ, tell us plainly." Jesus answered them, "I told you, and you don't believe. The works that I do in my Father's name, these testify about me.

Acts 20:28
Take heed, therefore, to yourselves, and to all the flock, in which the Holy Spirit has made you overseers, to shepherd the assembly of the Lord and God which he purchased with his own blood.

1 Peter 5:2
Shepherd the flock of God...among you, exercising the oversight, not under compulsion, but voluntarily, not for dishonest gain, but willingly.

John 15:1-2
I am the true vine, and my Father is the farmer. Every branch in me that doesn't bear fruit, he takes away. Every branch that bears fruit, he prunes, that it may bear more fruit.

A Biblical Explanation

The plan of redemption is quite an amazing story and has many parts. In this chapter, we will discuss the creation of the Earth and its highest occupant (man), the fall through the Serpent's trickery of Eve and Adam's own rebellion, and the plan conceived in eternity past for his redemption through Christ. Then we will examine the brand-new creation man can become by receiving Christ as Savior and Lord. Sharing this plan is one of our great tasks as believers.

The Creation of Man

In Genesis chapter two, God created the earth, sun, moon, stars, the plants, and animals. After this, He proceeded to fashion His highest creation – man. In verse 7, Moses writes that God formed man out of the dust of the ground and then breathed into him the breath of life. As a result, man became a living being. The important question then arises, "Why did God create man?" The answers are found all over Scripture. In Romans 8:29-30 the apostle Paul explains, "For whom he foreknew, he also predestined to be conformed to the image of his Son, that he might be the firstborn [means preeminent one] among many brothers. Whom he predestined, those he also called. Whom he called, those he also justified. Whom he justified, those he also glorified." Here Paul indicates that Christians were given as a gift to the Son so He might be the prominent one among a great kingdom of brothers. The term "given" signals a gift. The saints are gifts to the Son. Men were primarily created to be the gift of a kingdom from God the Father to God the Son (John 3:35; 10:29; 13:3; 17:1-2, 6-7; Colossians 1:15-18).

John 3:35
The Father loves the Son, and has given all things into his hand.

John 10:29
My Father who has given them to me is greater than all. No one is able to snatch them out of my Father's hand.

John 13:3
Jesus, knowing that the Father had given all things into his hands, and that he came from God, and was going to God.

John 17:1-2
Jesus said these things, then lifting up his eyes to heaven, he said, "Father, the time has come. Glorify your Son, that your Son may also glorify you; even as you gave him authority over all flesh, so he will give eternal life to all whom you have given him.

John 17:6-7
I revealed your name to the people whom you have given me out of the world. They were yours, and you have given them to me. They have kept your word. Now they have known that all things whatever you have given me are from you.

Colossians 1:15-18
He is the image of the invisible God, the firstborn of all creation. For by him all things were created in the heavens and on the Earth, visible things and invisible things, whether thrones or dominions or principalities or powers. All things have been created through him and for him. He is before all things, and in him all things are held together. He is the head of the body, the assembly, who is the beginning, the firstborn from the dead, that in all things he might have the preeminence.

This brought forth the other purposes for which man was created. Those purposes are to give the Triune God great glory (Ephesians 1:11-12), to experience fellowship with Him (1 John 1:3; Genesis 3:8), to be holy, righteous, and blameless before Him (Ephesians 1:4), to serve Him through eternity (Genesis 1:26), to experience God's attributes (Romans 9:22), to reign and rule over Earth in honor of Him (Genesis 1:28), to live in harmony with other people and nature (Genesis 1:29-31), and to exist forever and ever (Genesis 3:22).

Ephesians 1:11-12
We {saints] were also assigned an inheritance in him, having been foreordained according to the purpose of him who does all things after the counsel of his will, to the end that we should be to the praise of his glory, we who had before hoped in Christ.

1 John 1:3
That which we have seen and heard we declare to you, that you also may have fellowship with us. Yes, and our fellowship is with the Father, and with his Son, Jesus Christ.

Genesis 3:8
They heard Yahweh God's voice walking in the garden in the cool of the day, and the man and his wife hid themselves from the presence of Yahweh God among the trees of the garden.

Ephesians 1:4
Even as he chose us in him before the foundation of the world, that we would be holy and without defect before him in love.

Genesis 1:26
God said, "Let's make man in our image, after our likeness. Let them have dominion over the fish of the sea, and over the birds of the sky, and over the livestock, and over all the Earth, and over every creeping thing that creeps on the Earth."

Romans 9:22
What if God, willing to show his wrath and to make his power known, endured with much patience vessels of wrath prepared for destruction.

Genesis 1:28
God blessed them. God said to them, "Be fruitful, multiply, fill the Earth, and subdue it. Have dominion over the fish of the sea, over the birds of the sky, and over every living thing that moves on the Earth."

Genesis 1:29-31
God said, "Behold, I have given you every herb yielding seed, which is on the surface of all the Earth, and every tree, which bears fruit yielding seed. It will be your food. 30 To every animal of the Earth, and to every bird of the sky, and to

everything that creeps on the Earth, in which there is life, I have given every green herb for food;" and it was so. God saw everything that he had made, and, behold, it was very good. There was evening and there was morning, a sixth day.

Genesis 3:22
Yahweh God said, "Behold, the man has become like one of us, knowing good and evil. Now, lest he reach out his hand, and also take of the tree of life, and eat, and live forever."

The Fall of Man

At first, things went well for man as he and God would walk and talk in the Garden of Eden. God had only given man one stipulation: if he was to continue to enjoy all that he had, he was not to eat of the Tree of Good and Evil (Genesis 2:16-17). The Serpent tempted and deceived Eve, and she ate of the fruit. Adam rebelled and ate the fruit also (Genesis 3:4-6). As a result, all mankind fell (1 Corinthians 15:22). No longer could man become the gift of a kingdom for His Son (Colossians 1:13), give God all glory (Romans 8:8), constantly fellowship with Him (Genesis 3:24), be holy, righteous, and blameless before the Holy One (Psalm 51:5; Romans 3:10-18), rule the Earth righteously (Ephesians 2:2), live in harmony with all other people (Genesis 4:7-8; 1 John 3:12) and nature (Genesis 3:7; Romans 8:20-21), and most of all, exist forever in their original human bodies (Ephesians 2:1; Romans 6:23).

Genesis 2:16-17
Yahweh God commanded the man, saying, "You may freely eat of every tree of the garden; but you shall not eat of the tree of the knowledge of good and evil; for in the day that you eat of it, you will surely die."

Genesis 3:4-6
The serpent said to the woman, "You won't really die, for God knows that in the day you eat it, your eyes will be opened, and you will be like God, knowing good and evil." When the woman saw that the tree was good for food, and that it was a delight to the eyes, and that the tree was to be desired to make one wise, she

took some of its fruit, and ate. Then she gave some to her husband with her, and he ate it, too.

1 Corinthians 15:22
For as in Adam all die, so also in Christ all will be made alive.

Colossians 1:13
Who delivered us out of the power of darkness, and translated us into the Kingdom of the Son of his love.

Romans 8:8
Those who are in the flesh can't please God.

Genesis 3:24
So he drove out the man; and he placed cherubim at the east of the garden of Eden, and a flaming sword which turned every way, to guard the way to the tree of life.

Psalm 51:5
Behold, I was born in iniquity. My mother conceived me in sin.

Ephesians 2:2
In which you once walked according to the course of this world, according to the prince of the power of the air, the spirit who now works in the children of disobedience.

Genesis 4:7-8
If you do well, won't it be lifted up? If you don't do well, sin crouches at the door. Its desire is for you, but you are to rule over it." Cain said to Abel, his brother, "Let's go into the field." While they were in the field, Cain rose up against Abel, his brother, and killed him.

1 John 3:12
Unlike Cain, who was of the evil one, and killed his brother. Why did he kill him? Because his deeds were evil, and his brother's righteous.

Genesis 3:7
Their eyes were opened, and they both knew that they were naked. They sewed fig leaves together, and made coverings for themselves.

Romans 8:20-21
For the creation was subjected to vanity, not of its own will, but because of him who subjected it, in hope that the creation itself also will be delivered from the bondage of decay into the liberty of the glory of the children of God.

Ephesians 2:1
You were made alive when you were dead in transgressions and sins,

Romans 6:23
For the wages of sin is death, but the free gift of God is eternal life in Christ Jesus our Lord.

Man would die. Also, man came under the wrath of God (Romans 1:18; Ephesians 2:3; Hebrews 9:27). People would now experience spiritual death and punishment for all their sins in a hell of fire (Matthew 5:22), a place of unquenchable fire (Matthew 9:23), a furnace of fire (Matthew 13:42), a lake of fire (Revelation 20:10), a place which was created for the Serpent of old and his evil demons (Matthew 25:41). When Christians encounter unbelievers, who appear to them as if all is so well, they must remember these truths. Things are not going well for them; they are in a difficult and desperate situation due to sin.

Romans 1:18
For the wrath of God is revealed from heaven against all ungodliness and unrighteousness of men...suppress the truth in unrighteousness.

Ephesians 2:3
We also all once lived among them in the lusts of our flesh, doing the desires of the flesh and of the mind, and were by nature children of wrath, even as the rest.

Hebrews 9:27
Inasmuch as it is appointed for men to die once...after this, judgment.

Matthew 5:22
But I tell you that everyone who is angry with his brother without a cause will be in danger of the judgment. Whoever says to his brother, "Raca!" will be in danger of the council. Whoever says, "You fool!" will be in danger of the fire of Gehenna.

Matthew 9:23
When Jesus came into the ruler's house and saw the flute players and the crowd in noisy disorder.

Matthew 13:42
And will cast them into the furnace of fire. There will be weeping and gnashing of teeth.

Revelation 20:10
The devil who deceived them was thrown into the lake of fire...sulfur, where the beast and the false prophet are also. They will be tormented day and night forever and ever.

Matthew 25:41
Then he will say also to those on the left hand, "Depart from me, you cursed, into the eternal fire which is prepared for the devil and his angels."

The Redemption of Man

Man no longer functioned according to the purposes for which God had created him. The entire human race was now destined for a life of rebellion and an eternity of hell. As a result, instead of God destroying Adam and Eve, the plan of redemption came into effect. Before the very foundation of the world, this plan was worked out in eternity past in the mind of the Triune God (Ephesians 1:3-6, 11-12). This plan took into account man's sin. Though man did not have to, nor should he have, nor did God want him to, yet God knew man would. God allowed man to rebel and determined that His divine response would be to pour out onto man even more love, goodness, mercy, grace, wisdom, and blessing.

Ephesians 1:36
Blessed be the God and Father of our Lord Jesus Christ, who has blessed us with every spiritual blessing in the heavenly places in Christ, even as he chose us in him before the foundation of the world, that we would be holy and without defect before him in love, having predestined us for adoption as children through Jesus Christ to himself, according to the good pleasure of his desire, to the praise of the glory of his grace, by which he freely gave us favor in the Beloved.

Ephesians 1:11-12
We were also assigned an inheritance in him, having been foreordained according to the purpose of him who does all things after the counsel of his will,

to the end that we should be to the praise of his glory, we who had before hoped in Christ.

This would bring greater glory to the Father, His Son, and Spirit and blessing to man (Ephesians 1:6). This would also allow the Lord God to display all of His attributes as He delivered man from his own rebellion and sin. In Ephesians 3:10, Paul describes this, "To the intent that now through the assembly [church] the manifold wisdom of God might be made known." It is through the Lord's work of salvation in His people that the many aspects of His wisdom and nature may be displayed. Then, the apostle Paul continues, "To the principalities and the powers in the Heavenly places." The angels and demons (in conjunction with mankind) become the divine audience for God's demonstration of all that He is. This plan portrays every aspect of His divine character.

Ephesians 1:6
To the praise of the glory of his grace, by which he freely gave us favor in the Beloved.

Ephesians 3:10
To the intent that now through the assembly the manifold wisdom of God might be made known to the principalities and the powers in the heavenly places.

God almighty displayed His love as He sent His Son to die (Romans 5:8), His mercy in turning people away from the punishment of fire (Titus 3:5), His grace as He offered an eternity in heaven (Titus 3:7), His patience as He restrained Himself from the destruction of humanity (1 Timothy 1:16), and His eternal power as He destroyed the evil works of darkness (Hebrews 2:14) and death (1 Corinthians 15:55). Also, God even demonstrated His justice and wrath, which are also two of His attributes. These were displayed as He was compelled within Himself to condemn man to eternal punishment (Romans 9:21-23). This ultimate portrayal of His many qualities brings Him more glory from His creation, which includes the angels and man.

Romans 5:8
But God commends his own love toward us, in that while we were yet sinners, Christ died for us.

Titus 3:5
Not by works of righteousness which we did ourselves, but according to his mercy, he saved us through the washing of regeneration and renewing by the Holy Spirit.

Titus 3:7
That being justified by his grace, we might be made heirs according to the hope of eternal life.

1 Timothy 1:16
However, for this cause I obtained mercy, that in me first, Jesus Christ might display all his patience for an example of those who were going to believe in him for eternal life.

Hebrews 2:14
Since then the children have shared in flesh and blood, he also himself in the same way partook of the same, that through death he might bring to nothing him who had the power of death, that is, the devil.

1 Corinthians 15:55
Death, where is your sting? Hades, where is your victory?

Romans 9:21-23
Or hasn't the potter a right over the clay, from the same lump to make one part a vessel for honor, and another for dishonor? What if God, willing to show his wrath and to make his power known, endured with much patience vessels of wrath prepared for destruction, and that he might make known the riches of his glory on vessels of mercy, which he prepared beforehand for glory.

The New Creation of Man

This wonderful plan not only gave God more glory, but it gave people more benefits. It did not simply restore man to his original state but gave to him a better and more excellent existence. Man would be given a brand-new and better earth to rule (2 Peter 3:10; Revelation 21:1). He would have a closer fellowship with God through the Holy Spirit inside of him (1 Corinthians 3:16; Philippians 2:13). People would be clothed in Christ's righteousness becoming like Him (1 John 3:2-3).

2 Peter 3:10
But the day of the Lord will come as a thief in the night; in which the heavens will pass away with a great noise, and the elements will be dissolved with fervent heat, and the Earth and the works that are in it will be burned up.

Revelation 21:1
I saw a new heaven and a new Earth: for the first heaven and the first Earth have passed away, and the sea is no more.

1 Corinthians 3:16
Don't you know that you are a temple of God, and that God's Spirit lives in you?

1 Corinthians 3:16
Don't you know that you are a temple of God, and that God's Spirit lives in you?

Philippians 2:13
For it is God who works in you both to will and to work, for his good pleasure.

1 John 3:2-3
Beloved, now we are children of God. It is not yet revealed what we will be; but we know that when he is revealed, we will be like him; for we will see him just as he is. 3 Everyone who has this hope set on him purifies himself, even as he is pure.

They would now be able to give God more glory because they had become the objects of His grace (Ephesians 5:18; 1 John 2:27). There would be a much deeper fellowship with each other in Christ (1 John 1:3-4). They could ultimately face death with hope in His Son Jesus who overcame death (John 5:29). A new immortal body would be provided for His own (1 Corinthians 15:20-27). All who know and love Him would inherit all the riches that are in Christ (1 Peter

1:4). These are just a few of the abundant blessings that were given to those in His kingdom.

Ephesians 5:18
Don't be drunken with wine, in which is dissipation, but be filled with the Spirit.

1 John 2:27
As for you, the anointing which you received from him remains in you, and you don't need for anyone to teach you. But as his anointing teaches you concerning all things, and is true, and is no lie, and even as it taught you, you will remain in him.

1 John 1:3-4
That which we have seen and heard we declare to you, that you also may have fellowship with us. Yes, and our fellowship is with the Father, and with his Son, Jesus Christ. And we write these things to you, that our joy may be fulfilled.

John 5:29
And will come out; those who have done good, to the resurrection of life; and those who have done evil, to the resurrection of judgment.

1 Peter 1:4
To an incorruptible and undefiled inheritance that doesn't fade away, reserved in Heaven for you.

All this was God's gracious and loving plan in response to man's sinful actions. It had been determined that the Second Person of the Trinity would cloth Himself in humanity and come to Earth to pay the penalty for sin (Philippians 2:5-8; Isaiah 53:6). In Romans 3:23-24, the apostle Paul writes, "For all have sinned, and fall short of the glory of God." Every man and woman sins and deserves punishment. Then, the apostle Paul continues with God's solution, "Being justified freely by his grace through the redemption that is in Christ Jesus." When the Lord Jesus came, He proclaimed this plan of redemption which involved His death on the cross and His resurrection. After this, He recruited others to proclaim this good news for all people (Matthew 28:19-20; Acts 1:1-8). Every Christian is to be an important part of sharing the gospel message. The saints will encounter people who may be searching for Jesus Christ and need to hear the plan of redemption and be saved.

Philippians 2:5-8
Have this in your mind, which was also in Christ Jesus, who, existing in the form of God, didn't consider equality with God a thing to be grasped, but emptied himself, taking the form of a servant, being made in the likeness of men. And being found in human form, he humbled himself, becoming obedient to the point of death, yes, the death of the cross.

Isaiah 53:6
All we like sheep have gone astray. Everyone has turned to his own way; and Yahweh has laid on him the iniquity of us all.

Romans 3:23-24
For all have sinned, and fall short of the glory of God; 24 being justified freely by his grace through the redemption that is in Christ Jesus.

Matthew 28:19-20
Go and make disciples of all nations, baptizing them in the name of the Father and of the Son and of the Holy Spirit, teaching them to observe all things that I commanded you. Behold, I am with you always, even to the end of the age. Amen.

An Ancient Portrait

No one understood the plan of redemption better than our redeemer Himself. For even at His own death in His final moments, Christ extended God's grace to a repentant thief dying next to Him. In Luke 23:35-43, the Lord Jesus was hanging on the cross while two others were being crucified next to him. These were real criminals on either side of Him, not a God-Man. The two of them were hurling the same kind of abuse as those below. Like the people all around Jesus, these two thieves had scorned Jesus for claiming to be the Christ, the chosen one of God, the long-awaited Messiah, and the one who fulfilled all the prophecies from ancient days. On the sign, just above the Lord's head on the cross, were the words, "The King of the Jews." His disciples, who had witnessed all of the miracles He had done, were just below his hanging body, and they still believed.

Suddenly, one of the two thieves grew silent as the other continued his mockery. As he prepared himself for death and considered his wicked life, he saw before his own eyes a perfect and innocent man. He must have taken a moment to ponder the very words he had spoken about Jesus' deity, the sign of His dignity, and the belief of His disciples in His divinity that was on display before him. In that moment, through the power of the Holy Spirit his blinders from Satan fell off, his prideful rationalizations for his own sins tumbled from his broken flesh, and he repented and believed. He grew sorrowful and mournful for his sins and believed that Jesus was indeed who He claimed to be. He was the Son of the living God and Savior of the world. Then deep within his heart he submitted to His Lordship.

Moments before, this man had cursed and criticized Jesus, now he turned toward the other thief and robber and cried out for him to stop his abusive words. The thief declared that they deserved everything they had gotten, but Jesus had done nothing wrong. In this statement, the thief affirmed his new belief that Jesus was a righteous and holy God. Before Him, these two criminals were utterly without any merit. He questioned the other condemned outlaw as to whether he feared God. Judgment was coming; it was at their door. The physical life was draining from their bodies and their eternal spirits would face an almighty God. As Jews, they knew the law and would have a greater judgment than the Gentiles. These two thieves lived sin-filled lives and now had been blaspheming God's anointed Messiah. This condemnation would be unimaginable. This other thief must stop before he says anything else to make his damnation even worse.

Then he turned toward Jesus Christ and asked the saving question that demonstrated all that the Holy Spirit had done in His life. He asked the Lord to remember him when He came into His Kingdom. There it was: a recognition of who Jesus was and what He was doing on the cross that day. He was not saving Himself so He could save others and the thief desperately desired that deliverance. So, at the moment of his death, the man cried out for forgiveness and salvation. When Jesus gives up His spirit and enters the abode of His Father will He please remember this repentant criminal and bring his unworthy soul into His heaven.

As the life was slowly pouring out of Him, Jesus looked at the man, and declared on that very day this repentant sinner and now saint would be with Him in paradise. This moment between the Savior and this repentant sinner is a wonderful picture of the plan of redemption lived out. The Lord Jesus knew He was the redeemer and offered that redemption to that desperate man. We must also live out the plan of God in the lives of others as we share the gospel with them.

A Modern Anecdote

Over the years, I have taught weekly Bible studies on a variety of topics. On one such evening, we actually studied the above story of Jesus and the two thieves. We learned that each thief responded differently to Jesus Christ while He was on the cross. One thief continued to taunt Jesus telling Him to save Himself if He was indeed the Son of God, while the other chastised the first and proclaimed their guilt for the crimes. He begged Jesus to remember him when He entered His kingdom. Jesus responded by telling him that very day he would be with the Lord in paradise.

After the description of the mercy and grace shown the repentant thief that night as the man anticipated paradise forever with his new Savior and Lord, everyone was deeply moved. After the evening was over, April, one of the women who attended, began to tell me the story of her grandmother. She was visiting from a small mountain community across the state and had recently lost her husband. She had flown down to see her family and friends in our area, then April had felt a deep burden for her salvation.

The woman tried to share the gospel with her but could not seem to articulate it clearly enough. She realized that she needed some serious training in evangelism and by the time she received it, it would be too late. Her grandmother was older, and it was becoming more and more difficult to make the trip down. April had several small children at home, and it would be extremely difficult to leave them to make the trip to the mountains for even a short time. Then she begged me to speak with her grandmother. I told her that I would share the gospel with her if April would watch and learn. I wanted April to have the privilege of bringing people to Christ and feeling the thrill of being used by God.

We decided that April would invite me over for coffee on the following Saturday and her husband would take the kids to the park while we visited with her grandmother. When I arrived, April introduced me to her grandmother, Donna. After a few minutes of casual conversation, I inquired about her religious background and her understanding of Christ. She explained that her parents had never gone to any type of church. Donna also knew that her daughter believed in Jesus and was attending a church. Since I could not find a specific way within the conversation to introduce the good news, I went to my back up plan.

I just simply asked, "In our Bible study we discussed last week the story of the thief on the cross, and it was amazing. Would you like to study that same story with us for a few minutes?" When the Holy Spirit has truly prepared a heart for salvation, it is like a piece of fruit falling effortlessly into your hand. The fruit doesn't have to be yanked and pulled. We began by reading the story with each of us taking a turn. Periodically, I would stop the reading and explain the verse bringing in every point of the good news. Since Donna was listening so intensely, I could tell the Spirit was at work and preparing her to receive Christ.

When we finished, I then asked her if she would desire to receive Christ as Savior and Lord. Donna looked at me and smiled saying, "I have been waiting for Him my whole life. Yes, I would." We prayed the prayer of salvation as April, her granddaughter, prayed silently and rejoiced. I wrote in the Bible I had given her the date of her salvation. We talked together about her new life in Christ and the importance of finding a group of believers in her area to support her.

When I left, I was once again amazed at what God could do in a person's heart. She went back to her little mountain town and got involved with a local Bible believing church and made many friends and served the Lord. Several years after, I performed her memorial service describing that day she came to our Lord. We rejoiced knowing that she was in heaven. The granddaughter told me that now that she had seen with her own eyes the plan at work, she couldn't wait to share the gospel. To do this, we must know the plan.

A Personal Response

Dear Heavenly Father,

Please help me to know and understand your kingdom plan. I believe You are raising up a kingdom of priests for Your Son, and I thank you for allowing me to be a member of that kingdom with all the blessings that go with it. I do not want to miss any opportunities you may bring to share the gospel with people so they may enter Your kingdom. Help me to proclaim to (add names) and others I know and meet that they too can have salvation in Your Son. Open my eyes to see the opportunities with them and others to share Your redemptive plan and motivate me through Your Holy Spirit to present it. I pray this in the name of Jesus. Amen.

Instructor's Notes

AN INSTRUCTOR'S MANUAL

Chapter 1

Know the Kingdom Plan

For Christians to share the gospel they must know and understand the kingdom plan. This includes the creation, fall, and redemption of all mankind.

In the section, "A Typical Scenario," the author describes how Christians can share the gospel with their neighbors who live near them.

What is the scenario about?

A Christian sees his neighbor almost every day and knows he or she should witness to the person.

What held the believer back from sharing the gospel?

They were unsure of the kingdom plan and did not view the neighbor correctly.

What finally led the Christian to share the good news and how did it occur?

Once he learned the kingdom plan, he used an open garage door to begin a conversation about Christ.

Have you had a similar experience?

(Various answers should be shared including yours.)

LEADING THE WAY

In the section, "A Scriptural Principle" the author presents an important biblical principle in evangelism which concerns our knowledge and understanding of God's kingdom plan.

How would you express this principle in your own words?

This first principle is "we must know the kingdom plan."

(Various answers should be shared including yours.)

How would you rewrite this principle to make it even more personal to your life (using your name and situation)?

(Various answers should be shared including yours.)

Why do you think this principle might be important in your life right now as you share the gospel?

(Various answers should be shared including yours.)

How would you rate yourself on the percentage of times you followed this principle in the past as a believer?

(Various answers should be shared including yours.)

Directions: Put a horizontal mark and your name where you see yourself on the percentage line.

| 0% | 25% | 50% | 75% | 100% |

In the section, "A Biblical Explanation," the author explains the gift of God's kingdom to His Son and its importance in sharing the gospel effectively.

What is the primary reason God, the Father, created human beings according to Romans 8:29-30?

Here Paul indicates that Christians were given as a gift to the Son so He might be the prominent one among a great kingdom of brothers. The term "given" signals a gift. The saints are gifts to the Son. Men were primarily created to be the gift of a kingdom from God the Father to God the Son (John 3:35; 10:29; 13:3; 17:1-2, 6-7; Colossians 1:15-18).

What are three other reasons, God created people and what bible passages describe them?

This brought forth the other purposes for which man was created. Those purposes are to give the Triune God great glory (Ephesians 1:11-12), to experience fellowship with Him (1 John 1:3; Genesis 3:8), to be holy, righteous, and blameless before Him (Ephesians 1:4), to serve Him through eternity (Genesis 1:26), to experience God's attributes (Romans 9:22), to reign and rule over Earth in honor of Him (Genesis 1:28), to live in harmony with other people and nature (Genesis 1:29-31), and to exist forever and ever (Genesis 3:22).

After Adam and Eve sinned against God, what are some of the blessings (name two) that people could no longer enjoy (provide verses)?

As a result, all mankind fell (1 Corinthians 15:22). No longer could man become the gift of a kingdom for His Son (Colossians 1:13), give God all glory (Romans 8:8), constantly fellowship with Him (Gen. 3:24), be holy, righteous, and blameless before the Holy One (Psalm 51:5; Romans 3:10-18), rule the Earth righteously (Ephesians 2:2), live in harmony with all other people (Genesis 4:7-8; 1 John 3:12) and nature (Genesis 3:7; Romans 8:20-21), and most of all, exist forever in their original human bodies (Ephesians 2:1; Romans 6:23).

Man would die. Also, man came under the wrath of God (Romans 1:18; Ephesians 2:3; Hebrews 9:27). People would now experience spiritual death and punishment for all their sins in a hell of fire (Matthew 5:22), a place of unquenchable fire (Matthew 9:23), a furnace of fire (Matthew 13:42), a lake of fire (Revelation 20:10), a place which was created for the Serpent of old and his evil demons (Matthew 25:41).

After Adam and Eve sinned against God and came under His wrath, what was the result in this life and the next?

Man would die. Also, man came under the wrath of God (Romans 1:18; Ephesians 2:3; Hebrews 9:27). People would now experience spiritual death and punishment for all their sins in a hell of fire (Matthew 5:22), a place of unquenchable fire (Matthew 9:23), a furnace of fire (Matthew 13:42), a lake of fire (Revelation 20:10), a place which was created for the Serpent of old and his evil demons (Matthew 25:41).

What greater blessings (name three) can people now enjoy because of God's plan of redemption (provide verses)?

Man would be given a brand-new and better Earth to rule (2 Peter 3:10; Revelation 21:1). He would have a closer fellowship with God through the Holy Spirit inside of him (1 Corinthians 3:16; Philippians 2:13). People would be clothed in Christ's righteousness becoming like Him (1 John 3:2-3).

They would now be able to give God more glory because they had become the objects of His grace (Ephesians 5:18; 1 John 2:27). There would be a much deeper fellowship with each other in Christ (1 John 1:3-4). They could ultimately face death with hope in His Son Jesus who overcame death (John 5:29). A new immortal body would be provided for His own (1 Corinthians 15:20-27). All who know and love Him would inherit all the riches that are in Christ (1 Peter 1:4). These are just a few of the abundant blessings that were given to those in His kingdom.

In what ways might these truths impact your life?

(Various answers should be shared including yours.)

In the section, "An Ancient Portrait," the author provides a unique portrayal of how one of the thieves hanging next to our Lord became a believer.

Can you briefly describe the setting of this real-life ancient drama?

The setting is found in Luke 23. In Luke 23:35-43, the Lord Jesus was hanging on the cross while two others were being crucified next to him. These were real criminals on either side of Him, not a God-Man. The two of them were hurling the same kind of abuse as those below. Like the people all around Jesus, these two thieves had scorned Jesus for claiming to be the Christ, the chosen one of God, the long awaited Messiah, and the one [Jesus] who fulfilled all the prophecies from ancient days. On the sign, just above the Lord's head on the cross, were the words, "The King of the Jews." His disciples, who had witnessed all of the miracles He had done, were just below his hanging body, and they still believed.

Can you describe the major characters involved?

The major characters are Jesus Christ and the two thieves.

How did the evangelist initiate the gospel presentation?

He initiated the gospel by His previous proclamations of His deity and His unwillingness to revile in return.

What was result of this evangelistic presentation?

As he prepared himself for death and considered his wicked life, he saw before his own eyes a perfect and innocent man. He must have taken a moment to ponder the very words he had spoken about Jesus' deity, the sign of His dignity, and the belief of His disciples in His divinity that was on display before him.

In that moment, through the power of the Holy Spirit his blinders from Satan fell off, his prideful rationalizations for his own sins tumbled from his broken flesh, and he repented and believed. He grew sorrowful and mournful for his sins and believed that Jesus was indeed who He claimed to be. He was the Son of the living God and Savior of the world. Then deep within his heart he submitted to His Lordship.

Then he turned toward Jesus Christ and asked the saving question that demonstrated all that the Holy Spirit had done in His life. He asked the Lord to remember him when He came into His Kingdom. There it was: a recognition of who Jesus was and what He was doing on the cross that day. He was not saving Himself so He could save others and the thief desperately desired that deliverance.

How was the principle explained in this chapter applied to the situation?

Throughout the ministry of Jesus, He preached the kingdom plan. This thief knew this plan and that Jesus was the Messiah.

Based on the truths learned in this chapter, what would you have done differently if you were the evangelist or how would you have responded if you were the recipient?

(Various answers should be shared including yours.)

In the section, "A Modern Anecdote," the author discusses a situation in which a woman in his bible study group needed assistance in sharing the gospel with her grandmother.

Can you briefly describe the setting of this real-life modern drama?

The setting is at the home of April's grandmother.

We decided that April would invite me over for coffee on the following Saturday and her husband would take the kids to the park while we visited with her grandmother. When I arrived, April introduced me to her grandmother, Donna. After a few minutes of casual conversation, I inquired about her religious background and her understanding of Christ. She explained that her parents had never gone to any type of church. Donna also knew that her daughter believed in Jesus and was attending a church. Since I could not find a specific way within the conversation to introduce the good news, I went to my back up plan.

Can you describe the major characters involved?

The major characters are the author, the grand-daughter April, and the grandmother Donna.

How did the author initiate the gospel presentation?

I just simply asked, "In our Bible study we discussed last week the story of the thief on the cross, and it was amazing. Would you like to study that same story with us for a few minutes?" When the Holy Spirit has truly prepared a heart for salvation, it is like a piece of fruit falling effortlessly into your hand.

AN INSTRUCTOR'S MANUAL

What was result of this evangelistic presentation?

When we finished, I then asked her if she would desire to receive Christ as Savior and Lord. Donna looked at me and smiled saying, "I have been waiting for Him my whole life. Yes, I would." We prayed the prayer of salvation as April, her granddaughter, prayed silently and rejoiced. I wrote in the Bible I had given her the date of her salvation. We talked together about her new life in Christ and the importance of finding a group of believers in her area to support her.

When I left, I was once again amazed at what God could do in a person's heart. She went back to her little mountain town and got involved with a local Bible believing church and made many friends and served the Lord.

How was the principle explained in this chapter applied to the situation?

The author knew the kingdom plan and explained it.

Based on the truths learned in this chapter, what would you have done differently if you were the author or how would you have responded if you were the recipient?

(Various answers should be shared including yours.)

In the section, "A Personal Response," the author provides a model you may use for prayer if you find it necessary after discovering the truths in this chapter.

Are you presently attempting to present the gospel of Jesus to someone? If not, are there some in your immediate family who may not know Jesus Christ and may need prayer for an opportunity for you to share with them and open hearts to receive Him?

(Various answers should be shared including yours.)

Based on the truths you have just learned, what will you continue to do in your current evangelistic efforts and what might you do differently?

(Various answers should be shared including yours.)

What additional thoughts would you like to share with the others?

(Various answers should be shared including yours.)

Chapter 2

Herald the Epic Message

Christians have been given this message of creation, the fall, and God's redemption through Jesus Christ to proclaim. According to Hebrews 1:1-4, God communicated this plan to His people through the fathers and the prophets in the Old Testament. After a period of silence, God spoke through His beloved Son, in the New Testament. His disciples wrote His true story down so it could be passed from one generation to another. We now have it and must also pass it on.

Hebrews 1:1-4
God, having in the past spoken to the fathers through the prophets at many times and in various ways, has at the end of these days spoken to us by his Son, whom he appointed heir of all things, through whom also he made the worlds. His Son is the radiance of his glory, the very image of his substance, and upholding all things by the word of his power, who, when he had by himself purified us of our sins, sat down on the right hand of the Majesty on high, having become as much better than the angels as the more excellent name he has inherited is better than theirs.

A Typical Scenario

Have you ever been in a situation that was something like the following? You walk into a local coffee shop and get in line to purchase a cup of coffee. As you are standing there, you look around the place. It is filled with people sitting by themselves, and you really do not know anyone in there. You have heard somebody say, "A Christian has to earn the right to share the gospel, so you think, 'Well, I guess though these people are all lost, I better not say anything because I haven't earned the right through my example and friendship to speak to them about Christ.'" You feel somewhat relieved.

Then you sit down at a table and read the newspaper. Later, you walk out the door, and the opportunity is gone. No one will ever know that a Christian had been in their midst.

In this chapter, we will learn that Christians are heralds of the epic message of salvation from the God of the universe. Believers are to announce, preach, teach, proclaim, testify, deliver, and comfort with the gospel. They are not required by their God to have a relationship with anyone in order to declare His good news of salvation. After you learn these powerful truths, perhaps this same encounter could be quite different.

Now that you know you are a herald, you decide that you will get your coffee, sit down at a table, and ask the Lord to prepare the heart of someone to whom you will share the gospel. You determine to begin with a simple conversation about something they are reading. Since the conversation might be interrupted or could require a follow-up discussion at a later date, it should be someone who comes in fairly regularly. After some thought, you conclude that it should be someone of the same gender, so you do not look like you have other motives for speaking to them.

You casually stroll among the tables and begin to observe what people are reading that might aid in a conversation starter. You are under no pressure. God is sovereign so you can always start a conversation and pick it up later. Perhaps, you will walk by while you pray for each person present to receive Jesus Christ. Finally, you notice a person reading a book that you are very familiar with. As you walk by, you casually comment, "That's a great book, isn't it?" If they don't make much of a response, you can walk on. If they do, you begin a conversation. As you discuss the book, you connect one of the concepts to a truth in the gospel and present your epic message of salvation.

Though this is an imaginary scenario, it is typical of the many different situations we may find ourselves in where the good news could be shared, but it is not due to a lack of understanding concerning who we are in Christ. We must realize that we are heralds of an epic message from the King of Kings and Lord of Lords and can at any time share the gospel. This can create within us a strong interest in sharing the gospel. This leads us to a second principle that involves this great identity and responsibility of ours.

A Scriptural Principle

For Christians to share the gospel, they must understand that they are messengers of a powerful declaration. This is truly good news for all men and women to hear. This brings us to principle number two which is "we must herald the epic message." Christians are to be presenting the gospel everywhere they go to everyone they meet at any time they choose as the Lord leads them. It is the responsibility and right that has been given to all believers.

A Biblical Explanation

This right and responsibility for the declaration of God's plan of redemption is described using several crucial Greek words filled with great meaning in the New Testament. As has been mentioned, believers are commanded to announce it, preach it, comfort with it, proclaim it, testify of it, teach it, and deliver it. Each word views evangelism from a different perspective. They present to the Christian their divine right and responsibility to share the good news of salvation.

To further enhance the understanding of this joyous task of evangelism, the Greek words used in the New Testament to describe evangelism will be studied in their historical, grammatical, and scriptural contexts. Before we approach their use in the New Testament, we will study their use in the Old Testament. How is this possible since it was written in primarily Hebrew? A large part of the Jewish population spoke only Greek because they had been occupied by Greek speaking people for a long time. As a result, a translation of the Hebrew Bible into the Greek language was needed. This Greek translation is called the Septuagint and is referred to by the three letters LXX in academic writing.

The Septuagint was in wide use in the time of Christ and was often cited by the Lord and His apostles. The particular Greek words that were chosen to translate the different Hebrew words in the LXX can provide much insight into the Greek words used to describe the presentation of the gospel in the New Testament. To study the Hebrews words and discern the various historical, grammatical, and scriptural contexts of each of them affords us a deeper understanding of this momentous supernatural endeavor Christians are to be involved in. We will study each individual Greek word that is utilized to describe the sharing of the gospel by the New Testament writers. This will be in no particular order; all are equally significant.

The Announcement of the Plan

The good news is to be announced. The Greek word that is translated "announce" is used in many places in the LXX. The term that is translated "announce" has the connotation of a declaration from God by His messenger. It is used in 2 Samuel 15:13, when David's own servant came to announce to him that his son Absalom had won the hearts of many of the people of Israel. In Exodus 9:16, Moses tells Pharaoh that the Lord God will send many plagues upon Egypt to show

God's power and announce His presence in the midst of the Hebrew nation.

2 Samuel 15:13
A messenger came to David, saying, "The hearts of the men of Israel are after Absalom."

Exodus 9:16
But indeed for this cause I have made you stand: to show you my power, and that my name may be declared throughout all the earth.

The Psalmists also utilized this word "to announce" the Lord God's holiness and righteousness (Psalm 22:30-31), His faithfulness (Psalm 30:9), His wondrous deeds (Psalm 71:17), and His steadfast love (Psalm 92:2). In Isaiah 42:9, the Lord God announces that He will bring new things through His coming Messiah.

Psalm 22:30-31
Future generations shall be told about the Lord. They shall come and shall declare his righteousness to a people that shall be born, for he has done it.

Psalm 71:17
God, you have taught me from my youth. Until now, I have declared your wondrous works.

Psalm 92:2
To proclaim your loving kindness in the morning, and your faithfulness every night.

Isaiah 42:9
Behold, the former things have happened and I declare new things. I tell you about them before they come up.

In the New Testament, the Greek word is used in John's description of the words of the woman at the well in John 4:25. She declares that the Messiah, when He comes, will announce all things. In John 1:18, John explains that no man has seen God at any time, but the Lord Jesus has announced Him. Christ as the divine messenger of God announced that the kingdom of God had come. In 1 John 1:2-3, the apostle writes to his readers that the message they received from the Lord was announced (declared) to them. Now His disciples are to be the messengers who are to go out and announce the divine message from God.

John 4:25
The woman said to him, "I know that Messiah comes, he who is called Christ. When he has come, he will declare to us all things."

John 1:18
No one has seen God at any time. The one and only Son, who is in the bosom of the Father, has declared him.

1 John 1:2-3
(And the life was revealed, and we have seen, and testify, and declare to you the life, the eternal life, which was with the Father, and was revealed to us); that which we have seen and heard we declare to you, that you also may have fellowship with us. Yes, and our fellowship is with the Father, and with his Son, Jesus Christ.

In Acts 20:20, Paul told the elders in Ephesus that he did not ever shrink from announcing to them anything that was profitable. Then in Acts 26:20, Paul told King Agrippa that he kept announcing (declaring) the message (they should repent and turn to God - the plan of redemption) to those at Damascus, in Jerusalem, in the entire region of Judea, and even to the Gentiles. He explained that he had "declared first to them of Damascus, at Jerusalem, and throughout all the country of Judea, and also to the Gentiles, that they should repent and turn to God, doing works worthy of repentance." One facet of evangelism is an announcement by Christians on behalf of the Lord God that His beloved Son has come, and salvation is in Him. Christians are to go out into to the world and announce this sacred message and plan.

Acts 20:20
How I didn't shrink from declaring to you anything that was profitable, teaching you publicly and from house to house.

Acts 26:20
But declared first to them of Damascus, at Jerusalem, and throughout all the country of Judea, and also to the Gentiles, that they should repent and turn to God, doing works worthy of repentance.

The Preaching of the Plan

The good news is to be preached. The Greek word that is translated "preach" is used in many places in the Septuagint. The word was used to speak of good news that a new era had begun. The word was used in 1 Kings 1:42 to refer to the good news that a king had been anointed, and a new rule had arrived. In Jeremiah 20:15, it's used to speak of the birth of a baby and the new life that had come.

1 Kings 1:42
While he yet spoke, behold, Jonathan the son of Abiathar the priest came; and Adonijah said, "Come in; for you are a worthy man, and bring good news."

Jeremiah 20:15
Cursed is the man who brought news to my father, saying, "A boy is born to you," making him very glad.

The word's most significant use is in the preaching of a new era of salvation that would be brought by Yahweh and His Messiah. This would fulfill the longings of Israel and sinful man for his own happiness and peace. In Psalm 96:2, the psalmist exhorts his audience to sing and bless the name of God. They were to preach good tidings of salvation from day to day. In Isaiah 41:27, God assures His people, Israel, of their future redemption in the midst of present punishment. He promised that He would send a messenger of good news, the Messiah. In Isaiah 61:1, the pre-incarnate Jesus Christ is speaking and declares to Israel that He will come to preach the good news to the humble.

Psalm 96:2
Sing to Yahweh! Bless his name! Proclaim his salvation from day to day!

Isaiah 41:27
I am the first to say to Zion, "Behold, look at them;" and I will give one who brings good news to Jerusalem.

Isaiah 61:1
The Lord Yahweh's Spirit is on me, because Yahweh has anointed me to preach good news to the humble. He has sent me to bind up the broken hearted, to proclaim liberty to the captives and release to those who are bound.

The Greek word is used similarly in the New Testament. In Luke 4:17-21, Jesus entered the synagogue on the Sabbath and stood up to read. The Lord read the passage from Isaiah which stated that the promised Messiah with the Spirit upon Him would preach good news. After this reading, Jesus told the congregation that this passage had at that moment been fulfilled in Him. He was preaching the good news that the era of the kingdom of God had begun. Mark describes Jesus as coming into Galilee preaching the gospel of the kingdom of God (Mark 1:14-15).

Luke 4:17-21
The book of the prophet Isaiah was handed to him. He opened the book, and found the place where it was written, "The Spirit of the Lord is on me, because he has anointed me to preach good news to the poor. He has sent me to heal the broken hearted, to proclaim release to the captives, recovering of sight to the blind, to deliver those who are crushed, and to proclaim the acceptable year of the Lord." He closed the book, gave it back to the attendant, and sat down. The eyes of all in the synagogue were fastened on him. He began to tell them, "Today, this Scripture has been fulfilled in your hearing."

Mark 1:14-15
Now after John was taken into custody, Jesus came into Galilee, preaching the Good News of God's Kingdom, and saying, "The time is fulfilled, and God's Kingdom is at hand! Repent, and believe in the Good News."

In Acts 5:42, the apostles carried on this preaching daily in the temple and from house to house. The inspired writer Luke records, "Every day, in the temple and at home, they never stopped teaching and preaching Jesus, the Christ." In Acts 8:4, Luke also explains that the saints were preaching the good news when they were scattered from Jerusalem. Their "preaching" involved the message that a new era was beginning. When true Christians encounter unsaved people, they must realize these people are desperate for a new era in their lives. They are dead in their sins (Ephesians 2:1), are walking according to the course of this world and its dark prince (Ephesians 2:2), are sons of disobedience (Ephesians 2:2), are living in the lusts of their flesh (Ephesians 2:3), and are by nature, children of wrath (Ephesians 2:3). People are filled with the cancer of sinfulness which is ruining their lives now and will destroy their lives beyond the grave.

Acts 5:42
Every day, in the temple and at home, they never stopped teaching and preaching Jesus, the Christ.

Acts 8:4
Therefore those who were scattered abroad went around preaching the word.

Ephesians 2:1
You were made alive when you were dead in transgressions and sins.

Ephesians 2:2
In which you once walked according to the course of this world, according to the prince of the power of the air, the spirit who now works in the children of disobedience.

Ephesians 2:3
We also all once lived among them in the lusts of our flesh, doing the desires of the flesh and of the mind, and were by nature children of wrath, even as the rest.

When unbelievers become Christians, a brand-new era is ushered into their lives. This brand-new era is characterized by these lost souls becoming brand-new creatures in Christ (2 Corinthians 5:17), children of the true God (John 1:12), and alive together with Him (Ephesians 2:5). They will walk in newness of life (Galatians 5:16), experience peace with God (Romans 10:15), and find a true joy from the Spirit (Galatians 5:22). Most of all, they will have eternal life (1 John 5:11-12).

2 Corinthians 5:17
Therefore if anyone is in Christ, he is a new creation. The old things have passed away. Behold, all things have become new.

John 1:12
But as many as received him, to them he gave the right to become God's children, to those who believe in his name.

Ephesians 2:5
Even when we were dead through our trespasses, made us alive together with Christ – by grace you have been saved.

Galatians 5:16
But I say, walk by the Spirit, and you won't fulfill the lust of the flesh.

Romans 10:15
And how will they preach unless they are sent? As it is written: "How beautiful are the feet of those who preach the Good News of peace, who bring glad tidings of good things!"

Galatians 5:22
But the fruit of the Spirit is love, joy, peace, patience, kindness, goodness, faith.

1 John 5:11-12
The testimony is this, that God gave to us eternal life, and this life is in his Son. He who has the Son has the life. He who doesn't have God's Son doesn't have the life.

The Comfort of the Plan

The good news is to comfort people. The Greek word that is translated "comfort" literally means to come along the side of someone and help. Its various forms are used in many places in the Septuagint. It was used to speak of comfort and showing pity (Psalm 119:50) and of compassion and sorrow (Psalm 135:14). It also refers to coming alongside others and encouraging them (Deuteronomy 3:24; Job 4:3). It involves the comfort that the gospel of salvation can bring. In Isaiah 40:1, God exhorts the prophets to comfort his people. They were to declare that He would deliver the nation after His wrath had come. This was such a great message of comfort to people who were experiencing the wrath of God. This was good news which brought comfort.

Psalm 119:50
This is my comfort in my affliction, for your word has revived me.

Psalm 135:14
For Yahweh will judge his people and have compassion on his servants.

Deuteronomy 3:24
Lord Yahweh, you have begun to show your servant your greatness, and your strong hand. For what god is there in heaven or in Earth that can do works like yours, and mighty acts like yours?

Job 4:3
Behold, you have instructed many, you have strengthened the weak hands.

Isaiah 40:1
Comfort, comfort my people," says your God.

In the New Testament, Jesus is called the Consolation of Israel by Luke as he describes the waiting of Simeon for the Messiah (Luke 2:25). In John 16:7, Jesus told His disciples that He would leave them and send another Comforter (the Holy Spirit). In verse 8, the Lord explains that this coming Comforter would bring conviction of sin, righteousness, and judgment. In other words, He would comfort them in the conviction of their sin with the gospel.

Luke 2:25
Behold, there was a man in Jerusalem...Simeon. This man was righteous and devout, looking for the consolation of Israel, and the Holy Spirit was on him.

John 16:7
Nevertheless I tell you the truth: It is to your advantage that I go away, for if I don't go away, the Counselor won't come to you. But if I go, I will send him....

John 16:8
When he has come, he will convict the world about sin, about righteousness, and about judgment.

LEADING THE WAY

This word is used for evangelism in several places in the New Testament. In Acts 2:40, Luke describes the comforting of the people through the preaching of the gospel by Peter. Luke records this, "With many other words he testified, and exhorted them, saying, 'Save yourselves from this crooked generation!'" On the day of Pentecost, this apostle continued to solemnly testify and to exhort (comfort) the people to be saved. The gospel of Christ brings an amazing amount of comfort as people trust Jesus for their salvation.

Acts 2:40
With many other words he testified, and exhorted them, saying, "Save yourselves from this crooked generation!"

In Acts 13:14-17, Paul arrived in Antioch of Pisidia and entered the temple. Since he was a rabbi, they asked him to give a word of exhortation (comfort), and Paul preached the gospel. He comforted them with the gospel. Then Paul told the Corinthians that his affliction was for their comfort and salvation. Comfort and salvation go hand in hand. A good example is found in 1 Thessalonians 2:7-12, where Paul tells the Thessalonians that he comforted them in the gospel as a mother nurses her newborn baby. Christians can bring great comfort with the gospel.

Acts 13:14-17
But they, passing on from Perga, came to Antioch of Pisidia. They went into the synagogue on the Sabbath day, and sat down. After the reading of the law and the prophets...rulers of the synagogue sent to them, saying, "Brothers, if you have...word of exhortation for the people, speak." Paul stood up, and beckoning with his hand said, "Men of Israel, and you who fear God, listen. The God of this people chose our fathers, and exalted the people when they stayed as aliens in the land of Egypt, and with an uplifted arm, he led them out of it.

1 Thessalonians 2:7-12
But we were gentle among you, like a nursing mother cherishes her own children. Even so, affectionately longing for you, we were well pleased to impart to you, not the Good News of God only, but also our own souls, because you had become very dear to us. For you remember, brothers, our labor and travail; for

working night and day, that we might not burden any of you, we preached to you the Good News of God. You are witnesses with God how holy, righteously, and blamelessly we behaved ourselves toward you who believe. As you know, we exhorted, comforted, and implored every one of you, as a father does his own children...you...walk worthily of God...calls you into his own Kingdom....

What more comfort could one give then offering peace with the almighty God (Romans 5:1)? When people come to Christians for advice in the hope of finding peace in their troubled lives, they can find an eternal one. This provides comfort to them in not only a temporal way on this Earth but an everlasting way.

Romans 5:1
Being therefore justified by faith, we have peace with God through our Lord Jesus Christ.

The Proclamation of the Plan

The good news is to be proclaimed. The Greek word that is translated "proclaim" is used in many places in the LXX. The Old Testament connotation for the word is to officially herald important news or announce an arrival of a dignitary. The Hebrew word is used to speak of Moses proclaiming to the people that they had brought enough offerings for the tabernacle (Exodus 36:6). In another instance, the new king, Josiah, had found a copy of the Scriptures in the temple. He then heralded the news, proclaiming that the people of Judah and Jerusalem were to bring to the Lord God the levy fixed by Moses, the servant of God (2 Chronicles 24:9). This official proclamation from a ruler and the binding character of his vital message demanded that the people comply.

Exodus 36:6
Moses gave a commandment, and they caused it to be proclaimed throughout the camp, saying, "Let neither man nor woman make anything else for the offering for the sanctuary." So the people were restrained from bringing.

LEADING THE WAY

2 Chronicles 24:9
They made a proclamation through Judah and Jerusalem, to bring in for Yahweh the tax that Moses the servant of God laid on Israel in the wilderness.

Cyrus, ruler of the Persian Empire, made a proclamation that God desired for him to build a temple in Jerusalem and released all the Jews to return to their land if they desired (2 Chronicles 36:22-23). This was an official proclamation from a supreme ruler which demanded immediate obedience and compliance. The word is used of Jonah's proclamation from God to Nineveh, when he told them to repent, or God would destroy them in forty days (Jonah 3:4). The word is used to proclaim God's future judgments upon the nations by the prophet Joel (Joel 3:9-13). The connotation is very clear: the prophet Joel is heralding a message that the ruler of the universe will bring judgment on the nations. It is binding, and the nations are expected to respond. Zephaniah uses the word to speak of the cry of triumph at the future restoration and salvation of Israel as a nation (Zephaniah 3:14).

2 Chronicles 36:22-23
Now in the first year of Cyrus king of Persia, that Yahweh's word by the mouth of Jeremiah might be accomplished, Yahweh stirred up the spirit of Cyrus king of Persia, so that he made a proclamation throughout all his kingdom, and put it also in writing, saying, "Cyrus king of Persia says, 'Yahweh, the God of heaven, has given all the kingdoms of the Earth to me; and he has commanded me to build him a house in Jerusalem, which is in Judah. Whoever there is among you of all his people, Yahweh his God be with him, and let him go up.'"

Jonah 3:4
Jonah began to enter into the city a day's journey, and he cried out, and said, "In forty days, Nineveh will be overthrown!"

Joel 3:9-13
Proclaim this among the nations: "Prepare for war! Stir up the mighty men. Let all the warriors draw near. Let them come up. Beat your plowshares into swords, and your pruning hooks into spears. Let the weak say, 'I am strong.' Hurry and come, all you surrounding nations, and gather yourselves together." Cause your mighty ones to come down there, Yahweh. "Let the nations arouse themselves, and come up to the valley of Jehoshaphat; for there I will sit to judge

all the surrounding nations. Put in the sickle; for the harvest is ripe. Come, tread, for the wine press is full, the vats overflow, for their wickedness is great."

Zephaniah 3:14
Sing, daughter of Zion! Shout, Israel! Be glad and rejoice with all your heart, daughter of Jerusalem.

Zachariah proclaimed that Israel's future King would be righteous bringing salvation and humbly riding on a donkey (Zachariah 9:9). This prophet is heralding the coming of a king who would bring salvation. It was serious and binding upon his hearers who were to respond with real repentance and acceptance of this message. This prophet became the official herald of God Almighty with an announcement that was so binding that their eternal destiny would be affected.

Zechariah 9:9
Rejoice greatly, daughter of Zion! Shout, daughter of Jerusalem! Behold, your King comes to you! He is righteous, and having salvation; lowly, and riding on a donkey, even on a colt, the foal of a donkey.

In the New Testament, Jesus was God's official herald, so God calls Him "My Servant" in Isaiah 42:1. Jesus declared that the Father had sent Him down from heaven (John 6:38). In Matthew 28:18, He proclaimed that He had all authority in heaven and on Earth. Jesus Christ came as God's official emissary to proclaim the message of redemption from the ruler of the universe. Jesus told His followers that He was speaking the things that He heard directly from God, His Father (John 8:26). The message of Jesus came from the lips of God Himself, and it was a message of sin, judgment, and also salvation. In Matthew 4:17, the author describes Jesus as heralding (preaching) a message of repentance (judgment) and the imminent coming of the kingdom of God.

Isaiah 42:1
Behold, my servant, whom I uphold, my chosen, in whom my soul delights: I have put my Spirit on him. He will bring justice to the nations.

John 6:38
For I have come down from heaven, not to do my own will, but the will of him who sent me.

Matthew 28:18
Jesus came to them and spoke to them, saying, "All authority has been given to me in heaven and on earth."

John 8:26
I have many things to speak and to judge concerning you. However he who sent me is true; and the things which I heard from him, these I say to the world.

Matthew 4:17
From that time, Jesus began to preach, and to say, "Repent! For the Kingdom of Heaven is at hand."

This heralding ministry of Jesus was then turned over to His disciples. In Mark 6:7-12, Jesus called His disciples, gave them His authority, and sent them out to herald the good news of salvation. In Acts 8:5, Luke writes that Philip went into Samaria and proclaimed (heralded) Christ to the people. In 1 Corinthians 1:23, Paul describes the proclamation of the disciples of Christ using this term. This was a message from God, the very king of the universe, which was brought by a group of heralds to proclaim to all the world.

Mark 6:7-12
He called to himself the twelve, and began to send them out two by two; and he gave them authority over the unclean spirits. He commanded them that they should take nothing for their journey, except a staff only: no bread, no wallet, no money in their purse, but to wear sandals, and not put on two tunics. He said to them, "Wherever you enter into a house, stay there until you depart from there. Whoever will not receive you nor hear you, as you depart from there, shake off the dust that is under your feet for a testimony against them. Assuredly, I tell you, it will be more tolerable for Sodom...Gomorrah in the day of judgment....

Acts 8:5
Philip went down to the city of Samaria, and proclaimed to them the Christ.

1 Corinthians 1:23
But we preach Christ crucified: a stumbling block to Jews, and foolishness to Greeks.

In 1 Thessalonians 2:9, though he had been working night and day, Paul told the church at Thessalonica that he had proclaimed (heralded) to them the gospel of God. He wrote these words, "For you remember, brothers, our labor and travail; for working night and day, that we might not burden any of you, we preached to you the good news of God." In Acts 10:42-43, Peter, as God's herald, arrived at the home of the Gentile Cornelius, and he declared that Christ is the one who will judge the living and the dead. This unbelieving man was to receive Jesus as Savior and Lord.

1 Thessalonians 2:9
For you remember, brothers, our labor and travail; for working night and day, that we might not burden any of you, we preached to you the Good News of God.

Acts 10:42-43
He commanded us to preach to the people and to testify that this is he who is appointed by God as the Judge of the living and the dead. All the prophets testify about him, that through his name everyone who believes in him will receive remission of sins.

Judgment and salvation were the message to herald. This message from the lips of a Christian becomes binding on all who hear. If they do not comply, they shall be punished in hell for all eternity. In Romans 10:16, Paul asks how people will believe if they have not heard. How will they hear if someone does not tell them? Christians can tell them. At times, unbelievers, who do not know our glorious Lord, will come to Christians asking for help and advice with a myriad of issues. These Christians must herald the message that the ultimate solution to every one of their problems begins with Jesus Christ, then provide biblical solutions to their many temporal problems.

Romans 10:16
But they didn't all listen to the glad news. For Isaiah says, "Lord, who has believed our report?"

The Testimony of the Plan

Christians should bear witness of the gospel. The Greek word translated "bear witness" literally means to testify in a court of law, or to be a witness. In the Septuagint, the noun form is used to speak of a piece of evidence which calls to mind a particular event. The stones on which Almighty God wrote the Ten Commandments were also called the Tablets of Testimony (Exodus 31:18). The Tent of Meeting was also called the Tent of Testimony (Exodus 29:4, 10). The Ark was referred to as the Ark of the Testimony Exodus 40:3).

Exodus 31:18
When he finished speaking with him on Mount Sinai, he gave Moses the two tablets of the covenant, stone tablets....

Exodus 29:4
You shall bring Aaron and his sons to the door of the Tent of Meeting, and shall wash them with water.

Exodus 29:10
You shall bring the bull before the Tent of Meeting; and Aaron and his sons shall lay their hands on the head of the bull.

Exodus 40:3
You shall put the ark of the covenant in it, and you shall screen the ark with the veil.

All of these objects were the evidence testifying to God's existence and His communication to man. The verb form is used in a legal sense all over the Old Testament. In the book of Numbers 35:30, it is used to speak of the witnesses in a murder trial. In Deuteronomy 19:15, Moses warns against the condemnation of a man based on insufficient testimony. This word always deals with certifiable, objective evidence, not simply unverifiable, subjective evidence. The concept of subjective feelings being used as evidence is foreign to the Old Testament. It had no place among the thinking of the Hebrews. One must keep this in mind.

Numbers 35:30
Whoever kills any person, the murderer shall be slain based on the testimony of witnesses; but one witness shall not testify alone against any person so that he dies.

Deuteronomy 19:15
One witness shall not rise up against a man for any iniquity, or for any sin that he sins. At the mouth of two witnesses, or at the mouth of three witnesses, shall a matter be established.

To bear witness or testify of the gospel meant to proclaim the gospel with evidence. It has absolutely nothing to do with any subjective feeling or experience. Also, it meant to substantiate the claims of Jesus Christ with evidence. This is exactly what God intended and His Christ was meant to do. Throughout the Old Testament, God told His people, the Jews, He would send His Messiah, and they would know Him through signs. The Messiah would be born in the city of Bethlehem (Micah 5:2), from a virgin (Isaiah 7:14), receive vinegar to drink at His own death (Psalm 9:21), and perform many miracles (Isaiah 6:1), to name a few. The purpose of the signs was to testify that Christ was the true Messiah.

Micah 5:2
But you, Bethlehem Ephrathah, being small among the clans of Judah, out of you one will come out to me that is to be ruler in Israel; whose goings out are from of old, from ancient times.

Isaiah 7:14
Therefore the Lord himself will give you a sign. Behold, the virgin will conceive, and bear a son, and shall call his name Immanuel.

Isaiah 6:1
In the year that king Uzziah died, I saw the Lord sitting on a throne, high and lifted up; and his train filled the temple.

The signs bore witness and testified to man that He was the Christ of God. Jesus told His people that he had not come to abolish the law and the prophets but to fulfill them (Matthew 5:17). All throughout His ministry, He appealed to that evidence. Christ did not expect people to simply believe His words but to see His works and the prophecies that He fulfilled. In Matthew 11:4-5, John the Baptist sent several of his disciples to confirm that Christ was indeed the Messiah. Jesus did not tell them to just believe His words. He told John's disciples to go and tell him that the blind see, the lame walk, and the lepers are cleansed.

Matthew 5:17
Don't think that I came to destroy the law or the prophets. I didn't come to destroy, but to fulfill.

Matthew 11:4-5
Jesus answered them, "Go and tell John the things which you hear and see: the blind receive their sight, the lame walk, the lepers are cleansed, the deaf hear, the dead are raised up, and the poor have good news preached to them.

These indicators would attest to His true identity. These signs would bear witness and testify to His anointing from God and that He is truly the Messiah. He specifically stated that His works bore witness that He was from the Father (John 5:36). In John 10:24-25, the Jewish people came and asked Him directly if He was the Christ (Messiah). Jesus told them to look at His works because they testified that He was the Christ.

John 5:36
But the testimony which I have is greater than that of John, for the works which the Father gave me to accomplish, the very works that I do, testify about me, that the Father has sent me.

John 10:24-25
The Jews therefore came around him and said to him, "How long will you hold us in suspense? If you are the Christ, tell us plainly." Jesus answered them, "I told you, and you don't believe. The works that I do in my Father's name, these testify about me.

The bearing witness and testifying was turned over to His disciples. In Acts 1:8, as Jesus was about to depart from the Earth, He taught His disciples that they were to be His witnesses. They were to testify of the resurrection, the many miracles and fulfilled prophecies (what they saw and heard). This is why Luke explains that Jesus remained forty days and provided them with many convincing proofs (Acts 1:3). The sermons that the apostle Peter preached which began in Acts 2:14, Acts 3:12, and Acts 4:8 clearly demonstrate that Peter did provide plenty of evidence concerning Jesus Christ being the Messiah through the Lord's resurrection, mighty works, and fulfilled prophecy.

Acts 1:8
But you will receive power when the Holy Spirit has come upon you. You will be witnesses to me in Jerusalem, in all Judea and Samaria, and to the uttermost parts of the Earth."
Acts 1:3
To these he also showed himself alive after he suffered, by many proofs, appearing to them over a period of forty days....

Acts 2:14
But Peter, standing up with the eleven, lifted up his voice and spoke out to them, "You men of Judea, and all you who dwell at Jerusalem, let this be known to you, and listen to my words.

Acts 3:12
When Peter saw it, he responded to the people, "You men of Israel, why do you marvel at this man? Why do you fasten your eyes on us, as though by our own power or godliness we had made him walk?

Acts 4:8
Then Peter, filled with the Holy Spirit, said to them, "You rulers of the people, and elders of Israel.

In 1 John 1:2, John declared that the apostles proclaimed what they had heard, seen, and touched concerning Jesus, the Word of Life. He wrote, "And the life was revealed, and we have seen, and testify, and declare to you the life, the eternal life, which was with the Father, and was revealed to us." No feelings were described. They never said, "I know Jesus is real because I can feel His presence in my life and talk to Him every day." They always appealed to evidence.

1 John 1:2
(And the life was revealed, and we have seen, and testify, and declare to you the life, the eternal life, which was with the Father, and was revealed to us).

When Christians proclaim the plan, they must testify and bear witness of the good news. The Christian is to share the testimony of actual eyewitnesses, miracles, and fulfilled prophecies of Christ to demonstrate Christ's true identity. This is the witness that will bring salvation to the unsaved through the power of the Spirit. Often times, Christians are told to speak of their personal experience or their journey with God. Though this is admirable, it is not biblical. In fact, any committed cultist or member of a religion could recount a great experience. God desires a testimony of facts.

The Teaching of the Plan

The good news is to be taught. The Greek word translated "teach" literally means to extend the hand for acceptance. A teacher extended his hand with instruction and the student accepted it. In the Septuagint, the term was used to denote instruction with life applications. It entails the many truths of the Scriptures. In Deuteronomy 4:1, 10, and 14, it is used of God's instruction to His people. The teaching concerned His history with His people and His numerous commandments. In Deuteronomy 11:19, the word is used to speak of Jewish fathers teaching their sons the commands of God and His history with them so they would not fall into idolatry.

Deuteronomy 4:1
Now, Israel, listen to the statutes...ordinances which I teach you, to do them; that you may live...possess the land which...the God of your fathers, gives you.

Deuteronomy 4:10
The day that...Yahweh said to me, "Assemble the people to me, and I will make them hear my words, that they may learn to fear me all the days that they live on the Earth, and that they may teach your children.

Deuteronomy 4:14
Yahweh commanded me at that time to teach you statutes and ordinances, that you might do them in the land where you go over to possess it.

Deuteronomy 11:19
You shall teach them to your children, talking of them when you sit in your house, when you walk by the way, when you lie down, and when you rise up.

Anyone who reads the New Testament will see that Jesus taught the people and instructed them concerning the many truths of the kingdom of God (Matthew 5-7). In Matthew 4:23, the apostle Matthew records that Jesus was teaching in the synagogues and proclaiming the gospel of the kingdom of God all throughout Galilee. In Matthew 11:1, the author describes it this way, "When Jesus had finished directing his twelve disciples, he departed from there to teach and preach in their cities." Jesus taught the gospel. He also explained many different aspects of it especially in regard to the fruits one bears once one is saved. In Luke 24:27, Jesus taught the two on the road to Emmaus the detailed truths concerning the Messiah in the Old Testament. Then, the Lord declared that He was the anointed one and described the signs and miracles that proved it. The disciples were to do the very same thing. They were not to speak of feelings but present the evidence that confirmed the deity of Jesus.

Matthew 4:23
Jesus went about in all Galilee, teaching in their synagogues, preaching the Good News of the Kingdom, and healing every disease and every sickness among the people.

Matthew 11:1
When Jesus had finished directing his twelve disciples, he departed from there to teach and preach in their cities.

Luke 24:27
Beginning from Moses and from all the prophets, he explained to them in all the Scriptures the things concerning himself.

The gospel presentation involves much instruction from the Bible. In Matthew 28:19-20, a passage known as the Great Commission, the Lord told His followers "to make disciples." The term translated "disciples" literally means learners. The concept of evangelism is not telling people to accept Christ tacked on at the end of a sermon, but it is the teaching of the Word concerning the plan of redemption and then making a plea for acceptance. This is very important for the Christian. When an unbeliever comes to a Christian for help, a simple plea for salvation will not be enough. The unbeliever should be taught from the Scriptures the true gospel and entreated to accept Christ as Lord and Savior as a result. There should never take a shortcut in the proclaiming of the gospel.

Matthew 28:19-20
Go and make disciples of all nations, baptizing them in the name of the Father and of the Son and of the Holy Spirit, teaching them to observe all things that I commanded you. Behold, I am with you always, even to the end of the age." Amen.

The Deliverance of the Plan

The gospel is to be passed on from one person to the next. The Greek word translated "deliver" literally means to hand something down, to pass something on, or even to deliver something to another. In the Septuagint, fathers are exhorted in Psalm 78:3-4 not to hide the knowledge of God from their children. These fathers were to deliver to the next generation the holy praises of God. God set up memorials, testimonies, and celebrations all throughout Israel's history, so the next generation would set their hope on Him.

Psalm 78:3-4
Which we have heard and known, and our fathers have told us. We will not hide them from their children, telling…the generation to come the praises of Yahweh, his strength, and his wondrous deeds that he has done.

The Lord did not want his divine works forgotten as their fathers stubbornly had done. The New Testament uses this word and concept often. In 1 Corinthians 11:2, Paul lauds the church and commends it for holding firmly to the traditions delivered to them. Later in the letter, he again uses the word when he reminds them that he delivered to them the gospel (1 Corinthians 15:3). The gospel of Christ which was handed down to the apostles has been handed down to all believers to deliver. Luke opens his book writing to Theophilus all those who were witnesses handed the gospel down to him. The writer in turn was handing it down to him and all other Christians (Luke 1:1-2). They in turn handed it down to us. Now, we pass it on to the next generation and so forth.

1 Corinthians 11:2
Now I praise you, brothers, that you remember me in all things, and hold firm the traditions, even as I delivered them to you.

1 Corinthians 15:3
For I delivered to you first of all that which I also received: that Christ died for our sins according to the Scriptures.

Luke 1:1-2
Since many have undertaken to set in order a narrative concerning those matters which have been fulfilled among us, even as those who from the beginning were eyewitnesses and servants of the word delivered them to us.

In 1 Corinthians 9:16-17, Paul utilizes this word when he describes his divine compulsion to preach. He writes, "For if I preach the Good News, I have nothing to boast about; for necessity is laid on me; but woe is to me, if I don't preach the Good News. For if I do this of my own will, I have a reward. But if not of my own will, I have a stewardship entrusted to me." Paul explained that he delivered the gospel to them.

1 Corinthians 9:16-17
For if I preach the Good News...for necessity is laid on me; but woe is to me if I don't preach the Good News. For if I do this of my own will, I have a reward. But if not of my own will, I have a stewardship entrusted to me.

It was a stewardship entrusted to him. Now, Christians have this critical stewardship entrusted to them. They can spend of hours with unbelieving friends, neighbors, or co-workers, but if they never "deliver" the gospel to them, what have they really done? This beloved person will perish and spend an eternity without God. James says that a man does not know what his life will be like tomorrow, for his life is but a vapor which appears for a time and then vanishes away (James 4:14). Christians can help people become the very best they can be, but they will still fade away. The true gospel will allow men to fade from this life into an eternity of blessing, rather than condemnation.

James 4:14
Whereas you don't know what your life will be like tomorrow. For what is your life? For you are a vapor that appears for a little time, and then vanishes away.

An Ancient Portrait

The good news of Jesus Christ is meant to be announced, preached, proclaimed, testified to, taught, delivered, and to bring comfort to the world. In Acts 14, the inspired historian Luke describes the heralding ministry of Paul and Barnabas as they announced God's plan of redemption in several cities in the region known as Galatia. Paul, this great messenger of the Lord, usually followed the same evangelistic approach as Jesus. They were both rabbis. Any traveling rabbi was given an opportunity to speak some words of encouragement in the synagogue service to the Jews and God-fearing Gentiles. Then Paul, as with Jesus, would also go to the marketplace and preach the good news of a new era in Jesus Christ to all others in a city. Barnabas accompanied him as his partner in ministry. As we know there was always a mixed reaction.

The author opens the chapter with the apostle's testimony in a city called Iconium. The two missionaries had just been driven out of the region of Pisidian Antioch by a faction of hostile Jews because of their blasphemous proclamation and many conversions. In Iconium, Paul and Barnabas as usual entered the synagogue, and Paul announced the important news of God's kingdom as His messenger. Once again, many of the Jews and Gentiles received Jesus Christ. Then he spent a long time in the city teaching and instructing the Iconium people concerning the truths of the grace of God.

They were also providing the important necessary signs and wonders to verify it. Another mob of angry Hebrews who had rejected his good news of God's comfort began stirring up the unbelieving Gentiles. They planned to stone the both of them to death for blasphemy. Since the city was so divided, Paul and Barnabas were able to flee the people and save their lives. This threat did not thwart their intent to deliver the gospel. These two heralds were determined to proclaim the message from the King of Kings.

In the city of Lystra, a lame man who had been crippled since birth was listening to the testimony of Paul. When the apostle noticed him and saw that he had faith to be healed, he cried out for him to stand up. Immediately, the lame man leaped to his feet and began to walk. When the people saw this amazing miracle, which could not be denied, they screamed that the gods had come down from their high places to visit them. They traveled throughout entire city shouting that their own gods Zeus (Barnabas) and Hermes (Paul) had appeared. Instantly, the high priest of Zeus, whose temple was just outside the town, brought oxen to sacrifice and garlands to place upon their heads in order for the people to honor and worship these gods.

When the two discovered what the citizens were saying and doing, they tore their robes and ran out announcing that they were mere men. Then they made a great proclamation from the true God. These heralds of the new era in Christ testified of the blessings of God in His creation and His true blessing in Jesus. Though it became difficult to restrain the crowd from sacrificing to them, the people began to listen to their words of testimony. Many people came to Christ.

During these days of preaching, some of the hostile Jews came down from Pisidian Antioch and Lystra and were able to turn the people against them. The crowds stoned Paul and dragged his supposedly lifeless body out of the city and left it there. While his disciples stood around him, he suddenly got up and walked back into Lystra. The following day, Paul traveled to Derbe to proclaim God's message of a new life in Christ. He established a church, appointed elders, and then taught the new Christians. After this, they returned to the cities of Lystra, Iconium, and Antioch and did the same as in Derbe. Throughout these cities, he explained to the believers that through many tribulations and difficulties people enter into the kingdom of God. What wonderful examples of what all believers are to do as they announce, preach, proclaim, testify, teach, and comfort with the plan of redemption.

A Modern Anecdote

As a pastor, one had many responsibilities but can never forget the most important one: to share the gospel. Some think when people become pastors, they automatically want to share the gospel with everyone they see and have no fear or other feelings which may impede them. This simply is not true. We have all the same kinds of concerns all Christians have. When I was a Senior Pastor, I remember sitting in my office looking out the window enjoying the sunshine as I was studying the Word. Suddenly, I saw two women drive up and get out of their car. When I opened the door, the daughter introduced herself as Shirley, and her mother was Virginia. She had tears in her eyes while her mother's head was slumped over with her face to the ground. Shirley went on to explain that her father, Robert, had just passed away. The daughter looked in her sixties and the mother in her eighties. Both of them were utterly devastated. The father had just passed away from a sudden and unexpected heart attack. Her parents attended our church occasionally many years back.

They had nowhere else to go for help with the planning of a religious service. Virginia indicated that they had never really been "church people," but this was the only church she knew. The daughter asked if I could help her mother with the funeral arrangements and then preside over the funeral service. From that moment forward, I began to pray for their salvation as I attended to the arrangements. The daughter did not live in the town or area, so it was just Virginia and I planning the many arrangements with the funeral home.

Knowing that God had called me (as every Christian) to share the gospel and offer the light to heaven to everyone, I decided that I would ask her a few questions to determine if either of them had ever received Jesus Christ. They had not. I prayed that God would give me the opportunity to share the gospel with her. I also had to determine the kind of service I would have for Robert. Perhaps, he had become a Christian near the end, and no one knew it.

When the night of viewing her husband's body arrived, I sat next to Virginia and tried to comfort her. Many people came to pay their respects to her and left in a steady stream. Since the daughter could not make it, it left me alone with her to present the gospel. I felt like it was a divine moment. Deep within my heart and soul I was praying fervently for the opportunity to speak with her that night. I must admit I was extremely fearful as to how I would actually begin the conversation, how I would then proceed, and how she may respond. Would the Lord even give me the opportunity that night and would I be courageous enough to take it?

Then the strangest thing happened. After everyone had come and gone, I looked at my watch and there was about ten minutes remaining. I thought, "I better say something quick, or it will be too late!" Suddenly, a tall, large, muscular man walked into the room, looked at her husband's body in the casket, and began frantically pacing the parlor. In a loud, high-pitched, cracking voice, he kept saying, "I don't know what to say. I don't know what to say. I don't know what to say." He walked back and forth from the casket to the door, over and over again, uttering those fateful words, "I don't know what to say." Then, he walked out.

I remember thinking, "Wait a minute, I do know what to say. I have a message from the King of Kings and Lord of Lords for this woman." I turned to Virginia and whispered, "Virginia, I would like to leave your wonderful husband into the hands of a holy loving God for eternity. Now, I would like to talk about your relationship to God and the life to come. Would that be okay?" She grabbed my arm, squeezed it, and began to cry. After a few moments, she looked at me and whispered, "Please do. I need to know." Right there in the viewing room of her deceased husband, while her tears were flowing, I announced the message that God had for her. That night, she received Jesus Christ as Savior and Lord. I became the herald in her life who had the privilege of ushering her into a new era. When she trusted Jesus Christ, I could see the comfort and peace that came over her from the good news. Before we departed, she declared to me, "Please, Pastor, share that gospel message in the memorial service on Saturday; I want everybody to have the hope that Jesus has now given to me." We can provide that hope to anyone who will hear as we herald the epic message.

A Personal Response

Dear Heavenly Father,

I now know that I am Your messenger to announce the plan of redemption to (add names) and others I know and meet. I do desire to speak to them of the good news that a new era of forgiveness and eternal life can begin in their lives. I realize that (add names) and others I know and meet are facing many difficulties in life. They need the comfort of a relationship with Jesus Christ so they will also know that no matter what life brings their way eternal blessing await them. Give me the motivation to be Your herald in their lives so I can testify to them as Your witness. As I teach them your truths and deliver your plan to them, I ask that through the power of the Spirit their eyes will be opened, and they will receive Your Son. I pray this in the name of Jesus. Amen.

Instructor's Notes

AN INSTRUCTOR'S MANUAL

Chapter 2

Herald the Epic Message

For Christians to share the gospel, they must understand that they are messengers of a powerful declaration given by God. They can witness anywhere, anytime, to anyone.

In the section, "A Typical Scenario," the author explains how the saints might begin a conversation about Christ in a local coffee shop they may frequent.

What is the scenario about?

A Christian desires to share the gospel with the patrons in a coffee shop he frequents.

What held the believer back from sharing the gospel?

He did not realize who he was in Christ: a herald of the King of Kings.

What finally led the Christian to share the good news and how did it occur?

He walked among the patrons and began a conversation based on what they were reading.

Have you had a similar experience?

(Various answers should be shared including yours.)

LEADING THE WAY

In the section, "A Scriptural Principle" the author presents an important biblical principle in evangelism which concerns our right and responsibility to share the gospel.

How would you express this principle in your own words?

This brings us to principle number two which is "we must herald the epic message."

(Various answers should be shared including yours.)

How would you rewrite this principle to make it even more personal to your life (using your name and situation)?

(Various answers should be shared including yours.)

Why do you think this principle might be important in your life right now as you share the gospel?

(Various answers should be shared including yours.)

How would you rate yourself on the percentage of times you followed this principle in the past as a believer?

(Various answers should be shared including yours.)

Directions: Put a horizontal mark and your name where you see yourself on the percentage line.

| 0% | 25% | 50% | 75% | 100% |

In the section, "A Biblical Explanation," the author explains our unique position as heralds of the King of Kings and its importance in sharing the gospel effectively.

What are the differences between "announcing" the plan and "preaching" the plan?

For Christians to share the gospel, they must understand that they are messengers of a powerful declaration given to them by God.

The term that is translated "announce" has the connotation of a declaration from God by His messenger.

The word was used to speak of good news that a new era had begun.

How does someone actually "comfort" with the message of the gospel?

The good news is to comfort people. The Greek word that is translated "comfort" literally means to come along the side of someone and help. Its various forms are used in many places in the Septuagint. It was used to speak of comfort and showing pity (Psalm 119:50) and of compassion and sorrow (Psalm 135:14). It also refers to coming alongside others and encouraging them (Deuteronomy 3:24; Job 4:3). It involves the comfort that the gospel of salvation can bring. In Isaiah 40:1, God exhorts the prophets to comfort his people.

What does it mean "to proclaim" the plan of redemption and give an example from the Bible?

The Old Testament connotation for the word is to officially herald important news or announce an arrival of a dignitary.

The Hebrew word is used to speak of Moses proclaiming to the people that they had brought enough offerings for the tabernacle (Exodus 36:6).

In another instance, the new king, Josiah, had found a copy of the Scriptures in the temple. He then heralded the news, proclaiming that the people of Judah and Jerusalem were to bring to the Lord God the levy fixed by Moses, the servant of God (2 Chronicles 24:9).

Cyrus, ruler of the Persian Empire, made a proclamation that God desired for him to build a temple in Jerusalem and released all the Jews to return to their land if they desired (2 Chronicles 36:22-23).

The word is used of Jonah's proclamation from God to Nineveh, when he told them to repent or God would destroy them in forty days (Jonah 3:4).

The word is used to proclaim God's future judgments upon the nations by the prophet Joel (Joel 3:9-13).

What are the differences between "testifying" and "teaching" the plan of redemption?

To bear witness or testify of the gospel meant to proclaim the gospel with evidence. It has absolutely nothing to do with any subjective feeling or experience. Also, it meant to substantiate the claims of Jesus Christ with evidence.

The good news is to be taught. The Greek word translated "teach" literally means to extend the hand for acceptance. A teacher extended his hand with instruction and the student accepted it. In the Septuagint, the term was used to denote instruction with life applications. It entails the many truths of the Scriptures.

How was the gospel message "delivered" to us and what are we supposed to do about it?
The gospel is to be passed on from one person to the next. The Greek word translated "deliver" literally means to hand something down, to pass something on, or even to deliver something to another.

The apostle Paul explained that he delivered the gospel to them.

It was a stewardship entrusted to him. Now, Christians have this critical stewardship entrusted to them.

In what ways might these truths impact your life?

(*Various answers should be shared including yours.*)

In the section, "An Ancient Portrait," the author provides a unique portrayal of an incident of mistaken identity when Paul shared the gospel.

Can you briefly describe the setting of this real-life ancient drama?

In Iconium, Paul and Barnabas as usual entered the synagogue, and Paul announced the important news of God's kingdom as His messenger. Once again, many of the Jews and Gentiles received Jesus Christ. Then he spent a long time in the city teaching and instructing the Iconium people concerning the truths of the grace of God.

Can you describe the major characters involved?

The major characters are Paul, Barnabas, the synagogue members, citizens of Lystra, and townspeople of Derbe.

How did the evangelist initiate the gospel presentation?

In Iconium he spoke as a Rabbi in the synagogue. In Lystra he healed a lame man. In Derbe, he just preached the gospel.

What was result of this evangelistic presentation?

Many came to Christ, some persecuted him.

How was the principle explained in this chapter applied to the situation?

Paul and Barnabas saw themselves as heralds of the King of Kings and shared the kingdom God and gospel.

Based on the truths learned in this chapter, what would you have done differently if you were the evangelist or how would you have responded if you were the recipient?

(Various answers should be shared including yours.)

In the section, "A Modern Anecdote," the author discusses a situation in which he was able to present the good news to a woman who had come to his church in the past.

Can you briefly describe the setting of this real-life modern drama?

The setting is the office of the author. When I was a Senior Pastor, I remember sitting in my office looking out the window enjoying the sunshine as I was studying the Word. Suddenly, I saw two women drive up and get out of their car.

Can you describe the major characters involved?

The major characters are the pastor, Shirley, the daughter, and Virginia, her mother.

How did the author initiate the gospel presentation?

Suddenly, a tall, large, muscular man walked into the room, looked at her husband's body in the casket, and began frantically pacing the parlor. In a loud, high-pitched, cracking voice, he kept saying, "I don't know what to say. I don't know what to say. I don't know what to say." He walked back and forth from the casket to the door, over and over again, uttering those fateful words, "I don't know what to say." Then, he walked out.

I remember thinking, "Wait a minute, I do know what to say. I have a message from the King of Kings and Lord of Lords for this woman." I turned to Virginia and whispered, "Virginia, I would like to leave your wonderful husband into the hands of a holy loving God for eternity. Now, I would like to talk about your relationship to God and the life to come. Would that be okay?" She grabbed my arm, squeezed it, and began to cry. After a few moments, she looked at me and whispered, "Please do. I need to know."

What was result of this evangelistic presentation?

That night, she received Jesus Christ as Savior and Lord. I became the herald in her life who had the privilege of ushering her into a new era. When she trusted Jesus Christ, I could see the comfort and peace that came over her from the good news.

How was the principle explained in this chapter applied to the situation?

Knowing that God had called me (as every Christian) to share the gospel and offer the light to heaven to everyone, I decided that I would ask her a few questions to determine if either of them had ever received Jesus Christ. They had not. I prayed that God would give me the opportunity to share the gospel with her. I also had to determine the kind of service I would have for Robert. Perhaps, he had become a Christian near the end, and no one knew it.

Based on the truths learned in this chapter, what would you have done differently if you were the author or how would you have responded if you were the recipient?

(Various answers should be shared including yours.)

LEADING THE WAY

In the section, "A Personal Response," the author provides a model you may use for prayer if you find it necessary after discovering the truths in this chapter.

Are you presently attempting to present the gospel of Jesus to someone? If not, are there some in your extended family who may not know Jesus Christ and may need prayer for an opportunity for you to share with them and open hearts to receive Him?

(Various answers should be shared including yours.)

Based on the truths you have just learned, what will you continue to do in your current evangelistic efforts and what might you do differently?

(Various answers should be shared including yours.)

What additional thoughts would you like to share with the others?

(Various answers should be shared including yours.)

Chapter 3

Accept the Divine Mandate

Surrounding the saints is a spiritually desperate world. Though believers often hear from the pulpits that people are "hurting" and are in physical, emotional, psychological, and financially need, this is not their fundamental problem. All people are caught in the grip of spiritual death, and this must be dealt with first. In Ephesians 2:1, the apostle Paul says that those without Christ are spiritually dead in their sins and their trespasses. In Romans 6:16, he adds that they are in slavery to sin which results in spiritual death. Christ sends every believer into the spiritually dying world with the only solution that can heal them from their greatest ill which is the gospel of Jesus. This is one of our chief goals as believers.

Ephesians 2:1
You were made alive when you were dead in transgressions and sins.

A Typical Scenario

Have you ever been in a situation that was something like the following? Every day you come into your high school or college classroom to hear the same mantra: all religions are the same and people throughout history have used them to harm others. Religion has caused wars, ruined cultures, and even enslaved people, so what is the point of believing in any religion. You want to respond but are not sure what you could possibly say to change their thinking. You think in your mind, "Why say something because they won't listen anyway. No one will agree with me, and I will cause a big commotion. Then my classmates will look at me differently, and the teacher will probably lower my grade. It isn't worth the trouble. Besides, it is not my problem."

In this chapter, we will learn that Christians have a divine mandate to share the good news of Jesus. They have been called, commanded, and given this great stewardship. Those unbelievers in that classroom are desperate for forgiveness leading to eternal life rather than everlasting condemnation. If some of those students' names have been written in the Book of Life, they may be waiting for you to share the gospel with them. They must have the works of Satan destroyed in their lives and God finally glorified through them. After you learn these powerful truths, perhaps this same situation could look very different.

Now, you walk into the classroom silently praying for all. Whenever a comment is made, you ask the Lord to provide wisdom and courage to speak His Word and correct them in gentleness. In the evenings, you study the various religions and prepare a simple answer that will be appropriate when the time comes. Then you wait, you are completely free to share or not to share. You feel no pressure, but you pray. You keep looking around the room wondering who may be the one God may have called. Finally, one day, after one of his religious tirades, the teacher says, "Well, what do you think? Am I wrong here?"

You raise your hand and respond, "Yes, I think you may be. It is unfair to lump all religions into the same bag. Each has its own beliefs, history, and contributions it has made to the world. There are those in the name of a religion who abuse people. I can only speak to my religious faith which is Christianity. The Lord Jesus never caused a war, destroyed a culture, or enslaved a people. Instead, He, as the Son of God and only Savior of the world, came to bring peace between

God and man and to free man from the slavery of sin." The class became absolutely silent. The teacher's mouth dropped open. He had never heard such conviction spoken with such clarity and boldness. After the class, a quiet student comes up to you and says, "Listen, I was raised in the church, but I do not think I have the kind of relationship you have with Jesus. Could you explain it to me?" So, I take the time over coffee to describe what it means to be a Christian and how to become one.

Though this is an imaginary scenario, it is typical of the kind of situations we may find ourselves in where the good news could be shared with people, but we miss many critical moments to proclaim the gospel due to an ignorance of our divine mandate. When we understand this supernatural directive, it provides an important catalyst for presenting the redemptive plan. Here is a third principle which involves recognizing, accepting, and acting on this command.

A Scriptural Principle

After His resurrection, Jesus told his disciples that as His Father had sent Him into the world, so He sent them (John 17:18). Christians have been sent with the gospel; there is no other cure. The salvation of the unsaved must be the priority of God's children. Jesus told his disciples that He was the way, truth, and life that all men and women must come to God through Him (John 14:6). The Lord could have selected a wide variety of ways in which He could have revealed His plan of redemption to a dying world, yet He chose for His people to proclaim it. The third biblical principle is "we must accept the divine mandate." This is our mandate.

John 17:18
As you sent me into the world...so I have sent them into the world.

John 14:6
Jesus said to him, "I am the way, the truth, and the life. No one comes to the Father, except through me."

A Biblical Explanation

Some Christians may feel inadequate to share the gospel. Others may be unwilling to take the time or make the effort to share the good news. Christians can easily fall into the slumber of not witnessing and merely hope that unbelievers come to Christ based solely on their examples! How will they come to Christ, if no one tells them? Most Christians just bring the unsaved into the church and hope the pastor will save them when he preaches his sermon. How many people could they possibly reach, even if, they shared the true gospel every Sunday for over forty years? Evangelism is every believer's responsibility. Individual Christians must recognize, accept, and act upon this divine endeavor.

In Romans 9:1-3, the apostle described the great sorrow and grief that filled his heart for his unbelieving Hebrew brethren in the nation of Israel. He penned, "I tell the truth in Christ. I am not lying, my conscience testifying with me in the Holy Spirit, that I have great sorrow and unceasing pain in my heart. For I could wish that I myself were accursed from Christ for my brothers' sake, my relatives according to the flesh." Paul would have gladly been condemned to hell for the sake of His lost countrymen. Why did he have such persistence in winning them to Christ?

Romans 9:1-3
I tell the truth in Christ. I am not lying, my conscience testifying with me in the Holy Spirit that I have great sorrow and unceasing pain in my heart. For I could wish that I myself were accursed from Christ for my brothers' sake, my relatives according to the flesh.

He told the church in Thessalonica that he was mistreated at Philippi. Yet, Paul pressed on to preach the gospel to them against much opposition (1 Thessalonians 2:2). The apostle was impelled to act. He declared to the Corinthians that he had nothing to boast about for he was under compulsion to preach the gospel (1 Corinthians 9:16). Why did he press on?

1 Thessalonians 2:2
But having suffered before and been shamefully treated, as you know, at Philippi, we grew bold in our God to tell you the Good News of God in much conflict.

1 Corinthians 9:16
For if I preach the Good News, I have nothing to boast about; for necessity is laid on me; but woe is to me if I don't preach the Good News.

The Scriptures provide reasons why Christians should be compelled to proclaim the redemptive plan. These reasons clearly cover the critical part evangelism must play in time spent with unbelievers. The saved cannot deny or dismiss this critical and important responsibility. It is a powerful and exciting mandate for all believers. Remember, it is not to be a burden thrust upon people from the church's pulpit. God never intended this. Yet, Christians must realize that they are deeply indebted to the ones who took their responsibility to share the gospel. Without these faithful people who were willing to accept the divine mandate and share the gospel with us, we may be living a very different life with a very different destiny.

The Glory of God

The theme of the universe, the reason for which all things were created, was, and is, and always will be, to give God glory. In Psalm 29:1-2, King David proclaims that all should ascribe to the Lord glory and strength. He must be given the glory that is due His name. David indicates that the Lord God by His very nature deserves glory. In Psalm 145:3, the psalmist proclaims that the Lord is magnificent and is to be greatly praised. The Lord is so grand, so awesome, and so powerful that He deserves praise from every human being on Earth (all of His creation). Yet, there is a vast majority of unsaved people on Earth who cannot glorify Him in their words or actions!

Psalm 29:1-2
Ascribe to Yahweh, you sons of the mighty, ascribe to Yahweh glory and strength. Ascribe to Yahweh the glory due to his name. Worship Yahweh in holy array.

Psalm 145:3
Great is Yahweh, and greatly to be praised! His greatness is unsearchable.

In John 5:23, Jesus declared emphatically, if one does not honor the son, one does not honor the Father who sent Him. Those who have not heard the gospel cannot know Christ and cannot glorify God. In Romans 3:23, Paul sets forth the problem when he states that all men have sinned and have fallen short of God's glory. If one has not been cleansed with the blood of the Lamb, he cannot give God glory (1 John 1:7). Without faith in God through Jesus Christ no one can please God (Hebrews 11:6). This is such a critical understanding for Christians.

John 5:23
That all may honor the Son, even as they honor the Father. He who doesn't honor the Son doesn't honor the Father who sent him.

Romans 3:23
For all have sinned, and fall short of the glory of God.

1 John 1:7
But if we walk in the light, as he is in the light, we have fellowship with one another, and the blood of Jesus Christ, his Son, cleanses us from all sin.

Hebrews 11:6
Without faith it is impossible to be well pleasing to him, for he who comes to God must believe that he exists, and that he is a rewarder of those who seek him.

Every day, God is faced with a massive sea of humanity, numbering in the billions, who will not and cannot give him the honor, praise, glory, and exaltation worthy of his person. Yet, Christians through the power of Christ can remedy such a despicable and horrendous situation. Christians can do this by proclaiming the plan to the small, but significant portion of humanity that could be found in their neighborhoods, schools, workplaces, and cities.

Through their witness, they can bring someone into the kingdom of God producing a lifetime of glorifying God in thought, word, and deed. Through the process of sharing the gospel, coming to Christ, and living a holy life afterwards, God receives a tremendous amount of glory and honor. In 2 Corinthians 2:14-16, Paul pronounces that in every place he shares the gospel a sweet aroma is sent to God giving Him glory. In Romans 15:9, the apostle explains that when Christ accepts people (saves them), even though they are all sinners and deserve nothing, the Lord God will receive glory and honor. Why? God demonstrates His great mercy and grace. It puts on display these beautiful attributes.

2 Corinthians 2:14-16
Now thanks be to God, who always leads us in triumph in Christ, and reveals through us the sweet aroma of his knowledge in every place. For we are a sweet aroma of Christ to God, in those who are saved and in those who perish: to the one a stench from death to death, to the other a sweet aroma from life to life. Who is sufficient for these things?

Romans 15:9
And that the Gentiles might glorify God for his mercy. As it is written, "Therefore I will give praise to you among the Gentiles and sing to your name."

In 2 Corinthians 4:15, when Paul proclaimed the gospel and people came to Christ, they responded with the giving of thanks to God. The inspired writer pens, "For all things are for your sakes, that the grace, being multiplied through the many, may cause...thanksgiving to abound to the glory of God." This gave God glory. In Ephesians 2:7, Paul asserts that those who come to Christ will forever be the trophies of God's grace. When Christians display God's grace, He is glorified. In Ephesians 1:6, 12, and 14, the apostle, who was sent to the Gentiles, affirms that the saints are redeemed for God's glory.

2 Corinthians 4:15
For all things are for your sakes, that the grace, being multiplied through the many, may cause the thanksgiving to abound to the glory of God.

Ephesians 2:7
That in the ages to come he might show the exceeding riches of his grace in kindness toward us in Christ Jesus.

Ephesians 1:6
To the praise of the glory of his grace, by which he freely gave us favor in the Beloved.

Ephesians 1:12
To the end that we should be to the praise of his glory, we who had before hoped in Christ.

Ephesians 1:14
Who is a pledge of our inheritance, to the redemption of God's own possession, to the praise of his glory.

Then, believers can spend an entire lifetime giving God glory through praying (John 14:13), doing good deeds (John 15:8), living righteously (Philippians 1:9-11), confession of sin (Luke 23:41), seeking unity with all the brethren (Romans 15:5-7), sharing the good news (Galatians 1:23), and suffering for Christ (John 21:19). Sharing the good news with others, bringing them to salvation, and knowing our Lord will be glorified throughout their lives is what life is all about.

John 14:13
Whatever you will ask in my name, I will do it, that the Father may be glorified in the Son.

Philippians 1:9-11
This I pray, that your love may abound yet more and more in knowledge and all discernment, so that you may approve the things that are excellent, that you may be sincere and without offense to the day of Christ, being filled with the fruits of righteousness, which are through Jesus Christ, to the glory and praise of God.

Luke 23:41
And we indeed justly, for we receive the due reward for our deeds, but this man has done nothing wrong."

Romans 15:5-7
Now the God of perseverance and of encouragement grant you to be of the same mind with one another according to Christ Jesus, that with one accord you may with one mouth glorify the God and Father of our Lord Jesus Christ. Therefore accept one another, even as Christ also accepted you, to the glory of God.

Galatians 1:23
But they only heard: "He who once persecuted us now preaches the faith that he once tried to destroy."

John 21:19
Now he said this, signifying by what kind of death he would glorify God. When he had said this, he said to him, "Follow me."

Christians have the great privilege of bringing people into a relationship with God, which will produce a lifetime and eternity of glorifying Him. Since believers seek to glorify God in everything, then bringing others to Christ will satisfy this great longing. What a blessing for Christians to be able stand before their God and Father and glorify Him through the bringing of others into His kingdom to do the same!

The Command of Christ

Christians are commanded to proclaim the gospel. This is obvious, but it is so essential to living the Christian life. In Matthew 28:19-20, Matthew records the final words of Jesus Christ before His departure from the Earth. Jesus begins by acknowledging that He has divine authority. In that very authority, He commands His followers "to make disciples" of Him (main verb: make learners), by going (proclamation of the gospel), baptizing (belief with its sign), and teaching (obedient lifestyle, building up in the faith).

Matthew 28:19-20
Go and make disciples of all nations, baptizing them in the name of the Father and of the Son and of the Holy Spirit, teaching them to observe all things that I commanded you. Behold, I am with you always, even to the end of the age." Amen.

Mark records the exact same event, though he provides an additional detail. In Mark 16:15, he writes, "He said to them, 'Go into all the world, and preach the Good News to the whole creation.'" They were commanded by their Lord to travel throughout the entire world and proclaim the gospel. Jesus exhorted His disciples to speak in the light what they had heard from Him in the darkness. His followers were entreated to declare what was whispered in their ears upon the housetops (Matthew 10:27). The good news is not God's private little message that He gave to His Son Jesus and His followers alone. It is for public consumption. It should also be spoken in the light and shouted from the roofs of homes (an ancient custom for announcing good news). If the Lord commands it, the saints are to do it. In Jude 1:22-23, Jude essentially commands believers to proclaim the plan, when he states that all believers are to show mercy (a command) to some doubters and to save (a command) others from the fire. The Lord explains to His disciples that loving Him involves obeying Him.

Mark 16:15
He said to them, "Go into all the world, and preach the Good News to the whole creation.

Matthew 10:27
What I tell you in the darkness, speak in the light; and what you hear whispered in the ear, proclaim on the housetops.

Jude 1:22-23
On some have compassion, making a distinction, and some save, snatching them out of the fire with fear, hating even the clothing stained by the flesh.

This means keeping His commandments (John 14:15). One of the many commandments of Jesus was to share the good news. God's children are compelled to share the gospel of Jesus Christ with all their unbelieving friends, neighbors, co-workers, and fellow students. The specifics of who, when, and where is left up to each individual believer. The Holy Spirit will work in their desires and put them into a variety of different circumstances that will allow them to share the good news that they have been given.

John 14:15
If you love me, keep my commandments.

The Call of God

All Christians are called by God to proclaim the plan. This is not just a serious command but a high calling. In Romans 1:6-7, Paul opened his letter by greeting the church as those who are "called to be his saints." Here is the critical truth that Christians are called to belong to Jesus Christ and are called to be His holy ones (saints who are set apart). This word "call" means to call out, to summon. What does this "calling" involve? What attitudes or actions spring from this call?

Romans 1:6-7
Among whom you are also called to belong to Jesus Christ; to all who are in Rome, beloved of God, called to be saints: Grace to you and peace from God our Father and the Lord Jesus Christ.

According to 1 Corinthians 1:9, Paul states that Christians were called into fellowship with His Son. He explained to them, "God is faithful, through whom you were called into the fellowship of his Son, Jesus Christ, our Lord." The word translated "fellowship" speaks of real or joint participation in something. Believers are called into joint participation with His Son. This entails so much more than just personal time with Christ. What is the Son of God doing that involves a saint's participation? He is calling those who were written in the book of life before the foundation of the world to Him. Then Jesus is building them up in the faith (Ephesians 1:15). This is essentially evangelism and edification. These are the two pillars of the church (Ephesians 4:11; Acts 2:41-42).

1 Corinthians 1:9
God is faithful, through whom you were called into the fellowship of his Son, Jesus Christ, our Lord.

Ephesians 1:15
For this cause I also, having heard of the faith in the Lord Jesus which is among you, and the love which you have toward all the saints.

Ephesians 4:11
He gave some to be apostles; and some, prophets; and some, evangelists; and some, shepherds and teachers.

Acts 2:41-42
Then those who gladly received his word were baptized. There were added that day about three thousand souls. They continued steadfastly in the apostles' teaching and fellowship, in the breaking of bread, and prayer.

Christians are to be regularly involved in edification, but it should begin with evangelism. After Christ's resurrection, Jesus conveyed to His disciples that the Father had sent Him into the world to proclaim the kingdom of God. Jesus was now sending them to do the exact same thing. Sharing the gospel is a responsibility of all who fellowship with Christ.

In 2 Corinthians 5:18-19, Paul describes it clearly when he explains that the Lord God reconciled or restored the union with the world through Christ. The Lord then gave him the word of reconciliation, the gospel, commissioning him as an ambassador of Christ to the world. Christians have the same commission (calling) of proclaiming God's plan in order to reconcile the unsaved. Paul's ambassadorship in the gospel is not the same as his apostleship. It extends to all believers.

2 Corinthians 5:18-19
But all things are of God, who reconciled us to himself through Jesus Christ, and gave to us the ministry of reconciliation; namely, that God was in Christ reconciling the world to himself, not reckoning to them their trespasses, and having committed to us the word of reconciliation.

The Characteristic of Christians

Proclaiming the gospel is a characteristic of Christians. In Acts 1:8, the Lord revealed that the disciples would receive power when the Holy Spirit came upon them. This would result in a very powerful testimony of Him all throughout the region and beyond to the farthest reaches of the Earth. He informed them that they would be His witnesses. It was not up for negotiation but would happen. Their testimony of His Word would be a common characteristic in their lives.

Acts 1:8
But you will receive power when the Holy Spirit has come upon you. You will be witnesses to me in Jerusalem, in all Judea and Samaria, and to the uttermost parts of the earth.

One of the clearest statements concerning this important quality can be found in Matthew 5:14-15. In this passage, the Lord Jesus is speaking to the Jews as a nation and reaffirms to them something they already should have known; they were lights to the world. Now, they should begin acting like lamps bringing light into the darkness for all unbelievers.

Matthew 5:14-15
You are the light of the world. A city located on a hill can't be hidden. Neither do you light a lamp and put it under a measuring basket, but on a stand; and it shines to all who are in the house.

The concept of light in the Scriptures always entailed the revelation of God's truth or holy living. This is diametrically opposed to the darkness which spoke of Satan's lies or evil living. To be a light to the world meant to show forth God's truth and holiness to the world, in other words, the gospel. When God's people, the Jews, rejected Christ, He established the church to take on that mantle. This mantle of evangelism is an amazing opportunity to participate in something truly meaningful.

In Philippians 2:14-15, the apostle validated this truth to the church at Philippi. He declared that the saints appeared as lights in the world and were to be holding forth the Word of Truth. He wrote, "Do all things without murmurings and disputes, that you may become blameless and harmless, children of God without blemish in the midst of a crooked and perverse generation, among whom you are seen as lights in the world." Paul writes this injunction in a matter-of-fact tone. This is what all Christians are to do. They are to be lights in their world. Believers should live in harmony, without disputes or grumbling, and with holy habits in the midst of a world that is perverse, sinful, and crooked. This means that we act differently than society at large.

Philippians 2:14-15
Do all things without complaining and arguing, that you may become blameless and harmless, children of God without defect in the middle of a crooked and perverse generation, among whom you are seen as lights in the world.

In John 12:35-36, Jesus refers to Himself as the light of the world and those who believe in Him as sons of light. When unsaved people come into the lives of Christians (the light), they come enveloped by complete darkness (Colossians 1:13) and they constantly stumble in total blindness (1 John 2:11). Christians are to be the light shining through that darkness with the good news. This good news will place them on the path of light, where they will not stumble in lies and sin any longer. The saints might not always display this important characteristic due to a **rebellious flesh (Romans 7). Often, the** flesh will desire to criticize and berate unbelievers in their minds, rather than feel deep compassion for their horrible lost condition. Beware the flesh!

John 12:35-36
Jesus therefore said to them, "Yet a little while the light is with you. Walk while you have the light, that darkness doesn't overtake you. He who walks in the darkness doesn't know where he is going. While you have the light, believe in the light, that you may become children of light." Jesus said these things, and he departed and hid himself from them.

Colossians 1:13
Who delivered us out of the power of darkness, and translated us into the Kingdom of the Son of his love.

1 John 2:11
But he who hates his brother is in the darkness, and walks in the darkness, and doesn't know where he is going...the darkness has blinded his eyes.

The Result of Maturity

Proclaiming the plan is a natural outgrowth of maturity. Paul affirms that Christians are to build themselves up into a mature man. This spiritual maturity must measure up to the stature of the fullness of Christ. This is found in Ephesians 4:13-14). Then, in Ephesians 4:15, he explains that Christians should no longer behave like children, who are tossed back and forth by false doctrines, but should speak God's truth in love. Paul explains, "But speaking truth in love, we may grow up in all things into him, who is the head, Christ." This important concept of "speaking the truth" must encompass the sharing of the gospel. This is the first truth anyone must know. Isn't it?

Ephesians 4:13-14
Until we all attain to the unity of the faith and of the knowledge of the Son of God, to a full grown man, to the measure of the stature of the fullness of Christ, that we may no longer be children, tossed back and forth and carried about with every wind of doctrine...trickery of men, in craftiness, after the wiles of error.

Ephesians 4:15
But speaking truth in love, we may grow up in all things into him who is the head, Christ.

In Jude 1:17-21, the author describes clearly the spiritual growth process. He identified the elements of this growth as building oneself up in the faith, praying in the Holy Spirit, keeping oneself in love, waiting for Christ, and having mercy on those who doubt. After this, the author issues the command that they are to save some by snatching them and pulling them out of the fire (Jude 1:23). This absolutely refers to evangelism; the fire is hell (Matthew 18:9). Sharing Christ and bringing them into the kingdom snatches them out of that fire. The apostles had been trained by the Lord Jesus before and after His resurrection and had spent much time with Him. They grew and matured in the faith resulting in a dynamic witness for Christ (Acts 3:4-9, 12). Their maturity was expressed in their growing desire to share the gospel as they became more like Him in His compassion, mercy, and grace. As they are increasingly filled by the Spirit, Christians should commit themselves to increasingly sharing the gospel (Ephesians 5:18).

Jude 1: 17-21
But you, beloved, remember the words which have been spoken before by the apostles of our Lord Jesus Christ. They said to you, "In the last time there will be mockers, walking after their own ungodly lusts." These are those who cause divisions and are sensual, not having the Spirit. But you, beloved, keep building up yourselves on your most holy faith, praying in the Holy Spirit. Keep yourselves in God's love, looking for the mercy of our Lord Jesus Christ to eternal life.

Jude 1:23
And some save, snatching them out of the fire with fear, hating even the clothing stained by the flesh.

Matthew 18:9
If your eye causes you to stumble, pluck it out and cast it from you. It is better for you to enter into life with one eye, rather than having two eyes to be cast into the Gehenna of fire.

Ephesians 5:18
Don't be drunken with wine, in which is dissipation, but be filled with the Spirit.

The Divinely Chosen Method

Proclaiming the good news by Christians is God's chosen method of evangelism. There are many ways in which God could have ordained to bring people into His kingdom. Yet, He decided to have His followers share His good news. In Galatians 3:1-2, Paul challenges his readers to remember that they were all saved by hearing accompanied by faith, not by works which is what the Judaizers had said. The Galatians had heard the gospel from Paul, and they had believed. In Romans 10:14, the apostle questioned the Romans as to how unbelievers could call upon the Lord, if they had not heard. Then, how could they hear without a preacher? A preacher going out to proclaim the gospel is the method of God. This preacher, who heralds the gospel, is the average believer.

Galatians 3:1-2
Foolish Galatians, who has bewitched you not to obey the truth, before whose eyes Jesus Christ was openly portrayed among you as crucified? I just want to learn this...Did you receive the Spirit by...works...or...hearing of faith?

Romans 10:14
How then will they call on him in whom they have not believed? How will they believe in him whom they have not heard? How will they hear without a preacher?

There are numerous ways in which God could reveal His plan, but he chose the simple sharing of the gospel by His followers. People should be talking and sharing with other people. Jude demands that Christians earnestly contend for the faith once and for all delivered to the church (Jude 1:3). Christians should take the Holy Scriptures and share this redemptive plan. In Romans 10:15, Paul questioned, "And how will they preach unless they are sent? As it is written: 'How beautiful are the feet of those who preach the Good News of peace, who bring glad tidings of good things!'" Paul asserts that those who bring the glad tidings of His salvation have very beautiful feet. It is the feet that must be used to approach the unsaved. What a blessing it would be to say at the end of a day, "The Lord made my feet beautiful today!"

Jude 1:3
Beloved, while I was very eager to write to you about our common salvation, I was constrained to write to you exhorting you to contend earnestly for the faith which was once for all delivered to the saints.

Romans 10:15
And how will they preach unless they are sent? As it is written:
"How beautiful are the feet of those who preach the Good News of peace, who bring glad tidings of good things!"

The proclamation of the good news was always shared in the Old Testament from person to person as well. Abraham's son heard it from Abraham. Isaac proclaimed it to Jacob. His sons heard it from him. The people of Israel heard it from

Moses and the other prophets. The saints in the first century heard it from other Christians, who had heard it from the apostles. They then told others.

In Matthew 16:18, Jesus declared to Peter that He, Christ, would build His church. Christ is the one who causes numerical growth in the church. In Revelation 1:10-13, John views Christ walking among lamp stands, which represent the churches. This portrays the Lord Jesus ministering and building up His churches. In Colossians 1:18, the apostle Paul emphatically declares that Christ is the head of the church and has the preeminence above all. The question then arises, how does Christ build His church numerically? The church experiences numerical growth through sharing the gospel.

Matthew 16:18
I also tell you that you are Peter, and on this rock I will build my assembly, and the gates of Hades will not prevail against it.

Revelation 1:10-13
I was in the Spirit on the Lord's day, and I heard behind me a loud voice, like a trumpet saying, "What you see, write in a book and send to the seven assemblies: to Ephesus, Smyrna, Pergamum, Thyatira, Sardis, Philadelphia, and to Laodicea." I turned to see the voice that spoke with me. Having turned, I saw seven golden lamp stands. And among the lamp stands was one like a son of man, Daniel.

Colossians 1:18
He is the head of the body, the assembly, who is the beginning, the firstborn from the dead, that in all things he might have the preeminence.

Two familiar passages teach this critical truth: Matthew 28:19-20 and Acts 1:8. Here He announces to his disciples that they are to be His witnesses and are to make disciples throughout the entire world. In 1 Corinthians 3:6, the apostle explains to the saints in Corinth that they should not group themselves according to the person who brought them to

Christ. Paul might have planted the seed of the gospel, but Apollos watered, and God caused the growth (1 Corinthians 3:6). The Lord God causes people to receive the gospel unto eternal life; no one else. The Lord God Almighty builds His church as Christians are willing to be faithful to bear witness of the gospel; no one else.

Matthew 28:19-20
Go and make disciples of all nations, baptizing them in the name of the Father and of the Son and of the Holy Spirit, teaching them to observe all things that I commanded you. Behold, I am with you always, even to the end of the age." Amen.

Acts 1:8
But you will receive power when the Holy Spirit has come upon you. You will be witnesses to me in Jerusalem, in all Judea and Samaria, and to the uttermost parts of the Earth."

1 Corinthians 3:6
I planted. Apollos watered. But God gave the increase.

Witnessing churches are growing churches. Witnessing ministries are growing ministries. This is the New Testament pattern. This is shown powerfully through the actions of the early church, which is found in Acts 5:42-6:1. In this passage, the saints proclaimed Jesus as the Christ, and God increased their number. The growth plan of the Lord was incredibly simple: people are to proclaim the good news of Jesus with other people. The saints should be spending time with the unsaved people everywhere they go and share the gospel. Believers must constantly remember this sharing person to person is the divine method God has chosen. They receive the privilege of utilizing this simple, but profound method of delivering the great plan of redemption from Him to the lost world of man.

Acts 5:4
While you kept it, didn't it remain your own? After it was sold, wasn't it in our power? How is it that you have conceived this thing in your heart? You haven't lied to men, but to God."

Acts 6:1
Now in those days, when the number of the disciples was multiplying, a complaint arose from the Hellenists against the Hebrews, because their widows were neglected in the daily service.

The Chosen Await the Proclamation

Those who have been chosen are awaiting the coming of Christians. Why? They must share the gospel with them. Who else will? In Ephesians 1:3-4, Paul opens his letter by describing the tremendous blessings that Christians possess. These divine blessings come to those chosen by God before the foundation of the world. In Colossians 3:12, the apostle calls Christians "the ones who have been chosen of God." In 1 Thessalonians 1:4, he specifies that his readers are beloved by God, chosen of Him. Christians must acknowledge that all around them are the elect waiting for their proclamation. In 2 Timothy 2:10, Paul reiterated this concept to the young pastor Timothy. He described his great passion and concern, "Therefore I endure all things for the chosen ones' sake, that they also may obtain the salvation which is in Christ Jesus with eternal glory." Here the apostle encouraged Timothy to remember that he had endured many difficulties for the sake of those who had been chosen. He would endure anything that they might find salvation in Christ (2 Timothy 2:7-9).

Ephesians 1:3-4
Blessed be the God...Father of our Lord Jesus Christ, who has blessed us with every spiritual blessing in the heavenly places in Christ, even as he chose us in him before the foundation of the world, that we would be holy and without defect before him in love.

Colossians 3:12
Put on therefore, as God's chosen ones, holy and beloved, a heart of compassion, kindness, lowliness, humility, and perseverance.

1 Thessalonians 1:4
We know, brothers loved by God, that you are chosen.

2 Timothy 2:10
Therefore I endure all things for the chosen ones' sake, that they also may obtain the salvation which is in Christ Jesus with eternal glory.

2 Timothy 2:7-9
Consider what I say, and may the Lord give you understanding in all things. Remember Jesus...risen from the dead, of the offspring[a] of David, according to my Good News, in which I suffer hardship to the point of chains as a criminal. But God's word isn't chained.

Paul saw the potentially chosen in every encounter with unbelievers. He was willing to suffer any difficulty, endure any kind of hardship, and handle any persecution in order to proclaim the plan to the chosen. Since the chosen could not be identified, Paul recognized that he would have to share the gospel with everyone. Christians must realize that people, who enter their lives, may have their names written in the Lord's book of life. This is so important to understand. The unsaved people that saints encounter in their everyday life may have their names written in the book of life. Is it possible that an unsaved person may walk into our lives to hear the good news of Jesus specifically from us (Phil. 4:3)?

Philippians 4:3
Yes, I beg you also, true partner, help these women, for they labored with me in the Good News with Clement also, and the rest of my fellow workers, whose names are in the book of life.

The Exaltation of Christ

The church has been given as a gift to the Son from God, the Father, for Christ's exaltation and glory for all eternity. In Romans 8:28-30, Paul describes it, "For whom he foreknew, he also predestined to be conformed to the image of his Son, that he might be the first born among many brothers. Whom he predestined, those he also called. Whom he called, those he also justified. Whom he justified, those he also glorified." Here, the inspired apostle recounts God's purpose for His Son. The Lord is to be the "first-born" of many brethren. This means the Lord is to be preeminent among a great host of brothers and sisters. All Christians are predestined, called, justified, glorified, and conformed to Christ's image for this purpose.

Romans 8:28-30
We know that all things work together for good for those who love God, for those who are called according to his purpose. For whom he foreknew, he also predestined to be conformed to the image of his son, that he might be the firstborn among many brothers. Whom he predestined, those he also called. Whom he called, those he also justified. Whom he justified...glorified.

In Colossians 1:18, the saints in Colossae were taught that Christ is the head of His body (church). He is the beginning and first born from the dead. As a result, Christ will have first place in everything. This first place speaks of exaltation and glory. Earlier in the same letter, it was presented that all things had been created for Jesus Christ and through Jesus Christ (Colossians 1:16). In his letter to the Philippians, Paul declares with great excitement that every knee will bow, and every tongue will confess that Jesus Christ is the Lord and Master of all (Philippians 2:9-11).

Colossians 1:18
He is the head of the body, the assembly, who is the beginning, the firstborn from the dead, that in all things he might have the preeminence.

Philippians 2:9-11
Therefore God also highly exalted him, and gave to him the name which is above every name, that at the name of Jesus every knee should bow, of those in heaven, those on Earth, and those under the Earth, and that every tongue should confess that Jesus Christ is Lord, to the glory of God the Father.

In John 3:35, John the Baptist proclaimed that the Father loved the Son and gave all things into His hand. All that one sees is given as a gift to Christ from the Father. In John 10:29, Jesus confirmed this when He told His followers that His Father, who was greater than all, had given His disciples to Him. No one could snatch them out of the Father's hand. It is critical that those in the church realize that every unbeliever will either bend the knee in salvation or in judgment. In either divine instance, the Son will be glorified. Therefore, receiving Christ must be the first step for Christ's exaltation now and at His coming.

John 3:35
The Father loves the Son, and has given all things into his hand.

John 10:29
My Father who has given them to me is greater than all. No one is able to snatch them out of my Father's hand.

The Stewardship of the Proclamation

The gospel is a stewardship that has been entrusted to the church. This stewardship is the church's main priority. The church is always to be proclaiming the plan of redemption. In 1 Corinthians 4:1-2, Paul declares that he saw himself as God's steward of the mysteries of Jesus Christ requiring Him to be faithful to that task. He asserts, "For if I do this of my own will, I have a reward. But if not of my own will, I have a stewardship entrusted to me."

1 Corinthians 4:1-2
So let a man think of us as Christ's servants, and stewards of God's mysteries. Here, moreover, it is required of stewards that they be found faithful.

In 1 Corinthians 9:17, Paul asserts that God had entrusted a stewardship to him. This servant knew that he would be held accountable for his faithfulness to this. Now this critical guardianship is entrusted to the church of Jesus Christ. How do we know this? In 1 Timothy 3:15, the apostle describes the universal church as the pillar and support of the truth. In 2 Timothy 1:13-14, Paul encourages Timothy to hold onto the pattern of sound words that the pastor had heard from the apostle Paul. These sound words and doctrine had been committed to him and were to be guarded in the power of the Holy Spirit who had already indwelt him. In chapter 2, verse 2, Paul commanded his son in the faith, Timothy, to commit all that he had taught him (the doctrine) to faithful men. These would teach it to many others. This stewardship was to be passed down from one person to another.

1 Corinthians 9:17
For if I do this of my own will, I have a reward. But if not of my own will, I have a stewardship entrusted to me.

1 Timothy 3:15
But if I wait long, that you may know how men ought to behave themselves in God's house, which is the assembly of the living God, the pillar and ground of the truth.

2 Timothy 1:13-14
Hold the pattern of sound words which you have heard from me, in faith and love which is in Christ Jesus. That good thing which was committed to you, guard through the Holy Spirit who dwells in us.

2 Timothy 2:2
The things which you have heard from me among many witnesses, commit the same things to faithful men, who will be able to teach others also.

In 2 Timothy 2:15, Paul alluded to this stewardship of the truth, when he pronounced that Timothy was to be handling the Word of God properly, as a diligent workman who was not ashamed of his use of it. In this same letter, Timothy was to use the Word of God to correct, rebuke, and instruct with patience and carefulness (2 Timothy 3:16), while he preached in season and out of season (2 Timothy 4:2).

2 Timothy 2:15
Give diligence to present yourself approved by God, a workman who doesn't need to be ashamed, properly handling the Word of Truth.

2 Timothy 3:16
Every Scripture is God-breathed and profitable for teaching, for reproof, for correction, and for instruction in righteousness.

2 Timothy 4:2
Preach the word; be urgent in season and out of season; reprove, rebuke, and exhort with all patience and teaching.

This stewardship of the truth had to do with the mystery mentioned in 1 Timothy 3:16. In this passage, Paul states that the mystery of godliness is that God was revealed in the flesh, justified in the spirit, seen by angels, proclaimed unto the nations, believed in the world, and received up in glory. This is the essence of the gospel. So, what does this mean to the average believer? If Christians are indeed the church, then all the followers of Christ are the pillar and support of the truth both individually and corporately. They do not volunteer for this crucial stewardship. Instead, it is one of the foundations of Christian living.

1 Timothy 3:16
Without controversy, the mystery of godliness is great: God was revealed in the flesh, justified in the spirit, seen by angels, preached among the nations, believed on in the world, and received up in glory.

The Need of the World

The world is desperate for the proclamation of the plan of redemption. Consider the condition of those who come into a Christian's life and do not know Christ. First, they are born in rebellion to God. David declared in Psalm 51:5 that he was brought forth in iniquity and conceived in sin. Mankind is born with the sin principle, an innate propensity to sin. In Romans 7:14, Paul felt such a conflict within himself that he described it as being of the flesh, sold into bondage to sin.

Psalm 51:5
Behold, I was born in iniquity. My mother conceived me in sin.

Romans 7:14
For we know that the law is spiritual, but I am fleshly, sold under sin.

Second, unbelievers live lives devoted and committed to sin. The unsaved live by sinful values and attitudes resulting in sinful actions. In Romans 6:17, Paul describes this sinful lifestyle, when he declares that the Roman Christians were slaves to sin in their former lives before Christ. In Ephesians 2:2, Paul describes the constant sin of the unsaved by stating that they walk according to the course of this world, which is according to the Devil, the prince of the power of the air, and are sons of disobedience. When people do not know Christ, they are following the Devil and his ways. Though they may not be fully cognizant of it, he is their ruler, and they are his slaves.

Romans 6:17
But thanks be to God, that, whereas you were bondservants of sin, you became obedient from the heart to that form of teaching to which you were delivered.

Ephesians 2:2
In which you once walked according to the course of this world, according to the prince of the power of the air, the spirit who now works in the children of disobedience.

Third, Satan's kingdom is called the domain of darkness in Colossians 1:13. Every unbeliever lives in this domain and behaves in this darkness. 1 John 1:6 states, "If we say that we have fellowship with him and walk in the darkness, we lie, and don't tell the truth." The apostle John calls this walking in darkness. Therefore, they are completely spiritually dead. In Ephesians 2:1, Paul reveals to the Ephesians that they had been dead in their trespasses and sin before coming to the Savior. Later in the letter, chapter 4:17-18, he explains this condition as being futile in their own minds, darkened in understandings, and alienated from God's life.

Colossians 1:13
Who delivered us out of the power of darkness, and translated us into the Kingdom of the Son of his love.

1 John 1:6
If we say that we have fellowship with him and walk in the darkness, we lie, and don't tell the truth.

Ephesians 2:1
You were made alive when...dead in transgressions and sins.

Ephesians 4:17-18
This I say therefore, and testify in the Lord, that you no longer walk as the rest of the Gentiles also walk, in the futility of their mind, being darkened in their understanding, alienated from the life of God because of the ignorance that is in them, because of the hardening of their hearts.

The Scriptures describe with many details this terrifying condition that unbelief produces. These poor people have no forgiveness of sins (Colossians 1:14). They are unrighteous (Romans 3:10), children of God's wrath (Ephesians 2:3), and captive by their own desires (Galatians 5:19-21). They have problems but no real solutions to their difficulties (James 1:2-4). They have human friendships but no bond that is eternal and spiritual (1 Corinthians 12:25).

Colossians 1:14
In whom we have our redemption, the forgiveness of our sins.

Romans 3:10
As it is written, "There is no one righteous; no, not one."

Ephesians 2:3
We also all once lived among them in the lusts of our flesh, doing the desires of the flesh and of the mind, and were by nature children of wrath, even as the rest.

Galatians 5:19-21
Now the deeds of the flesh are obvious, which are: adultery, sexual immorality, uncleanness, lustfulness, idolatry, sorcery, hatred, strife, jealousies, outbursts of anger, rivalries, divisions, heresies, envy, murders, drunkenness, orgies, and things like these; of which I forewarn you, even as I also forewarned you, that those who practice such things will not inherit God's Kingdom.

James 1:2-4
Count it all joy, my brothers, when you fall into various temptations, knowing that the testing of your faith produces endurance. Let endurance have its perfect work, that you may be perfect and complete, lacking in nothing.

1 Corinthians 12:25
That there should be no division in the body, but that the members should have the same care for one another.

When true believers come to Christ through the power of the Holy Spirit, their whole lives change. Christ transforms them from rebellion to praise (Ephesians 1:12), turns them from a life totally devoted to sin to a life devoted to holiness (Romans 7:24-25), and turns them from captivity to sin to freedom in the Holy Spirit (Romans 8:9-10). They are made spiritually alive (Ephesians 2:5) and given the forgiveness of sins (Acts 10:43). These children of wrath become children of God (John 1:12), are declared righteous before Him (Romans 5:19), and will now experience love, joy, peace and the rest of the fruits of the Spirit (Galatians 5:22-23).

Ephesians 1:12
To the end that we should be to the praise of his glory, we who had before hoped in Christ.

Romans 7:24-25
What a wretched man I am! Who will deliver me out of the body of this death? I thank God through Jesus Christ, our Lord! So then with the mind, I myself serve God's law, but with the flesh, sin's law.

Romans 8:9-10
But you are not in the flesh but in the Spirit, if it is so that the Spirit of God dwells in you. But if any man doesn't have the Spirit of Christ, he is not his. If Christ is in you, the body is dead because of sin, but the spirit is alive because of righteousness.

Ephesians 2:5
Even when we were dead through our trespasses, made us alive together with Christ – by grace you have been saved.

Acts 10:43
All the prophets testify about him, that through his name everyone who believes in him will receive remission of sins.

John 1:12
But as many as received him, to them he gave the right to become God's children, to those who believe in his name.

Romans 5:19
For as through the one man's disobedience many were made sinners, even so through the obedience of the one, many will be made righteous.

Galatians 5:22-23
But the fruit of the Spirit is love, joy, peace, patience, kindness, goodness, faith, gentleness, and self-control. Against such things there is no law.

The person who does not know the Lord must live a life centered on sinful values, motivated by sinful attitudes, and committed to sinning as a pattern of their lives. Christians know that He is the solution to every problem, the answer to every dilemma, and the way of coping with every difficulty (Philippians 1:20). As a result, in all their relationships with unbelievers, the sharing of the good news must come first. Trouble will never leave a life filled with sin that is destined for judgment. These dear people are desperate for Christ to meet their innermost longings and outer most needs.

Philippians 1:20
According to my earnest expectation and hope, that I will in no way be disappointed, but with all boldness, as always, now also Christ will be magnified in my body, whether by life or by death.

The Judgment to Come

The previous point dealt with unbelievers in his present life and condition, but without Christ their future eternity is worse. The intense emotional, psychological, physical, and intellectual torment that they may feel while on this Earth is nothing compared to what awaits them at death. In Romans 2:12-16, Paul presents a very important fact: all men will be judged. The Jews will be judged with the law and by the law in the Scriptures. The Gentiles will be judged without the written law of God but by this law within them. This law is the conscience within a man. Both will be judged by a law. No man will escape judgment out of ignorance of God's law.

Romans 2:12-16
For as many as have sinned without the law will also perish without the law. As many as have sinned under the law will be judged by the law. For it isn't the hearers of the law who are righteous before God, but the doers of the law will be justified (for when Gentiles who don't have the law do by nature the things of the law, these, not having the law, are a law to themselves, in that they show the work of the law written in their hearts, their conscience testifying with them...their thoughts among themselves accusing or else excusing them) in the day when God will judge the secrets of men, according to my Good News....

Paul discloses to the Romans that unbelievers are storing up for themselves wrath for the day of God's righteous and holy judgment. This will be a time of tremendous anguish, agony, torment, and pain. This will be a day that will bring eternal condemnation to the unsaved. In Romans 2:5-6, Paul explains, "But according to your hardness and unrepentant heart you are treasuring up for yourself wrath in the day of wrath, revelation, and of the righteous judgment of God; 'who will pay back to everyone according to their works.'" The author declares that they will be judged according to their deeds. Basically, these will be compared to God's law and judgment will come. Every day unbelievers remain in their unbelief; they sin again and again storing up additional wrath for the Day of Judgment. This wrath will be displayed on that day of righteous justice.

Romans 2:5-6
But according to your hardness and unrepentant heart you are treasuring up for yourself wrath in the day of wrath, revelation, and of the righteous judgment of God; who "will pay back to everyone according to their works:"

In Revelation 19:11-15, the apostle John compares the Day of Judgment upon the world to a winepress crushing grapes. The winepress was simply an enclosure, where grapes were placed to be crushed under the feet of men. When Christ returns and pours out His wrath, men will be crushed under His powerful and mighty feet. This judgment will occur world-wide at the second coming of Christ and individually at the great white throne. In Revelation 20:12-15, John writes that he saw death, Hades, and the sea give up their dead, both great and small. Each one stood before Christ's white throne and books were opened in which were written all their works. Each person was judged according to each and every sin. Can anyone imagine being judged for every single sin that one commits in a lifetime? All those whose names were not written in the book of life were cast into a lake of fire. This is a deeply frightening future for those who come to believers in friendship or for help, comfort, or solace. These must resist sharing only the wisdom from the world; instead, they must share the gospel at this critical moment in their lives.

Revelation 19:11-15
I saw the heaven opened, and behold, a white horse, and he who sat on it is called Faithful and True. In righteousness he judges and makes war. His eyes are a flame of fire, and on his head are many crowns. He has names written and a name written which no one knows but he himself. He is clothed in a garment sprinkled with blood. His name is called "The Word of God." The armies which are in heaven followed him on white horses, clothed in white, pure, fine linen. Out of his mouth proceeds a sharp, double-edged sword, that with it he should

strike the nations. He will rule them with an iron rod. He treads the wine press of the fierceness of the wrath of God, the Almighty.

Revelation 20:12-15
I saw the dead, the great and the small, standing before the throne, and they opened books. Another book was opened, which is the book of life. The dead were judged out of the things which were written in the books, according to their works. The sea gave up the dead who were in it. Death and Hades gave up the dead who were in them. They were judged, each one according to his works. Death and Hades were thrown into the lake of fire. This is the second death, the lake of fire...he was cast into the lake of fire.

The Destruction of Satan's Works

At the fall of man, God promised Satan that he would be dealt a crushing blow upon the head by the seed of Eve (Genesis 3:15). The blow came at the resurrection of Christ (her seed) as He ultimately rendered Satan powerless. As the world comes to an end, Satan will be thrown into a lake of fire which ends his influence and power forever (Revelation 20:10). Until this time, Satan is allowed to continue his evil ways, but he is powerless over believers. He can only control them if they allow him too (Ephesians 4:27). Since he fully controls unbelievers as their own father (John 8:44) and the world they live in as its prince, these people must come to Jesus Christ for Satan to be rendered powerless in their lives. Christians should share the gospel in order to destroy the works of the Devil in the lives of the unsaved.

Genesis 3:15
I will put hostility between you and the woman, and between your offspring and her offspring. He will bruise your head, and you will bruise his heel."

Revelation 20:10
The devil who deceived them was thrown into the lake of fire and sulfur, where the beast and the false prophet are also. They will be tormented day and night forever and ever.

Ephesians 4:27
And don't give place to the devil.

John 8:44
You are of your father, the devil, and you want to do the desires of your father. He was a murderer from the beginning, and doesn't stand in the truth, because there is no truth in him. When he speaks a lie, he speaks on his own; for he is a liar, and the father of lies.

One of his works is physical death. As people come into the kingdom of God, they are no longer held in the fearful lifelong bondage of death. In 1 Corinthians 15:54-57, Paul asserts that believers have victory over death through the resurrection. Since Christians have been freed from sin and now have the victory of eternal life, Paul declares that death has lost its sting!

1 Corinthians 15:54-57
But when this perishable body will have become imperishable, and this mortal will have put on immortality, then what is written will happen: "Death is swallowed up in victory. Death, where is your sting? Hades, where is your victory?" The sting of death is sin, and the power of sin is the law. But thanks be to God, who gives us the victory through our Lord Jesus Christ.

1 John 3:8
He who sins is of the devil, for the devil has been sinning from the beginning. To this end the Son of God was revealed: that he might destroy the works of the devil.

In 1 John 3:8, John emphatically states that the Son of God came upon the Earth for the purpose of destroying the works of the Devil. The Devil has been sinning and attempting to ruin everything God has been doing since He created man. Christ came to annihilate these evil works. In Hebrews 2:14-15, the author states, "Since then the children have shared in flesh and blood, he also himself in the same way partook of the same, that through death he might bring to nothing him who had the power of death, that is, the Devil." The Lord Christ rendered the Devil powerless, the one who had the power of death. Death was this evil being's ultimate weapon, and he lost it at the resurrection.

1 John 3:8
He who sins is of the devil, for the devil has been sinning from the beginning. To this end the Son of God was revealed: that he might destroy the works of the devil.

Hebrews 2:14-15
Since then the children have shared in flesh and blood, he also himself in the same way partook of the same, that through death he might bring to nothing him who had the power of death, that is, the devil, and might deliver all of them who through fear of death were all their lifetime subject to bondage.

In John 16:33, Christ declared that he had overcome the world. Christ had overcome the system that Satan controls upon the Earth. How? Believers no longer are controlled by its evil system through the lusts of the flesh. They have the power necessary within them through the Spirit to resist sin and find victory in Christ. This is taught in such passages as Romans 6:17-19 and Galatians 5:16-18.

John 16:33
I have told you these things, that in me you may have peace. In the world you have trouble; but cheer up! I have overcome the world."

Romans 6:17-19
But thanks be to God, that, whereas you were bondservants of sin, you became obedient from the heart to that form of teaching to which you were delivered. Being made free from sin, you became bondservants of righteousness. I speak in human terms because of the weakness of your flesh, for as you presented your members as servants to uncleanness and to wickedness upon wickedness, even so now present your members as servants to righteousness for sanctification.

Galatians 5:16-18
But I say, walk by the Spirit, and you won't fulfill the lust of the flesh. For the flesh lusts against the Spirit, and the Spirit against the flesh; and these are contrary to one another, that you may not do the things that you desire. But if you are led by the Spirit, you are not under the law.

The apostle John declares that this constant accuser, his world system, and his false prophets no longer have any power over believers. In 1 John 4:4, the apostle encourages his readers to stand against the influence of false prophets. Why? The God, who is in them, is greater than the Devil (implied), who is in the false prophets. In 1 John 5:4, John writes that Christians, who are born of God, have overcome the world. The entire world system of Satan no longer has a death grip of lust and temptation on them.

1 John 4:4
You are of God, little children, and have overcome them; because greater is he who is in you than he who is in the world.

1 John 5:4
For whatever is born of God overcomes the world. This is the victory that has overcome the world: your faith.

In 1 John 5:18, John announces that people who are born of God do not continually sin. Why? God keeps them, and they cannot be touched by the Evil One. Satan no longer has power over them. When unbelievers come to Christ, they are freed from the evil clutches of all these terribly destructive enemies. Many problems are derived from these adversaries. The gospel can release people from their clutches and bring them into the freedom of Christ.

1 John 5:18
We know that whoever is born of God doesn't sin, but he who was born of God keeps himself, and the evil one doesn't touch him.

The Joy of Heaven

When the plan of redemption is proclaimed and someone is saved, there is great joy in heaven. In Luke 15:2-7, Jesus speaks of this rejoicing in the Parable of the Lost Sheep. He describes the joy in heaven when one sinner comes to Christ What an amazing thought? The angels rejoice over a human being becoming a Christian. As the lost come to believers for relief from their ultimate spiritual burden of their sin and unbelief, Christians should proclaim to them the good news. When they turn to Jesus as their Savior and Lord, those in the heavenly places rejoice with great and exceeding joy.

Luke 15:2-7
The Pharisees and the scribes murmured, saying, "This man welcomes sinners, and eats with them." He told them this parable. "Which of you men, if you had one hundred sheep, and lost one of them, wouldn't leave the ninety-nine in the wilderness, and go after the one that was lost, until he found it? When he has found it, he carries it on his shoulders, rejoicing. When he comes home, he calls together his friends and his neighbors, saying to them, 'Rejoice with me, for I have found my sheep which was lost!' I tell you that even so there will be more joy in heaven over one sinner who repents, than over ninety-nine righteous people who need no repentance.

In Luke 15:9-10, Jesus tells a powerful story about a lost coin. A woman lost one coin, even though she had ten. She lit a lamp, swept the floor, and looked diligently for the coin. When she had found it, she called together all her friends and rejoiced with them. Here, Jesus asserts that the angels of heaven rejoice over one repentant sinner in the same way. Luke described it in these words, "Rejoice with me, for I have found the drachma which I had lost." Then the Lord Jesus commented, "Even so, I tell you, there is joy in the presence of the angels of God over one sinner repenting."

Luke 15:9-10
When she has found it, she calls together her friends and neighbors, saying, "Rejoice with me, for I have found the drachma which I had lost." Even so, I tell you, there is joy in the presence of the angels of God over one sinner repenting."

The Blessing of Proclamation

As Christians proclaim the gospel of Jesus, they will bring upon themselves great blessing. Jesus professed in Matthew 5:9 that peacemakers are blessed, for they shall be called sons of God. The word "blessed" denotes happiness and joy. In the Beatitudes, Jesus is describing the characteristics of those in the kingdom of God. One of those characteristics is making peace. The Lord Jesus was speaking spiritually of those who bring others to peace with God through Him. The peacemakers are the proclaimers of the good news of peace. (Ephesians 6:15). In that peacemaking, there is great joy. In that peacemaking, Christians demonstrate to their God, the world, the angels, and themselves that they are truly His. This is part of the fruit that comes from a true branch from the Vine of Christ (Matthew 7:20). It will be one of the ways the saints demonstrate their true faith by works (James 2:18).

Matthew 5:9
Blessed are the peacemakers, for they shall be called children of God.
Ephesians 6:15
And having fitted your feet with the preparation of the Good News of peace.

Matthew 7:20
Therefore by their fruits you will know them.

James 2:18
Yes, a man will say, "You have faith, and I have works." Show me your faith without works, and I will show you my faith by my works."

There are many other blessings involved in sharing the gospel. In Philippians 1:12-13, Paul was a prisoner in chains awaiting trial before Caesar. This was the worst situation of his life, yet God was still using him in mighty ways. He was chained night and day to members of the Praetorian Guard and took this opportunity to share the gospel with them. Many became believers. As he encountered those of Caesar's household, the plan was proclaimed and many of them came to Christ. The saints in Rome were awakening from their spiritual slumber and becoming bolder in their witness for Christ. The entire city was hearing the good news through one chained prisoner (Philippians 1:14). As a result of this,

Paul declared that he rejoiced and would continue to rejoice (Philippians 1:18).

Philippians 1:12-13
Now I desire to have you know, brothers, that the things which happened to me have turned out rather to the progress of the Good News, so that it became evident to the whole palace guard, and to all the rest, that my bonds are in Chris.
Philippians 1:14
And that most of the brothers in the Lord, being confident through my bonds, are more abundantly bold to speak the word of God without fear.

Philippians 1:18
What does it matter? Only that in every way, whether in pretense or in truth, Christ is proclaimed. I rejoice in this, yes, and will rejoice.

There is blessing in seeing God work through a believer. There is blessing in watching someone come to Christ. There is blessing in viewing a supernatural work of God. There is blessing in observing people's lives change. There is blessing in knowing that someone has been snatched from the fire of hell. There is blessing as Christians become spiritual parents and rejoice in their own children's birth and growth. Paul describes himself to the Corinthians as their spiritual father because he proclaimed the gospel of Jesus Christ to them and established their church (1 Corinthians 4:15). Joy comes in all the fathering, nourishing, and encouraging of spiritual children. What joy would it be to fellowship with one's own spiritual children (Romans 15:32; Philippians 1:4; 2:17)! Then we could enjoy their fellowship forever.

1 Corinthians 4:15
For though you have ten thousand tutors in Christ, you don't have many fathers. For in Christ Jesus, I became your father through the Good News.

Romans 15:32
That I may come to you in joy through the will of God, and together with you, find rest.

Philippians 1:4
Always in every request of mine on behalf of you all, making my requests with joy,

Philippians 2:17
Yes, and if I am poured out on the sacrifice and service of your faith, I rejoice, and rejoice with you all.

In 1 Thessalonians 2:19, Paul rejoiced that the members of the church in that city were his hope, crown, and happiness. Why? He looked forward to rejoicing with them in heaven as their spiritual father. He describes it so beautifully, "For what is our hope, or joy, or crown of rejoicing? Isn't it even you, before our Lord...at his coming?" This blessing would be at the coming of Jesus Christ. This is the future aspect of the blessing that the saints will receive as they proclaim the good news. All believers will be rejoicing together with those who have received Jesus Christ through their ministry. These are only a few of the many blessings for those who accept the divine mandate and share the good news of Jesus.

1 Thessalonians 2:19
For what is our hope, or joy, or crown of rejoicing? Isn't it even you, before our Lord Jesus at his coming?

An Ancient Portrait

So many amazing events were occurring in the early days of the church which were written for our instruction. Often times, people focus on the physical miracles in those days, but the spiritual miracles were even more spectacular. When the saints took their divine mandate seriously the Lord God worked mighty miracles in the lives of unbelievers as their eternity was forever changed from the judgment of hell to the blessings of heaven.

One such person was a Christian named Philip. This was not the apostle but a committed disciple in the church of Jerusalem. In Acts 8:26-40, Luke describes Philip's sharing of the good news with an Ethiopian Eunuch. This man was in charge of the treasury of Candace of Ethiopia. This was not her name but a designation (like Pharaoh or Caesar) of the queen mother. Ethiopia was the empire that claimed most of Africa at the time. She was ruling behind her son who was worshiped as a god. The eunuch had authority, respect, and power. Yet, he was returning from the worship of the God of Israel in Jerusalem. This would have been a twelve-hundred-mile journey on foot. The Greek word translated "chariot" would be most likely the single or double seated platform with their poles extended to be carried by servants on their shoulders.

On his return home this Gentile was reading a portion of the Hebrew Scriptures. All of the wealth, riches, authority, and power could not satisfy his unfulfilled heart except the true God. He could find peace in the worship of some man who claimed to be a god. As a read, he turned to a portion of the prophet Isaiah which described the coming Messiah but was having a difficult time understanding it. As the Holy Spirit was working on the heart of this important official and preparing him to receive Jesus Christ as Savior and Lord, it became necessary to provide a Christian who would follow the divine mandate and share the gospel with him. Philip had already been evangelizing in Samaria. In the early days of the church, many miracles occurred to authenticate the truth preached but sometimes they were used to move the good news quickly to other regions. This eunuch actually represented the gospel spreading to the entire country of Ethiopia. So, God sent an angel to inform Philip that he was to travel to a desert road that led to the city of Gaza. This evangelist knew the gospel would be involved.

Without hesitation, Philip obeyed the divine command then arose and left. When he arrived on the road, there were caravans traveling from Jerusalem to Gaza. It was probably fairly busy at the time. As he was standing on the road, the Holy Spirit directed him to join the chariot of the Ethiopian Eunuch which had obviously passed by. Luke records that Philip had to run to join the chariot. This enthusiastic saint ran up and walked alongside this official's chariot. He hears him reading aloud from Isaiah. Most likely, he purchased it in Jerusalem and had begun reading it when he departed the city. Phillip begins the conversation with a question.

He inquired, "Do you understand what you are reading?" This prestigious man replied that he could not understand this passage without someone explaining it to him. So, he invited Phillip to join him in the chariot. After teaching him that the passage referred to Jesus and sharing the gospel with him, he received Christ as Savior and Lord. After this, Phillip was supernaturally transported to Azotus and began proclaiming the gospel there. Phillip had followed the divine mandate and not only did that man receive eternal life, but many would come to Christ in Ethiopia because of him. We are to do the very same thing.

A Modern Anecdote

Early on in my ministry as a Christian Pastoral Counselor, I made a commitment to the Lord that I would present the gospel with everyone that came into my office or confirm their faith. How can someone change without the power of the Spirit? Why solve temporal problems on this Earth and not solve the eternal problems? There is another distinction which is important. Since I practice "Christian" counseling, this involves principles from the Scriptures.

The Bible makes distinctions between Christians and non-Christians providing different standards, expectations and techniques for each. As a result, I must know whether my counselees are, or consider themselves to be, believers or not. Sometimes, this leads to awkwardness in situations when people are not sure of their own salvation. At times, they may not be sure of their children's faith whom I might be counseling. Whenever this occurs, I will utilize a simple strategy to assist in sharing the gospel.

I have the wonderful opportunity of dealing with all ages of people facing all kinds of issues in their lives. Over the course of weeks, I had been working with a couple who had faced some serious marriage problems. They had overcome these major difficulties and were growing rapidly in Christ. Also, the were growing closer to each other. Unfortunately, during the time that the two of them were having problems, their triplets (two boys and a girl) were acting out in school, not getting along with each other, and defying their parents.

Once the couple was on the right track, it became time to help their children do the same. I asked the parents if the children had received Christ, and they were not sure. I asked if anyone else would have shared the gospel with them and again, they were not sure. The parents had intermittently brought them to church but never mentioned Jesus Christ. I explained that counseling their three children would involve sharing the gospel and providing an opportunity for them to receive Christ as Savior and Lord. They gave me permission and I scheduled a meeting with the three of them together. I wanted to see the dynamics of their interaction together before I met with them separately. This was a time of great commotion, much chaos, constant vying for attention, and an unwillingness to listen.

I introduced myself and then provided some background about myself that I thought they could relate to. After this, I described what our individual times together would look like. When I met with them individually, my simple strategy came into play. Rather than force the issue, I simply asked each of them, "Since I am a Christian counselor, I normally give advice from the Scriptures. It provides help differently for Christians and non-Christians, so it is crucial that I know which you are so I can counsel you. Would you like me to counsel you as a Christian or as a non-Christian?" Michael responded, "Yeah, I guess so." His brother, Patrick asserted, "Absolutely, I love Jesus." His sister, Debbie said, "I don't know if I am a Christian or not."

This allowed me to individualize my gospel presentation to each. With Michael, I asked him to explain what he meant by "I guess so." With Patrick, I asked him if he could tell me who he thought Jesus was and how he loved Jesus. With Debbie, I began with the definition of what it means to be a true Christian and then asked her if she thought she was a believer. It turned out that not one of the three were true believers. When I asked each of them if they had wanted to receive Jesus Christ that very day and know for sure that they had eternal life with Him, all of them told me they did. I shared the gospel and they all received Christ as Savior and Lord. They now had the power from the Holy Spirit in their lives and a real commitment to follow His commandments. As a result, I was able to place them on a new Christian track of honoring and glorifying Him at home, school, and church. Of course, this did not happen overnight. Lives can be saved when we all accept the divine mandate to heart and commit ourselves to proclaiming the redemptive plan.

A Personal Response

Dear Heavenly Father,

   I now know that I am commanded, called, and been given the stewardship of sharing Your good news of salvation. Help me to be obedient to Your will and present Your plan of redemption to (add names) and others I know and meet. I do long for (add names) and others to glorify You and exalt Your Son for all eternity. I recognize that they desperately need their sins forgiven and eternal life with You rather than judgment. I want to destroy Satan's work in their lives and see them free. I also realize that at this moment they may have their names written in the Book of Life and just waiting for me to share Your good news with them. I would love to experience the blessings from witnessing for You and know that there is joy in heaven when they come to Christ. Give me the motivation and power through Your Holy Spirit to accept Your divinely chosen method of using me to be Your witness. I pray this in the name of Jesus. Amen.

LEADING THE WAY

Instructor's Notes

Chapter 3

Accept the Divine Mandate

Christians have been given a divine mandate to share the gospel of the kingdom of God. This involves recognizing, accepting, and acting upon this critical spiritual command.

In the section, "A Typical Scenario," the author discusses how believers might respond to criticisms of Jesus Christ in their classroom by their teacher or fellow classmates.

What is the scenario about?

In the classroom, a Christian has to constantly hear his faith blamed for wars and slavery, etc. and he won't speak up.

What held the believer back from sharing the gospel?

He did not understand the divine mandate and the fact that the teacher and students desperately needed forgiveness.

What finally led the Christian to share the good news and how did it occur?

He prayed and when the teacher asked the class if he was wrong, he spoke up and defended Jesus Christ. As a result, another student became interested in his faith.

Have you had a similar experience?

(Various answers should be shared including yours.)

In the section, "A Scriptural Principle" the author presents an important biblical principle in evangelism which concerns our commission as divine emissaries of Jesus Christ.

How would you express this principle in your own words?

The third biblical principle is "we must accept the divine mandate." This is our mandate.

(Various answers should be shared including yours.)

How would you rewrite this principle to make it even more personal to your life (using your name and situation)?

(Various answers should be shared including yours.)

Why do you think this principle might be important in your life right now as you share the gospel?

(Various answers should be shared including yours.)

How would you rate yourself on the percentage of times you followed this principle in the past as a believer?

(Various answers should be shared including yours.)

Directions: Put a horizontal mark and your name where you see yourself on the percentage line.

0%   25%   50%   75%   100%

In the section, "A Biblical Explanation," the author explains the divine mandate that all believers have been given and its importance in sharing the gospel effectively.

In what ways do Christians glorify God in their presenting of the plan of redemption and unbelievers in their reaction to the plan presented?

In 2 Corinthians 2:14-16, Paul pronounces that in every place he shares the gospel a sweet aroma is sent to God giving Him glory.

In Romans 15:9, the apostle explains that when Christ accepts people (saves them), even though they are all sinners and deserve nothing, the Lord God will receive glory and honor.

In 2 Corinthians 4:15, when Paul proclaimed the gospel and people came to Christ, they responded with the giving of thanks to God.

In Ephesians 2:7, Paul asserts that those who come to Christ will forever be the trophies of God's grace.

(These are just of the answers provided in the book.)

What is the difference between God's "command" to share the good news and His "call" to do it?

Christians are commanded to proclaim the gospel. This is obvious, but it is so essential to living the Christian life.

All Christians are called by God to proclaim the plan. This is not just a serious command but a high calling. In Romans 1:6-7, Paul opened his letter by greeting the church as those who are "called to be his saints." Here is the critical truth that Christians are called to belong to Jesus Christ and are called to be His holy ones (saints who are set apart). This word "call" means to call out, to summon.

What does this "calling" involve? What attitudes or actions spring from this call?

What is the difference between our testimony about Jesus being a "characteristic" of our salvation and it being a result of our "spiritual maturity"?

He informed them that they would be His witnesses. It was not up for negotiation but would happen. Their testimony of His Word would be a common characteristic in their lives.

One of the clearest statements concerning this important quality can be found in Matthew 5:14-15. In this passage, the Lord Jesus is speaking to the Jews as a nation and reaffirms to them something they already should have known; they were lights to the world. Now, they should begin acting like lamps bringing light into the darkness for all unbelievers.

What is God's divinely chosen method of evangelism and how is it to be accomplished?

Proclaiming the good news by Christians is God's chosen method of evangelism. There are many ways in which God could have ordained to bring people into His kingdom. Yet, He decided to have His followers share His good news.

There are numerous ways in which God could reveal His plan, but he chose the simple sharing of the gospel by His followers.

What are two additional reasons Christians should present the gospel with the outside world (provide verses)?

Here are the answers they can choose from which come from the first sentence under each subheading.

Those who have been chosen are awaiting the coming of Christians.

The gospel is a stewardship that has been entrusted to the church. The church has been given as a gift to the Son from God, the Father, for Christ's exaltation and glory for all eternity.

The world is desperate for the proclamation of the plan of redemption.

The previous point dealt with unbelievers in his present life and condition, but without Christ their future eternity is   worse.

At the fall of man, God promised Satan that he would be dealt a crushing blow upon the head by the seed of Eve.

When the plan of redemption is proclaimed and someone is saved, there is great joy in heaven.

As Christians proclaim the gospel of Jesus, they will bring upon themselves great blessing.

In what ways might these truths impact your life?

(Various answers should be shared including yours.)

In the section, "An Ancient Portrait," the author provides a unique portrayal of the salvation of the Ethiopian eunuch on the road to Gaza.

Can you briefly describe the setting of this real-life ancient drama?

The setting is a road to Gaza. Without hesitation, Philip obeyed the divine command then arose and left. When he arrived on the road, there were caravans traveling from Jerusalem to Gaza. It was probably fairly busy at the time. As he was standing on the road, the Holy Spirit directed him to join the chariot of the Ethiopian Eunuch which had obviously passed by.

Can you describe the major characters involved?

The major characters are the Ethiopian Eunuch, Phillip, and the Holy Spirit.

How did the evangelist initiate the gospel presentation?

Luke records that Philip had to run to join the chariot. This enthusiastic saint ran up and walked alongside this official's chariot. He hears him reading aloud from Isaiah. Most likely, he purchased it in Jerusalem and had begun reading it when he departed the city. Phillip begins the conversation with a question.

He inquired, "Do you understand what you are reading?" This prestigious man replied that he could not understand this passage without someone explaining it to him.

What was result of this evangelistic presentation?

So, he invited Phillip to join him in the chariot.

How was the principle explained in this chapter applied to the situation?

After teaching him that the passage referred to Jesus and sharing the gospel with him, he received Christ as Savior and Lord. After this, Phillip was supernaturally transported to Azotus and began proclaiming the gospel there. Phillip had followed the divine mandate and not only did that man receive eternal life, but many would come to Christ in Ethiopia because of him. We are to do the very same thing.

Based on the truths learned in this chapter, what would you have done differently if you were the evangelist or how would you have responded if you were the recipient?

(Various answers should be shared including yours.)

LEADING THE WAY

In the section, "A Modern Anecdote," the author discusses a situation in which he was able to share the gospel with a set of triplets.

Can you briefly describe the setting of this real-life modern drama?

The setting is a home of the triplets or the office of the author. Unfortunately, during the time that the two of them were having problems, their triplets (two boys and a girl) were acting out in school, not getting along with each other, and defying their parents.

Can you describe the major characters involved?

The major characters are the author, two parents, and the triplets (two boys and a girl) - Debbie, Michael, and Patrick.

How did the author initiate the gospel presentation?

Early on in my ministry as a Christian Pastoral Counselor, I made a commitment to the Lord that I would present the gospel with everyone that came into my office or confirm their faith. How can someone change without the power of the Spirit? Why solve temporal problems on this Earth and not solve the eternal problems?

Would you like me to counsel you as a Christian or as a non-Christian?" Michael responded, "Yeah, I guess so." His brother, Patrick asserted, "Absolutely, I love Jesus." His sister, Debbie said, "I don't know if I am a Christian or not."

AN INSTRUCTOR'S MANUAL

What was result of this evangelistic presentation?

When I asked each of them if they had wanted to receive Jesus Christ that very day and know for sure that they had eternal life with Him, all of them told me they did. I shared the gospel and they all received Christ as Savior and Lord.

How was the principle explained in this chapter applied to the situation?

This allowed me to individualize my gospel presentation to each. With Michael, I asked him to explain what he meant by "I guess so." With Patrick, I asked him if he could tell me who he thought Jesus was and how he loved Jesus. With Debbie, I began with the definition of what it means to be a true Christian and then asked her if she thought she was a believer. It turned out that not one of the three were true believers.

Based on the truths learned in this chapter, what would you have done differently if you were the author or how would you have responded if you were the recipient?

(Various answers should be shared including yours.)

In the section, "A Personal Response," the author provides a model you may use for prayer if you find it necessary after discovering the truths in this chapter.

Are you presently attempting to present the gospel of Jesus to someone? If not, are there some in your neighborhood who may not know Jesus Christ and may need prayer for an opportunity for you to share with them and open hearts to receive Him?

(Various answers should be shared including yours.)

Based on the truths you have just learned, what will you continue to do in your current evangelistic efforts and what might you do differently?

(Various answers should be shared including yours.)

What additional thoughts would you like to share with the others?

(Various answers should be shared including yours.)

Chapter 4

Allow God to Be Sovereign

As Christians proclaim the gospel, God is also at work. It takes a dynamic interaction between God and man to bring others to the gospel. In the Great Commission, Jesus told his followers to go out into all the world and make disciples for Him. This was their part. Then He asserted that He would be with them always, even to the very end. That was His part (Matthew 28:19-20). Sharing the gospel was always meant to be an interaction between the divine and human. The role of God will be discussed in this chapter and the role of man in the next.

Matthew 28:19-20
Go and make disciples of all nations, baptizing them in the name of the Father and of the Son and of the Holy Spirit, teaching them to observe all things that I commanded you. Behold, I am with you always, even to the end of the age....

A Typical Scenario

Have you ever been in a situation that was something like the following? Almost every day, you eat your lunch in the break room where your co-workers also sit and eat their lunches. The conversation is usually about things going on at work but sometimes strays into personal issues. Normally, you think to yourself that this would be a good opportunity to share the gospel, but you become afraid. You think, "How can I even get started? What could I possibly say? Will they negatively respond?" So, you quietly sit there while fear and guilt fill your heart. Perhaps, you simply do not think much about it at all. You have decided to leave the sharing of the gospel up to the pastor and other more gifted people.

In this chapter you will learn how to look at this situation differently. You do not have to be nervous or fearful because you serve a sovereign God who is in control of the situation. As you sit in that room day after day, God is at work. The Lord has ordained the plan of redemption, sent His Son to fulfill the plan, and has His Spirit right now working in various stages of the lives of these co-workers of yours. If they have been called and this is their time, you will share the gospel and they will believe. You are there because God desires a Christian witness in that place. If you ask the Lord, He will provide an opportunity to share the gospel or to get a simple conversation started for some future presentation. When the time comes, He will give you the wisdom to speak the words necessary and open their hearts to believe. If you choose not to share, He will send someone into their lives who will. His purpose will be accomplished with or without you, but you could be a part of His work at that time.

After you learn these powerful truths, perhaps this same situation would look quite different. Now, you begin to pray and wait. Then one day, only one of the usual people is in the break room when you enter. It is suddenly just the two of you. You start to talk and the conversation quickly goes to your co-worker's mother who has just been diagnosed with cancer. They were both terribly afraid but were trying to stay positive. You tell her that you will pray for them. Suddenly, you hear yourself saying, "My uncle, who is a Christian like me, went through this same kind of experience, but we had something much more powerful to depend on than positive thinking."

She inquires, "What was it?" You once again hear yourself saying, "It is not a "what but a who." He is Jesus Christ, my Savior and Lord. He was with both of us every step of the way. When we read His Word, it said that we never have to really worry because whether my uncle remained upon this

Earth or the Lord took Him home, we both knew He would now be safe. That is better than positive thinking." Then, the conversation continued toward the sharing of the gospel. As you finish and leave the room, you realize that the Lord just answered your prayers. You just experienced the Holy Spirit working through you.

Though this is an imaginary scenario, it is typical of the various situations we find ourselves in, where the gospel could be shared. Since we don't often recognize the crucial fact that presenting the plan of redemption is all God's work and power, we don't take opportunities God may provide. Also, acknowledging God's sovereignty in witnessing can encourage our hearts to share His blessed gospel message. This brings us to the fourth principle describing the role of God in evangelism.

A Scriptural Principle

In evangelism, God and man play distinctive roles, have different responsibilities, and perform divergent functions. It is crucial that Christians understand these differences. Any misunderstanding can leave believers immobilized, anxious, and discouraged. It can rob them of the joy that evangelistic encounters were meant to bring. If a saint shares the gospel, God will produce the growth. A reliance on God brings joy, confidence, and boldness.

The fourth principle is "we must allow the Lord God to be sovereign." Since the Lord God plays the critical role in the proclamation of the plan of redemption, then believers must understand the roles that each person of the Trinity plays and how the Godhead works through man to accomplish salvation in people's lives. It is His power that is always at work. When lives are so miraculously and supernaturally changed, then praise and thanksgiving are offered up to the Lord. It is all about Him. This is so comforting. God is at all times in control of every situation we find ourselves in.

A Biblical Explanation

Throughout the New Testament, as one carefully studies the various evangelistic encounters, one sees the beautiful and marvelous interaction between God and man. In Acts 2:1-6, it was the Lord God who sent a sound like the wind and brought the multitude together. In verse 14, it was Peter who preached to the gathered crowd. Yet, In Acts 2:41, His Holy Spirit brought many to Him that day. In Acts 3:6, it was the power of God that healed the lame man, and it was Peter who took the divine opportunity and shared the good news. Then the grace, mercy, and power from almighty God was unleashed and thousands were saved. In Acts 4:8, it was God who filled Peter with His Holy Spirit and the apostle spoke the gospel in boldness to the Sanhedrin. Then it was God who provided the courage to face their persecution. The Lord has been the major creator and implementer of His great redemptive plan from the beginning and will until its fulfillment.

Acts 2:1-6
Now when the day of Pentecost had come, they were all with one accord in one place. Suddenly there came from the sky a sound like the rushing of a mighty wind, and it filled all the house where they were sitting. Tongues like fire appeared and were distributed to them, and one sat on each of them. They were all filled with the Holy Spirit, and began to speak with other languages, as the Spirit gave them the ability to speak. Now there were dwelling in Jerusalem Jews, devout men, from every nation under the sky. When this sound was heard, the multitude came together and were bewildered, because everyone heard them speaking in his own language.

Acts 2:14
But Peter, standing up with the eleven, lifted up his voice and spoke out to them,

"You men of Judea, and all you who dwell at Jerusalem, let this be known to you, and listen to my words.

Acts 2:41
Then those who gladly received his word were baptized. There were added that day about three thousand souls.

Acts 3:6
But Peter said, "I have no silver or gold, but what I have, that I give you. In the name of Jesus Christ of Nazareth, get up and walk!"

Acts 4:8
Then Peter, filled with the Holy Spirit, said to them, "You rulers of the people, and elders of Israel."

The Ordination and Planning of God

The redemption of man was God's design from eternity past. In Ephesians 1:3-4, Paul opens his powerful letter with a description of the many blessings the saints have in Christ. One of these blessings was the election of believers into the kingdom of God. He explains that before the foundation of the world was laid and the universe created, Christians were chosen to be redeemed by Christ. The redemption of man was ordained and planned by God.

Ephesians 1:3-4
Blessed be the God and Father of our Lord Jesus Christ, who has blessed us with every spiritual blessing in the heavenly places in Christ, even as he chose us in him before the foundation of the world, that we would be holy and without defect before him in love.

In Ephesians 1:5-6, Paul writes, "Having predestined us for adoption as children through Jesus Christ to himself, according to the good pleasure of his desire, to the praise of the glory of his grace, by which he freely bestowed favor on us in the Beloved." In this passage, the apostle explains to the believers in Ephesus that Christians were predestined to be God's adopted sons. This adoption was through Christ and is according to His will and His kind intention, which is to the praise and glory of His grace. The Lord God wanted to demonstrate His grace and the plan to redeem man was conceived. Paul disclosed to the church in Corinth that there is only one true God, the Father, who was the originator of all things (1 Corinthians 8:6). This does include the plan of redemption.

Ephesians 1:5-6
Having predestined us for adoption as children through Jesus Christ to himself, according to the good pleasure of his desire, to the praise of the glory of his grace, by which he freely gave us favor in the Beloved.

The Revelation and Fulfillment in Christ

God's redemptive plan was to be revealed through Christ. In the letter of Hebrews 1:1-2, the author of Hebrews makes this crystal clear. He certifies that God revealed His plan in the past through the patriarchs and the prophets and now reveals Himself through His only Son. The New Testament is simply the revelation about the Father revealed in the Son written down by the apostles and others.

Hebrews 1:1-2
God, having in the past spoken to the fathers through the prophets at many times and in various ways, has at the end of these days spoken to us by his Son, whom he appointed heir of all things, through whom also he made the worlds.

In John 7:16, Jesus declared to the Jews that His teaching was not His own, but the Father who had sent Him. John records, "Jesus therefore answered them, and 'My teaching is not mine, but his [Father] who sent me.'" The Lord Jesus was continually disclosing everything that was being revealed to Him by God, His Father. In John 1:18, the beloved apostle confesses that no man has ever seen God at any time; Christ, the only begotten of God in His bosom, has explained Him. The explanation of the Father and His plan is found in the words and actions of Jesus Christ. In John 14:8-11, when Philip asked the Lord to show them the Father, Jesus became astonished. How could Philip have been with Jesus for so long and not realized that He was one with the Father? If they had seen Him, they had seen the Father. They were one.

John 7:16
Jesus therefore answered them, "My teaching is not mine, but his who sent me."

John 1:18
No one has seen God at any time. The one and only Son, who is in the bosom of the Father, has declared him.

John 14:8-11
Philip said to him, "Lord, show us the Father, and that will be enough for us." Jesus said to him, "Have I been with you such a long time, and do you not know me, Philip? He who has seen me has seen the Father. How do you say, 'Show us the Father?' Don't you believe that I am in the Father, and the Father in me? The words...I speak not from myself; but the Father who lives in me...Believe me that I am in the Father, and the Father in me...believe me for...works' sake.

Redemption was fulfilled in the Lord. In Matthew 5:17, Christ declared that He did not come to abolish the law or the prophets. Instead, he came upon the Earth to fulfill them. In Christ Jesus, the entire law of God was completely and totally fulfilled, so He went to the cross as a fully righteous, unblemished lamb. In Luke 24:44-47, after His resurrection, Jesus visited some of His disciples and explained to them, once again that He must fulfill all that was in the Law of Moses, the Prophets, and the Psalms. Then, the Lord opened their minds to show them that He had to die, rise, and bring redemption to man.

Matthew 5:17
Don't think that I came to destroy the law or the prophets. I didn't come to destroy, but to fulfill.

Luke 24:44-47
He said to them, "This is what I told you, while I was still with you, that all things which are written in the law of Moses, the prophets, and the psalms, concerning me must be fulfilled." Then he opened their minds, that they might understand the Scriptures. He said to them, "Thus it is written, and thus it was necessary for the Christ to suffer and to rise from the dead the third day, and that repentance and remission of sins should be preached in his name to all the nations, beginning at Jerusalem.

These important truths were found in the Scriptures and shown to them. Salvation was accomplished on the cross. When the Father had ordained the plan in eternity past, then His only Son came to Earth proclaiming and then fulfilling the plan.

The Witness and Testimony of the Spirit

In John 15:26-27, Jesus gave one of His final discourses to the disciples. He explained to them that the Holy Spirit was coming from the Father to bear witness of Him as the Son. God ordained the plan, Christ proclaimed and fulfilled the plan, and the Holy Spirit was to convict people of their sin and convince them to believe in the plan. In John 16:7-11, Jesus explains the role of the Spirit concerning this testimony of Christ in the world. The Holy Spirit will convict of sin, righteousness, and judgment. These terms have a deep, rich meaning. The Greek word that is translated "convicts" really contains two key ideas: convicting and convincing. First, the Holy Spirit convicts unbelievers that their unbelief is false, which is the sin that will condemn them. Then, the Spirit of God convinces unbelievers that Jesus is the Christ, the Son of God, which will save them from eternal judgment.

John 15:26-27
When the Counselor has come, whom I will send to you from the Father, the Spirit of truth, who proceeds from the Father, he will testify about me. You will also testify, because you have been with me from the beginning.

John 16:7-11
Nevertheless I tell you the truth: It is to your advantage that I go away, for if I don't go away, the Counselor won't come to you. But if I go, I will send him to you. When he has come, he will convict the world about sin, about righteousness, and about judgment; about sin, because they don't believe in me; about righteousness, because I am going to my Father, and you won't see me any more; about judgment, because the prince of this world has been judged.

Second, the Holy Spirit convicts the unsaved world of the insufficiency of their self-righteousness to save them. Then, He convinces them that Christ's righteousness is sufficient for their salvation. This was the responsibility of Jesus while on Earth, but He is now with the Father, so the Holy Spirit must assume the role. Third, the Spirit convicts the world concerning the lie of the Devil. Their judgment of Jesus as a false messiah (the lie) is untrue. Instead, the Spirit convinces unbelievers that Jesus is the Christ, who brings eternal life. The Spirit testifies and bears witness of Christ.

In 1 John 5:5-8, John records that there are three witnesses to the deity of Jesus Christ. He explains it in these words, "For there are three who testify: the Spirit, the water, and the blood; and the three agree as one. The water, which alludes to the baptism of Jesus, testifies of His deity because God Himself declared Jesus was His Son. The blood, which alludes to His death, testifies of His deity because He rose from the dead proving Christ is the Son of God. The Holy Spirit testifies of His deity because He is the Spirit of truth revealing and confirming the deity of Jesus. Christians should be assured that the good news they are sharing, was ordained by God, proclaimed and fulfilled in Christ, and is currently being testified by the Spirit. This is a powerful and encouraging biblical truth.

1 John 5:5-8
Who is he who overcomes the world...Jesus is the Son of God? This is he who came by water and blood, Jesus Christ...but with the water and the blood....For...three who testify: the Spirit, the water, and the blood....

The Election of Those Who Believe

Another role God plays in the evangelism process is the choosing of souls to be a part of the kingdom being given to His Son. Before the foundation of the world, the Lord God chose or elected every believer that He desired to be saved. In Ephesians 1:4, Paul conveys the truth that God chose all Christians in Him before the foundation of the world and predestined them for adoption as children. Colossians 3:12 again states that believers are chosen of God. God knows every person who will come to His Son because He chose them before the foundation of the world. It is these chosen or elected believers who will respond to your proclamation of the gospel.

Ephesians 1:4
Even as he chose us in him before the foundation of the world, that we would be holy and without defect before him in love.

Colossians 3:12
Put on therefore, as God's chosen ones, holy and beloved, a heart of compassion, kindness, lowliness, humility, and perseverance.

Sometimes, Christians become so worried about making some kind of mistake in the presentation, but those chosen will respond. Others will try and soften the discussion of sin thinking the unsaved will reject the gospel because it is too harsh. They are mistaken. The chosen will respond to the powerful work of the Holy Spirit in their hearts as they hear the Word preached.

In Acts 13:48, Luke wrote that Paul preached and as many of those who were appointed to receive eternal life believed. He describes it this way." As the Gentiles heard this, they were glad, and glorified the Word of God. As many as were appointed to eternal life believed." The apostle told Timothy that saints have a holy calling by God's grace given to them before time eternal (2 Timothy 1:9). Then, Paul declared to Titus, another companion in ministry that he was a servant and an apostle according to the faith of God's chosen ones (Titus 1:1). This is clear.

Acts 13:48
As the Gentiles heard this, they were glad, and glorified the word of God. As many as were appointed to eternal life believed.

2 Timothy 1:9
Who saved us and called us with a holy calling, not according to our works, but according to his own purpose and grace, which was given to us in Christ Jesus before times eternal.

Titus 1:1
Paul, a servant of God, and an apostle of Jesus Christ, according to the faith of God's chosen ones, and the knowledge of the truth which is according to godliness.

God appoints some to eternal life, and they are the ones who respond to the gospel. God does the calling and those who had been chosen will believe. All throughout the cities are people chosen of God, who have not yet heard nor have believed. The Lord will bring these individuals into the lives of Christians to be saved. Christians must share the gospel with all because they cannot determine who might be called. We can never assume just because people appear negative to the gospel that they are not elected. Keep sharing! As with the thief on the cross, they may come to Christ much later.

The Sending of Christians to Proclaim

God sends all Christians into the world to proclaim the plan of redemption. This is another important role He plays in the evangelistic process. It was God's idea to utilize man to share His good news. It was God's Son who commanded His followers to go and make disciples (Matthew 28:19).

Matthew 28:19
Go and make disciples of all nations, baptizing them in the name of the Father and of the Son and of the Holy Spirit.

Just before His ascension, the Lord repeated this mandate once again. This time with the promise of the power of the Holy Spirit associated with it. In Acts 1:8, Luke records, "But you will receive power when the Holy Spirit has come upon you. You will be witnesses to me in Jerusalem, in all Judea and Samaria, and to the uttermost parts of the Earth." In this passage, the Lord promised His disciples that they would receive power from the Spirit. After this, they were to be His witnesses in Jerusalem, Judea, Samaria, and throughout all the world. In John 20:21, Jesus told His disciples that as the Father sent Him, He was sending them.

Acts 1:8
But you will receive power when the Holy Spirit has come upon you. You will be witnesses to me in Jerusalem, in all Judea and Samaria, and to the uttermost parts of the Earth.

John 20:21
Jesus therefore said to them again, "Peace be to you. As the Father has sent me, even so I send you."

Do these exhortations include the average Christian? Of course, otherwise, the true gospel would have died out with the apostles. The exact opposite was true. Immediately, the Christians were out sharing the good news everywhere, and the church grew in leaps and bounds (Acts 2:41, 47). God's mandate applies to all believers…throughout the earth.

Acts 2:41
Then those who gladly received his word were baptized. There were added that day about three thousand souls.

Acts 2:47
Praising God, and having favor with all the people. The Lord added to the assembly day by day those who were being saved.

Though scattered from persecution, Christians in the first century still proclaimed Christ (Acts 8:4). It now becomes the privilege of Christians today to do the same. Believers must see themselves as divinely sent to share that truth. When a Christian shares the gospel, he does it as one sent from the King of Kings and Lord of Lords (Revelation 19:16). Every day the saints of God should be reminding themselves and each other of this critically important truth.

Acts 8:4
Therefore those who were scattered abroad went around preaching the word.

Revelation 19:16
He has on his garment and on his thigh a name written, "KING OF KINGS, AND LORD OF LORDS."

The Provision of Opportunities to Proclaim

God provides opportunities for his followers to proclaim the plan. Throughout the New Testament, God was active in directing the many evangelistic activities of the apostles and His church. Time and time again, they were provided with opportunities to proclaim the plan.

In Acts 2:2-6, God brought the sound of a wind and drew an immense crowd for Peter to share the gospel. In Acts 8:26, an angel of the Lord sent Philip to the road from Jerusalem to Gaza. There an angel directed him to an Ethiopian eunuch puzzling over a passage of Scripture, and Philip shared the gospel. The eunuch, one of the elect, was waiting (though he did not know it) for God to send a believer into his path with the gospel. In Acts 13:2, the Holy Spirit told the church at Antioch to set apart Paul and Barnabas for ministry. As they served the Lord and fasted, the Holy Spirit said, "Separate Barnabas and Saul for me, for the work to which I have called them." The Holy Spirit directed them all throughout their journeys and led them every step of the way.

Acts 2:2-6
Suddenly there came from the sky a sound like the rushing of a mighty wind, and it filled all the house where they were sitting. Tongues like fire appeared and were distributed to them, and one sat on each of them. They were all filled with the Holy Spirit, and began to speak with other languages, as the Spirit gave them the ability to speak. Now there were dwelling in Jerusalem Jews, devout men, from every nation under the sky. When this sound was heard, the multitude came together and were bewildered, because everyone heard them speaking in his own language.

Acts 8:26
But an angel of the Lord spoke to Philip, saying, "Arise, and go toward the south to the way that goes down from Jerusalem to Gaza. This is a desert."

Acts 13:2
As they served the Lord and fasted, the Holy Spirit said, "Separate Barnabas and Saul for me, for the work to which I have called them."

At the end of their first missionary journey, the apostle gathered the church together and told them of how God had opened many doors of faith to the nations (Acts 14:27). The apostle credited the Lord for creating the opportunities for the gospel to go to the world. In Acts 16:6-16, they traveled through the regions of Phrygia and Galatia, but the Spirit of God would not allow them to proclaim the good news in Asia. They attempted to enter Bithynia, but the Spirit would not allow it. Then Paul had a vision that God desired him to go into Macedonia and followed it.

Acts 14:27
When they had arrived, and had gathered the assembly together, they reported all the things that God had done with them, and that he had opened a door of faith to the nations.

Acts 16:6-10
When they had gone through the region of Phrygia and Galatia, they were forbidden by the Holy Spirit to speak the word in Asia. When they had come opposite Mysia, they tried to go into Bithynia, but the Spirit didn't allow them. Passing by Mysia, they came down to Troas. A vision appeared to Paul in the night. There was a man of Macedonia standing, begging him, and saying, "Come over into Macedonia and help us." When he had seen the vision,

immediately we sought to go out to Macedonia, concluding that the Lord had called us to preach the Good News to them.

Over and over, God had put Paul in the right place at the right time. The Lord will do the same for every Christian who desires to share the good news and witness for Him. God will create numerous opportunities by opening doors into situations for the good news to be preached. Those Christians sharing the gospel should watch for these divine open doors. As will be discussed later, Paul asked the saints at Colossae to pray that God would open a door for the Word (Colossians 4:3). As a result, all Christians should be praying for open doors for the good news and watching for them to occur. Praying and watching are critical elements in the evangelistic process. In Psalm 5:3, David says he will pray to the Lord God and then eagerly watch for the divine response. Christians are to do the same in evangelism.

Colossians 4:3
Praying together for us also, that God may open to us a door for the word, to speak the mystery of Christ, for which I am also in bonds.

Psalm 5:3
Yahweh, in the morning you will hear my voice. In the morning I will lay my requests before you, and will watch expectantly.

The Provision of Wisdom to Proclaim

Most Christians do not share the gospel because they are fearful that their presentation will be inadequate. This was the fear of Moses, when God told him to speak to Pharaoh in Exodus 4:10-12. The Lord told Moses that he had made his mouth and would teach him what to say. God would give Moses wisdom as the leader spoke His words.

Exodus 4:10-12
Moses said to Yahweh, "O Lord, I am not eloquent, neither before now, nor since you have spoken to your servant; for I am slow of speech, and of a slow tongue." Yahweh said to him, "Who made man's mouth? Or who makes one mute, or deaf, or seeing, or blind? Isn't it I, Yahweh? Now therefore go, and I will be with your mouth, and teach you what you shall speak."

In Luke 12:11-12, Jesus told his disciples that they were not to worry when they were proclaiming the plan before the rulers and authorities. Luke records it in these words, "When they bring you before the synagogues, the rulers, and the authorities, don't be anxious [as to] how or what you will answer, or what you will say; for the Holy Spirit will teach you in that same hour what you must say." Of course, they knew the truth. The Lord prepared His disciples and trained them to share His good news (Luke 24:40; Acts 1:1-3). Once trained, the Holy Spirit would guide them as they spoke that truth. Is this not true for every Christian today? This promise brings confidence that as we witness in the most difficult of situations, God will be there with us providing the wisdom that we need through His Holy Spirit.

Luke 12:11-12
When they bring you before the synagogues, the rulers, and the authorities, don't be anxious how or what you will answer, or what you will say; for the Holy Spirit will teach you in that same hour what you must say.

Luke 24:40
When he had said this, he showed them his hands and his feet.

Acts 1:1-3
The first book I wrote, Theophilus, concerned all that Jesus began both to do and to teach, until the day in which he was received up, after he had given commandment through the Holy Spirit to the apostles whom he had chosen. To these he also showed himself alive after he suffered, by many proofs, appearing to them over a period of forty days, and speaking about God's Kingdom.

Christians should be fully prepared at any time to present the basic truths of the gospel. In the very moment of sharing the gospel, the Holy Spirit will take over. He will use the biblical truths of whatever words they speak to bring people to Christ. Of course, the better prepared Christians are the more truth the Spirit has to work with in the unbeliever's life. In Ephesians 6:19, Paul enjoins the saints to pray that the right words would be given to him as he opened his mouth to preach and teach the Word. All believers are to know the Word and rely on the Holy Spirit to use that knowledge in the lives of the unsaved. Christians don't have to depend on clever techniques of persuasion but on the simple truths of God's Word as His Spirit works. In 1 Corinthians 2:1-2, Paul acknowledged the fact that he did not come as the world did in superiority of speech or wisdom but simply proclaimed the testimony of God.

Ephesians 6:19.
On my behalf, that utterance may be given to me in opening my mouth, to make known with boldness the...Good News.

1 Corinthians 2:1-2
When I came to you, brothers, I didn't come with excellence of speech or of wisdom, proclaiming to you the testimony of God. For I determined not to know anything among you except Jesus Christ and him crucified.

Then Paul asserted that he purposely determined to know nothing, but Christ crucified. The testimony of God is found only in His Word. Christians need to stay within the bounds of the Scriptures. Paul exalts the Thessalonians because they accepted his word as God's Word which was doing its work in them who believed (1 Thessalonians 2:13). Christians need to stay within the scope of the Bible and the Spirit's work. When believers speak God's wisdom, it will be foolishness to the Gentiles or a stumbling block to the Jews Yet, it is the power of God to those being saved (1 Corinthians 1:23).

1 Thessalonians 2:13
For this cause we also thank God...when you received...the word of...God, you accepted it not as the word of men, but as it is in truth, the word of God, which also works in you who believe.

1 Corinthians 1:23
But we preach Christ crucified: a stumbling block to Jews, and foolishness to Greeks.

The Opening of Hearts to Believe

For people to believe in the gospel and receive the Lord, God must open up their hearts. In Acts 2:47, Luke declares that the Lord Jesus was adding to their number day by day. Christians can bring the good news, but the Holy Spirit must open their minds. Unbelievers are blinded in their spiritual eyes (2 Corinthians 4:4), cannot understand spiritual things (1 Corinthians 2:14), and are hardened in their hearts toward Him (Ephesians 4:19). God must change this through His Spirit. Luke describes the Lord Jesus opening the minds of His disciples, so that they could understand the Scriptures (Luke 24:45).

Acts 2:47
Praising God, and having favor with all the people. The Lord added to the assembly day by day those who were being saved.

2 Corinthians 4:4
In whom the god of this world has blinded the minds of the unbelieving, that the light of the Good News of the glory of Christ, who is the image of God, should not dawn on them.

1 Corinthians 2:14
Now the natural man doesn't receive the things of God's Spirit, for they are foolishness to him, and he can't know them, because they are spiritually discerned.

Ephesians 4:19
They, having become callous, gave themselves up to lust, to...all uncleanness with greediness.

Luke 24:45
Then he opened their minds, that they might understand the Scriptures.

In John 6:44, Jesus declared that no one can come to Him unless the Father draws Him. Jesus brought the Word, and the Father through His Holy Spirit opened their minds. Paul declared that the good news came to the Thessalonians not just in words but in the full conviction, in the Spirit, and in power (1 Thessalonians 1:5). Once again, Paul brought the Word, but the Holy Spirit opened the minds. This opening of the minds involves the softening of their hearts, the removal of their spiritual blinders, and the ability to understand the gospel.

John 6:44
No one can come to me unless the Father who sent me draws him, and I will raise him up in the last day.

1 Thessalonians 1:5
And that our Good News came to you not in word only, but also in power, and in the Holy Spirit, and with much assurance. You know what kind of men we showed ourselves to be among you for your sake.

In Acts 16:14, Paul preached to a woman named Lydia, a seller of purple fabrics, in Philippi. Luke describes it in these words, "A certain woman named Lydia, a seller of purple, of the city of Thyatira, one who worshiped God, heard us; whose heart the Lord opened to listen to the things which were spoken by Paul." Luke discloses that the Lord opened her heart to listen to the things which Paul spoke. He always depended on the Spirit to work in the hearts of his listeners. He knew he could not do this work on his own. Human effort cannot possibly compensate for the work of the Spirit.

Acts 16:14
A certain woman named Lydia, a seller of purple, of the city of Thyatira, one who worshiped God, heard us. The Lord opened her heart to listen to the things which were spoken by Paul.

The Accomplishment of God's Purpose

All unbelievers who are called to Christ will come to Him despite any contention or opposition from the world system, or even the unwillingness of Christians to share the gospel in a particular encounter with unbelievers. Often, Christians may worry that they missed opportunities to witness due to fear or inattentiveness, which may lead to the loss of eternal life for some. This simply is not true. God is an omnipotent and sovereign God, who calls the unsaved to Himself. God will work in any and every situation to bring them to His Son. If the Lord desires, they will come. There is nothing an unbeliever in his resistance, a saint in his unwillingness, the world in their antagonism, or the Devil in his opposition can do to stop someone from entering the kingdom, if God wills.

God has declared from ancient times that all His purposes come to pass. In Isaiah 46:10, the prophet describes God in these words, "Declaring the end from the beginning, and from ancient times things that are not yet done; saying, My counsel shall stand, and I will do all my pleasure. The Lord proclaims that His purpose will always be established, and He will accomplish all His good pleasure. In Daniel 4:34-35, after Nebuchadnezzar had returned from his punishment of insanity for his arrogance, he lifted up his eyes to heaven and blessed God. He declared that God acts according to His will in the host of heaven, the angels, and among the people on the Earth. No one can stop Him. In other words, God does exactly what He desires anytime and in any way He desires it. In Psalm 135:6, the psalmist reiterates this very concept, when he writes that Yahweh does whatever He pleases in heaven, on Earth, in the seas, and all the oceans. This would include the Christian's evangelistic encounters, would it not?

Isaiah 46:10
I declare the end from the beginning, and from ancient times things that are not yet done. I say: My counsel will stand, and I will do all that I please.

Daniel 4:34-35
At the end of the days I, Nebuchadnezzar, lifted up my eyes to heaven, and my understanding returned to me, and I blessed the Most High, and I praised and honored him who lives forever; for his dominion is an everlasting dominion, and his kingdom from generation to generation....the inhabitants of the Earth are reputed as nothing; and he does according to his will in the army of heaven, and among the inhabitants of the Earth; and no one can stop his hand, or ask him, "What are you doing?"

Psalm 135:6
Whatever Yahweh pleased, that he has done, in heaven and in Earth, in the seas and in all deeps.

Even if Christians are willing and share the gospel, there isn't a mistake, a blunder, anything the Christian can do that can stop someone from coming to Christ, if it is God's will. Also, if God is indeed sovereign, He knows the kinds of blunders Christians are capable of making, before He sends the unsaved into their paths. In Psalm 139:4, David utters that even before there is a word on a believer's tongue, the Lord knows it. Most Christians think that they need to bring the seeking unbeliever to someone else better qualified to share the gospel. This is not needed. God can compensate for the bumbling or ineptness Christians may have in sharing. God desires for all believers to share, not a professional few. He will do the rest that is needed.

Psalm 139:4
For there is not a word on my tongue, but, behold, Yahweh, you know it altogether.

LEADING THE WAY

An Ancient Portrait

Often times, Christians meet people that are so caught up in their own false religion that they spend their time not only proselytizing others but also persecuting Christians. It may appear as if they would never come to Christ, yet they do. God is in the divine business of turning those diametrically opposed to Him into faithful followers. He has done this miracle many times throughout Christian history. One of these remarkable conversions occurred with Saul from the city of Tarsus. His unique story is found in Acts 8-9.

Saul was an educated and zealous Jew. He called himself a "Hebrew of Hebrews" who so carefully and meticulously followed the Jewish law. This deeply religious man was so antagonized by the Christians and their blasphemous claims that he personally made it his life calling to track them down in order to kill them for their blasphemy against God. Saul hated them for proclaiming that Jesus of Nazareth was the Son of God and rose from the dead. He would hunt them down, attempt to force them to deny their Savior and Lord, and then when they refused, he would cast his vote as a member of the Jewish council to have them put to death. This was his goal, his delight, and his service to his God. As soon as the death of Stephen had occurred, which he most likely instigated, Saul began his ravaging of the church. In Jerusalem, he went from house to house stalking all those who believed in Jesus and dragged them off to prison. This frightened the saints, and they ran for their lives.

Next, Saul asked the high priest permission to travel the long distance to Damascus to search for Christians. When he found them, Saul wanted authority to drag the idolatrous blasphemers back bound in chains to Jerusalem and force them to recant their beliefs. If they refused, they would be imprisoned, tried, and put to death. When this impassioned persecutor of Christians was granted the approval that he desired with the authenticating letters, he was immediately off to this foreign city to find them wherever they were. It was a long and arduous journey but not for this group of treacherous men. When Saul approached the city, a brilliant light (as bright as the sun) flashed around them. The group immediately fell to the ground. Then a voice out of heaven asked, "Saul, Saul why are you persecuting me?"

Stunned by all that was happening, he requested for this divine being to identify Himself and it turned out to be Jesus of Nazareth. It was the Jesus who died on that cursed cross and rose again exactly as his disciples had declared all along. Saul must have been terrified and mortified because this Jesus, whom he thought was dead and buried, was alive and the true God. He may be dead at any moment and this Son of God would now judge him. He was humiliated because he had thought all along that he was truly serving God when in reality he was persecuting His only Son. He was hurting those that loved Him. These were the same disciples that he hunted, tormented, and ultimately killed.

The men all around knew that some supernatural event was occurring but could not understand the voice nor see the being that was speaking. They heard Saul address Him as Lord and ask Him what he now wanted him to do. Jesus declared that he was now appointed to be His minister and witness to the Gentiles. Through Saul, soon to be called Paul, the Lord would open their eyes from the darkness to light, take them from the domain of Lucifer to God, and forgive their sins and provide an inheritance in the heavenly places through faith in Him. Though the men around him could not comprehend the commissioning Saul had just received, they were required to lead this humbled, blinded, and now believing man to the city of Damascus to await the arrival of the prophet Agabus for further directions. Rather than be struck dead on the spot, he was soon to serve his Savior and Lord. All Christians must remember that God is sovereign and can bring anyone to His Son that He has chosen. We must allow God to fulfill His role in salvation.

A Modern Anecdote

I became a Christian many years ago at the University of Southern California. I'll never forget that day. I thought I was so important because I had an academic scholarship to USC. I was young and so excited, thinking I had the whole world in front of me. In fact, when I looked into my future, I saw everything I could ever want: power, prestige, fame, money, happiness, and fulfillment. On October third of my sophomore year, I began wondering around the campus of USC at lunch time. I was doing what I normally did at this time which was looking for a place to sit. Often, numerous campus groups would sponsor speakers at lunch.

So, I had about an hour and a half between classes to find something to do. While I was eating a sandwich in one hand and munching on a bag of chips in the other, I walked by an auditorium on campus and saw a sign that said, "How to Have A Fulfilling Marriage." I figured, since I was planning on becoming a psychologist, I should know something about marriage, so in I walked. There were almost 200 students there. After a few moments, an evangelist from a Christian group walked on the stage. Later, he would become a highly prominent writer and speaker in Christian apologetics. At this time, he was just a young guy sharing his faith for a Christian organization on campus.

Scott presented many principles and examples on how to have a truly fulfilling marriage from his own relationship with his spouse. After about twenty minutes, he explained to the student audience the real reason he and his wife had such an amazing marriage. He declared that it was because they both knew and loved the Lord Jesus Christ. He told the students that he would like to share the gospel with them but did not want to force them, so they could leave if they wanted. As a result, most got up and walked out. I had not finished my sandwich or my chips, and it was hot outside, so I stayed with about three other students scattered about the theater.

Scott began sharing the gospel of Jesus Christ with the principle that God loves you and has a wonderful plan for your life. He said that the Bible indicated that there was a great chasm between man and God and that chasm was sin. God, being absolutely holy, must judge those sins; no one was exempt. In Romans 3:23, Paul wrote that all had sinned and fallen short of the glory of God. The wages (payment) for sin would be spiritual death in an eternity of punishment (Romans 6:23). All of a sudden, I realized that I had already committed a huge number of sins since I was a young child. There was still the possibility of committing a so many more. Right there, the weight of about ninety years of sin came upon me, and I knew there was no way that any prestige, fame, power, accomplishment, money, or even doing good works in this life could compensate for my sins. There was and would be too many! In fact, one was enough.

Romans 3:23
For all have sinned, and fall short of the glory of God.

Romans 6:23
For the wages of sin is death, but the free gift of God is eternal life in Christ Jesus our Lord.

Then Scott shared God's holy solution, which was His Son, Jesus Christ. God had so loved the world (including you and me) that He had given His only Begotten Son to die on the cross for us (John 3:16). If we would believe in Him, our sins would be forgiven, and we would be possessors of eternal life with Him. After proclaiming the entire gospel, he asked if any of the students would like to stay and receive Jesus Christ as their Savior and Lord.

John 3:16
For God so loved the world, that he gave his one and only Son, that whoever believes in him should not perish, but have eternal life.

With that question, the other three students got up and walked out. Suddenly, I was left there alone in that large auditorium at lunch time that day and I raised my hand. I wanted desperately to be forgiven. I wanted desperately to have this eternal life. While Scott was standing on the stage and I was sitting in the chair, I prayed a prayer declaring Jesus Christ to be the Son of God and only Savior of the world. I acknowledged that Jesus had risen from the dead, then I relinquished my will and life to Him as Lord.

I see now that the Lord God was sovereignly at work as one student looking for some place to sit to eat his lunch. Scott simply shared the gospel and let God be God (John 6:44-46).

John 6:44-46
No one can come to me unless the Father who sent me draws him, and I will raise him up in the last day. It is written in the prophets, They will all be taught by God. Therefore everyone who hears from the Father and has learned, comes to me.

A Personal Response

Dear Heavenly Father,

I acknowledge that this massive plan of redemption is all Your work and power. You ordained this from eternity past and sent Your only Son to reveal and fulfill it. Lord, use the Holy Spirit powerfully in my testimony to (add names) and others I know and meet. Please have Him convict them of their sinfulness and convince them of Your message about salvation in Your Son. Please do not let them rely on their own self-righteousness but on the righteousness of Jesus, as they find faith in Him. Use me to proclaim the gospel to them by providing the opportunity to share or giving me the wisdom to make the opportunity. I know that if they are elected, they will come to Christ whether I witness to them or someone else does. Give me the motivation and especially courage to be the one to have the privilege of sharing your good news. Please Lord, open their hearts to the message. I pray this in the name of Jesus. Amen.

LEADING THE WAY

Instructor's Notes

Chapter 4

Allow God to Be Sovereign

As Christians proclaim the gospel, God is also at work. It takes a dynamic interaction between God and man to bring others to the gospel. In this chapter, we focus on God's role.

In the section, "A Typical Scenario," the author mentions ways in which believers might share their faith in Christ in the employee's lunchroom.

What is the scenario about?

A Christian is afraid to start a conversation about Christ in his employee's lunchroom thinking he is in control.

What held the believer back from sharing the gospel?

He did not realize that God is able to make an opportunity to share the gospel occur and provide the courage and words to speak.

What finally led the Christian to share the good news and how did it occur?

An employee was alone in the company lunchroom, and he started a conversation about an uncle with cancer that trusted the Lord.

Have you had a similar experience?

(Various answers should be shared including yours.)

LEADING THE WAY

In the section, "A Scriptural Principle" the author presents an important biblical principle in evangelism which concerns God's sovereign role in the sharing or the gospel.

How would you express this principle in your own words?

The fourth principle is "we must allow the Lord God to be sovereign."

(Various answers should be shared including yours.)

How would you rewrite this principle to make it even more personal to your life (using your name and situation)?

(Various answers should be shared including yours.)

Why do you think this principle might be important in your life right now as you share the gospel?

(Various answers should be shared including yours.)

How would you rate yourself on the percentage of times you followed this principle in the past as a believer?

(Various answers should be shared including yours.)

Directions: Put a horizontal mark and your name where you see yourself on the percentage line.

0%   25%   50%   75%   100%

In the section, "A Biblical Explanation," the author explains the Lord God's role in evangelism and the importance of this knowledge in sharing the gospel effectively.

In what different ways are the Father, the Son, and the Holy Spirit involved in the sharing of the gospel?

The Trinity is involved in the ordination and planning of God, the revelation and fulfillment in Jesus Christ, and the witness and Testimony of the Spirit

Who ultimately sends believers to share the gospel?

God sends all Christians into the world to proclaim the plan of redemption. This is another important role He plays in the evangelistic process. It was God's idea to utilize man to share His good news. It was God's Son who commanded His followers to go and make disciples (Matthew 28:19).

What promise can believers claim if they feel too inadequate to share the gospel and does this mean they will not need to be trained?

Most Christians do not share the gospel because they are fearful that their presentation will be inadequate. This was the fear of Moses, when God told him to speak to Pharaoh in Exodus 4:10-12. The Lord told Moses that he had made his mouth and would teach him what to say. God would give Moses wisdom as the leader spoke His words.

Of course, they knew the truth. The Lord prepared His disciples and trained them to share His good news (Luke 24:40; Acts 1:1-3). Once trained, the Holy Spirit would guide them as they spoke that truth. Is this not true for every Christian today? This promise brings confidence that as we witness in the most difficult of situations, God will be there with us providing the wisdom that we need through His Holy Spirit.

Christians should be fully prepared at any time to present the basic truths of the gospel. In the very moment of sharing the gospel, the Holy Spirit will take over. He will use the biblical truths of whatever words they speak to bring people to Christ. Of course, the better prepared Christians are the more truth the Spirit has to work with in the unbeliever's life.

Why do we not have to worry about persuading people to open their hearts to God?

For people to believe in the gospel and receive the Lord, God must open up their hearts. In Acts 2:47, Luke declares that the Lord Jesus was adding to their number day by day.

Luke discloses that the Lord opened her heart to listen to the things which Paul spoke. He always depended on the Spirit to work in the hearts of his listeners. He knew he could not do this work on his own. Human effort cannot possibly compensate for the work of the Spirit.

Does a Christian have to be concerned that if they missed an opportunity to share the gospel with people, they may never come to Christ?

We must know that the accomplishment of God's purpose to save people will occur with or without us.

In what ways might these truths impact your life?

(Various answers should be shared including yours.)

In the section, "An Ancient Portrait," the author provides a unique portrayal of Saul's persecution of Christians and then his miraculous conversion to Christ.

Can you briefly describe the setting of this real-life ancient drama?

The setting is the road to Damascus. Next, Saul asked the high priest permission to travel the long distance to Damascus to search for Christians. When he found them, Saul wanted authority to drag the idolatrous blasphemers back bound in chains to Jerusalem and force them to recant their beliefs. If they refused, they would be imprisoned, tried, and put to death.

Can you describe the major characters involved?

The major characters are Saul and the Lord Jesus Christ.

How did the evangelist initiate the gospel presentation?

When Saul approached the city, a brilliant light (as bright as the sun) flashed around them. The group immediately fell to the ground. Then a voice out of heaven asked, "Saul, Saul why are you persecuting me?"

The men all around knew that some supernatural event was occurring but could not understand the voice nor see the being that was speaking.

What was result of this evangelistic presentation?

They heard Saul address Him as Lord and ask Him what he now wanted him to do.

Jesus declared that he was now appointed to be His minister and witness to the Gentiles. Through Saul, soon to be called Paul, the Lord would open their eyes from the darkness to light, take them from the domain of Lucifer to God, and forgive their sins and provide an inheritance in the heavenly places through faith in Him. Though the men around him could not comprehend the commissioning Saul had just received, they were required to lead this humbled, blinded, and now believing man to the city of Damascus to await the arrival of the prophet Agabus for further directions. Rather than be struck dead on the spot, he was soon to serve his Savior and Lord.

How was the principle explained in this chapter applied to the situation?

All Christians must remember that God is sovereign and can bring anyone to His Son that He has chosen. We must allow God to fulfill His role in salvation.

Based on the truths learned in this chapter, what would you have done differently if you were the evangelist or how would you have responded if you were the recipient?

(Various answers should be shared including yours.)

AN INSTRUCTOR'S MANUAL

In the section, "A Modern Anecdote," the author discusses his own conversion to Jesus Christ as a young man ready for adulthood.

Can you briefly describe the setting of this real-life modern drama?

The setting is many years ago at the University of Southern California. I'll never forget that day. I thought I was so important because I had an academic scholarship to USC.

While I was eating a sandwich in one hand and munching on a bag of chips in the other, I walked by an auditorium on campus and saw a sign that said, "How to Have A Fulfilling Marriage." I figured, since I was planning on becoming a psychologist, I should know something about marriage, so in I walked. There were almost 200 students there.

Can you describe the major characters involved?

The major characters are the author and Scott.

How did the author initiate the gospel presentation?

Scott presented many principles and examples on how to have a truly fulfilling marriage from his own relationship with his spouse. After about twenty minutes, he explained to the student audience the real reason he and his wife had such an amazing marriage. He declared that it was because they both knew and loved the Lord Jesus Christ. He told the students that he would like to share the gospel with them but did not want to force them, so they could leave if they wanted.

After proclaiming the entire gospel, he asked if any of the students would like to stay and receive Jesus Christ as their Savior and Lord.

What was result of this evangelistic presentation?

With that question, the other three students got up and walked out. Suddenly, I was left there alone in that large auditorium at lunch time that day and I raised my hand. I wanted desperately to be forgiven. I wanted desperately to have this eternal life. While Scott was standing on the stage and I was sitting in the chair, I prayed a prayer declaring Jesus Christ to be the Son of God and only Savior of the world. I acknowledged that Jesus had risen from the dead, then I relinquished my will and life to Him as Lord.

How was the principle explained in this chapter applied to the situation?

I see now that the Lord God was sovereignly at work as one student looking for some place to sit to eat his lunch. Scott simply shared the gospel and let God be God (John 6:44-46).

Based on the truths learned in this chapter, what would you have done differently if you were the author or how would you have responded if you were the recipient?

(Various answers should be shared including yours.)

In the section, "A Personal Response," the author provides a model you may use for prayer if you find it necessary after discovering the truths in this chapter.

Are you presently attempting to present the gospel of Jesus to someone? If not, are there some among your many friends who may not know Jesus Christ and may need prayer for an opportunity for you to share with them and open hearts to receive Him?

(Various answers should be shared including yours.)

Based on the truths you have just learned, what will you continue to do in your current evangelistic efforts and what might you do differently?

(Various answers should be shared including yours.)

What additional thoughts would you like to share with the others?

(Various answers should be shared including yours.)

LEADING THE WAY

Instructor's Notes

Chapter 5

Allow Man to Be Challenged

Not only does God have a part in the proclamation of the plan but man does to. As has been studied earlier, if God wanted to use a method other than people to proclaim the plan, He would have, but this is His only divine approach. Though God has an active role in bringing people to Christ so does His church. He requires every individual believer to participate. As the saints present the good news (man's part), they rely on God's work in the person's heart through His Holy Spirit (God's part). The role of God was discussed in the last chapter and the role of man will now be discussed.

A Typical Scenario

Have you ever been in a situation that was something like the following? You do not normally like to go to high school reunions, but you have not been to the first two. When the invitation to the third one arrives, you decide to go. When you enter the high school gym, you see an old band friend of yours. You actually taught him how to read music and play an instrument like yours so you could have someone else in your brass section. You played together in football games, marched in parades, and did concerts together. Yet, you had not seen each other in over fifteen years. He was an agnostic at the time, and you were a Christian. You had attempted to witness to him many times in high school, but he would have nothing to do with Christ. So, you think to yourself, "Well, he probably hasn't changed, and this is not the right place or time to share my faith." So, you have a conversation, but the Lord never comes up.

In this chapter you will learn how to look at this situation with a biblical viewpoint. You will learn that though sharing the gospel is all God's work and power, you also have been given a critical role. He desires for you to present His plan. You will need to know His plan well and then choose to proclaim it. He will provide opportunities for you to take and will ask that you also make your own opportunities in the various situations of life. After you learn these important truths, perhaps this same situation could look a bit different.

Now, you will attempt to rebuild your relationship and take the opportunity to share the gospel. When you see each other, you act as if you were right back in high school. Since the reunion happened to be at your old high school and the new principal was an old friend and classmate of yours, you talk her into letting you into the band room for a jam session with your friend. You grab your instrument and hope you can still play it. Though it had been such a long time, you weren't as awful as you had expected. After this, you ask him directly if he had ever changed his old agnostic position and embraced a faith. He replied that he never had, though he realized as he had gotten older that agnosticism was just his excuse for not believing in anything. You inquire as to what he had done with his life. He explains that after high school he went to college for a year and dropped out. Then he just got a job and has been hanging out ever since. He almost got engaged, but the woman did not think that he had any ambition. She told him that the relationship was over. He did admit that she was right and couldn't fault her. He shrugged his shoulders and uttered, "What can I do?"

You take that question and run with it. You tell him that it is not too late to conjure up some real ambition, get his life together, and make something of himself. Then he asks you what you think he could possibly do because he had no real purpose in life. You told him that the Lord God had created

Him for a purpose and that purpose wasn't to hang out until it was finally all over. You take him back to eternity past and explain that God desired to give a love gift to His Son. It was a kingdom of people who would live eternally for and with Him. You remind him that you are a Christian which makes you a member of that Kingdom. You indicate that you are now involved in something that is supernatural, powerful, and eternal. It is extremely motivating and exciting.

You are now involved in advancing this Kingdom of God on Earth and training His subjects to be like the Son of God. Nothing in the world is like it. He is intrigued. He says that he thought you would bring up Jesus again. You smile and nod your head in agreement. He says that he thinks it is nothing more than going to church, giving out a bunch of money, and being good. You dispel this simplistic belief by asserting that those things were only a small part of the big picture.

He says he wants to learn more about this "bigger picture" because deep down he knows there had to be something more than this life. He will be in town for a couple of days and asks to meet again. During this time, you explain the big eternal, everlasting kingdom picture that is found in Genesis chapter one and ends in Revelation chapter twenty-two. You then share the gospel with him. He receives Jesus as Savior and Lord. He thanks you for being so persistent and tells you he has finally found his purpose in life. He will dedicate himself to serving the Lord in His kingdom on Earth. You ask him to give you a call about finding a Bible believing church in his area to attend.

Though this is an imaginary scenario, it is typical of the different encounters Christians may have with people where the gospel could be shared. We do not take the chance to share the good news because we may not know the desire of the Lord to include us in the advancement of His kingdom on Earth. Comprehending this role we play can motivate and embolden all of us to present His plan regularly. This brings us to the fifth principle which concerns responding to this important challenge.

A Scriptural Principle

In 1 Peter 2:9, Peter explains to his readers that unique position in Christ. The apostle writes, "But you are a chosen race, a royal priesthood, a holy nation, a people for God's own possession." Then in the next part he describes the very purpose we have as a kingdom of His chosen people. He continues with our real purpose, "That you may proclaim the excellence [excellencies - plural] of him who called you out of darkness into his marvelous light." One of our key objectives is to proclaim the many excellent facets of God. This is essentially the gospel. What a wonderful role to play in this great redemptive drama! The fifth principle is "we must allow man to be challenged." As humans, we have a crucial role (though sharing the gospel is all about Him).

1 Peter 2:9
But you are a chosen race, a royal priesthood, a holy nation, a people for God's own possession, that you may proclaim the excellence of him who called you out of darkness into his marvelous light.

A Biblical Explanation

God and man participate as one team in the evangelistic encounter. This participation is the reality, not because God needs believers to share His gospel, Instead, He desires to give them the awesome privilege. In Acts 10:10-16, God sent a vision to Peter showing him there was no longer clean and unclean, but all who believe would receive the Spirit. Then in Acts 10:23-24, the apostle Peter journeyed to Caesarea and preached Christ to Cornelius and all of his household. Peter had to take his responsibility for sharing the gospel so the Lord could bring them to Himself. In Acts 6:3-8, it was God who filled Stephen with the Spirit, faith, wisdom, grace, and power to share the gospel. Yet, it was Stephen who preached Christ to the people. In Acts 8:26-29, it was God's Spirit who readied the heart of the Ethiopian court official of Candace and sent Philip miraculously to him. Though God worked, Philip had to start the initial conversation, preach Jesus, and baptize him.

Acts 10:10-16
He became hungry and desired to eat, but while they were preparing, he fell into a trance. He saw heaven opened and a certain container descending to him, like a great sheet let down by four corners on the Earth, in which were all kinds of four-footed animals of the Earth, wild animals, reptiles, and birds of the sky. A voice came to him, "Rise, Peter, kill and eat!" But Peter said, "Not so, Lord; for I have never eaten anything that is common or unclean." A voice came to him again the second time, "What God has cleansed, you must not call unclean." This was done three times, and immediately the vessel was received up into heaven.

Acts 10:23-24
So he called them in and provided a place to stay. On the next day Peter arose and went out with them, and some of the brothers from Joppa accompanied him. On the next day they entered into Caesarea. Cornelius was waiting for them, having called together his relatives and his near friends.

Acts 6:3-8
Therefore select from among you, brothers, seven men of good report, full of the Holy Spirit and of wisdom, whom we may appoint over this business. But we will continue steadfastly in prayer and in the ministry of the word. These words pleased the whole multitude. They chose Stephen, a man full of faith and of the Holy Spirit, Philip, Prochorus, Nicanor, Timon, Parmenas, and Nicolaus, a proselyte of Antioch; whom they set before the apostles. When they had prayed, they laid their hands on them. The word of God increased and the number of the disciples greatly multiplied in Jerusalem. A great company of the priests were obedient to the faith. Stephen, full of faith and power, performed great wonders and signs among the people.

Acts 8:26-29
But an angel of the Lord spoke to Philip, saying, "Arise, and go toward the south to the way that goes down from Jerusalem to Gaza. This is a desert." He arose and went; and behold, there was a man of Ethiopia, a eunuch of great authority under Candace, queen of the Ethiopians, who was over all her treasure, who had come to Jerusalem to worship. He was returning and sitting in his chariot, and was reading the prophet Isaiah. When The Spirit said to Philip, "Go near, and join yourself to this chariot."

Of course, there are the incredible missionary journeys of Paul. God sent Paul (Acts 13:1-2), guided him (Acts 16:6-8), empowered him (Acts 13:9), and brought miraculous results through him (1 Corinthians 3:6). Yet, Paul made the journeys (Acts 13:4), followed the Spirit (Acts 16:9-10), preached the plan of redemption (Acts 16:14), then taught and nurtured those who believed (1 Thessalonians 2:8). So, what exactly is God's role in the proclamation of the plan of redemption?

Acts 13:1-2
Now in the assembly that was at Antioch there were some prophets and teachers: Barnabas, Simeon who was called Niger, Lucius of Cyrene, Manaen the foster brother of Herod the tetrarch, and Saul. As they served the Lord and fasted, the Holy Spirit said, "Separate Barnabas and Saul for me, for the work to which I have called them."

Acts 16:6-8
When they had gone through the region of Phrygia and Galatia, they were forbidden by the Holy Spirit to speak the word in Asia. When they had come opposite Mysia, they tried to go into Bithynia, but the Spirit didn't allow them. Passing by Mysia, they came down to Troas.

Acts 13:9
But Saul, who is also called Paul, filled with the Holy Spirit, fastened his eyes on him.

1 Corinthians 3:6
I planted. Apollos watered. But God gave the increase.

Acts 13:4
So, being sent out by the Holy Spirit, they went down to Seleucia. From there they sailed to Cyprus.

Acts 16:9-10
A vision appeared to Paul in the night. There was a man of Macedonia standing, begging him, and saying, "Come over into Macedonia and help us." When he [Paul] had seen the vision, immediately we sought to go out to Macedonia, concluding that the Lord had called us to preach the Good News to them.

Acts 16:14
A certain woman named Lydia, a seller of purple, of the city of Thyatira, one who worshiped God, heard us. The Lord opened her heart to listen to the things which were spoken by Paul.

1 Thessalonians 2:8
Even so, affectionately longing for you, we were well pleased to impart to you, not the Good News of God only, but also our own souls, because you had become very dear to us.

The Need to Know the Plan

Christians cannot fulfill their responsibility in evangelism, if they do not know the plan that they must share. In Luke 9, the disciples had been with Jesus for quite a while and the time came for some missionary work. In verses 1-6, He sent them to preach the gospel throughout the villages in the area giving them power over demons and disease. This implies that they had knowledge of the good news that they were proclaiming. These followers of Jesus understood the good news of the kingdom.

Luke 9:1-6
He called the twelve together, and gave them power and authority over all demons, and to cure diseases. He sent them out to preach God's Kingdom and to heal the sick. He said to them, "Take nothing for your journey — no staffs, nor wallet, nor bread, nor money. Don't have two coats each. Into whatever house you enter, stay there, and depart from there. As many as don't receive you, when you depart from that city, shake off even the dust from your feet for a testimony against them." They departed and went throughout the villages, preaching the Good News and healing everywhere.

This is rather obvious, yet many Christians do not really know the simple truths that must be proclaimed to preach the gospel. Jesus had taught all of them the plan. In Luke 8:1, the disciples heard and saw Him proclaiming the gospel from city to city. Then, Jesus preached the parables to the Jews and explained it them to them afterward (Luke 8:9-10).

Luke 8:1
Soon afterwards, he went about through cities and villages, preaching and bringing the good news of God's Kingdom. With him were the twelve.

Luke 8:9-10
Then his disciples asked him, "What does this parable mean?" He said, "To you it is given to know the mysteries of God's Kingdom, but to the rest in parables; that 'seeing they may not see, and hearing they may not understand.'"

In Matthew 10:27, Jesus declared to his disciples that they were to speak in the light and on the housetops what they had heard in the darkness and whispered in their ears. The apostle Matthew records, "What I tell you in the darkness, speak in the light; and what you hear whispered in the ear, proclaim on the housetops." Jesus was proclaiming to them the mysteries of the kingdom of God. Once learned, they were to share the good news in every place. The mysteries were to be declared for all to hear and see. For the disciples to accomplish this task, they would have to listen and learn everything the Lord had taught them about the gospel and kingdom. After His resurrection, the Lord showed Himself alive by many proofs for over a period of forty days to His disciples and spoke to them about God's kingdom (Acts 1:3).

Matthew 10:27
What I tell you in the darkness, speak in the light; and what you hear whispered in the ear, proclaim on the housetops.

Acts 1:3
To these he also showed himself alive after he suffered, by many proofs, appearing to them over a period of forty days, and speaking about God's Kingdom.

Christ taught His disciples the gospel, its many facets and truths, and its proofs until He was taken up to be with the Father. Christians must know the key points of the gospel, the Scriptures to back them up, and have enough knowledge to answer questions. People have nowhere else to find the truth except to go to Christians. If Christians do not know these truths and proofs, where will the unbeliever go? They are to be found nowhere else in the world.

The Choice to Proclaim the Plan

God commands Christians to proclaim the plan, but they must respond to this critical precept. Believers must choose to take their role and responsibility for sharing the gospel. The New Testament is filled with saints responding to God's command by presenting the good news. In Acts chapter 2, after the Spirit had come upon those who were at Pentecost, which was manifested by tongues of fire, Peter preached a great sermon. This message was not the only preaching that went occurred. According to verse one, there were 119 other people in the same upper room who received the miracle. He describes that the one hundred and nineteen also began speaking in other languages the mighty works of God (Acts 2:1-4). They were basically testifying of God's work in Jesus.
In Acts 6-8, Luke speaks of the evangelistic ministries of two great men of faith, Stephen and Philip. Yet, in Acts 8:4, Luke mentions that the Christians, who had been scattered due to persecution, went about preaching the Word. Though the impact of these two men was great, it would never have equaled the impact of these scattered Christians taking their responsibility and proclaiming the plan.

Acts 2:1-4
Now when the day of Pentecost had come, they were all with one accord in one place. Suddenly there came from the sky a sound like the rushing of a mighty

wind, and it filled all the house where they were sitting. Tongues like fire appeared and were distributed to them, and one sat on each of them. They were all filled with the Holy Spirit, and began to speak with other languages, as the Spirit gave them the ability to speak.

Acts 8:4
Therefore those who were scattered abroad went around preaching the word.

Once Paul, the apostle, had planted a church in a city, he usually left. Who won others to Christ and built the church? The saints in that church did this. They were responsible for carrying the presentation of the gospel to the next level. This involved the evangelism of the entire city. In 1 Thessalonians 1:8, Paul writes how much he rejoiced over the dynamic witness of the Thessalonians. He praises, "For from you the Word of the Lord has been declared, not only in Macedonia and Achaia, but also in every place your faith toward God has gone out; so that we need not to say anything." Paul applauds them because the gospel had gone forth from them into Macedonia, Achaia, and many other places.

1 Thessalonians 1:8
For from you the word of the Lord has been declared, not only in Macedonia and Achaia, but also in every place your faith toward God has gone out, so that we need not to say anything.

Those believers did not just leave the responsibility for evangelism up to the chosen apostles. When the Lord sends those searching for Christ into the path of believers at work, school, or in their neighborhood, those believers must accept their own responsibility and share the good news. Christians could provide many unbelievers with a helping hand, some clothes, food, money, or some other resource, but without the gospel, these people will never have eternal life. A warm meal cannot save one's soul. Also, the average saints cannot just leave it up to pastors to do this work. Christians must also share the gospel with others.

The Opportunities to Be Taken

In the first century, God created many opportunities for a Christian to proclaim the eternal plan of redemption. When God provides evangelistic opportunities, believers must act. The Spirit of God is constantly working in people's lives to bring them to Christ. He must lead them into the path of a believer to bring them into the kingdom. Once again, in Romans 10:13-15, the apostle Paul argues that people cannot believe unless they hear, and they cannot hear unless they have a preacher. Christians are those preachers.

Romans 10:13-15
For, "Whoever will call on the name of the Lord will be saved." How then will they call on him in whom they have not believed? How will they believe in him whom they have not heard? How will they hear without a preacher? And how will they preach unless they are sent? As it is written: "How beautiful are the feet of those who preach the Good News of peace, who bring glad tidings of good things!"

In Acts 8:29-30, Philip was sent by the Holy Spirit to the Ethiopian eunuch. Luke writes, "The Spirit said to Philip, 'Go near, and join yourself to this chariot.' Philip ran to him, and heard the man reading Isaiah the prophet, and said, "Do you understand what you are reading?"' The Scriptures were opened, but Philip had to take it from there and preach the gospel. Had Philip refused, out of fear or lack of motivation, the unbelieving eunuch would have had to come to Jesus Christ through another preacher. The Lord would have sent someone else, and he would not have had the privilege.

Acts 8:29-30
The Spirit said to Philip, "Go near, and join yourself to this chariot." Philip ran to him, and heard him reading Isaiah the prophet, and said, "Do you understand what you are reading?"

In Acts 10, Cornelius received a dream from God and sent for Peter. When the apostle Peter arrived at the house of

Cornelius, everyone had gathered to hear his message. God had set up the entire opportunity. Yet, Peter had to actually travel to the home of Cornelius and share the gospel with him. The opportunity God provided had to be taken. This is man's role in evangelism. Man must act in the preaching of the gospel for someone to be saved. This is and has always been God's way. In Acts 9:15-16, God told Paul through a prophet, whose name was Ananias that Paul would speak before governors and kings. In Acts 21:23 when Paul was finally arrested in the city of Jerusalem, God began fulfilling that prophecy and opening up opportunities for the gospel.

Acts 10:1-5
Now there was a certain man in Caesarea, Cornelius by name, a centurion of what was called the Italian Regiment, 2 a devout man, and one who feared God with all his house, who gave gifts for the needy generously to the people, and always prayed to God. 3 At about the ninth hour of the day, he clearly saw in a vision an angel of God coming to him, and saying to him, "Cornelius!" 4 He, fastening his eyes on him, and being frightened, said, "What is it, Lord?" He said to him, "Your prayers and your gifts to the needy have gone up for a memorial before God. 5 Now send men to Joppa, and get Simon, who is also called Peter.

Acts 9:15-16
But the Lord said to him, "Go your way, for he is my chosen vessel to bear my name before the nations and kings, and the children of Israel. For I will show him how many things he must suffer for my name's sake."

Acts 21:23
Therefore do what we tell you. We have four men who have taken a vow.

In Acts 22:1, he spoke before a Roman centurion and a large gathering of the Jews. In Acts 23:1, Paul proclaimed his message before the Jewish counsel. In Acts 24:10, Paul spoke before Governor Felix. In Acts 25:6, Felix left Paul in prison, and he preached the gospel to Festus, Felix's next successor. In Acts 26:1, Paul was sent to King Herod Agrippa, leader of the Jewish nation, and preached the gospel. Paul was able to share the good news with the highest Jewish official.

Acts 22:1
Brothers and fathers, listen to the defense which I now make to you.

Acts 23:1
Paul, looking steadfastly at the council, said, "Brothers, I have lived before God in all good conscience until today."

Acts 24:10
When the governor had beckoned to him to speak, Paul answered, "Because I know that you have been a judge of this nation for many years, I cheerfully make my defense."

Acts 25:6
When he had stayed among them more than ten days, he went down to Caesarea, and on the next day he sat on the judgment seat, and commanded Paul to be brought.

Acts 26:1
Agrippa said to Paul, "You may speak for yourself." Then Paul stretched out his hand, and made his defense.

Yet, the Lord God was not done, in Acts 28:16, Paul was sent to Rome to speak before the emperor (Philippians 1:12). The apostle knew he had to appeal to the emperor to keep from going back to the Jews. The Jews would have killed him. It had been prophesied that he preach to Caesar, so the apostle exercised his Roman right.

In every instance, the apostle Paul had to make a choice to seize the opportunity that God had given him and share the gospel. Paul could have chosen not to proclaim the plan, and the Book of Acts would have been written differently. Many opportunities to share can be brought by God to Christians (the divine role), but they must proclaim the gospel (the human role).

Philippians 1:12
Now I desire to have you know, brothers, that the things which happened to me have turned out rather to the progress of the Good News.

The Opportunities to Be Made

Not only are Christians to take the opportunities that God provides to share the gospel, but they are to make their own opportunities to share the gospel. In Acts 3:10-11, Peter and John saw a lame man who was begging in the temple. When they healed the man, a large crowd gathered. Peter preached the good news, which brought over 5,000 people to Christ. Peter created this opportunity to share the gospel by healing the lame man. He knew a crowd would be gathered. In Acts 4:8-11, the apostles of the Lord were taken into custody and brought before the Sanhedrin. Rather than remaining silent, Peter created an opportunity and shared the good news.

Acts 3:10-11
They recognized him, that it was he who used to sit begging for gifts for the needy at the Beautiful Gate of the temple. They were filled with wonder and amazement at what had happened to him. As the lame man who was healed held on to Peter and John, all the people ran together to them in the porch that is called Solomon's, greatly wondering.

Acts 4:8-11
Then Peter, filled with the Holy Spirit, said to them, "You rulers of the people, and elders of Israel, if we are examined today concerning a good deed done to a crippled man, by what means this man has been healed, may it be known to you all, and to all the people of Israel, that in the name of Jesus Christ of Nazareth, whom you crucified, whom God raised from the dead, this man stands here before you whole in him. He is 'the stone which was regarded as worthless by you, the builders, which has become the head of the corner.'"

In Acts 5:29-32, after many in Jerusalem were healed of their physical infirmities, the apostles were dragged before the council and commanded by them not to preach. After being miraculously released, they went out preaching the gospel in defiance of the council's command. They would obey the Lord God, rather than man. They were once again arrested. This time Peter preached the gospel. He created an opportunity as they stood before the council.

Acts 5:29-32
But Peter and the apostles answered, "We must obey God rather than men. The God of our fathers raised up Jesus, whom you killed, hanging him on a tree. 31 God exalted him with his right hand to be a Prince and...Savior, to give repentance to Israel, and remission of sins. We are his witnesses of these things; and so also is the Holy Spirit, whom God has given to those who obey him."

In Acts 6-7, Stephen went about preaching the good news and performing many miracles. Each time, he was creating an opportunity. Even when he was arrested, he stood before the Sanhedrin as Peter did and proclaimed the good news brought through Christ. Stephen created an opportunity to share the gospel out of his arrest.

This instigated Saul to begin his persecution of Christians in Acts 8. When this occurred, many Christians ran for their lives. In Acts 8:4, Luke records what happened, "Therefore those who were scattered abroad went around preaching the Word." Everywhere they traveled, these Christians created opportunities to share the gospel. They did not wait around for God to hand deliver a situation for them to speak. They shared the good news of the Lord Jesus Christ with anyone who would listen.

Acts 8:4
Therefore those who were scattered abroad went around preaching the word.

During his persecutions, Saul was converted on the road to Damascus. Sometime after, Saul, who became Paul, began his three missionary journeys that Luke begins to describe in Acts thirteen and continues to the end of the book. Each of his gospel journeys involved many opportunities Paul made to share the gospel. Paul's strategy was simple: go into the synagogue or into the marketplace and present the gospel to anyone who would listen (Acts 17:17). Christians need to do the same. The Lord does not direct every single evangelistic encounter as He did with Cornelius or the eunuch. Most of the time, evangelistic opportunities were simply created. The good news can be brought into numerous situations, with some forethought or prayerful consideration, by Christians while a situation is unfolding.

Acts 17:17
So he reasoned in the synagogue with the Jews and the devout persons, and in the marketplace every day with those who met him.

An Ancient Portrait

Sometimes becoming a Christian may require a series of steps and some time to journey to the cross. There will be those who will immediately believe and others who must go through a pilgrimage of their own making or of others who may stand in their way. God may have to remove various obstacles for them to enter His eternal kingdom. One such individual was the powerful governor of Cyprus named Sergius Paulus. The thirteenth chapter of Acts opens with Paul and Barnabas being affirmed by the Holy Spirit and then commissioned by the church. They were to go out in their behalf and share the good news of Christ. This was Paul's first missionary journey. The group had determined that their initial stop would be a small island not too far away called Cyprus.

Acts 13:1-3
Now in the assembly that was at Antioch there were some prophets and teachers: Barnabas, Simeon who was called Niger, Lucius of Cyrene, Manaen the foster brother of Herod the tetrarch, and Saul. As they served the Lord and fasted, the Holy Spirit said, "Separate Barnabas and Saul for me, for the work to which I have called them." Then, when they had fasted and prayed and laid their hands on them, they sent them away.

After they picked up John Mark (the author of the gospel Mark), they set sail from the port of Seleucia for the island in the Mediterranean Sea. There first destination was the city of

Salamis. This was the biggest city on the island with a large Jewish population and would have had several synagogues. Here, Paul and his companions entered the synagogues and began proclaiming the Word. Luke does not describe what happened in that city, but the author does indicate that they were preaching all the way to Paphos. This city was across the island on the west coast and was the seat of the Roman governor. This city was also the center of the worship of the goddess of love, Venus. It was a place of sexual promiscuity. and every kind of vice imaginable.

The Roman proconsul of Cyprus was Sergius Paulus. When he heard that Paul had arrived, he sent for him. Luke describes him as a man of great intelligence. The Greek word which is translated "intelligence" in the English indicates the governor was wise, discerning, smart, and learned. I am sure by the time this group of missionaries had finally entered his city, he had been presented with much of the message and results of Paul's evangelistic efforts. A man like this always knows what is occurring on his island. This initial response was God at work in his heart. He sought a word from God.

The governor was already in Satan's domain of darkness and kept there by a Jewish sorcerer who falsely claimed to be a prophet of God. His name was Bar-Jesus which means "son of salvation." He was the official medium of the royal court. He practiced dark magic and had a hold on the whole island through this official that had just sent for Paul and Barnabas. Since Elymas (another name for Bar-Jesus) had claimed to be a prophet, perhaps proconsul Paulus thought he could get another word from God. We know he believed that these men did speak the Word of God because Luke explains that he was seeking that from them. This demon empowered emissary could not allow them to influence his disciple, the governor, and lose his hold on him. So, he stood against Paul and attempted to turn Sergius away from the faith that Paul was declaring. This immediately called for a divine intervention by Paul and a miraculous authentication of his gospel. Paul had the real truth as opposed to the lies Elymas had been teaching in the Roman court. There was a confrontation in the same way as Elijah had with the false prophets of Baal.

This time, Christ's apostle fixed his gaze on Elymas and announced that he was a fraud, a liar, a son of the Devil, an enemy of righteousness, and a man who would never cease making crooked the straight ways of the Lord. Then Paul, filled with the Spirit, struck him with blindness. Suddenly, a darkness and mist came over this deputy of the court and he sought to find someone to lead him around. When Sergius saw this miracle, his initial searching heart turned into a true believing one and the proconsul received Jesus as Savior and Lord. For Sergius several steps toward the cross had to be taken by both himself (as seeker) and Paul (as evangelist). Paul had to bring the gospel to him and share it. To do this, he had to take a stand against a powerful man who opposed this seeker from receiving Christ. In his searching for truth, Sergius had to send for Paul so he could hear the Word of God. His pilgrimage ended in eternal life.

A Modern Anecdote

I learned the power of God's challenge to take my role in the sharing of His plan of redemption early in my ministry as a Senior Pastor. I had only been in this ministry for two years when a wonderful, Spirit-filled elderly woman in my congregation came to me with a request. Elizabeth inquired, "Pastor, I have prayed persistently over thirty-four years for the salvation of my brother-in-law. He has lived a godless, sin-filled life of pleasure-seeking and wickedness. Now he is in the hospital dying of throat cancer. Could you possibly visit Joe and share the gospel with him? I am afraid soon it will be too late, and he will perish."

I immediately agreed, not knowing what I was about to encounter. I asked her to pray that I would receive from the Lord an opportunity to share the good news with him and would be bold and have clarity of speech. A couple of days later, I entered the hospital waiting room and saw Elizabeth with another woman standing together. As I greeted them, the woman, whose name was Brenda, introduced herself as Joe's wife. She walked us to the patio and pointed to a man sitting on a chair across the way and shouted, "Joey, Joey, Elizabeth's pastor has come by to see you, please say hello."

In front of me sat literally the shell of an eighty-five-year-old man with half of his face and lips eaten away by cancer. He was smoking a cigarette out of the other half of his lip. I was taken aback and uttered in the silence of my own soul, "Oh no, help me, Lord Jesus!" He looked up, took a puff of his cigarette, gave me the once over, and then growled in a nasal tone, "I know why you're here. Well, don't bother!" In shock, I stood there.

I was speechless. I began to pray for wisdom and waited for the Lord to work in some way. Then suddenly, I heard myself saying with great enthusiasm and vigor, "Well Joey, I can see this is not a good time, if I come back to see you, will you turn me away? He replied with a deep grown, "Noooo." As I passed the two welcoming ladies saying my good-byes, I whispered, "Pray, Pray hard!" At first, I thought to myself, "I never want to see that man again." Then I remembered the role God had given me to play in His redemptive plan: Joey could not be saved if I did not share the good news with him. God would not drop a message from heaven. I was His instrument.

I recommitted myself to my role in his possible salvation. I had planned on visiting him about four days later after more prayer, but on the second day, the phone rang. It was Joey's wife explaining to me that Joey had wanted to see me right away. I was utterly stunned and awestruck at God's sovereignty. He really was in control. I replied that I would be by the next day. I walked into Joey's hospital room, and he motioned me to come over to him.

He muttered, "Pastor, come close and talk into my right ear. It's the good one and tell me what you have to say!" This was like a dream which was born out of thirty-four years of prayer and God's wondrous work. I began to share with him the full gospel of Jesus Christ. Joey sat there for a good thirty minutes, never saying a word, only quietly listening and weeping. Sometimes, I had to shout over his sobbing.

When I got to the end, my heart was pounding in my chest, and I boldly asked, "Well, would you like to become a Christian? Joey shook his head and whimpered, "Yeahhhh." And right then and there, this dying man became a believing and trusting Christian in the great forgiving work of Jesus. I visited Joey every other day speaking of the hope he now had in heaven. Tears of joy were always in his eyes as he asked question after question about his new eternity.

Three weeks later, I went to fellowship with him, and his bed was empty. Joey had passed away and into the arms of His Savior and Lord (2 Corinthians 5:6-8). He had heard the good news just in time through God's grace. I was thankful that I had taken my role and been a part of bringing another person into the kingdom to glorify the Son for all eternity.

AN INSTRUCTOR'S MANUAL

2 Corinthians 5:6-8
Therefore we are always confident and know that while we are at home in the body, we are absent from the Lord; for we walk by faith, not by sight. We are courageous, I say, and are willing rather to be absent from the body and to be at home with the Lord.

A Personal Response

Dear Heavenly Father,

    I understand that this great plan of redemption is all Your work and power, yet I also have been given an important role. Please motivate me to study and learn all the aspects of the true gospel. I ask that You help me to choose to accept my full responsibility and share the good news with (add names) and others I know and meet it. Give me the wisdom I need to discern the opportunities you have provided for me to share with them. Also, I request that you give me the courage and boldness to make opportunities every chance I get to present to them Your beautiful plan of salvation. Fill me with Your Spirit and a wonderful enthusiasm for sharing the gospel. Please soften their hearts and bring them to Your beloved Son. Father, help me to encourage other Christians I know to share with their friends and those they know and meet. I pray this in the name of Jesus. Amen.

LEADING THE WAY

Instructor's Notes

Chapter 5

Allow Man to Be Challenged

Not only does God have a part in the proclamation of the plan but man also. In His infinite wisdom, God decided to use people to proclaim His plan to other people.

In the section, "A Typical Scenario," the author demonstrates how the followers of Jesus Christ can share the gospel with old high school friends at their reunions.

What is the scenario about?

A Christian wants to witness at his reunion to an agnostic friend but decides he won't because he probably hasn't changed his mind.

What held the believer back from sharing the gospel?

He did not realize that he had to know God's plan and then chose to share it by creating an opportunity for the gospel.

What finally led the Christian to share the good news and how did it occur?

When the friends reunited, the agnostic described his directionless life, and he took the opportunity to share the gospel.

Have you had a similar experience?

(Various answers should be shared including yours.)

LEADING THE WAY

In the section, "A Scriptural Principle" the author presents an important biblical principle in evangelism which concerns the believer's role in sharing the gospel.

How would you express this principle in your own words?

This fifth principle is "we must allow man to be challenged."

(Various answers should be shared including yours.)

How would you rewrite this principle to make it even more personal to your life (using your name and situation)?

(Various answers should be shared including yours.)

Why do you think this principle might be important in your life right now as you share the gospel?

(Various answers should be shared including yours.)

How would you rate yourself on the percentage of times you followed this principle in the past as a believer?

(Various answers should be shared including yours.)

Directions: Put a horizontal mark and your name where you see yourself on the percentage line.

0%   25%   50%   75%   100%

In the section, "A Biblical Explanation," the author explains the role believers play in evangelism and their willingness to accept it and take action to share the gospel effectively.

What is a major obstacle that keeps Christians from sharing the gospel?

This is rather obvious, yet many Christians do not really know the simple truths that must be proclaimed to preach the gospel. Jesus had taught all of them the plan. In Luke 8:1, the disciples heard and saw Him proclaiming the gospel from city to city.

According to Acts 1:3, what two things did Jesus Christ do to prepare His disciples for ministry before his ascension?

After His resurrection, the Lord showed Himself alive by many proofs for over a period of forty days to His disciples and spoke to them about God's kingdom (Acts 1:3).

According to Acts 2, who chose to share the gospel after the Spirit manifested the tongues of fire?

In Acts chapter 2, after the Spirit had come upon those who were at Pentecost, which was manifested by tongues of fire, Peter preached a great sermon. This message was not the only preaching that went occurred. According to verse one, there were 119 other people in the same upper room who received the miracle.

According to Acts 8:4, what did the Christians choose to do after they were scattered?

In Acts 6-8, Luke speaks of the evangelistic ministries of two great men of faith, Stephen and Philip. Yet, in Acts 8:4, Luke mentions that the Christians, who had been scattered due to persecution, went about preaching the Word. Though the impact of these two men was great, it would never have equaled the impact of these scattered Christians taking their responsibility and proclaiming the plan.

What is the main difference in evangelism between choosing an opportunity God provides and making one?

In the first century, God created many opportunities for a Christian to proclaim the eternal plan of redemption. When God provides evangelistic opportunities, believers must act. The Spirit of God is constantly working in people's lives to bring them to Christ.

Not only are Christians to take the opportunities that God provides to share the gospel, but they are to make their own opportunities to share the gospel. In Acts 3:10-11, Peter and John saw a lame man who was begging in the temple. When they healed the man, a large crowd gathered.

In what ways might these truths impact your life?

(Various answers should be shared including yours.)

In the section, "An Ancient Portrait," the author provides a unique portrayal of Paul's sharing of the gospel with Sergius Paulus.

Can you briefly describe the setting of this real-life ancient drama?

The setting is the small island of Cypress. Here, Paul and his companions entered the synagogues and began proclaiming the Word. Luke does not describe what happened in that city, but the author does indicate that they were preaching all the way to Paphos. This city was across the island on the west coast and was the seat of the Roman governor.

Can you describe the major characters involved?

The major characters are Paul, Sergius Paulus, and Elymas the Magician.

How did the evangelist initiate the gospel presentation?

This demon empowered emissary could not allow them to influence his disciple, the governor, and lose his hold on him. So, he stood against Paul and attempted to turn Sergius away from the faith that Paul was declaring. This immediately called for a divine intervention by Paul and a miraculous authentication of his gospel. Paul had the real truth as opposed to the lies Elymas had been teaching in the Roman court. There was a confrontation in the same way as Elijah had with the false prophets of Baal.

This time, Christ's apostle [Paul] fixed his gaze on Elymas and announced that he was a fraud, a liar, a son of the Devil, an enemy of righteousness, and a man who would never cease making crooked the straight ways of the Lord. Then Paul, filled with the Spirit, struck him with blindness. Suddenly, a darkness and mist came over this deputy of the court and he sought to find someone to lead him around.

What was result of this evangelistic presentation?

When Sergius saw this miracle, his initial searching heart turned into a true believing one and the proconsul received Jesus as Savior and Lord.

How was the principle explained in this chapter applied to the situation?

For Sergius several steps toward the cross had to be taken by both himself (as seeker) and Paul (as evangelist). Paul had to bring the gospel to him and share it. To do this, he had to take a stand against a powerful man who opposed this seeker from receiving Christ. In his searching for truth, Sergius had to send for Paul so he could hear the Word of God. His pilgrimage ended in eternal life.

Based on the truths learned in this chapter, what would you have done differently if you were the evangelist or how would you have responded if you were the recipient?

(Various answers should be shared including yours.)

In the section, "A Modern Anecdote," the author discusses a situation where he, as a pastor, met with a man who was dying in the hospital.

Can you briefly describe the setting of this real-life modern drama?

The setting is a hospital. I asked her to pray that I would receive from the Lord an opportunity to share the good news with him and would be bold and have clarity of speech. A couple of days later, I entered the hospital waiting room and saw Elizabeth with another woman standing together.

Can you describe the major characters involved?

The major characters are Elizabeth, the author, Brenda, and Joey.

How did the author initiate the gospel presentation?

He looked up, took a puff of his cigarette, gave me the once over, and then growled in a nasal tone, "I know why you're here. Well, don't bother!" In shock, I stood there.

I was speechless. I began to pray for wisdom and waited for the Lord to work in some way. Then suddenly, I heard myself saying with great enthusiasm and vigor, "Well Joey, I can see this is not a good time, if I come back to see you, will you turn me away? He replied with a deep grown, "Noooo." As I passed the two welcoming ladies saying my good-byes, I whispered, "Pray, Pray hard!"

I recommitted myself to my role in his possible salvation. I had planned on visiting him about four days later after more prayer, but on the second day, the phone rang. It was Joey's wife explaining to me that Joey had wanted to see me right away. I was utterly stunned and awestruck at God's sovereignty.

He muttered, "Pastor, come close and talk into my right ear. It's the good one and tell me what you have to say!" This was like a dream which was born out of thirty-four years of prayer and God's wondrous work. I began to share with him the full gospel of Jesus Christ. Joey sat there for a good thirty minutes, never saying a word, only quietly listening and weeping.

What was result of this evangelistic presentation?

When I got to the end, my heart was pounding in my chest, and I boldly asked, "Well, would you like to become a Christian? Joey shook his head and whimpered, "Yeahhhh." And right then and there, this dying man became a believing and trusting Christian in the great forgiving work of Jesus.

How was the principle explained in this chapter applied to the situation?

Joey had passed away and into the arms of His Savior and Lord (2 Corinthians 5:6-8). He had heard the good news just in time through God's grace. I was thankful that I had taken my role and been a part of bringing another person into the kingdom to glorify the Son for all eternity.

Based on the truths learned in this chapter, what would you have done differently if you were the author or how would you have responded if you were the recipient?

(Various answers should be shared including yours.)

AN INSTRUCTOR'S MANUAL

In the section, "A Personal Response," the author provides a model you may use for prayer if you find it necessary after discovering the truths in this chapter.

Are you presently attempting to present the gospel of Jesus to someone? If not, are there some among your classmates who may not know Jesus Christ and may need prayer for an opportunity for you to share with them and open hearts to receive Him?

(Various answers should be shared including yours.)

Based on the truths you have just learned, what will you continue to do in your current evangelistic efforts and what might you do differently?

(Various answers should be shared including yours.)

What additional thoughts would you like to share with the others?

(Various answers should be shared including yours.)

LEADING THE WAY

Instructor's Notes

Chapter 6

Persist in Watchful Prayer

Prayer is one of the most effective and powerful tools for bringing people to Christ. Unfortunately, it is probably the most neglected method utilized in evangelism. The saints should pray consistently and persistently for the unsaved. Prayer can and will move the hand of an all-powerful God. Since the Bible is filled with examples of prayer having very powerful effects on the lives of people and nations. Why not the salvation of souls?

A Typical Scenario

Have you ever been in a situation that was something like the following? When you were growing up, perhaps you had an uncle who was like a second father to you. At every single Thanksgiving, Christmas, Easter, three-day weekend, and vacation, he, his wife, and kids would travel to your house to bring all the families together. He would gather up you, your siblings, and cousins, and take you all shopping at the mall, to play at the park, or go to the movies. At night, he would talk his brother (your dad) into letting all the kids sleep in sleeping bags in the living room like a camp out.

As the kids got older, he would attend plays, concerts, and whatever else you participated in. He always made you feel like you were the best person in the group. He was always happy and always encouraging. Then you received Christ as Savior and Lord and suddenly realized he was not a believer and not going to heaven. Once you tried to share Christ with him, then he brought up dinosaurs, evolution, and spun off in a million directions. These discussions went nowhere. His happiness never left and neither did his sins. Whenever he was around, you thought about his salvation; whenever he was gone, it left your mind.

In this chapter you learn that you are to be committed to praying for the salvation of souls and should expect God to work mighty miracles by bringing those people to His Son. When you feel burdened and sense a kindred spirit toward those you love or meet, you should respond through prayer. You should ask God to provide an open door to share the gospel with others and to give you courage and wisdom to speak the truth. You must also be praying for others to take the challenge and present God's plan. God desires for people to be saved and praying for this will please Him. After you learn these biblical truths, perhaps this same situation might proceed differently.

You realize that you love your uncle deeply and ask God to give you a burden to pray for him. You do not want to see him perish, so you decide to rely upon the power of prayer to move the hand of God in his life. You conclude that it is an opportune moment to develop a consistent daily time of prayer. So, every day on your way to or from work, rather than listen to talk radio or music, you pray. He is always the first name from your lips to the Lord. You ask the Lord, "Please bring my uncle to your Son. Please prepare his heart and give me an opportunity to share your gospel with him. Give me the wisdom and boldness that will be necessary when the time comes. In the name of Jesus. Amen."

The Lord does not answer your prayers at first. You see him but do not receive the opportunity to speak alone with him. You just keep praying. Finally, the opportunity arrives on one Thanksgiving Day. Since your uncle missed his son's birthday, he indicates that he is going out to his car to get a gift he had purchased for him. You yell, "I'll go with you." You prayed silently, "Lord, please help me." When you get to the car, he opens the trunk, takes out the gift, and starts walking in. Then he stops suddenly, turns to you and says, "I want to ask you a question and I want an honest answer. Will you give it to me?"

You gulp and reply that you will, if you can. He explains that on the way to the party, he could not get the radio talk show he was used to listening to. He flipped through the stations and landed on what he thought was an alternate talk show, but it turned out to be a preacher. He tells you that he was so bored he decided to listen. Then your uncle sternly asks, "Do you think I am going to hell?" Since you had been praying for this moment for so long, you boldly look at him and say, "Yes, may I explain why?" When he answers in the affirmative, you share the gospel with him. Right there in the driveway of your own house, your most beloved uncle receives Jesus as Savior and Lord.

Though this is an imaginary scenario, it is very typical of the kinds of encounters Christians have with unbelievers. We might not take an opportunity to share the gospel with loved ones or those we meet because we have not prayed for them. We need to begin the sharing of the gospel standing before the throne of God begging for Him to unleash His power and bring many people to His Son through us. This leads us to the sixth principle which involves praying for the unsaved.

A Scriptural Principle

Many of us are afraid of sharing the gospel because of we may have never actually seen someone come to Christ and it becomes an unknown. Yet, we ourselves were there when we became Christians. When we remember our experience, it seemed so simple, and it was. The reason it is so simple is because the power of the Holy Spirit had supernaturally worked for someone to share the gospel with us and for us to respond. To unleash this power God has determined that the saints should pray and ask Him for it. The sixth principle is "we must persist in watchful prayer."

A Biblical Explanation

At numerous times in King David's life, he needed God's power and prayed for it. He persisted in his requests and then watched for God to answer them. In Psalm 5:1-3, the leader of Israel and psalmist writes, "Give ear to my words, Yahweh. Consider my meditation. Listen to the voice of my cry, my King and my God; for to you do I pray. Yahweh, in the morning you shall hear my voice. In the morning I will lay my requests before you, and will watch expectantly." Here, David describes his pattern of prayer. Every morning, he would go before the throne of God with his requests and eagerly watch for His divine work. He had persistence and watchfulness. Why? David knew His God and understood that His God responds to the prayers of His people in great power.

Psalm 5:1-3
Give ear to my words, Yahweh. Consider my meditation. Listen to the voice of my cry, my King and my God; for I pray to you. Yahweh, in the morning you will hear my voice. In the morning I will lay my requests before you, and will watch expectantly.

In Ephesians 3:20, the apostle Paul, who had seen God do amazing things in his evangelistic efforts, describes God's power in these words, "Now to him who is able to do exceedingly abundantly above all that we ask or think." The Lord can work in our sharing of the gospel way beyond even what we could conceive of or ask from Him. Then Paul concludes, "According to the power that works in us." This power is in us. When we pray and then share the gospel, the power that we need is inside us. When the unsaved hear our good news (and it is time for them to receive Christ), the power of the Spirit destroys their blinders from the Devil, the hardness of their hearts melt away, faith in Jesus comes, and the Holy Spirit enters them. This is the power we can see as we share the message of salvation.

Ephesians 3:20
Now to him who is able to do exceedingly abundantly above all that we ask or think, according to the power that works in us.

The Power of Prayer in the Proclamation

Prayer unleashes God's power. In Genesis 18:22, when Abraham prayed for Lot, his life was spared from the fire of Sodom and Gomorrah. In Exodus 14:10, when Moses prayed for God's people to be delivered from Egypt, God parted the Red Sea. In Exodus 15:25, when Moses cried out to God for the starving Hebrews, God provided manna from heaven.

Genesis 18:22
The men turned from there, and went toward Sodom, but Abraham stood yet before Yahweh.

Exodus 14:10
When Pharaoh came near, the children of Israel lifted up their eyes, and behold, the Egyptians were marching after them; and they were very afraid. The children of Israel cried out to Yahweh.

Exodus 15:25
Then he cried to Yahweh. Yahweh showed him a tree, and he threw it into the waters, and the waters were made sweet. There he made a statute and an ordinance for them, and there he tested them.

In 1 Kings 17:1, When Elijah, the prophet, prayed for the rain to cease in judgment upon God's people, it did not rain for three-and-one-half years. In 1 Kings 18:38, When Elijah asked God to consume his water drenched offering before the 850 prophets of Baal and Asherah, fire came from heaven and burned up his offering while leaving theirs untouched. In Daniel 9:3, when Daniel, the prophet, prayed for Israel's release from Babylonian captivity, God delivered His people through King Cyrus (Ezra 1:1-4). In Luke 1:13, when the priest Zacharias prayed for his barren wife Elizabeth, she conceived John the Baptist. In Acts 12:5, when the saints prayed for Peter who was guarded by trained soldiers in a prison, he was rescued by an angel.

1 Kings 17:1
Elijah the Tishbite, who was one of the settlers of Gilead, said to Ahab, "As Yahweh, the God of Israel, lives, before whom I stand, there shall not be dew nor rain these years, but according to my word."

1 Kings 18:38
Then Yahweh's fire fell, and consumed the burnt offering, the wood, the stones, and the dust, and licked up the water that was in the trench.
Daniel 9:3
I set my face to the Lord God, to seek by prayer and petitions, with fasting and sackcloth and ashes.

Ezra 1:1-4
Now in the first year of Cyrus king of Persia, that Yahweh's word by Jeremiah's mouth might be accomplished, Yahweh stirred up the spirit of Cyrus king of Persia, so that he made a proclamation throughout all his kingdom, and put it also in writing, saying, "Cyrus king of Persia says, 'Yahweh, the God of heaven, has given me all the kingdoms of the Earth; and he has commanded me to build him a house in Jerusalem, which is in Judah. Whoever there is among you of all his people, may his God be with him, and let him go up to Jerusalem, which is in Judah, and build the house of Yahweh, the God of Israel (he is God), which is in Jerusalem. Whoever is left, in any place where he lives, let the men of his place help him with silver, with gold, with goods, and with animals, in addition to the free will offering for God's house which is in Jerusalem.'"

Luke 1:13
But the angel said to him, "Don't be afraid, Zacharias, because your request has been heard. Your wife, Elizabeth, will bear you a son, and you shall call his name John."

Acts 12:5
Peter therefore was kept in the prison, but constant prayer was made by the assembly to God for him.

The prayers of believers can be an effective and powerful means for accomplishing the work of God. In 1 Corinthians 2:1-3, Paul tells the Corinthians that his gospel did not come to them in persuasive words of man's wisdom but "in power and the Spirit." Power through the Spirit can be unleashed through prayer. In 1 Thessalonians 1:5-6, Paul rejoices and thanks his God, the Father, for the Word coming into their lives in His power through the Holy Spirit. This power could produce a mighty witness for the Lord Jesus throughout the whole region.

1 Corinthians 2:1-3
When I came to you, brothers, I didn't come with excellence of speech or of wisdom, proclaiming to you the testimony of God. For I determined not to know anything among you except Jesus Christ and him crucified. I was with you in weakness, in fear, and in much trembling.

1 Thessalonians 1:5-6
And that our Good News came to you not in word only, but also in power, and in the Holy Spirit, and with much assurance. You know what kind of men we showed ourselves to be among you for your sake. You became imitators of us and of the Lord, having received the word in much affliction, with joy of the Holy Spirit.

In 2 Thessalonians 1:11-12, Paul discusses the persecution that resulted from their witness and prays that God would grant them power in their work of faith. The main work of faith was their witness for Christ. Here Paul is praying that their witness would go forth in power. Prayer has a definite role in evangelism. It can provide power to save.

2 Thessalonians 1:11-12
To this end we also pray always for you, that our God may count you worthy of your calling, and fulfill every desire of goodness and work of faith with power, that the name of our Lord Jesus may be glorified in you, and you in him, according to the grace of our God and the Lord Jesus Christ.

The Importance of the Proclamation in Prayer

Prayer is very important in evangelism. Prayer should be involved intimately and intricately in every aspect of sharing the good news. This importance is described in two different ways. First, praying for the salvation of others is an essential part of prayer. Second, praying for the salvation of others is an essential part of evangelism. These are two sides of the same gospel coin. The personal and congregational prayers of the saints must involve evangelism and the salvation of the unsaved. To win others to Christ begins on one's knees.

Evangelism is an essential part of our prayers. Whenever saints pray, they should include prayer for the salvation of the unsaved and for those who share the gospel. Prayer for all the physical needs of unbelievers is important, but prayer for their eternal destiny should be the priority. In Matthew 6, the Lord's disciples approached Jesus and asked Him how to pray. In verses 8-13, Jesus composed a prayer that included the salvation of the lost. Out of the many subjects for prayer the Lord Jesus could have chosen, He spoke of evangelism. In Matthew 6:10, Jesus commands them to pray that His Father's kingdom will come. The apostle wrote these words of the Lord, "Let your kingdom come. Let your will be done, as in Heaven, so on Earth." According to Jesus, an essential element of one's prayer life is a request that the Lord God establish His kingdom. God will build His church upon the Earth. How does God build His kingdom?

Matthew 6:8-13
Therefore don't be like them, for your Father knows what things you need before you ask him. Pray...this: "Our Father in heaven, may your name be kept holy. Let your Kingdom come. Let your will be done on Earth as it is in heaven. Give us today our daily bread. Forgive us our debts, as we also forgive our debtors. Bring us not into temptation, but deliver us from the evil one. For yours is the Kingdom...power, and the glory forever. Amen."

Matthew 6:10
Let your Kingdom come. Let your will be done on Earth as it is in heaven.

In Colossians 1:13, the apostle declares that unbelievers, who become Christians, are transferred from Satan's domain of darkness to the kingdom of Christ. The kingdom of Jesus is the kingdom of God. Any time a believer shares the gospel and brings an unbeliever to Christ - the kingdom of God is advanced. Why? Christians comprise this kingdom. They are its temple, priests, and building blocks (1 Corinthians 3:17; 1 Peter 2:9; Ephesians 2:21).

Colossians 1:13
Who delivered us out of the power of darkness, and translated us into the Kingdom of the Son of his love.

1 Corinthians 3:17
If anyone destroys God's temple, God will destroy him; for God's temple is holy, which you are.

1 Peter 2:9
But you are a chosen race, a royal priesthood, a holy nation, a people for God's own possession, that you may proclaim the excellence of him who called you out of darkness into his marvelous light.

Ephesians 2:21
In whom the whole building, fitted together, grows into a holy temple in the Lord.

Therefore, to pray for the kingdom of God to come, one is praying for believers who are sharing the gospel and for unbelievers who are being saved. In Romans 10:1, Paul cried out that his heart's true desire and prayer was for the Jews to be saved. This prayer for their salvation was a prayer for the advancement of the kingdom.

Romans 10:1
Brothers, my heart's desire and my prayer to God is for Israel, that they may be saved.

The Importance of Prayer in the Proclamation

Prayer is an essential part of sharing the gospel of Jesus. Whenever we proclaim the plan, we need to pray. In Luke 5:15-17, the author describes the ministry of Jesus as healing the people and proclaiming the kingdom of God. He was out teaching the multitudes and confronting the Pharisees. Then he would often slip away to pray. What would have been the subject of His prayers? He was praying for His ministry which was proclaiming the gospel (evangelism).

Luke 5:15-17
But the report concerning him spread much more, and great multitudes came together to hear, and to be healed by him of their infirmities. But he withdrew himself into the desert, and prayed. On one of those days, he was teaching; and there were Pharisees and teachers of the law sitting by, who had come out of every village of Galilee, Judea, and Jerusalem. The power of the Lord was with him to heal them.

In Mark 1:35, Jesus left His disciples early in the morning to pray. The gospel writer records, "Early in the morning, while it was still dark, he [Jesus] rose up and went out, and departed into a deserted place, and prayed there." Christ's disciples came and told Him that many were looking for Him, but the Lord desired to preach to the towns nearby. Obviously, He prayed for His Father to bless His preaching in the towns where he shared the gospel. In Acts 6:4, Paul described the work of the apostles as the work of ministry and prayer. The primary ministry of the twelve apostles was evangelism. Preaching and praying go hand in hand.

Mark 1:35
Early in the morning, while it was still dark, he rose up and went out, and departed into a deserted place, and prayed there.

Acts 6:4
But we will continue steadfastly in prayer and in the ministry of the word.

Christians need to be constantly preaching and praying. As has been seen earlier, preaching and praying was done by regular, ordinary saints, not just the pastor and church staff. As we do this, we will see God work in mighty ways.

The Motivation for Prayer in the Proclamation

There are many reasons why one should be proclaiming the plan and praying for the salvation of others. First, saints are encouraged and exhorted to pray for the salvation of souls. In 1 Timothy 2:1-2, Paul discusses with Timothy how people are to conduct themselves in the church. He urges Timothy to have all the saints pray for all men and kings in authority, so that the saints may lead quiet, peaceful lives in godliness and dignity. In verses 3-4, Paul writes the reason. The entreating, prayers, petitions, and thanksgivings, which were in behalf of all men, were for their salvation. Christians are to clearly be praying for the salvation of souls.

1 Timothy 2:1-2
I exhort therefore, first of all, that petitions, prayers, intercessions, and givings of thanks be made for all men: for kings and all who are in high places, that we may lead a tranquil and quiet life in all godliness and reverence.

1 Timothy 2:3-4
For this is good and acceptable in the sight of God our Savior, who desires all people to be saved and come to full knowledge of the truth.

Second, when believers pray for the salvation of others, it pleases God. In that same passage, Paul asserts to his fellow worker that this is good and acceptable to God. To pray for the salvation of all men is a good thing and God accepts it. Why? It pleases Him. Third, God desires people to be saved. Once again, in that same passage, Paul gives the reason that it is acceptable to God because He desires all people to come to a saving knowledge of Him. Peter told his readers that God is patient, and He does not wish for any to perish, so the second coming of Christ had not occurred yet (2 Peter 2:9). God is delaying the coming of His only Son because He wants more people to become His children.

2 Peter 2:9
The Lord knows how to deliver the godly out of temptation and to keep the unrighteous under punishment for the Day of Judgment.

Fourth, prayer for the unsaved is the natural result of a burdened heart. In Romans 9:1-3, Paul declares his burden for the salvation of the Jewish people. It brought him great sorrow and constant grief. In Romans 10:1, this deep burden poured forth in prayer for these people. The apostle wrote, "Brothers, my heart's desire and my prayer to God is for Israel, that they may be saved." Paul was so troubled that he was actually willing to trade his own salvation if he could see his Hebrew brothers saved.

Romans 9:1-3
I tell the truth in Christ. I am not lying, my conscience testifying with me in the Holy Spirit that I have great sorrow and unceasing pain in my heart. For I could wish that I myself were accursed from Christ for my brothers' sake, my relatives according to the flesh.

Romans 10:1
Brothers, my heart's desire and my prayer to God is for Israel, that they may be saved.

Fifth, prayer is the natural result of a kindred heart. In that same passage, Paul calls the Jews his brethren and his kinsmen according to the flesh. Paul felt a human bond to the Jews. He was born of their nation (Acts 22:3). Christians are to take all of these reasons for prayer in the proclamation of the good news to heart. Petitions for the salvation of others should be an important part of prayer.

Acts 22:3
I am indeed a Jew, born in Tarsus of Cilicia, but brought up in this city at the feet of Gamaliel, instructed according to the strict tradition of the law of our fathers, being zealous for God, even as you all are today.

The Content of Prayer in the Proclamation

The Scriptures clearly delineate the content of prayer that involves the evangelistic process. First, Christians are to pray for the salvation of particular souls. This concept has been discussed. Second, believers are to pray for an open door to share their testimony. In Colossians 4:2-3, Paul requests the Colossians to ask God for an open door for the good news. As was seen previously, the Father creates opportunities for Christians to witness for Him. That is God's part. The part Christians play is to pray for those very opportunities to be created. Also, these prayers should be made by Christians on behalf of their fellow believers, not just for themselves. Paul was asking for prayer on his own behalf because he wanted many people praying for him.

Colossians 4:2-3
Continue steadfastly in prayer, watching in it with thanksgiving, praying together for us also, that God may open to us a door for the word, to speak the mystery of Christ, for which I am also in bonds.

Third, Christians should pray for God's wisdom in their witnessing. In Colossians 4:4-6, Paul exhorted the church at

Colossae to pray so he would know how he ought to speak. Then he discussed being wise toward outsiders and having speech that is gracious, seasoned with salt. Not only are the saints to pray for opportunities to speak but the wisdom to be gracious and kind. Fourth, Christians are to pray that the gospel will spread rapidly. Paul encourages the church in Thessalonica to pray that God would multiply the fruits of his evangelistic efforts and spread the good news quickly (2 Thessalonians 3:1). Fifth, saints are to be praying for great boldness. Paul entreated the church to request the Lord God to give him courage in sharing the mystery of the gospel of Jesus Christ (Ephesians 6:19).

Colossians 4:4-6
That I may reveal it as I ought to speak. Walk in wisdom toward those who are outside, redeeming the time. Let your speech always be with grace, seasoned with salt, that you may know how you ought to answer each one.

2 Thessalonians 3:1
Finally, brothers, pray for us, that the word of the Lord may spread rapidly and be glorified, even as also with you.

Ephesians 6:19
On my behalf, that utterance may be given to me in opening my mouth, to make known with boldness the mystery of the Good News.

Sixth, believers are to pray for additional workers to share the gospel. In Matthew 9:37-38, Matthew records it this way, "Then he [Jesus] said to his disciples, 'The harvest indeed is plentiful, but the laborers are few. Pray therefore that the Lord of the harvest will send out laborers into his harvest.'" Here the Lord gazed out at all the people and saw crops of souls ripe for harvest. He asked his disciples to pray that the Lord of the harvest would send out workers to share the gospel. Christians need to be praying that the Lord would provoke the hearts of others to share the gospel.

Matthew 9:37-38
Then he said to his disciples, "The harvest indeed is plentiful, but the laborers are few. Pray therefore that the Lord of the harvest will send out laborers into his harvest."

An Ancient Portrait

When Paul, Luke, Timothy, and Silas entered the Roman city of Philippi recorded in Acts 16:1-40, little did they know that the Lord was about to do some strange and wondrous things in this city in response to their prayers. These men were on the move and depended on their prayers to unleash the power of God in their many evangelistic efforts. When Paul arrived in the city, there were no Jewish men to open a synagogue, so they went to the town's riverbank hoping that some women may be there praying. This was the usual Jewish custom. During this encounter, the Lord brought a woman named Lydia to Christ, and she offered her home to begin their church.

While traveling through the city ministering to all, they began to be harassed by a fortune-telling slave girl who was demon-possessed. Every time that the group journeyed to the place of prayer, this woman of divination would follow them. She would be constantly declaring that Paul and his companions were bondservants of the Most High God and were proclaiming the way of salvation. Paul knew that this demon was attempting to associate their holy and righteous efforts with his dark and profiteering work.

Finally, Paul became so annoyed that he cast the demon out of her. Not only did the demon depart but so did her powers and the great profit to her handlers. The merchants became very enraged and seized Paul and Silas. Then, they dragged them before the governing authorities and accused them falsely of throwing the city into chaos. They claimed the two were promoting customs contrary to Roman laws. As the crowds became more and more hostile and upset, the magistrates responded by tearing their robes in a powerful display of disgust and commanded the two to be beaten.

Right there on the street in front of this hostile crowd, they were beaten with an instrument made of wooden rods strapped together. After this they were to be thrown into the innermost dungeon of the prison. With this direction, the jailer in charge had them put both in the stocks to stretch out their legs until they cramp. Then he left them in the darkest, dirtiest, animal infested area of the prison. Then he locked them up as securely as he could. Luke records that about midnight, the two of them were praying and singing hymns of praise to the Lord as the other prisoners were listening. These believers were sharing the good news through their singing and praying for God to work. This must have caught the attention of the other captive prisoners. The jailer was asleep expecting a quiet evening.

As their prayers and praise ascended into the heavens, the Lord God responded with a great Earthquake. The whole foundation of the prison was shaken, the doors opened, their chains were broken, and escape became imminent. The Jailer prepared to commit suicide because death was the penalty for allowing any prisoner to escape. When Paul realized that his prayers had been answered with a chance to share the gospel, he shouted for the jailer to stop. All the prisoners were still there. God had made sure that no one could or would escape.

Paul called for the lights to be turned on and the man in trembling and fear fell before Paul and uttered, "What must I do to be saved?" It was obvious to all that his Lord God was the true and almighty one. In almost unison, Paul and Silas declared that he and his entire household must believe in Jesus. They shared the good news of salvation in Jesus Christ and Him alone.

Then, this jailer took them into his own home, cleaned their wounds, fed them, and asked them to present the good news to his family and servants. Everyone in his household believed and then was baptized. The final puzzle piece was set into place to begin to church at Philippi as God answered the prayers of these men. Evangelism includes in prayer.

A Modern Anecdote

One of the ministries I enjoyed when I was a bit younger was as a camp speaker for junior high and high school at winter and summer Christian camps. I remember these big church buses rolling in on a Saturday afternoon to stay for a whole week of teaching, activities, and relaxation. I would preach Saturday night, Sunday morning, Sunday evening, and then every single morning and evening until they left the following Saturday. It was a very exciting and yet very tense time speaking to about two hundred young people that much. I spent much time praying for boldness, wisdom, and clarity of speech.

I remember as soon as the camp was over that week, I would begin praying every single day for the next year those busses would come rolling in again. So, for one whole year, I would pray every day for the salvation of every young person or for each one's growth in Christ, even though I did not even know their names yet. As a result, I saw God do amazing things at those camps. One time, about mid-week, I had been speaking on the great difference between being a member of a church or attending youth group and being a Christian with a personal relationship to Jesus Christ.

After the talk, as the teens were leaving the amphitheater, two young ladies approached me. One of them, whose name was Kim, said very straightforwardly, "Hi Pastor Don (my title in those days), I am a Catholic, am I saved?" Wow, that was a powerful question. I prayed to the Lord for wisdom. I looked at her and replied, "It doesn't matter whether you are Catholic, Presbyterian, Methodist, Baptist, or a member of any other religious group, you must have a personal, saving relationship with Jesus Christ just as I have been speaking about for the last several days? Do you have this kind of relationship with Him?"

The second girl silently standing next to her friend looked shocked. Kim thought for a moment and said, "No, I don't think so." I looked at the other young lady, whose name was Angie, and asked her, "Do you?" And she replied, "Yes, I really do." Then she smiled. I turned once again to Kim and asked, "Would you like to become a Christian and enter into a personal relationship with Jesus Christ as Savior and Lord right now? The young lady looked at me very solemnly and said, "Yes, I do." Angie's face turned white, like a ghost.

As I led her friend Kim into the kingdom of God, Angie stood there with a stunned look on her face. Then as we prayed the prayer, Angie kept shaking her head in disbelief. Afterward, the two were rejoicing which such joy as they walked away. Then Angie turned back and walked over to me and said, "Pastor Don, I have been praying for my friend Kim to become a Christian, since I was a little girl.

Now I was able to see God answer my prayer right before my eyes. This was awesome!" I replied, "I have been praying for your friend for a year, and I got to watch God answer my prayer right before my eyes also. That is awesome too!" It brought a joy that neither had felt before. What amazement and a powerful sense of blessing we had that day. In a sense, our persistent prayers gave Kim supernatural life. Though Kim was living her life and enjoying her family and friends, many prayers were ascending to heaven in her behalf. Even as she arrived at camp that week, she could have foreseen the power that was about to be unleashed in her behalf. When she sat down that day with no expectation as to what might happen, God was preparing to do a great work in her life. That young Christian and I accomplished something utterly "above and beyond" this life (Ephesians 3:20). We both did it first on our knees before the Almighty. Then as I received the opportunity to present the gospel in boldness and clarity of speech at this camp, God did the rest.

A Personal Response

Dear Heavenly Father,

Please help me to pray consistently for the salvation of (add names) and others I know and meet. I believe all the powerful miracles you did in the Bible in answer to prayer. I ask that you a miracle in each of their lives to bring every one of them to Your beloved Son. Develop a deep burden in me to pray and share the gospel with not only (add names) but my (other) family members and friends as well. I realize that You desire all men to hear the gospel and receive Your Son as Savior and Lord. I acknowledge that my praying for them pleases You. I ask that You provide an open door to present the plan of redemption to them. Give me courage and boldness to share the gospel with them. Then provide me the wisdom of mind and clarity of speech I will need. I request that will provoke other Christians to also share Your mighty Word with others who do not know You. I pray this in the name of Jesus. Amen.

Instructor's Notes

AN INSTRUCTOR'S MANUAL

Chapter 6

Persist in Watchful Prayer

Prayer is one of the most effective and powerful tools for bringing people to Christ. Believers should pray consistently and persistently for the unsaved.

In the section, "A Typical Scenario," the author shows how believers can share their Christian testimonies to the beloved members of their extended family.

What is the scenario about?

A nephew tries to share the gospel with his beloved uncle, but the uncle always brings up evolution and other issues to distract him.

What held the believer back from sharing the gospel?

The nephew did not understand the power of prayer and its work in evangelism.

What finally led the Christian to share the good news and how did it occur?

After much prayer, on a holiday the nephew accompanied the uncle to his car and was asked if he thought the uncle was going to hell.

Have you had a similar experience?

(Various answers should be shared including yours.)

In the section, "A Scriptural Principle" the author presents an important biblical principle in evangelism which concerns the power of prayer as believers share the gospel.

How would you express this principle in your own words?

This sixth principle is "we must persist in watchful prayer."

(Various answers should be shared including yours.)

How would you rewrite this principle to make it even more personal to your life (using your name and situation)?

(Various answers should be shared including yours.)

Why do you think this principle might be important in your life right now as you share the gospel?

(Various answers should be shared including yours.)

How would you rate yourself on the percentage of times you followed this principle in the past as a believer?

(Various answers should be shared including yours.)

Directions: Put a horizontal mark and your name where you see yourself on the percentage line.

| 0% | 25% | 50% | 75% | 100% |

In the section, "A Biblical Explanation," the author explains how to move the hand of God in prayer and its importance in sharing the gospel effectively.

What are two examples in the Bible of the power of prayer?

Prayer unleashes God's power. In Genesis 18:22, when Abraham prayed for Lot, his life was spared from the fire of Sodom and Gomorrah. In Exodus 14:10, when Moses prayed for God's people to be delivered from Egypt, God parted the Red Sea. In Exodus 15:25, when Moses cried out to God for the starving Hebrews, God provided manna from heaven.

In 1 Kings 17:1, When Elijah, the prophet, prayed for the rain to cease in judgment upon God's people, it did not rain for three-and one-half years. In 1 Kings 18:38, When Elijah asked God to consume his water drenched offering before the 850 prophets of Baal and Asherah, fire came from heaven and burned up his offering while leaving theirs untouched. In Daniel 9:3, when Daniel, the prophet, prayed for Israel's release from Babylonian captivity, God delivered His people through King Cyrus (Ezra 1:1-4).

Does God desire us to pray for the unsaved? Why or why not?

Evangelism is an essential part of our prayers. Whenever saints pray, they should include prayer for the salvation of the unsaved and for those who share the gospel. Prayer for all the physical needs of unbelievers is important, but prayer for their eternal destiny should be the priority. In Matt. 6, the Lord's disciples approached Jesus and asked Him how to pray. In verses 8-13, Jesus composed a prayer that included the salvation of the lost. Out of the many subjects for prayer the Lord Jesus could have chosen, He spoke of evangelism.

According to Mark 1:35, what was an essential part of the Lord's gospel ministry?

In Mark 1:35, Jesus left His disciples early in the morning to pray. The gospel writer records, "Early in the morning, while it was still dark, he [Jesus] rose up and went out, and departed into a deserted place, and prayed there." Christ's disciples came and told Him that many were looking for Him, but the Lord desired to preach to the towns nearby.

What are at least three reasons for prayer as Christians share the gospel?

First, saints are encouraged and exhorted to pray for the salvation of souls. Second, when believers pray for the salvation of others, it pleases God. Third, God desires people to be saved. Fourth, prayer for the unsaved is the natural result of a burdened heart. Fifth, prayer is the natural result of a kindred heart.

What are at least three prayer requests as believers present God's plan of redemption?

First, Christians are to pray for the salvation of particular souls. This concept has been discussed. Second, believers are to pray for an open door to share their testimony. Third, Christians should pray for God's wisdom in their witnessing. Fourth, Christians are to pray that the gospel will spread rapidly. Fifth, saints are to be praying for great boldness. Sixth, believers are to pray for additional workers to share the gospel.

In what ways might these truths impact your life?

(Various answers should be shared including yours.)

In the section, "An Ancient Portrait," the author provides a unique portrayal of Paul's imprisonment in Philippi and what God was able to accomplish.

Can you briefly describe the setting of this real-life ancient drama?

The setting is the city of Philippi. Right there on the street in front of this hostile crowd, they were beaten with an instrument made of wooden rods strapped together. After this they were to be thrown into the innermost dungeon of the prison. With this direction, the jailer in charge had them put both in the stocks to stretch out their legs until they cramp. Then he left them in the darkest, dirtiest, animal infested area of the prison.

Can you describe the major characters involved?

The major characters are Paul, Silas, and the Philippian Jailer.

How did the evangelist initiate the gospel presentation?

The Jailer prepared to commit suicide because death was the penalty for allowing any prisoner to escape. When Paul realized that his prayers had been answered with a chance to share the gospel, he shouted for the jailer to stop. All the prisoners were still there. God had made sure that no one could or would escape.

Paul called for the lights to be turned on and the man in trembling and fear fell before Paul and uttered, "What must I do to be saved?" It was obvious to all that his Lord God was the true and almighty one. In almost unison, Paul and Silas declared that he and his entire household must believe in Jesus. They shared the good news of salvation in Jesus Christ and Him alone.

What was result of this evangelistic presentation?

Then, this jailer took them into his own home, cleaned their wounds, fed them, and asked them to present the good news to his family and servants. Everyone in his household believed and then was baptized.

How was the principle explained in this chapter applied to the situation?

The final puzzle piece was set into place to begin to church at Philippi as God answered the prayers of these men. Evangelism includes in prayer.

Based on the truths learned in this chapter, what would you have done differently if you were the evangelist or how would you have responded if you were the recipient?

(Various answers should be shared including yours.)

AN INSTRUCTOR'S MANUAL

In the section, "A Modern Anecdote," the author discusses a situation where he was able to proclaim the kingdom of God at a camp for teens.

Can you briefly describe the setting of this real-life modern drama?

The setting is a teen Christian camp.

Can you describe the major characters involved?

The major characters are the author, Angie, and Kim.

How did the author initiate the gospel presentation?

I remember these big church buses rolling in on a Saturday afternoon to stay for a whole week of teaching, activities, and relaxation. I would preach Saturday night, Sunday morning, Sunday evening, and then every single morning and evening until they left the following Saturday. It was a very exciting and yet very tense time speaking to about two hundred young people that much. I spent much time praying for boldness, wisdom, and clarity of speech.

I remember as soon as the camp was over that week, I would begin praying every single day for the next year those busses would come rolling in again. So, for one whole year, I would pray every day for the salvation of every young person or for each one's growth in Christ, even though I did not even know their names yet. As a result, I saw God do amazing things at those camps. One time, about mid-week, I had been speaking on the great difference between being a member of a church or attending youth group and being a Christian with a personal relationship to Jesus Christ.

After the talk, as the teens were leaving the amphitheater, two young ladies approached me. One of them, whose name was Kim, said very straightforwardly, "Hi Pastor Don (my title in those days), I am a Catholic, am I saved?" Wow, that was a powerful question. I prayed to the Lord for wisdom.

The second girl silently standing next to her friend looked shocked. Kim thought for a moment and said, "No, I don't think so." I looked at the other young lady, whose name was Angie, and asked her, "Do you?" And she replied, "Yes, I really do." Then she smiled. I turned once again to Kim and asked, "Would you like to become a Christian and enter into a personal relationship with Jesus Christ as Savior and Lord right now? The young lady looked at me very solemnly and said, "Yes, I do." Angie's face turned white, like a ghost.

What was result of this evangelistic presentation?

As I led her friend Kim into the kingdom of God, Angie stood there with a stunned look on her face. Then as we prayed the prayer, Angie kept shaking her head in disbelief. Afterward, the two were rejoicing which such joy as they walked away.

How was the principle explained in this chapter applied to the situation?

Then Angie turned back and walked over to me and said, "Pastor Don, I have been praying for my friend Kim to become a Christian, since I was a little girl.

Now I was able to see God answer my prayer right before my eyes. This was awesome!" I replied, *"I have been praying for your friend for a year, and I got to watch God answer my prayer right before my eyes also. That is awesome too!"*

Based on the truths learned in this chapter, what would you have done differently if you were the author or how would you have responded if you were the recipient?

(Various answers should be shared including yours.)

In the section, "A Personal Response," the author provides a model you may use for prayer if you find it necessary after discovering the truths in this chapter.

Are you presently attempting to present the gospel of Jesus to someone? If not, are there some among your co-workers who may not know Jesus Christ and may need prayer for an opportunity for you to share with them and open hearts to receive Him?

(Various answers should be shared including yours.)

Based on the truths you have just learned, what will you continue to do in your current evangelistic efforts and what might you do differently?

(Various answers should be shared including yours.)

What additional thoughts would you like to share with the others?

(Various answers should be shared including yours.)

Chapter 7

Proclaim the Proper Message

One of the greatest joys Christians have the privilege of experiencing is people receiving the Lord as they share the gospel. They will view up front and personal a supernatural work of the Holy Spirit in the hearts of people as He literally opens their blind eyes (2 Corinthians 4:4) and provides the faith they need to respond to Him (Ephesians 2:8). They will have a front row seat to people being transferred from the domain of darkness to the kingdom of light (1 Peter 2:9). For this momentous occasion to occur in one's life, the proper message of salvation must be proclaimed. This involves the presentation of certain key elements of the good news.

2 Corinthians 4:4
In whom the god of this world has blinded the minds of the unbelieving, that the light of the Good News of the glory of Christ, who is the image of God, should not dawn on them.

Ephesians 2:8
For by grace you have been saved through faith, and that not of yourselves; it is the gift of God.

1 Peter 2:9
But you are a chosen race, a royal priesthood, a holy nation, a people for God's own possession, that you may proclaim the excellence of him who called you out of darkness into his marvelous light.

A Typical Scenario

Have you ever been in a situation that was something like the following? You frequently hear sermons about how you need to be sharing the good news but aren't sure how to get started. Every once in a while, you think that there must be something you can do. You see other religions on the street passing out pamphlets and think, "Why am I not doing that for my faith?" This thought keeps coming in and out of your mind, but nothing happens. Year after year goes by and still nothing happens. You think, "Well, maybe someday." Yet, "someday" never actually comes. When you finally sit down and analyze why you aren't witnessing, you must admit to yourself that you don't really know the gospel message in its entirety. You have heard parts of it here and there but do not really understand the full message enough to share it. You become used to the guilt of not witnessing and it fades away.

In this chapter, you will learn the full gospel presentation. It encompasses the proclamation of sin and man's judgment, the declaration of Christ's deity, His saving work on the cross, and the need to receive Him as both Savior and Lord. The good news includes the testimony of His many miracles, fulfilled prophecies, and His resurrection from the dead. It involves a relationship by faith, not feeling and its outward sign is water baptism. After you learn these spiritual truths, perhaps this same situation could look quite different.

Now that you understand the gospel presentation, you become excited about sharing it with everyone. You realize that one of the times unbelievers are often thinking about the Lord at Christmas time. Also, for those who have lost a loved one, are facing the perils of old age or death, or have estranged families, the holidays are especially difficult. So, you gather a group of Christians together from your church, practiced some familiar Christmas carols (specifically about Christ), obtain a portable CD player, purchase some gospel pamphlets, and then start walking around the neighborhood singing carols for Christ the week before Christmas.

You hand out a small bag of candy canes, a church service invite, and the salvation message brochure. After you sing three songs, you or one of the others ask if they would like to know more about the child born that Christmas morn who was now your Savior and Lord. Everybody is kind at first, but no one takes you up on your offer. Finally, a man opens the door with a huge smile on his face. He explains that his wife had just passed away, and he had nowhere to go. He invites the whole group into his home after you sing. Then you say boldly, "Listen sir, I know this must be a difficult time for you and you may feel all alone, but you are not. In Psalm 146:9, it says that God upholds and supports the fatherless and the widow. God will comfort you if you will seek Him out. He can be found only through His Son Jesus Christ. In John 14:6, Jesus Christ said that He was the way, the truth, and the life, and no one comes to the Father except through Him."

Then you present the full gospel message. Everyone sits silent and prays. When you ask the man if he would like to receive Christ right now, he looks at you with tears in his eyes, and replies, "Yes, I have no one else to go to but Him. I am alone." Almost in complete unison, everyone shouted, "Not any longer, you have a new family." From that time on he is baptized and becomes a ministering member of your church. He is now surrounded by many members of his new family of God.

Though this is an imaginary scenario, it is typical of the kinds of opportunities we can create, when we feel confident in our knowledge of the gospel message. We will miss many moments to share the gospel because we simply do not know what to say. Also, when the saints understand and are able to present God's redemptive plan, it might encourage them to become continual witnesses of Him. We now come to the seventh principle involving the elements of the true message of salvation.

A Scriptural Principle

Jesus presents a startling concept when He speaks of the narrow road to life. There will be some who call Him Lord on judgment day and will not enter His kingdom. They may have prophesied in His name, cast out demons in His name, and even done mighty works, but he will tell all of them to depart for He never knew them (Matthew 7:22-23). How is this possible? Can some claim the name of Christ and not be one of His? Yes! It simply is not enough to just name His name or serve Him; one must have a genuine, saving faith. This involves trusting in Him and Him alone for their salvation and living for the Lord. In 1 John 2:19, the apostle describes this phenomenon. Some in the churches claimed to be true Christians and had departed. This exodus prompted similar questions by the believers. John denounced those who had left as never really being a part of the true church. They were not saved at all.

Matthew 7:22-23
Many will tell me in that day, "Lord, Lord, didn't we prophesy in your name, in your name cast out demons, and in your name do many mighty works?" Then I will tell them, "I never knew you. Depart from me, you who work iniquity."

1 John 2:19
They went out from us, but they didn't belong to us; for if they had belonged to us, they would have continued with us. But they left, that they might be revealed that none of them belong to us.

Why does this happen? The key resides in the fact that a saving relationship comes directly from the presentation of a true gospel and a proper response to it. Sometimes, people do not hear the true gospel, so they cannot respond in a true saving way. If the saints proclaim an incomplete, distorted, or different message, it will only result in a "good news" that cannot deliver from eternal judgment. Therefore, the seventh principle is "we must proclaim the proper message." When the clear and exact message is proclaimed with its essential elements explained, a true salvation can occur.

A Biblical Explanation

Why do thousands receive the Lord in a great evangelistic crusade, yet few join or remain in a church for any length of time? Why does the church appear to be growing in size in leaps and bounds, but the saints don't seem to be maturing in Christ? Why do many seem to come to Christ when they are young, fall away in their teens, then later rededicate their lives to Christ? Was this actually their initial salvation? Why do others spend their Christian lives receiving Christ over and over again? Why do many others appear to have very dramatic conversion with weeping and great joy then fall away a short time afterward? Why do others claim to know Christ, yet produce little or no fruit year after year? These questions become all the more relevant in the light of several Bible passages which speak of the change that occurs when someone moves from darkness into light (John 3:20; 11:10; 1 John 2:9-10). Why do some appear as if they are still living in the darkness when they are supposed to be in the light?

John 3:20
For everyone who does evil hates the light, and doesn't come to the light, lest his works would be exposed.

John 11:10
But if a man walks in the night, he stumbles, because the light isn't in him."

LEADING THE WAY

1 John 2:9-10
He who says he is in the light and hates his brother is in the darkness even until now. He who loves his brother remains in the light...stumbling in him.

In Matthew 9:37, Jesus Christ compared the whole world to a field of wheat ready for harvest. Why does much of the wheat harvested seem so weak and brittle? In John 3:3, the Lord compared salvation to being born again. Why do many born again Christians appear stillborn or so immature, frail, and weak in their faith that they appear to have never grown up in Christ? In 2 Corinthians 5:17, Paul declares that those who become Christians are new creations. He says that the old things have passed away and new things have come. Why do many appear to have little "new things" and are still filled with the "old things"? In John 1:12, the people who become Christians are called the children of God. They now belong to the family of God. Why then do many after only a few months forsake their new family and return to the Devil (1 John 3:10)? Were they in God's family or not?

Matthew 9:37
Then he said to his disciples, "The harvest indeed is plentiful, but the laborers are few."

John 3:3
Jesus answered him, "Most certainly, I tell you, unless one is born anew, he can't see God's Kingdom."

2 Corinthians 5:17
Therefore if anyone is in Christ, he is a new creation. The old things have passed away. Behold, all things have become new.

John 1:12
But as many as received him, to them he gave the right to become God's children, to those who believe in his name.

1 John 3:10
In this the children of God are revealed, and the children of the devil. Whoever doesn't do righteousness is not of God, neither is he who doesn't love his brother.

These questions have various answers. Certainly, Satan is prowling about like a roaring, hungry lion seeking as many saints as possible to devour (1 Peter 5:8). Certainly, there is mounting pressure from the world to stay within its realm of influence. In James 4:4, James sternly warned his readers not to be friends with the world system. This would be spiritual adultery and hostility toward God. Also, there is a real battle within Christians against their flesh. In Romans 7:23, Paul recognized this when he described the waging of war within him. His mind was in constant battle with his flesh.

1 Peter 5:8
Be sober...self-controlled. Be watchful. Your adversary, the devil, walks around like a roaring lion, seeking whom he may devour.

James 4:4
You adulterers and adulteresses, don't you know that friendship with the world is hostility toward God? Whoever therefore wants to be a friend of the world makes himself an enemy of God.

Romans 7:23
But I see a different law in my members, warring against the law of my mind, and bringing me into captivity under the law of sin which is in my members.

He desired good, but his flesh desired evil. Though these are acceptable answers, they cannot account for the small amount of "spiritual fruit" or the lack of it altogether. Fruit is always the sign of true faith (these are good works produced from true faith). Consider another reason: they were not at all saved. There was no harvest of wheat in the first place. These unhealthy spiritual births of "newborn babes in Jesus Christ" were not births at all. Those who demonstrate only the deeds of the old creation have never become new. Some will appear to be Christians when they are not. There is no real battle against the Devil, the world, or the flesh because they simply are not saved. Numerous Christians, including some leaders, may not even know the key components that must be in a gospel message to bring an unbeliever to a saving knowledge.

All of these critical elements must come directly from the Scriptures, not emotion or experience. To put "Jesus in one's heart" is not the true gospel message of salvation. To "accept Christ as Savior" is only a part of the good news. To "love Jesus" is important but it will not admit someone into the kingdom of God. Others might be sincere about their faith in Jesus but be "sincerely wrong." They believed in the wrong Jesus, or a false gospel message, or really gave only a partial response. When the members of numerous cults come to the door of Christians today, they claim that they have "accepted Jesus into their hearts." Have they? No, they have not.

When Paul preached in the Berean church in Acts 17:11, they responded to him by searching the Scriptures to see if what he was saying was true. Then, they reacted in saving faith. The proper proclamation of the gospel must come out of Scripture, not Scripture plus other writings. Neither will inspirational stories, emotional appeals, meaningful music, and spectacular events or presentations save, only the true gospel proclaimed through the power of the Spirit saves. This section will elucidate the essential elements of the good news of the proclamation of the plan of redemption. Later, the responses to the gospel that bring eternal salvation will be considered. These should be studied very carefully as one prepares to share one's faith. Corners cannot be cut due to time, fear of a negative response, or a desire to take away the offense of the gospel. The salvation of souls is on the line, and they must hear a clear and complete gospel.

Acts 17:11
Now these were more noble than those in Thessalonica, in that they received the word with all readiness of mind, examining the Scriptures daily to see whether these things were so.

The Declaration of the Kingdom

The message begins with a declaration of the kingdom of God. Christians should begin by identifying themselves as believers and explaining briefly the redemptive plan of God discussed in chapter one. This would include the four parts discussed: the creation of man in order to create a kingdom of priests to God's Son (John 3:35; Colossians 1:16; John 17:2, 6, 7,9,12); the temptation of man and his fall (Genesis 3:4-6; 1 Timothy 2:14), the plan to redeem man through Jesus Christ (Ephesians 1:7, 14; Colossians 1:14), and the eternal life that comes (John 6:40, 47, 68; 1 John 5:11-12).

John 3:35
The Father loves the Son, and has given all things into his hand.

Colossians 1:16
For by him all things were created in the heavens and on the Earth, visible things and invisible things, whether thrones or dominions or principalities or powers. All things have been created through him and for him.

John 17:2
Even as you gave him authority over all flesh, so he will give eternal life to all whom you have given him.

John 17:6
I revealed your name to the people whom you have given me out of the world. They were yours, and you have given them to me. They have kept your word.

John 17:7
Now they have known that all things whatever you have given me are from you.

John 17:9
I pray for them. I don't pray for the world, but for those whom you have given me, for they are yours.

John 17:12
While I was with them in the world, I kept them in your name. I have kept those whom you have given me. None of them is lost except the son of destruction, that the Scripture might be fulfilled.

Genesis 3:4-6
The serpent said to the woman, "You won't really die, 5 for God knows that in the day you eat it, your eyes will be opened, and you will be like God, knowing good and evil." When the woman saw that the tree was good for food, and that it was a delight to the eyes, and that the tree was to be desired to make one wise, she took some of its fruit, and ate. Then she gave some to her husband with her, and he ate it, too.

1 Timothy 2:14
Adam wasn't deceived, but the woman, being deceived, has fallen into disobedience.

Ephesians 1:7
In whom we have our redemption through his blood, the forgiveness of our trespasses, according to the riches of his grace.

Ephesians 1:14
Who is a pledge of our inheritance, to the redemption of God's own possession, to the praise of his glory.

Colossians 1:14
In whom we have our redemption, the forgiveness of our sins.

John 6:40
This is the will of the one who sent me, that everyone who sees the Son, and believes in him, should have eternal life; and I will raise him up at the last day.

John 6:47
Most certainly, I tell you, he who believes in me has eternal life.

John 6:68
Simon Peter answered him, "Lord, to whom would we go? You have the words of eternal life.

1 John 5:11-12
The testimony is this, that God gave to us eternal life, and this life is in his Son. He who has the Son has the life. He who doesn't have God's Son doesn't have the life.

This presentation of the Lord God's redemptive plan is called preaching the kingdom of God by the New Testament writers (Matthew 3:2; 9:35; Luke 4:43). Jesus then passed on this ministry of proclamation to His disciples. In Matthew

10:7, Jesus calls His twelve disciples and gives them the commission to preach the kingdom of heaven just as He was doing. Matthew records His words, "As you go, preach, saying, 'The Kingdom of Heaven is at hand!'

Matthew 3:2
Repent, for the Kingdom of Heaven is at hand!

Matthew 9:35
Jesus went about all the cities and the villages, teaching in their synagogues and preaching the Good News of the Kingdom, and healing every disease and every sickness among the people.

Luke 4:43
But he said to them, "I must preach the good news of God's Kingdom to the other cities also. For this reason I have been sent."

Matthew 10:7
As you go, preach, saying, "The Kingdom of Heaven is at hand!"

This is reiterated and described in numerous places in the New Testament (Luke 9:2; Acts 8:12; 14:22; 19:8; 28:31). Once the gift of the kingdom from God the Father to God the Son is explained then it should be offered to the unbelievers to whom the Christian is speaking. They should be asked if they desire to become a part of God's Kingdom on Earth and then into eternity. Do they want eternal life now? Do they want to live forever with God or without God? Do they want to be a part of this kingdom?

Luke 9:2
He sent them out to preach God's Kingdom and to heal the sick.

Acts 8:12
But when they believed Philip preaching good news concerning God's Kingdom and the name of Jesus Christ, they were baptized, both men and women.

Acts 14:22
Strengthening the souls of the disciples, exhorting them to continue in the faith, and that through many afflictions we must enter into God's Kingdom.

Acts 19:8
He entered into the synagogue and spoke boldly for a period of three months, reasoning...persuading about the things concerning God's Kingdom.

Acts 28:31
Preaching God's Kingdom, and teaching the things concerning the Lord Jesus Christ with all boldness, without hindrance.

The Proclamation of Sin and Judgment

Proclaiming sin and judgment is absolutely critical when the gospel is shared. Today, many people believe they are basically good and will be in a better place when they die. Others believe that they do not have to worry about death because somehow it will all work out to a happy conclusion. Still others simply do not concern themselves about death because they feel nothing can be done to prevent it. Some have decided that they will not worry since no one knows what will happen anyway.

These denials cannot change the reality of their judgment and condemnation for a lifetime of sin. Those who have not received Christ, thus appropriating His death on the cross for their wicked deeds, will not be saved from this judgment. Unfortunately, this life is not a fairy tale with an imaginary, happy ending. This harsh and terrifying reality must be declared to unbelievers. Yes, it is offensive, but much more offensive would be an eternity of hell and punishment.

In Romans 3:10-11, Paul explains that there is no one who is righteous or understands God. In Romans 3:23, he asserts that all have sinned and fall short of God's glory. This sin brought God's condemnation. In Romans 1:18, the apostle Paul describes the wrath of God, which is revealed in heaven against man's sin and unrighteousness. In Hebrews 9:27, the inspired author explains that people will die once and then judgment will come. In 2 Peter 2:9, Peter asserts that there will be judgment and destruction of ungodly people. This condemnation is very real and eternal. People cannot escape its clutches for God is just and righteous.

Romans 3:10-11
As it is written, "There is no one righteous; no, not one.
There is no one who understands. There is no one who seeks after God.

Romans 3:23
For all have sinned, and fall short of the glory of God.

Romans 1:18
For...wrath of God [His anger] is revealed from heaven against all ungodliness and unrighteousness of men who suppress the truth in unrighteousness.

Hebrews 9:27
Inasmuch as it is appointed for men to die once, and after this, judgment.

2 Peter 2:9
The Lord knows how to deliver the godly out of temptation and to keep the unrighteous under punishment for the day of judgment.

The proclamation of sin and judgment began with John the Baptist in the New Testament. In Mark 1:4, the inspired writer explains, "John came baptizing in the wilderness and preaching the baptism of repentance for forgiveness of sins." This prophet came and preached repentance. One cannot share the good news without declaring sin and judgment! In Luke 3:10-14, Luke describes more fully John's message. To answer their many questions of what they must do in their repentance, John the Baptist implied that the multitudes had to stop being selfish and start caring for the numerous needs of others. They had to begin to make sacrifices for others. They had to turn from their evil deeds.

Mark 1:4
John came baptizing in the wilderness and preaching the baptism of repentance for forgiveness of sins.

LEADING THE WAY

Luke 3:9-14
Even now the ax...lies at the root of the trees. Every tree therefore that doesn't produce good fruit is cut down, and thrown into the fire." The multitudes asked him, "What then must we do?" He answered them, "He who has two coats, let him give to him who has none. He who has food, let him do likewise." Tax collectors also came to be baptized, and they said to him, "Teacher, what must we do?" He said to them, "Collect no more than that which is appointed to you." Soldiers also asked him, saying, "What about us? What must we do?" He said to them, "Extort from no one by violence, neither accuse anyone wrongfully. Be content with your wages."

He accused the tax-collectors of gauging the people by overcharging them. He blamed the soldiers for their constant false charges against people, extorting others by threatening them with violence, and not being content with their wages. He even indicted Herod the Tetrarch for having an illicit relationship with his brother's wife who got him thrown in jail and ultimately beheaded. In Matthew 3:7-9, the apostle records that he called the Pharisees and Sadducees offspring of snakes and vipers who depended on being descendants of Abraham to save them from their constant wickedness.

Matthew 3:7-9
But when he saw many of the Pharisees and Sadducees coming for his baptism, he said to them, "You offspring of vipers, who warned you to flee from the wrath to come? Therefore produce fruit worthy of repentance! Don't think to yourselves, 'We have Abraham for our father,' for I tell you that God is able to raise up children to Abraham from these stones."

Jesus, the greatest evangelist of them all, indicted people for their sin. We must remember the Lord's question to the woman at the well when she was asked for living water. In John 4:16-18, Jesus responded with a scathing description of her sin, "Jesus said to her, 'Go, call your husband, and come here.' The woman answered, 'I have no husband.' Jesus said to her, 'You said well, 'I have no husband,' for you have had five husbands; and he whom you now have is not your husband. This you have said truly.'" Here was a crystal-clear indictment for her sin and an opportunity for her to repent.

Often, this is missed in this important story and is a critical truth.

John 4:16-18
Jesus said to her, "Go, call your husband, and come here." The woman answered, "I have no husband." Jesus said to her, "You said well, 'I have no husband,' for you have had five husbands; and he whom you now have is not your husband. This you have said truly."

The Lord Jesus commanded the adulterous woman to "Go your way. From now on, sin no more." (John 8:11). This was His judgment of her sin. They both knew that the men who brought her before Him were correct in their accusations. She had committed adultery, probably often, and Jesus did not attempt to conceal their allegations. The point of Christ commanding the men to cast the first stone, if they had not sinned, was to indict them also. Jesus most certainly wrote on the ground each of their sins one by one. All the men left because the Lord had exposed their sins. This whole scene involved the exposure of sin and the opportunity given to find salvation through the Lord Jesus, not condemnation. Judgment comes when one does not embrace their sin and receive Jesus Christ as Savior and Lord.

John 8:11
She said, "No one, Lord." Jesus said, "Neither do I condemn you. Go your way. From now on, sin no more."

In Matthew 23:13-36, the Lord Jesus called the Pharisees and scribes hypocrites, pretenders, blind fools and guides, cups which are only clean on the outside and dirty on the inside, and white tombs full of dead men's bones. Of course, His harsher language was reserved for the hypocritical false enslaving teachers, but Jesus always indicted people for their sin. The gospel writers mention his constant proclamation for people to repent (Matthew 4:17; 12:41; Luke 5:32; Luke 13:3-5), does this not imply an indictment for sin?

Matthew 4:17
From that time, Jesus began to preach, and to say, "Repent! For the Kingdom of Heaven is at hand."

Matthew 12:41
The men of Nineveh will stand up in the judgment with this generation and will condemn it, for they repented at the preaching of Jonah; and behold, someone greater than Jonah is here.

Luke 5:32
I have not come to call the righteous, but sinners to repentance.

Luke 13:3-5
I tell you, no, but unless you repent, you will all perish in the same way. Or those eighteen, on whom the tower in Siloam fell and killed them; do you think that they were worse offenders than all the men who dwell in Jerusalem? I tell you, no, but, unless you repent, you will all perish in the same way.

Every evangelist who preached in the book of Acts spoke of this condemnation, and it was never left out. In Acts 14:15, the apostle arrives in Lystra, heals a crippled man, and Paul and Barnabas are hailed as gods. Paul was given a chance to speak and entreats them to turn from their useless and vain idol worship. In Acts 26:18, Paul is preaching the gospel to King Agrippa and explains that belief in Christ will bring the forgiveness of sins and an inheritance in heaven. How can Christians speak of forgiveness without first speaking of sin and God's judgment? People are not being forgiven for their unmet needs or brokenness but for their sinful thoughts, unrighteous words, and wicked deeds. This is what must be preached by Christians everywhere.

Acts 14:15
Men, why are you doing these things? We also are men of like passions with you, and bring you good news, that you should turn from these vain things to the living God, who made the sky, the Earth, the sea, and all that is in them.

Acts 26:18
To open their eyes, that they may turn from darkness to light and from the power of Satan to God, that they may receive remission of sins and an inheritance among those who are sanctified by faith in me.

In Acts 17:30-31, Paul travels to Athens and he preaches that they must repent of their sin for judgment is coming. Paul proclaimed the gospel and continually indicted people for their sin and proclaimed a coming judgment. Sin is the major issue that faces man. With it comes condemnation.

Acts 17:30-31
The times of ignorance therefore God overlooked. But now he commands that all people everywhere should repent, because he has appointed a day in which he will judge the world in righteousness by the man whom he has ordained; of which he has given assurance to all men, in that he has raised him from the dead.

This cannot be replaced by the proclamation that the Lord can fulfill the felt needs of people. To ask people to place their faith in Jesus Christ because the Lord will satisfy all their needs is preaching contrary to the message of Jesus and the apostles. God does not always fulfill one's felt needs. Often, Christianity brings persecution and trials from the Devil, the world (society), and the flesh. Often one's life becomes more complicated with more problems because he is now moving against the flow of the whole world. Some might say that Jesus did miracles to fulfill needs to prepare people for the gospel. Jesus performed miracles primarily to substantiate His claims. This is a critical distinction!

Believers must remember that Revelation ends with the judgment of unbelievers. This judgment can only be avoided through a gospel that proclaims it. In Revelation 20:12, the apostle John describes it, "I saw the dead, the great and the small, standing before the throne, and they opened books. Another book was opened, which is the book of life. The dead were judged out of the things which were written in the books, according to their works." In the future, there is coming a punishment for all the sins unbelievers commit.

Revelation 20:12
I saw the dead, the great and the small, standing before the throne, and they opened books. Another book was opened, which is the book of life. The dead were judged out of the things which were written in the books, according to their works.

Christians who share the gospel must address personal sin and its resultant judgment to see their desperate need for salvation. This does not mean an evangelist has to deal with specific sins. This will be done by the conviction of the Spirit. We must ask again what Jesus asked, "What does it really profit a man, if he gains the whole world (has all his needs fulfilled), but loses his soul?"

The Proclamation of Christ as God

There is no true gospel message without the proclamation of Christ as the true God. The essential message of the Lord is that He is the Son of God and equal with God in His deity. In John 8:58, Jesus told the Jews that before Abraham was born, He existed (I Am). This is a direct claim to be the God or Yahweh (I Am) of the Old Testament. The Jews knew this. In verse 59, they took up stones to kill him for blasphemy. In Mark 14:61, Jesus stood before the Sanhedrin. When asked if He was the Christ, the Son of the Blessed One, He replied by saying, "I Am." This was the designation of Yahweh of the Old Testament. The high priest's response was the tearing of his robes to signify blasphemy. Declaring oneself as the Son of God was a pronouncement of deity. In John 10:30, when Jesus declared that He and the Father were one (essence), He was proclaiming His deity.

John 8:58
Jesus said to them, "Most certainly, I tell you, before Abraham came into existence, I AM."
John 8:59

Therefore they took...stones to throw at him, but Jesus was hidden, and went out of the temple, having gone through the middle of them, and so passed by.

Mark 14:61
But he stayed quiet, and answered nothing. Again the high priest asked him, "Are you the Christ, the Son of the Blessed?"

John 10:30
I and the Father are one.

The apostles proclaimed His deity. In Acts 2:36, Peter said, "Let all the house of Israel therefore know certainly that God has made him both Lord and Christ, this Jesus whom you crucified." The apostle Peter, as he was speaking before the multitude at Pentecost, declared that Jesus was both Lord and Christ. In Acts 3:14-15, Peter healed the lame man and proclaimed Jesus as the Holy and Righteous One and the Prince of Life. These were all designations of His deity.

Acts 2:36
Let all the house of Israel therefore know certainly that God has made him both Lord and Christ, this Jesus whom you crucified.

Acts 3:14-15
But you denied the Holy and Righteous One and asked for a murderer to be granted to you, and killed the Prince of life, whom God raised from the dead, to which we are witnesses.

In Acts 4:12, Peter boldly announced to the Sanhedrin that only in the name of Jesus could one be saved! This can only be done by deity. In Acts 8:34-35, the eunuch from Ethiopia was reading a messianic passage from Isaiah. Philip revealed that it referred to Jesus. He showed him how Jesus was the promised Messiah which was a proclamation of His deity. In chapter nine Paul receives Jesus Christ as Savior and Lord. From that point on in Acts, the apostle preaches His deity. Everything hinges on the deity of Jesus Christ as God's Son.

Acts 4:12
There is salvation in no one else, for there is no other name under heaven that is given among men, by which we must be saved!

Acts 8:34-35
The eunuch answered Philip, "Who is the prophet talking about? About himself, or about someone else?" Philip opened his mouth, and beginning from this Scripture, preached to him about Jesus.

Now, Christ's humanity is assumed but critical. Though Christians must proclaim the Lord's deity, they may have to declare that He was also fully human, if it becomes an issue. Most have no problem with Jesus being a man of history. Jesus Christ was fully God and fully man. Belief in His full humanity as an essential was declared when aberrations of this truth arose (1 John 4:2; 2 John 1:7; Hebrews. 5:7).

1 John 4:2
By this you know the Spirit of God: every spirit who confesses that Jesus Christ has come in the flesh is of God.

2 John 1:7
For many deceivers have gone out into the world, those who don't confess that Jesus Christ came in the flesh. This is the deceiver and the Antichrist.

Hebrews 5:7
He, in the days of his flesh, having offered up prayers and petitions with strong crying and tears to him who was able to save him from death, and having been heard for his godly fear.

The Proclamation of Christ as Savior

Jesus must be proclaimed as the Savior of the world. In Luke 19:10, Jesus Himself said that He had come to save all those who were lost. In Matthew 1:21, an angel of the Lord told Joseph to name the baby in Mary's womb Jesus because He will save His people from their sins. In Romans 5:8-11, the apostle wrote that Christians were saved by His death on the cross, justified by His blood, reconciled to God, and also delivered from the wrath to come.

Luke 19:10
For the Son of Man came to seek and to save that which was lost.

Matthew 1:21
She shall give birth to a son. You shall name him Jesus, for it is he who shall save his people from their sins.

Romans 5:8-11
But God commends his own love toward us, in that while we were yet sinners, Christ died for us. Much more then, being now justified by his blood, we will be saved from God's wrath through him. For if while we were enemies, we were reconciled to God through the death of his Son, much more, being reconciled, we will be saved by his life. Not only so, but we also rejoice in God through our Lord Jesus Christ, through whom we have now received the reconciliation.

Paul told the Corinthians he desired only to preach Jesus Christ and Him crucified (1 Corinthians 2:2). Jesus was His humanity and Christ was His deity. The cross spoke of Jesus being the Savior. In Colossians 2:13-15, Paul declared that though believers were dead in their sins, Christ made them alive. Jesus forgave all their trespasses and took all of the ordinances of God which was against them and nailed them to the cross. All of their sins, whether they are in the past, in the present, or in the future, are forgiven.

1 Corinthians 2:2
For I determined not to know anything among you except Jesus Christ and him crucified.

Colossians 2:13-15
You were dead through your trespasses and the uncircumcision of your flesh. He made you alive together with him, having forgiven us all our trespasses, wiping out the handwriting in ordinances which was against us. He has taken it out of the way, nailing it to the cross. Having stripped the principalities and the powers, he made a show of them openly, triumphing over them in it.

Yet, this is not enough. Jesus must be proclaimed as the only Savior and the only way to heaven. In John 14:6, John writes, "Jesus said to him, 'I am the way, the truth, and the life. No one comes to the Father, except through me." The Lord explained to his disciples that He was about to go into heaven to prepare a place for them all. When Thomas asked what the way was to get there, Jesus testified that He was the way, truth, and life. Then Jesus pronounced that no one came to the Father, except through Him.

John 14:6
Jesus said to him, "I am the way, the truth, and the life. No one comes to the Father, except through me."

In Acts 4:12, Peter preached to the Sanhedrin that Christ had the full authority to save. He asserted that there was no other name that men could call upon to be saved. In John 5:23, Jesus explicitly stated that unless He was honored as the Son, no one could honor the Father who sent Him. Jesus Christ is to be proclaimed the only Savior of the world. As Christians share the gospel, they must let the unsaved know that Christ died for all their sins on the cross and is the only way to heaven. Often, believers are accused of being narrow in the faith, when it was actually Jesus Himself who claimed to be the narrow way. So, they simply declare what He said!

Acts 4:12
There is salvation in no one else, for there is no other name under heaven that is given among men, by which we must be saved!

John 5:23
That all may honor the Son, even as they honor the Father. He who doesn't honor the Son doesn't honor the Father who sent him.

The Proclamation of Christ as Lord

Jesus must be proclaimed as Lord. This speaks of Christ's authority in relationship to His people. It speaks of entering into a relationship of obedience with Jesus Christ. He is not only the Savior but also the Lord. The key word referring to Jesus in the New Testament is "Lord." This literally means "master." The proclamation of the gospel involves declaring Jesus as Lord as well as Savior. In Matthew 3:3, the author describes John the Baptist as preparing the way for the Lord. In Matthew 7:20, Jesus refers to Himself as Lord. In Matthew 28:18, Jesus asserted that all authority had been given to Him on Earth and in heaven. This refers to His Lordship overall.

Matthew 3:3
For this is he who was spoken of by Isaiah the prophet, saying, "The voice of one crying in the wilderness, make the way of the Lord ready! Make his paths straight!"

Matthew 7:20
Therefore by their fruits you will know them.

Matthew 28:18
Jesus came to them and spoke to them, saying, "All authority has been given to me in heaven and on Earth."

There are numerous passages where Jesus declared and demonstrated His full authority over nature (John 6:16-21; Mark 11:14, 20), disease (Matthew 4:23-24; Luke 6:17-19), sin (Mark 2:5; Luke 7:49), evil angels (Matthew 8:16), and death (John 11:43-44; Luke 7:14). His Lordship is a critical part of the message of the good news and cannot be left out. In Acts 2:36, Peter declared that all of Israel needed to know that God had made Jesus both Christ and Lord. Both terms are used. In Acts 4:33, Luke describes the apostles' proclamation of the good news. He says that they testified of the "Lord's" resurrection. They referred to Him as "Lord."

LEADING THE WAY

John 6:16-21
When evening came, his disciples went down to the sea. They entered into the boat, and were going over the sea to Capernaum. It was now dark, and Jesus had not come to them. The sea was tossed by a great wind blowing. When therefore they had rowed about twenty-five or thirty stadia, they saw Jesus walking on the sea, and drawing near to the boat; and they were afraid. But he said to them, "It is I. Don't be afraid." They were willing therefore to receive him into the boat. Immediately the boat was at the land where they were going.

Mark 11:14
Jesus told it, "May no one ever eat fruit from you again!" and his disciples heard it.

Mark 11:20
As they passed by in the morning, they saw the fig tree withered away from the roots.

Matthew 4:23-24
Jesus went about in all Galilee, teaching in their synagogues, preaching the Good News of the Kingdom, and healing every disease and every sickness among the people. The report about him went out into all Syria. They brought to him all who were sick, afflicted with various diseases and torments, possessed with demons, epileptics, and paralytics; and he healed them.

Luke 6:17-19
He came down with them, and stood on a level place, with a crowd of his disciples, and a great number of the people from all Judea and Jerusalem, and the seacoast of Tyre and Sidon, who came to hear him and to be healed of their diseases; as well as those who were troubled by unclean spirits, and they were being healed. All the multitude sought to touch him, for power came out of him and healed them all.

Mark 2:5
Jesus, seeing their faith, said to the paralytic, "Son, your sins are forgiven you."

Luke 7:49
Those who sat at the table with him began to say to themselves, "Who is this who even forgives sins?"

Matthew 8:16
When evening came, they brought to him many possessed with demons. He cast out the spirits with a word, and healed all who were sick.

John 11:43-44
When he had said this, he cried with a loud voice, "Lazarus, come out!" He who was dead came out, bound hand and foot with wrappings, and his face was wrapped around with a cloth. Jesus said to them, "Free him, and let him go."

Luke 7:14
He came near and touched the coffin, and the bearers stood still. He said, "Young man, I tell you, arise!"

Acts 2:36
Let all the house of Israel therefore know certainly that God has made him both Lord and Christ, this Jesus whom you crucified.

Acts 4:33
With great power, the apostles gave their testimony of the resurrection of the Lord Jesus. Great grace was on them all.

In Acts 11:20, witnessing is termed preaching the Lord Jesus. Luke writes, "But there were some of them, men of Cyprus and Cyrene, who, when they had come to Antioch, spoke to the Hellenists, preaching the Lord Jesus." In Acts 13:12, the gospel is also called the preaching of the Lord. In Ephesians 1:20-23, Paul asserts that Christ is the Lord of all. He is the only one with the authority to save, judge, and rule forever. Jesus Christ is the only one with the right to demand allegiance and obedience. This critical element produces the obedience that is the foundation of Christian life.

Acts 11:20
But there were some of them, men of Cyprus and Cyrene, who, when they had come to Antioch, spoke to the Hellenists, preaching the Lord Jesus.

Acts 13:12
Then the proconsul, when he saw what was done, believed, being astonished at the teaching of the Lord.

Ephesians 1:20-23
Which he worked in Christ, when he raised him from the dead and made him to sit at his right hand in the heavenly places, far above all rule, authority, power, dominion, and every name that is named, not only in this age, but also in that which is to come. He put all things in subjection under his feet, and gave him to

be head over all things for the assembly, which is his body, the fullness of him who fills all in all.

In James 2:17, the brother of Jesus declared that true faith without works is dead, being by itself. Faith always brings forth obedience. Jesus told his followers that the proof of a saint's true discipleship would be the bearing of much fruit (John 15:8) and would be the natural result of their love for Him (John 14:23). John the Baptist told his audience to bring forth fruit in keeping with their true repentance (Matthew 3:8). The Lordship of Jesus must be declared to bring forth not only true repentance but also obedience. Acknowledging that "Jesus is Lord" will produce the fruit of obedience as the saints put themselves in submission to Him. That obedience will become the sign of their salvation.

James 2:17
Even so faith, if it has no works, is dead in itself.

John 15:8
In this my Father is glorified, that you bear much fruit; and so you will be my disciples.

John 14:23
Jesus answered him, "If a man loves me, he will keep my word. My Father will love him, and we will come to him, and make our home with him."

Matthew 3:8
Therefore produce fruit worthy of repentance!

The Defense of Christ as God

In the gospel message, the presentation of evidence for the deity of Christ is a given. Jesus proved His deity through the performance of miracles, the fulfillment of prophecies (both Old Testament and His own), and His resurrection from the dead. Of course, His resurrection was his greatest miracle and fulfillment of prophecy. It is the demonstration of His power....

First, Jesus performed numerous miracles to confirm His deity. In Matthew 4:23, the apostle records that the Lord preached the gospel and healed the sick. This was His usual method of evangelism. The Lord would proclaim His deity and prove it through miracles. In Matthew 11:4-6, when John the Baptist sent his followers to inquire as to Christ's deity, Jesus spoke of the miracles that He performed: He healed the sick, made the lame walk, the blind to see, the deaf to hear, and the mute to speak. In John 5:36, the Lord challenged the Jewish people to consider the works (miracles) He had done as a testimony to His deity.

Matthew 4:23
Jesus went about in all Galilee, teaching in their synagogues, preaching the Good News of the Kingdom...healing every disease and every sickness among the people.

Matthew 11:4-6
Jesus answered them, "Go and tell John the things which you hear and see: the blind receive their sight, the lame walk, the lepers are cleansed, the deaf hear, the dead are raised up, and the poor have good news preached to them. Blessed is he who finds no occasion for stumbling in me."

John 5:36
But the testimony which I have is greater than that of John, for the works which the Father gave me to accomplish, the very works that I do, testify about me, that the Father has sent me.

Second, Jesus fulfilled numerous prophecies in order to demonstrate that He was the Son of God. The Lord fulfilled most Old Testament prophecies through God's providence (Micah 5:2; Psalm 72:10; Jeremiah 31:15; Hosea 11:1; Isaiah 9:1-2). Others, Christ fulfilled intentionally and deliberately (Luke 4:21; John 2:22; 13:18; 17:12; 19:28). He also predicted events that would occur that were fulfilled in His final week (Matthew 26:1-2, 6-12; John 3:14-15; 8:28-29; 12:23-24).

LEADING THE WAY

Micah 5:2
But you, Bethlehem Ephrathah, being small among the clans of Judah, out of you one will come out to me that is to be ruler in Israel; whose goings out are from of old, from ancient times.

Psalm 72:10
The kings of Tarshish and of the islands will bring tribute. The kings of Sheba and Seba shall offer gifts.

Jeremiah 31:15
Yahweh says: "A voice is heard in Ramah, lamentation and bitter weeping, Rachel weeping for...children. She refuses to be comforted for her children, because they are no more."

Hosea 11:1
When Israel was a child, then I loved him, and called my son out of Egypt.

Isaiah 9:1-2
But there shall be no more gloom for her who was in anguish. In the former time, he brought into contempt the land of Zebulun and the land of Naphtali; but in the latter time he has made it glorious, by the way of the sea, beyond the Jordan, Galilee of the nations. The people who walked in darkness have seen a great light. The light has shined on those who lived in the land of the shadow of death.

Luke 4:21
He began to tell them, "Today, this Scripture has been fulfilled in your hearing."

John 2:22
When therefore he was raised from the dead, his disciples remembered that he said this, and they believed the Scripture, and the word which Jesus had said.

John 13:18
I don't speak concerning all of you. I know whom I have chosen. But that the Scripture may be fulfilled, "He who eats bread with me has lifted up his heel against me."

John 17:12
While I was with them in the world, I kept them in your name. I have kept those whom you have given me. None of them is lost except the son of destruction, that the Scripture might be fulfilled.

John 19:28
After this, Jesus, seeing that all things were now finished, that the Scripture might be fulfilled, said, "I am thirsty."

Matthew 26:1-2
When Jesus had finished all these words, he said to his disciples, "You know that after two days the Passover is coming, and the Son of Man will be delivered up to be crucified."

Matthew 26:6-12
Now when Jesus was in Bethany, in the house of Simon the leper, a woman came to him having an alabaster jar of very expensive ointment, and she poured it on his head as he sat at the table. But when his disciples saw this, they were indignant, saying, "Why this waste? For this ointment might have been sold for much and given to the poor." However, knowing this, Jesus said to them, "Why do you trouble the woman? She has done a good work for me. For you always have the poor with you, but you don't always have me. For in pouring this ointment on my body, she did it to prepare me for burial.

John 3:14-15
As Moses lifted up the serpent in the wilderness, even so must the Son of Man be lifted up, that whoever believes in him should not perish, but have eternal life.

John 8:28-29
Jesus therefore said to them, "When you have lifted up the Son of Man, then you will know that I am he, and I do nothing of myself, but as my Father taught me, I say these things. He who sent me is with me. The Father hasn't left me alone, for I always do the things that are pleasing to him."

John 12:23-24
Jesus answered them, "The time has come for the Son of Man to be glorified. Most certainly I tell you, unless a grain of wheat falls into the Earth and dies, it remains by itself alone. But if it dies, it bears much fruit."

Third, Jesus resurrected from the dead to demonstrate His deity. This fulfilled many prophecies and proved His deity. His resurrection was predicted in the Old Testament (Job 19:25-26; Psalm 16:8-11; 22:19-24; Isaiah 53:10-11) and it was fulfilled with evidence in the New Testament (1 Corinthians 15:5-11; Matthew 28:9-10). Luke begins Acts by stating that the Lord appeared to His disciples after His resurrection for a period of forty days and provided many proofs that He was truly alive from the dead (Acts 1:3).

Job 19:25-26
But as for me, I know that my Redeemer lives. In the end, he will stand upon the Earth. After my skin is destroyed, then I will see God in my flesh,

Psalm 16:8-11
I have set Yahweh always before me. Because he [God] is at my right hand, I shall not be moved. Therefore my heart is glad, and my tongue rejoices. My body shall also dwell in safety. For you will not leave my soul in Sheol neither will you allow your holy one to see corruption. You will show me the path of life. In your presence is fullness of joy. In your right hand there are pleasures forever more.

Psalm 22:19-24
But don't be far off, Yahweh. You are my help. Hurry to help me! Deliver my soul from the sword, my precious life from the power of the dog. Save me from the lion's mouth! Yes, you have rescued me from the horns of the wild oxen. I will declare your name to my brothers. Among the assembly, I will praise you. You who fear Yahweh, praise him! All you descendants of Jacob, glorify him! Stand in awe of him, all you descendants of Israel! For he has not despised nor abhorred the affliction of the afflicted, Neither has he hidden his face from him; but when he cried to him, he heard.

Isaiah 53:10-11
Yet it pleased Yahweh to bruise him. He has caused him to suffer. When you make his soul an offering for sin, he will see his offspring. He will prolong his days and Yahweh's pleasure will prosper in his hand. After the suffering of his soul, he will see the light and be satisfied. My righteous servant will justify many by the knowledge of himself; and he will bear their iniquities.

1 Corinthians 15:5-11
And that he [Jesus] appeared to Cephas [Peter], then to the twelve. Then he appeared to over five hundred brothers at once, most of whom remain until now, but some have also fallen asleep. Then he appeared to James, then to all the apostles, and last of all, as to the child born at the wrong time, he appeared to me also. For I am the least of the apostles, who is not worthy to be called an apostle, because I persecuted the assembly of God. But by the grace of God I am what I am. His grace which was given to me was not futile, but I worked more than all of them; yet not I, but the grace of God which was with me. Whether then it is I or they, so we preach, and so you believed.

Matthew 28:9-10
As they went to tell his disciples, behold, Jesus met them, saying, "Rejoice!" They came and took hold of his feet, and worshiped him. Then Jesus said to them, "Don't be afraid. Go tell my brothers that they should go into Galilee, and there they will see me."

Acts 1:3
To these he also showed himself alive after he suffered, by many proofs, appearing to them over a period of forty days, and speaking about God's Kingdom.

Before His resurrection, Christ proclaimed to the Jewish people that He would fulfill a critical prophecy from their Scriptures which would be a sign for them identifying Him as the true Messiah. The prophecy was the sign of Jonah. As Jonah was in the sea creature three days and three nights, so would He be in the Earth three days and three nights. The implication was that as Jonah was spewed forth onto the sand, so would Christ be spewed forth from the Earth and rise from the dead (Matthew 12:39-40; 16:4; Luke 11:29). This was an important element in His gospel message.

Matthew 12:39-40
But he answered them, "An evil and adulterous generation seeks after a sign, but no sign will be given to it but the sign of Jonah the prophet. For as Jonah was three days and three nights in the belly of the huge fish, so will the Son of Man be three days and three nights in the heart of the Earth."

Matthew 16:4
"An evil and adulterous generation seeks after a sign, and there will be no sign given to it, except the sign of the prophet Jonah." He left them and departed.

Luke 11:29
When the multitudes were gathering together to him, he began to say, "This is an evil generation. It seeks after a sign. No sign will be given to it but the sign of Jonah, the prophet.

On other occasions, He predicted His own resurrection. Jesus declared that if they destroyed the temple, He would rebuild it in three days. Jesus was referring to His death and resurrection. This simple but important analogy confounded the Jewish people because they thought the Lord meant their physical temple. Yet, this prediction was often mentioned in His preaching. This is obvious because the prophecy was so well known among the people.

The knowledge of this prediction about the temple was so widespread that it was used by the false witnesses against the Lord Jesus at His trial as words of sedition against the Jews (Matthew 26:61; Mark 14:58). These words were a part of the insults by the people walking by Jesus while He was hanging on the cross. The two gospel writers mentioned this prediction of people passing by and demanding He prove He was the Son of God by coming down from the cross (Matthew 27:39-40; Mark 15:29).

Matthew 26:61
And said, "This man said, 'I am able to destroy the temple of God, and to build it in three days.'"

Mark 14:58
We heard him say, "I will destroy this temple that is made with hands, and in three days I will build another made without hands."

Matthew 27:39-40
Those who passed by blasphemed him, wagging their heads and saying, "You who destroy the temple and build it in three days, save yourself! If you are the Son of God, come down from the cross!"

Mark 15:29
Those who passed by blasphemed him, wagging their heads, and saying, "Ha! You who destroy the temple, and build it in three days."

In John 2:22, John acknowledges that when Christ had risen from the dead, the disciples remembered this prophecy and believed in Him. He wrote, "When therefore he was raised from the dead, his disciples remembered that he had said this, and they believed the Scripture, and the word which Jesus had said." The resurrection brought belief.

John 2:22
When therefore he was raised from...dead, his disciples remembered that he said this, and they believed the Scripture, and the word which Jesus had said.

In Luke 24:25-27, there were two on the road to Emmaus who encountered the risen Christ, but they did not know it. These two men were confused as to who Christ was and the events that had just unfolded in Israel. Jesus rebuked them because they did not believe the prophets and what had just been fulfilled concerning His suffering and resurrection. The chastisement did not happen because they did not know; it occurred because they did not believe.

Luke 24:25-27
He said to them, "Foolish men, and slow of heart to believe...! Didn't the Christ have to suffer these things and to enter into his glory?" Beginning from Moses...he explained...the Scriptures the things concerning himself.

These prophecies were well known in Israel. Then, He explained how Jesus had fulfilled many of the prophecies in the Old Testament. Later, He revealed Himself to them, and they went immediately to His disciples. The two described what happened and declared that Jesus was indeed alive. This proclamation of fulfilled prophecy and physical proof that He had risen from the dead was important to the Lord.

Not only did Jesus proclaim His deity and demonstrate it through His miracles, His fulfillment of prophecy, and His resurrection, but His disciples were told to proclaim what they had seen in Him. They were commanded to share His message and the proofs of His deity to those in Jerusalem, Judea, Samaria, and all the Earth (Acts 1:8). This is exactly what they did. He told them they would be His "witnesses." They were simply to share what they had seen and heard.

Acts 1:8
But you will receive power when the Holy Spirit has come upon you. You will be witnesses to me in Jerusalem, in all Judea and Samaria, and to the uttermost parts of the Earth.

John, the apostle explains this commission by Christ to his readers in 1 John 1:1-2 when he comments, "That which was from the beginning, that which we have heard, that which we have seen with our eyes, that which we saw, and our hands touched, concerning the Word of life (and the life was revealed, and we have seen, and testify, and declare to you the life, the eternal life, which was with the Father, and was revealed to us)." The disciples heard Christ's message and saw His plentiful miracles and His fulfillment of numerous prophecies. He gave them many convincing proofs.

1 John 1:1-2
That which was from the beginning, that which we have heard, that which we have seen with our eyes, that which we saw, and our hands touched, concerning the Word of life (and the life was revealed, and we have seen, and testify, and declare to you the life, the eternal life, which was with the Father, and was revealed to us).

All of this was experienced by all their senses. They saw Him with their own eyes, heard Him with their own ears, and touched Him with their own hands. Then they merely declared Christ, His message, and these proofs to everyone they encountered. The four gospel writers appealed to the miracles, fulfilled prophecies, and the resurrection of Jesus that confirmed His deity in their evangelistic messages. The gospels are filled with numerous examples.

Since Christians today are not eyewitnesses, what should they do about confirming and defending the faith? Consider Luke, who also was not an eyewitness. Yet, in Luke 1:1-4, the author explains that he investigated carefully all that had happened from actual eyewitness accounts. This way his readers would know with certainty that Christ was the Son of God. Christians should present these proofs as Luke did. These proofs are the substance which the Spirit uses to bring someone to belief in Christ. God chose this method, not man.

Luke 1:1-4
Since many have undertaken to set in order a narrative concerning those matters which have been fulfilled among us, even as those who from the beginning were eyewitnesses and servants of the word delivered them to us, it seemed good to me also, having traced the course of all things accurately from the first, to write to you in order...Theophilus; that you might know the certainty concerning the things in which you were instructed.

The Proclamation of a Relationship with Christ

Christ isn't simply an historical man of the past, nor is He a distant God of the present but the God-Man, risen, alive, and desirous of a real relationship with people. The essence of Christianity is not just obeying a list of precepts but, more importantly, following a person in a relationship with Him. Though the Scriptures do not utilize the word relationship, they assume it. John distinctly said in 1 John 5:11-13 that if one has (possesses) the Son, one has (possesses) eternal life.

1 John 5:11-13
The testimony is this, that God gave to us eternal life, and this life is in his Son. He who has the Son has the life. He who doesn't have God's Son doesn't have the life. These things I have written to you who believe in the name of the Son of God, that you may know that you have eternal life, and that you may continue to believe in the name of the Son of God.

In Matthew 7:23, Jesus speaks of the end, when some will come to Him and call for Him as Lord. He will say that they are to go away because He never "knew" them. The word "know" in that passage means an experiential knowledge which is more than intellectual. The Septuagint uses this key Greek term to characterize the intimacy between a man and woman. It is a relational knowing. Christians know of many historical figures, but they do not have a have a relationship of love, faith, and obedience with them. Some grow up with some knowledge of Jesus but do not trust Him as Savior or obey Him as Lord. They know only "of Him."

Matthew 7:23
Then I will tell them, "I never knew you. Depart from me, you who work iniquity"'

In Revelation, Jesus discusses His relationship with two churches. In Revelation 2:4, the Lord accuses the church at Ephesus of departing from their first love. Their motivation in their persistence and endurance was no longer love for Him. True Christians are in love with Jesus Christ. This is an authentic relationship. In Revelation 3:16, Jesus charges the church in Laodicea with being lukewarm. They were neither hot nor cold toward Him. In verse 20, He offers those in the church a relationship with Him when he proclaims that He is standing at the door and knocking. If people in the church "hear" His voice and "open" the door, Christ will "dine" with them. These are powerful relationship words. They signify the invitation to a relationship.

Revelation 2:4
But I have this against you, that you left your first love.

Revelation 3:16
So, because you are lukewarm, and neither hot nor cold, I will vomit you out of my mouth.

Revelation 3:20
Behold, I stand at the door and knock. If anyone hears my voice and opens the door, then I will come into him, and will dine with him, and he with me.

In 1 John 1:3, John indicates that he proclaimed the gospel to them so they could fellowship with the Lord Jesus Christ. He describes it this way, "That which we have seen and heard we declare to you, that you also may have fellowship with us. Yes, and our fellowship is with the Father, and with his Son, Jesus Christ." Fellowship speaks of a relationship.

1 John 1:3
That which we have seen and heard we declare to you, that you also may have fellowship with us. Yes, and our fellowship is with the Father, and with his Son, Jesus Christ.

In Matthew 22:37, when He was asked about the greatest commandment, the Lord declared that it was to love God with all of one's heart, soul, and mind. This is a beautiful and meaningful description of a relationship. When Christians share the gospel, they are offering a personal relationship with Jesus Christ and with His Father. No one can bypass Jesus Christ and go directly to the Father. In John 5:23, the Lord said that honoring Him honors the Father.

Matthew 22:37
Jesus said to him, "You shall love the Lord your God with all your heart, with all your soul, and with all your mind."

John 5:23
That all may honor the Son, even as they honor the Father. He who doesn't honor the Son doesn't honor the Father who sent him.

The Proclamation of Faith Alone

Another element in the proclamation of the gospel is the declaration that only faith in Jesus Christ alone saves. This is apart from works. People cannot work their way into God's heaven. Good works are always a result of salvation. Over and over, Jesus declared that one must believe in Him to be saved. In John 3:16, Jesus told Nicodemus, "For God so loved the world, that he gave his one and only Son, that whoever believes in him should not perish, but have eternal life." He claims that whoever believes in Him will have eternal life. In John 4:39, John describes the saving of the Samaritan people, who had been brought to the well by the Samaritan woman, as believing in Him. In John 6:29, Jesus told His listeners that they must believe in Him who God sent. In John 6:35, Jesus declared that He was the bread of life, and they must believe in Him for eternal life. Research in a concordance of the biblical word "believe" in the Gospel of John by itself will yield passage after passage which emphasizes belief alone.

John 3:16
For God so loved the world, that he gave his one and only Son, that whoever believes in him should not perish, but have eternal life.

John 4:39
From that city many of the Samaritans believed in him because of the word of the woman, who testified, "He told me everything that I did."

John 6:29
Jesus answered them, "This is the work of God, that you believe in him whom he has sent."

John 6:35
Jesus said to them, "I am the bread of life. Whoever comes to me will not be hungry, and whoever believes in me will never be thirsty.

The apostles claimed that belief was the essential element, not works. In Acts 4:4, Luke describes those who were saved as those who had believed. In Acts 5:14, Luke declares that multitudes had believed. In Acts 8:37, when the eunuch from Ethiopia heard the gospel, he confessed that he believed that Jesus Christ was the Son of God. Peter preached to Cornelius that anyone who believes in Christ receives forgiveness of sins. In Acts 16:36, Paul told the Philippian jailer and all in his household that they must believe in the Lord Jesus Christ to be saved. Belief in Jesus alone was constantly proclaimed.

Acts 4:4
But many of those who heard the word believed, and the number of the men came to be about five thousand.

Acts 5:14
More believers were added to the Lord, multitudes of both men and women.

Acts 16:36
The jailer reported these words to Paul, saying, "The magistrates have sent to let you go; now therefore come out and go in peace."

Yet, at the same time, the Lord spoke often concerning the producing of fruit in keeping with true faith. In Matthew 13:23, the Lord compared believers to good seeds that always produce the fruit of righteous deeds by their faith. In John 15:2, the Lord Jesus compares Himself to a vine and His true followers as those branches which produce fruit. If His branches abide in Him, they will bear fruit. Why? Apart from Him they can do nothing (John 15:5). This is different than submission to Christ as Lord.

Matthew 13:23
What was sown on the good ground, this is he who hears the word and understands it, who most certainly bears fruit and produces, some one hundred times as much, some sixty, and some thirty.

John 15:2
Every branch in me that doesn't bear fruit, he takes away. Every branch that bears fruit, he prunes, that it may bear more fruit.

John 15:5
I am the vine. You are the branches. He who remains in me and I in him bears much fruit, for apart from me you can do nothing.

The submission to Jesus as Lord is a true saving response and obedience is the result. Even though there has been controversy concerning whether one is saved if one believes but does not submit, the Bible is clear. Some desire to make distinctions in their minds to allow some they love into the kingdom who appear to profess Christ, but spiritual fruit from their words of declaration is completely lacking. The Scripture makes no such distinction. The distinction may lie in the amount of fruit, but there is always faith-based works.

If one falls away, then a Christian should expect the Lord to discipline his child back into obedience (Hebrews 12:4-7).

Hebrews 12:4-7
You have not yet resisted to blood, striving against sin. You have forgotten the exhortation which reasons with you as with children, "My son, don't take lightly the chastening of the Lord, nor faint when you are reproved...for whom the Lord loves, he disciplines, and chastises every son whom he receives." It is for discipline that you endure. God deals with you as with children, for what son is there whom his father doesn't discipline?

The Proclamation of Water Baptism

An additional element that is often left out in discussions of salvation messages is the teaching that Christians must immediately respond to their salvation by being baptized. Baptism in water does not save. God desires new believers to proclaim their new faith in Christ to the world through water baptism. It must become the initial response a believer makes in His obedience to Christ as Lord of his life.

Water baptism was continually declared and practiced as the initial response after someone became a Christian. One believes, and then one is baptized. When John the Baptist prepared the people for the coming Messiah, he proclaimed that all should repent and be baptized (Matthew 3:6, 11; Mark 1:5; Luke 3:2-3; John 1:26). In fact, John preached at the river Jordan, so he could baptize all those who responded immediately after their repentance. This was John's pattern.

Matthew 3:6
They were baptized by him in the Jordan, confessing their sins.

Matthew 3:11
I indeed baptize you in water for repentance, but he [Jesus] who comes after me is mightier than I, whose sandals I am not worthy to carry. He will baptize you in the Holy Spirit.

Mark 1:5
All the country of Judea and all those of Jerusalem went out to him. They were baptized by him in the Jordan river, confessing their sins.

Luke 3:2-3
In the high priesthood of Annas and Caiaphas, the word of God came to John, the son of Zacharias, in the wilderness. He came into all the region around the Jordan [river], preaching the baptism of repentance for remission of sins.

John 1:26
John answered them, "I baptize in water, but among you stands one whom you don't know."

There are many examples where water baptism is claimed as the initial response to salvation. In Acts 10:47, once the Holy Spirit had entered into Cornelius and his household, indicating belief in Christ, Peter ordered them to be baptized and they were. In Acts 8:35-36, Philip is sent to the Ethiopian eunuch and shares the good news with him. As soon as the eunuch believes, he asks Philip to be baptized. Luke records it this way, "Philip opened his mouth, and beginning from this Scripture, preached to him Jesus. As they went on the way, they came to some water, and the eunuch said, 'Behold, here is water. What is keeping me from being baptized?'" He knew he must be baptized. How did the eunuch know this? Philip must have explained this during his presentation of the gospel.

Acts 10:47
"Can anyone forbid these people from being baptized with water? They have received the Holy Spirit just like us."

Acts 8:35-36
Philip opened his mouth, and beginning from this Scripture, preached to him about Jesus. 36 As they went on the way, they came to some water, and the eunuch said, "Behold, here is water. What is keeping me from being baptized?"

In Acts 22:16, Paul describes his baptism by Ananias. As soon as Paul's blindness was removed by the prophet, he demanded that Paul rise and be baptized. In fact, he asked

Paul why he was delaying. Here this prophet proclaimed the baptism that was to proceed immediately after faith in Jesus Christ. Baptism follows but does not save.

Acts 22:16
Now why do you wait? Arise, be baptized, and wash away your sins, calling on the name of the Lord.

Then what is baptism, its purpose, and why is it so closely linked to salvation? The Lord Jesus Christ desires for His people to announce their newly obtained salvation to the saints and the world through the outward sign of baptism. Therefore, baptism was to be practiced in public for all to see. The immersion in the water was to signify that they had died to their old lives and been raised to new ones through Christ's death and resurrection (Romans 6:4). This becomes the concluding remarks in one's gospel presentation. Though not often done, it is the biblical pattern.

Romans 6:4
We were buried therefore with him through baptism into death, that just as Christ was raised from the dead through the glory of the Father, so we also might walk in newness of life.

Another important purpose is to have new saints publicly identify themselves with others in His church, the body of Christ (1 Corinthians 12:13). Wherever the unsaved travel in the world, they should constantly be viewing new Christians being baptized by believers in public view. This means in numerous streams, lakes, rivers, and oceans not in buildings that cannot be viewed by all whether they know the person or not. People should see the outward sign of other people being cleansed from sin and becoming brand-new creations. This is the testimony of baptism the Lord demands.

1 Corinthians 12:13
For in one Spirit we were all baptized into one body, whether Jews or Greeks, whether bond or free; and were all given to drink into one Spirit.

Then those same people should be able to watch the old lives of those being baptized pass away and their new lives come as they live righteously for Him (2 Corinthians 5:17)! This is what numerous people in the first century saw and should see today. Since water baptism should occur almost immediately after one is saved, some have mistakenly made baptism an actual element of the salvation process. This is a great error and could not be further from the truth.

2 Corinthians 5:17
Therefore if anyone is in Christ, he is a [brand] new creation. The old things have passed away. Behold, all things have become new.

Baptism cannot and does not save. It is the outward sign of the believer's inward faith. It was always proclaimed in the gospel as the initial act of obedience after salvation. As a result, all the saints should proclaim the gospel and explain baptism within it. Then, they should urge the new Christian to be baptized as soon as possible for the world to see.

An Ancient Portrait

The church of Jesus Christ had just begun, and the Spirit was at work in many miraculous ways. A short time before, Peter had preached a sermon on the day of Pentecost that brought three thousand souls to Christ. These and the other believers in Jerusalem were devoted to the apostles' teaching (the Word), prayer, fellowship, and the breaking of bread (communion) together. These believers were caring for each other's needs, and their love was flowing. Yet, this was only the beginning. The Holy Spirit was not finished.

In Acts 3:1-4:4, Luke gives us an account of the next great sharing of the message of salvation by the apostle Peter. In those days, the disciples often went to pray in the temple as both Christians and now believing Jews. While many devout Jews and Christians were entering the temple at this time, the friends and families of the crippled would place them in front of the gate. This way when the religious people saw these poor handicapped people begging for money, it would tug on their hearts, and they would give generously.

So, there would be many handicapped people present vying for the attention of all who came. When a lame man saw Peter and John, he begged them for financial help. On this particular occasion, the apostle Peter was obviously prompted through the Spirit and his compassion to relieve the suffering of one man and create an opportunity to share the good news with a large crowd. Since he would need a verifiable miracle to authenticate the message he desired to proclaim, he chose this lame man. The man would have been a perfect choice for a miracle. The reason is that out of this crippled throng of suffering people, everyone would have known that he had been handicapped since birth.

In this way, there would be no question as to whether a supernatural sign and wonder had occurred in the name of Jesus. This is exactly what the apostles of Christ had been commissioned to do in their preaching ministry (Hebrews 2:3-4; Matthew 10:5-8). So, Peter turned his attention fully on him and demanded that he look at the two men. Then with the confidence and determination of a true apostle, he told the man that he had no money but would give him a gift far greater. Then he commanded the man in the name of Jesus Christ to stand up and walk.

Hebrews 2:3-4
How will we escape if we neglect so great a salvation — which at the first having been spoken through the Lord, was confirmed to us by those who heard, God also testifying with them, both by signs and wonders, by various works of power and by gifts of the Holy Spirit, according to his own will?

Matthew 10:5-8
Jesus sent these twelve out and commanded them, saying, "Don't go among...Gentiles...don't enter into any city of the Samaritans. Rather, go to the lost sheep of the house of Israel. As you go, preach, saying, 'The Kingdom of Heaven is at hand!' Heal the sick, cleanse the lepers, and cast out demons. Freely you received, so freely give."

He grasped the hand of the man and raised him from the ground. Immediately, strength came into the man's legs and feet, and he stood up. They entered the temple with the man walking, jumping up and down, and praising God. All of the people recognized him and were filled with amazement and wonder. A crowd gathered and the apostle Peter took the opportunity and began to proclaim the good news.

He declared that this was not from the power of man but from the hand of God in the name of Jesus of Nazareth. Then he preached a true gospel message. First, he proclaimed that the God of Abraham, Isaac, and Jacob had glorified Jesus Christ (defense - a reference to resurrection) and the people were seeing the result through this miracle (defense). Even though they had crucified the Holy and Righteous One who is the Prince of Life (these three terms refer to Christ as God, Savior, and Lord), the Lord God had raised him from the dead (defense) and he and John were witnesses of this great event (defense).

This had fulfilled the prophecies God had given through all of His prophets (defense). They were to repent of their sinful deeds (sin and judgment) and embrace Jesus Christ by faith (only Savior, only by faith). Of course, since Jesus was alive, this implied a relationship with Him as both Savior and Lord. According to Acts 4:41 more than five thousand people received the Lord on that day. We can assume that all were baptized after belief to proclaim their faith to God, the church, and the world (Acts 2:41). We must understand that the proper message of salvation was always proclaimed.

Acts 4:4
But many of those who heard the word believed, and the number of the men came to be about five thousand.

Acts 2:41
So then, those who had received his word were baptized; and that day there were added about three thousand souls.

A Modern Anecdote

The Lord has given me the amazing privilege of leading my four children to Christ and then assisting my own grown daughter to lead her daughter (my granddaughter) to Jesus our Lord. The first responsibility the saints have as parents is to raise their children up in the discipline and instruction of the Lord (Ephesians 6:4). Does this not presuppose that they will at some time need to share the good news with them?

Ephesians 6:4
Fathers, do not provoke your children to anger, but bring them up in the discipline and instruction of the Lord.

As they were growing up, I made two commitments to the Lord. The first was to be an example of what a Christian should be. This did not mean living a perfect life before them which is impossible. Instead, it meant that I would attempt to live righteously and when I made mistakes, I would ask the Lord for forgiveness and then whomever I committed the sin against (including them) and start again. I would study the bible and pray in their presence as well as in my own personal time. I would serve the saints in ministry and share the gospel with unbelievers.

When things got hectic and I felt I wasn't going to get the time I needed to study the Word and pray, I would yell, "Coffee drive!" The kids would quickly gather their favorite toys, coloring books, and games; then, they would jump into the car to drive around the neighborhood while I listened to the audio Bible and prayed afterward. This went on for a long time and is spoken of fondly by all of them.

Second, I committed myself to teaching them the things of the Lord. I am not very good at a specific weekly study and prayer together though we did do this. It was easier for me to establish a simple weekend rule which was that anybody can go on an errand with daddy. Whenever I ran errands, they would all come. Then, I would speak to them about the things of the Lord (Deuteronomy 6:1-4). Whether we were at a shopping mall, a hardware store, or a supermarket, we talked about Him. This was not every time but consistently. I also took them to church regularly so they would hear the teaching of other Christians and have the influence of other Christian kids. As soon as they could do something in the church, I put them to work for the Lord.

Deuteronomy 6:1-4
Now these are the commandments...statutes, and the ordinances, which Yahweh your God commanded to teach you, that you might do them in the land that you go over to possess; that you might fear Yahweh your God, to keep all his statutes and his commandments, which I command you – you, your son, and your son's son, all the days of your life; and that your days may be prolonged. Hear therefore, Israel, and observe to do it, that it may be well with you,
and that you may increase mightily, as Yahweh, the God of your fathers, has promised to you, in a land flowing with milk and honey.

They all received the Lord about the same age. This was not directly instigated by me. Once each of them turned five years old, sometime during that fifth year they came to me one by one and told me they wanted to be Christians. One happened in the living room, one in our bedroom, one at the beach, and one at the park. When they asked me if they could become Christians, I told them that the bad things we all do is against God, and it broke His law. When we break God's law, we must go to a place of punishment forever. We could not live with Him. Instead of God punishing us, he punished His Son because they both loved us.

I explained that it would be like a brother saying to his daddy, "Father, will you punish me instead. I have done nothing wrong, but I love my sister and will do it for her." This is what Jesus did on the cross. He took the punishment for our sin. I described how we must be sorry for the bad things we do which is called "sin" and ask Jesus to forgive us and be our Savior. We must believe that he will forgive our sins and take us to heaven with Him when we die. We must also believe that Jesus Christ is the only way into heaven. No one can enter God's home without receiving Jesus as their only Savior.

Then I asserted that we must make Him the boss of our life even above me, their own daddy. We have to be willing to live our life by obeying His Words in the Bible. When I asked, "Do you still want to become a Christian?" Each said, "Yes!" So, I prayed this prayer as they repeated each sentence after me, "Dear God, I am so sorry for my sins." Then I told them to tell Jesus quietly what some of those sins were that they were sorry for.

We continued, "Jesus, I believe you are God's only Son. I believe you died on the cross and rose from the dead. I know you did this to take the punishment for my sins. I know you are the only way to heaven. Please forgive my sins and become my Savior. Please be the boss [Lord] of my life and help me to follow what you say you want me to do in the Bible. Amen." I would then joyfully announce, "You are now a Christian!"

Then for the next several years, we would all celebrate their "spiritual birthdays." Currently, they are grown up and married to Christian spouses, attending church, and serving the Lord. I look forward to seeing perhaps one or two more generations of my family come to Jesus Christ. This would be one of the greatest joys of my life. Through these many experiences, I learned to proclaim the proper message and depend on our sovereign God to do all the rest.

This is God's divine plan. Presenting the proper message of salvation cannot ever be overemphasized. The good news of Jesus must be shared in its fullness. This means that we must put some time into the explanation of the gospel. We cannot present it at the end of a sermon or in a tiny four-page booklet (Acts 17:1-3).

Acts 17:1-3
Now when they had passed through Amphipolis and Apollonia, they came to Thessalonica, where there was a Jewish synagogue. Paul, as was his custom, went in to them, and for three Sabbath days reasoned with them from the Scriptures, explaining and demonstrating that the Christ had to suffer and rise again from the dead, and saying, "This Jesus, whom I proclaim...is the Christ."

A Personal Response

Dear Heavenly Father,

I now realize that for (add name) and others I know and meet to become Christians, I must know and understand the true gospel message. Give me the diligence to study Your Word and learn the principles of the good news and Bible passages that support them. Make me bold but gentle as I discuss their sin and God's judgment. Help me to be clear in my proclamation of the deity of Christ. Please assist me as I explain to them the many truths concerning what Your Son Jesus accomplished on the cross for them. Lord, support me through Your Holy Spirit as I describe how Jesus fulfilled prophecy, performed numerous miracles, and then rose from the dead to demonstrate His deity to them. Use me to show them how to receive Your Son as Savior and submit to Him as Lord. Provide me with all the words necessary to explain how they have entered into a personal relationship with your Son by faith alone and how works will be the fruit. Then help me to guide them to be baptized in their newfound faith. I pray this in the name of Jesus. Amen.

Chapter 7

Proclaim the Proper Message

All people receive Jesus Christ through a clear and exact message of salvation proclaimed to them. This is a work of the Spirit not the persuasion of men.

In the section, "A Typical Scenario," the author presents an account of how the saints can testify of their faith during the Christmas season.

What is the scenario about?

A Christian wanted to share the gospel but was afraid to try since he did not know all its parts to present.

What held the believer back from sharing the gospel?

He did not know the basic elements of the gospel message in order to share it with others.

What finally led the Christian to share the good news and how did it occur?

Once he learned the proper message, he and others sang Christmas carols from house to house and shared the gospel.

Have you had a similar experience?

(Various answers should be shared including yours.)

LEADING THE WAY

In the section, "A Scriptural Principle" the author presents an important biblical principle in evangelism which concerns declaring the true gospel with all of its elements.

How would you express this principle in your own words?

This seventh principle is "we must proclaim the proper message."

(Various answers should be shared including yours.)

How would you rewrite this principle to make it even more personal to your life (using your name and situation)?

(Various answers should be shared including yours.)

Why do you think this principle might be important in your life right now as you share the gospel?

(Various answers should be shared including yours.)

How would you rate yourself on the percentage of times you followed this principle in the past as a believer?

(Various answers should be shared including yours.)

Directions: Put a horizontal mark and your name where you see yourself on the percentage line.

0%   25%   50%   75%   100%

In the section, "A Biblical Explanation," the author explains the elements of the plan of redemption and their importance in bringing true believers into the kingdom.

What are two New Testament examples of proclaiming sin and judgment in the gospel message?

The proclamation of sin and judgment began with John the Baptist in the New Testament.

To answer their many questions of what they must do in their repentance, John the Baptist implied that the multitudes had to stop being selfish and start caring for the numerous needs of others. They had to begin to make sacrifices for others. They had to turn from their evil deeds.

Here [asking the woman at the well to bring her husband] was a crystal-clear indictment for her sin and an opportunity for her to repent. Often, this is missed in this important story and is a critical truth.

The Lord Jesus commanded the adulterous woman to "Go your way. From now on, sin no more." (John 8:11). This was His judgment of her sin.

Every evangelist who preached in the book of Acts spoke of this condemnation and they never left it out.

What are two examples of the proclamation of Jesus as God by Jesus Himself and one of his apostles?

In John 8:58, Jesus told the Jews that before Abraham was born, He existed (I Am). This is a direct claim to be the God or Yahweh (I Am) of the Old Testament. The Jews knew this.

The apostle Peter, as he was speaking before the multitude at Pentecost, declared that Jesus was both Lord and Christ.

In Acts 8, the eunuch from Ethiopia was reading a messianic passage from Isaiah. Philip revealed that it referred to Jesus as the Messiah. This was the proclamation of His deity.

In Acts 8:34-35, the eunuch from Ethiopia was reading a messianic passage from Isaiah. Philip revealed that it referred to Jesus. He showed him how Jesus was the promised Messiah which was a proclamation of His deity.

Briefly, what does it mean to proclaim Jesus as both "Savior" and "Lord?"

Jesus must be proclaimed as the Savior of the world. In Luke 19:10, Jesus Himself said that He had come to save all those who were lost.

Yet, this is not enough. Jesus must be proclaimed as the only Savior and the only way to heaven. In John 14:6, John writes, "Jesus said to him, 'I am the way, the truth, and the life. No one comes to the Father, except through me.''

Jesus must be proclaimed as Lord. This speaks of Christ's authority in relationship to His people.

What three defenses for Christ's deity does the Holy Spirit utilize to bring people to Christ?

In the gospel message, the presentation of evidence for the deity of Christ is a given. Jesus proved His deity through the performance of miracles, the fulfillment of prophecies (both Old Testament and His own), and His resurrection from the dead.

What are three terms used in the Bible that indicate receiving Jesus as Savior and Lord involves a relationship with Jesus not just a cursory knowledge of Him?

In Matthew 7:23, Jesus speaks of the end, when some will come to Him and call for Him as Lord. He will say that they are to go away because He never "knew" them. The word "know" in that passage means an experiential knowledge which is more than intellectual.

In Revelation 2:4, the Lord accuses the church at Ephesus of departing from their first love.

In Revelation 3:16, Jesus charges the church in Laodicea with being lukewarm. They were neither hot nor cold toward Him. In verse 20, He offers those in the church a relationship with Him when he proclaims that He is standing at the door and knocking. If people in the church "hear" His voice and "open" the door, Christ will "dine" with them. These are powerful relationship words. They signify the invitation to a relationship.

In 1 John 1:3, John indicates that he proclaimed the gospel to them so they could fellowship with the Lord Jesus Christ.

In Matthew 22:37, when He was asked about the greatest commandment, the Lord declared that it was to love God with all of one's heart, soul, and mind.

In what ways might these truths impact your life?

(*Various answers should be shared including yours.*)

In the section, "An Ancient Portrait," the author provides a unique portrayal of Peter's encounter with a lame man on his way to the temple.

Can you briefly describe the setting of this real-life ancient drama?

The setting is at the temple in Jerusalem. The lame would sit next to the entrance begging for alms.

Can you describe the major characters involved?

The major characters are Peter, John, and the lame man.

How did the evangelist initiate the gospel presentation?

Then he commanded the man in the name of Jesus Christ to stand up and walk.

He grasped the hand of the man and raised him from the ground. Immediately, strength came into the man's legs and feet, and he stood up. They entered the temple with the man walking, jumping up and down, and praising God. All of the people recognized him and were filled with amazement and wonder. A crowd gathered and the apostle Peter took the opportunity and began to proclaim the good news.

What was result of this evangelistic presentation?

According to Acts 4:41 more than five thousand people received the Lord on that day. We can assume that all were baptized after belief to proclaim their faith to God, the church, and the world (Acts 2:41).

How was the principle explained in this chapter applied to the situation?

We must understand that the proper message of salvation was always proclaimed.

Based on the truths learned in this chapter, what would you have done differently if you were the evangelist or how would you have responded if you were the recipient?

(Various answers should be shared including yours.)

In the section, "A Modern Anecdote," the author discusses how his four children received Jesus Christ as Savior and Lord in their early years.

Can you briefly describe the setting of this real-life modern drama?

The setting is in the author's living room, bedroom, the beach, and the park.

Can you describe the major characters involved?

The major characters are the author and his four children.

How did the author initiate the gospel presentation?

As they were growing up, I made two commitments to the Lord. The first was to be an example of what a Christian should be. This did not mean living a perfect life before them which is impossible. Instead, it meant that I would attempt to live righteously and when I made mistakes, I would ask the Lord for forgiveness and then whomever I committed the sin against (including them) and start again.

When things got hectic and I felt I wasn't going to get the time I needed to study the Word and pray, I would yell, "Coffee drive!" The kids would quickly gather their favorite toys, coloring books, and games; then, they would jump into the car to drive around the neighborhood while I listened to the audio Bible and prayed afterward.

Second, I committed myself to teaching them the things of the Lord. I am not very good at a specific weekly study and prayer together though we did do this. It was easier for me to establish a simple weekend rule which was that anybody can go on an errand with daddy.

Once each of them turned five years old, sometime during that fifth year they came to me one by one and told me they wanted to be Christians.

What was result of this evangelistic presentation?

I know you did this to take the punishment for my sins. I know you are the only way to heaven. Please forgive my sins and become my Savior. Please be the boss [Lord] of my life and help me to follow what you say you want me to do in the Bible. Amen." I would then joyfully announce, "You are now a Christian!"

Then for the next several years, we would all celebrate their "spiritual birthdays." Currently, they are grown up and married to Christian spouses, attending church, and serving the Lord.

How was the principle explained in this chapter applied to the situation?

This is God's divine plan. Presenting the proper message of salvation cannot ever be overemphasized. The good news of Jesus must be shared in its fullness. This means that we must put some time into the explanation of the gospel. We cannot present it at the end of a sermon or in a tiny four-page booklet (Acts 17:1-3).

Based on the truths learned in this chapter, what would you have done differently if you were the author or how would you have responded if you were the recipient?

(*Various answers should be shared including yours.*)

In the section, "A Personal Response," the author provides a model you may use for prayer if you find it necessary after discovering the truths in this chapter.

Are you presently attempting to present the gospel of Jesus to someone? If not, are there some who may attend your local church who may not know Jesus Christ and may need prayer for an opportunity for you to share with them and open hearts to receive Him?

(Various answers should be shared including yours.)

Based on the truths you have just learned, what will you continue to do in your current evangelistic efforts and what might you do differently?

(Various answers should be shared including yours.)

What additional thoughts would you like to share with the others?

(Various answers should be shared including yours.)

Chapter 8

Utilize Your Interests and Skills

Deep down in the hearts of Christians is a great desire to share the gospel with others. We want to see many receive our Savior and Lord. We do not want to be spectators in the process. Though it may bring some joy to invite someone to a meeting, life group, bible study, or church service and watch someone else present the plan of redemption and them come to Christ. Would you like to jump into the game and watch God work through you as you witness for Him? This chapter explains how to become engaged in this very process. God's strategy has always been to use every single believer to share the gospel, not a chosen few. The chosen few were to equip the others, not to do all the work. Where is the personal blessing in that?

A Typical Scenario

Have you ever been in a situation that was something like the following? For a long time, you have wanted to be able to share the gospel on a regular basis but have never had a strategy to do it. Since door to door evangelism did not seem to be what you felt comfortable doing, for many years you did nothing. You could not remember sharing the gospel in its entirety to even one person since becoming a Christian. When you look around at your Christian friends, they seem to think that the best method is to invite people to church and let the pastor present the gospel. Yet, you want the thrill and blessing of being used by God in this way. You want the joy of having spiritual children in Christ. You desire to be able to use your spiritual gifts and abilities in this area.

LEADING THE WAY

In this chapter you will learn that every Christian has the individual responsibility of sharing the gospel. All the saints should develop an evangelistic strategy which is performed alone or with other believers. It should be created around their spiritual gifts, talents, abilities, backgrounds, desires, and ethnicities. Every encounter with an unsaved person is to be viewed as a potential evangelistic encounter. You could individually tailor a presentation to the situation at hand. To witness, you should not offend unbelievers in the area of your Christian liberty. This will involve your constant contact with those who are unsaved and a continual testimony to them by your love for others in the church. After you learn these spiritual truths, perhaps you could develop a strategy similar to this one.

Since you love golfing and need to spend time with those who do not know Christ, you decide to start playing golf more regularly. You call a Christian friend who also golfs and ask her if she would like to meet some people. You and she could share the gospel with them and play golf at the same time. It would provide a natural conversation starter and connection. This first thing you did was to start reading golf magazines so you could talk about current happenings in the world of golf. You decide to go to mixers with your friend and meet other golf enthusiasts. During his time, you put absolutely no pressure on yourself, except to pray for opportunities that you could make or opportunities that God would provide. As you play golf and go to mixers, people begin to open up to you about the many difficulties they are facing.

If they have a problem, you ask them if you could pray for them and then follow up to see how they are doing. If they have a need, you would try and meet that need. Then, you would explain that you try and honor the Lord Jesus in your life every day by doing good in His Name. You treat the staff with kindness and dignity as an example of Jesus. Then, you wear a small cross on the collar of a golf shirt. So, whenever someone used God or Christ's name in vain, you politely ask them to please refrain from those words. You explain that you worship Him as Savior and Lord, so it offends you. It is done very quietly, gently, and politely. You never do it in an overbearing way. It isn't long before people begin to come to and your friend to talk about the Lord.

Though this is an imaginary scenario, it is typical of the kinds of strategies we can utilize to share the good news of Jesus Christ. Understanding the following principles will help us develop personal evangelistic strategies that we are comfortable with. This allows us to create many of our own opportunities and take many of God's. What a marvelous stimulus we can have in our Christian lives to evangelize! Now, we arrive at the eighth principle which involves the development of these diverse methods we may use alone or with others.

A Scriptural Principle

The good news can be presented and shared in a variety of ways for many reasons. These methods and motivations can honor or dishonor the Lord. Some believers have the mistaken notion that the gospel can be presented with any motive or method as long as "people get saved." This could not be further from the truth. There are specific ways in which God desires His gospel to be proclaimed in Scripture.

This is the key: the Lord God chooses how He wants His good news to be presented. The methods and motives in which the good news is to be proclaimed are more important than the results of the proclamation. God does most of the work in salvation, and He desires things done His way. For

Christians to share the good news, they must know how to develop strategies to accomplish this exciting, supernatural, and critical kingdom task. Principle number eight is "we must utilize our interests and skills." Though on the surface, this may seem somewhat vague, we will dig into the New Testament to discover the numerous ways the background, skills, gifts, and interests of the saints were used.

A Biblical Explanation

Though this new chapter concerns itself with the proper methods to present the redemptive plan of God, we begin this discussion with some of the improper ways in which the plan should not be shared. This contrast will help clarify the numerous presentations we have all seen that appear as if something is not right with the presenter or the way they have chosen to proclaim His good news of salvation. Paul encountered many who shared the gospel in shameful ways and with unrighteous motives. In his letters, the apostle exposes, condemns, and warns believers to not follow them or duplicate their ways. Though each deserves a separate study, I will only introduce them and encourage the readers to study each of them further.

The first is found in Philippians 1:15-18. Paul describes a group of people who were sharing the gospel due to envy, rivalry, and selfish ambition. These evangelists wanted to see more people come to Christ and create a status above Paul in the Roman church. Paul exposes their sinful motives and condemns them. The gospel of Jesus Christ is a pure and holy message, which the Lord desires to be shared from pure and holy motives. Our intentions should always match the holiness of the message we have to proclaim. The next principles can be found in 1 Thessalonians 2:3-6. Here, Paul describes several other improper attitudes or presentations as the apostle clearly contrasts his method of righteous, holy preaching of the gospel with those who had wicked motives and inappropriate "gospel presentations" toward the church at Thessalonica.

Philippians 1:15-18
Some indeed preach Christ even out of envy and strife, and some also out of good will. The former insincerely preach Christ from selfish ambition, thinking that they add affliction to my chains; but the latter out of love, knowing that I am appointed for the defense of the Good News. What does it matter? Only that in every way, whether in pretense or in truth, Christ is proclaimed. I rejoice in this, yes, and will rejoice.

1 Thessalonians 2:3-6
For our exhortation is not of error, nor of uncleanness, nor in deception. But even as we have been approved by God to be entrusted with the Good News, so we speak: not as pleasing men, but God, who tests our hearts. For neither were we at any time found using words of flattery...nor a cloak of covetousness (God is witness), nor seeking glory from men (neither from you nor from others), when we might have claimed authority as apostles of Christ.

Second, the true gospel should be presented without error according to the truths in the Scriptures. Third, saints are not to announce the plan with impurity but with pure motives. Fourth, the gospel should not be shared in deceit or with trickery but in truthfulness. Fifth, believers should not seek the favor of men in the presentation of the gospel but seek the approval of the Lord. The offense of the gospel cannot be removed. Sixth, saints should not evangelize by relying on flattering speech but proclaim judgment for unbelief and salvation for belief. Seventh, the gospel should never be presented with a pretext for greed or for personal gain. The gospel should bring the gain of salvation for those who hear. Eighth, the gospel should never be heralded for personal glory but for the glory of the Almighty.

In 1 Corinthians 2:1-5, the apostle Paul describes several more inappropriate motives or behavior in the sharing of the gospel. Ninth, the gospel should not be presented in such a way as to appeal to the wisdom of man. The gospel is the wisdom of God and stands alone. Tenth, the gospel should not be shared in cleverness of speech. The Holy Spirit uses the simple message to convince and convert unbelievers not human persuasion. In 2 Corinthians 2:17, Paul discloses the eleventh. The gospel is not to be a money-making device which is sold like various wares. The apostle never shared the good news like some others who were simply peddling the Word of God. In 1 Thessalonians 1:5-7, the apostle Paul describes two more principles which govern the motives and behavior of those sharing the gospel. Twelfth, the good news should not be preached out of an unrighteous lifestyle but out of a holy life, providing many good examples to follow. Thirteen, the good news should not be shared out of pity or disgust but from real love and affection as a nursing mother cares for her babies.

1 Corinthians 2:1-5
When I came to you, brothers, I didn't come with excellence of speech or of wisdom, proclaiming to you the testimony of God. For I determined not to know anything among you except Jesus Christ and him crucified. I was with you in weakness, in fear, and in much trembling. My speech and my preaching were not in persuasive words of human wisdom, but in demonstration of the Spirit and of power, that your faith wouldn't stand in the wisdom of men, but in the power of God.

2 Corinthians 2:17
For we are not as so many, peddling the word of God. But as of sincerity, but as of God, in the sight of God, we speak in Christ.

1 Thessalonians 1:5-7
And that our Good News came to you not in word only, but also in power, and in the Holy Spirit, and with much assurance. You know what kind of men we showed ourselves to be among you for your sake. You became imitators of us and of the Lord, having received the word in much affliction, with joy of the Holy Spirit, so that you became an example to all who believe in Macedonia and in Achaia.

These are important considerations for Christians, who are constantly being recruited for a wide variety of so-called evangelistic efforts. As a result, there are great temptations to fall into one of these offenses. These errors ought to be carefully studied and avoided at all costs.

An Individual Responsibility for the Proclamation

Every believer should take their proper responsibility for proclaiming the plan of redemption. God's perfect plan for evangelism is very, very simple. It has several basic steps. A church sends an evangelist or missionary into an area where there are no Christians (or just a few). This evangelist or missionary wins people to Christ and equips the saints to win others to Christ. He might move on or remain. He then turns over the church to the pastor-teacher who equips the saints for the work of the ministry in the church.

The evangelist is a gifted believer in the church who wins people to Christ. In Acts 21:8 Philip is called an evangelist, and he went out sharing the good news all over Samaria. Paul explains to Timothy that he needs to accomplish the work of an evangelist (2 Timothy 4:5). This young pastor was to share Christ and bring them into his church and plant another one. Besides this crucial responsibility, Timothy, as an evangelist must equip individual saints for evangelism in their own community, region, and even to the remotest parts of the Earth. He was not to do evangelism all by himself.

Acts 21:8
On the next day, we who were Paul's companions departed, and came to Caesarea. We entered into the house of Philip the evangelist...the seven....

2 Timothy 4:5
But you be sober in all things, suffer hardship, do the work of an evangelist, and fulfill your ministry.

LEADING THE WAY

In Ephesians 4:11-12, Paul discusses exactly how Christ builds His body with the pastor-teacher and evangelist. He writes, "He gave some to be apostles; and some, prophets; and some, evangelists; and some, shepherds and teachers; for the perfecting of the saints, to the work of serving, to the building up of the body of Christ."

Ephesians 4:11-12
He gave some to be apostles; and some, prophets; and some, evangelists; and some, shepherds and teachers; for the perfecting of the saints, to the work of serving, to the building up of the body of Christ.

The real church of Jesus Christ should grow numerically through spiritual reproduction and then spiritually through the mutual ministry of believers. This is fully accomplished through the equipping of believers by these two gifted leaders in the church. The evangelist and pastor-teacher are to equip the saints for the work of service to build up the body. A biblical evangelist equips the saints for the work of service outside the church and the pastor-teacher inside the church. The saints being equipped by a true evangelist is absolutely essential in God's pattern of growth.

Then, the saints take over in the evangelistic process. This is found all throughout the book of Acts. In Acts 13:1-4, the church at Antioch sent Paul and Barnabas out to win people to Christ and plant churches. They went to Seleucia, then Cyprus (Acts 13:4). They preached the gospel in Salamis (Acts 13:5) then onto the island of Paphos (Acts 13:6). Then they traveled to Perga, and from there to Antioch of Pisidia (Acts 13:14). After these cities, Paul ventured into Iconium, Lycaonia, Lystra, Derbe, and the surrounding region (Acts 13:51-14:5). After Paul finished up in Derbe (Acts 14:20), he went back to those same cities. He desired to check on their progress, encourage them in their faith, warn them against false teachers, and appoint elders (Acts 14:21-23).

AN INSTRUCTOR'S MANUAL

Acts 13:1-4
Now in the assembly that was at Antioch there were some prophets and teachers: Barnabas, Simeon who was called Niger, Lucius of Cyrene, Manaen the foster brother of Herod the tetrarch, and Saul. As they served the Lord and fasted, the Holy Spirit said, "Separate Barnabas and Saul for me...." Then, when they had fasted and prayed and laid their hands on them, they sent them away. So, being sent out by the Holy Spirit, they went down to Seleucia. From there they sailed to Cyprus.

Acts 13:4
So, being sent out by the Holy Spirit, they went down to Seleucia. From there they sailed to Cyprus.

Acts 13:5
When they were at Salamis, they proclaimed God's word in the Jewish synagogues. They also had John as their attendant.

Acts 13:6
When they had gone through the island to Paphos, they found a certain sorcerer, a false prophet, a Jew, whose name was Bar Jesus.

Acts 13:14
But they, passing on from Perga, came to Antioch of Pisidia. They went into the synagogue on the Sabbath day, and sat down.

Acts 13:51-14:5
But they shook off the dust of their feet against them, and came to Iconium. The disciples were filled with joy and with the Holy Spirit. In Iconium, they entered together into the synagogue of the Jews, and so spoke that a great multitude both of Jews and of Greeks believed. But the disbelieving Jews stirred up and embittered the souls of the Gentiles against the brothers. Therefore they stayed there a long time, speaking boldly in the Lord, who testified to the word of his grace, granting signs and wonders to be done by their hands. But the multitude of the city was divided. Part sided with the Jews, and part with the apostles. When some of both the Gentiles and the Jews, with their rulers, made a violent attempt to mistreat and stone them.

Acts 14:20
But as the disciples stood around him, he rose up, and entered into the city. On the next day he went out with Barnabas to Derbe.

Acts 14:21-23
When they had preached the Good News to that city, and had made many disciples, they returned to Lystra, Iconium, and Antioch, strengthening the

souls of the disciples, exhorting them to continue in the faith, and that through many afflictions we must enter into God's Kingdom. When they had appointed elders for them in every assembly, and had prayed with fasting, they commended them to the Lord, on whom they had believed.

From this point, how did the churches really grow? Did they find friends going to another church and attract them to come to theirs? No, they went out and shared the gospel. It was the same in the city of Philippi. In Acts 16, Paul entered the busy city and began proclaiming the good news (verses 11-13). He won Lydia to Christ (verse 14), possibly a demon-possessed slave girl (verse 18), and definitely the Philippian jailer and his whole household (verses 31-33). These were the core members of the church in Philippi. How did this church grow from a small handful of people from there? Obviously, those saints shared the good news. Later, he went back to check on them (Acts 20:1-6) and even write them a letter.

Acts 16:11-13
Setting sail therefore from Troas, we made a straight course to Samothrace, and the day following to Neapolis; and from there to Philippi, which is a city of Macedonia, the foremost of the district, a Roman colony. We were staying some days in this city. On the Sabbath day we went outside of the city by a riverside, where we supposed there was a place of prayer, and we sat down and spoke to the women who had come together.

Acts 16:14
A certain woman named Lydia, a seller of purple, of the city of Thyatira, one who worshiped God, heard us. The Lord opened her heart to listen to the things which were spoken by Paul.

Acts 16:18
She was doing this for many days. But Paul, becoming greatly annoyed, turned and said to the spirit, "I command you in the name of Jesus Christ to come out of her!" It came out that very hour.

Acts 16:31-33
They said, "Believe in the Lord Jesus Christ, and you will be saved, you and your household." They spoke the word of the Lord to him, and to all who were in his house. He took them the same hour of the night and washed their stripes, and was immediately baptized, he and all his household.

Acts 20:1-6
After the uproar had ceased, Paul sent for the disciples, took leave of them, and departed to go into Macedonia. When he had gone through those parts, and had encouraged them with many words, he came into Greece. When he had spent three months there, and a plot was made against him by Jews as he was about to set sail for Syria.... These accompanied him as far as Asia: Sopater of Beroea; Aristarchus and Secundus of the Thessalonians; Gaius of Derbe; Timothy; and Tychicus and Trophimus of Asia. But these had gone ahead, and were waiting for us at Troas. We sailed away from Philippi after the days of Unleavened Bread, and came to them at Troas in five days, where we stayed seven days.

The clearest example of saints sharing the gospel is found in Acts 17:1-4. Paul arrived in Thessalonica, preached the good news and won people to Christ. Due to persecution, he stayed only a short time. He then left Timothy to equip all of them. What happened next is marveled at by the apostle. In 1 Thessalonians 1:8, the gospel had sounded out from them all over Macedonia and Achaia and everywhere their faith went. They were totally on fire for their Lord and took their individual responsibility for sharing the gospel.

Acts 17:1-4
Now when they had passed through Amphipolis and Apollonia, they came to Thessalonica, where there was a Jewish synagogue. Paul, as was his custom, went in to them, and for three Sabbath days reasoned with them from the Scriptures, explaining and demonstrating that the Christ had to suffer and rise again from the dead, and saying, "This Jesus, whom I proclaim to you, is the Christ." Some of them were persuaded and joined Paul and Silas, of the devout Greeks a great multitude, and not a few of the chief women.

1 Thessalonians 1:8
For from you the word of the Lord has been declared, not only in Macedonia and Achaia, but also in every place your faith toward God has gone out, so that we need not to say anything.

An Individual Personal Evangelistic Strategy

In the New Testament, there are examples of many saints who simply went about proclaiming the gospel in a simple, upfront way. In Acts 8:4, Luke writes that those who were scattered due to Saul's intense persecution went about and preached the gospel. The saints were scattered and shared the gospel. In the letter of 1 Thessalonians 1:8, Paul tells the church the Word of the Lord was declared in Macedonia and Achaia and wherever their faith toward God had gone out. Christians were sharing the gospel.

Acts 8:4
Therefore those who were scattered abroad went around preaching the word.

1 Thessalonians 1:8
For from you the word of the Lord has been declared, not only in Macedonia and Achaia, but also in every place your faith toward God has gone out, so that we need not to say anything.

Every New Testament example demonstrates a simple and up-front presentation. There are other saints (including the apostles) who had a personal evangelistic strategy. They desired to establish a regular plan of action. This usually consisted of determining to whom they would witness and how they would make the opportunity to present the gospel.

Matthew describes the evangelistic strategy of John the Baptist in Matthew 3:1-6. John went about in the wilderness of Judea dressed in camel's hair eating locusts and honey. Why? John was a prophet and took a Nazarite vow to live a life of purity and devotion to God (Matthew 11:9; Luke 1:13-15). This did not allow for the drinking of wine or the cutting of hair. He lived an austere life in the wilderness wearing the uncomfortable clothing made of camel's hair. This contrasted his humble lifestyle with the overindulgent religious leaders of the day. Then he preached repentance in preparation for the coming Messiah near a populated river where water was available for baptism. This was his method.

Matthew 3:1-6
In those days, John the Baptizer came, preaching in the wilderness of Judea, saying, "Repent, for the Kingdom of Heaven is at hand!" For this is he who was spoken of by Isaiah the prophet, saying, "The voice of one crying in the wilderness, make the way of the Lord ready! Make his paths straight!" Now John himself wore clothing made of camel's hair with a leather belt around his waist. His food was locusts and wild honey. Then people from Jerusalem, all of Judea, and all the region around the Jordan went out to him. They were baptized by him in the Jordan, confessing their sins.

Matthew 11:9
But why did you go out? To see a prophet? Yes, I tell you, and much more than a prophet.

Luke 1:13-15
But the angel said to him, "Don't be afraid, Zacharias, because your request has been heard. Your wife, Elizabeth, will bear you a son, and you shall call his name John. You will have joy and gladness, and many will rejoice at his birth. For he will be great in the sight of the Lord, and he will drink no wine nor strong drink. He will be filled with the Holy Spirit, even from his mother's womb.

The Lord Jesus had His personal strategy of evangelism, which He followed His entire ministry. In Matthew 4:23, the apostle describes it in these words, "Jesus went about in all Galilee, teaching in their synagogues, preaching the Good News of the Kingdom, and healing every disease and every sickness among the people. The Lord Jesus traveled to the synagogue and to the streets, healing people and preaching the kingdom of God. Paul's strategy was very similar. In Acts 17:1-2 and verse 17, Luke discloses that Paul's custom was to enter a city and begin preaching in the synagogue. Then he would go out into the marketplaces and proclaim the gospel. Why did Jesus (John 3:2) and Paul (Acts 22:3) have similar evangelistic strategies? The both of them were recognized as rabbis. A visiting rabbi was allowed to speak in the synagogues. They went to the streets during the week to reach the Gentiles also. In the streets and market places much discussion of events, religion, and politics occurred.

Matthew 4:23
Jesus went about in all Galilee, teaching in their synagogues, preaching the Good News of the Kingdom, and healing every disease and every sickness among the people.

Acts 17:1-2
Now when they had passed through Amphipolis and Apollonia, they came to Thessalonica, where there was a Jewish synagogue. Paul, as was his custom, went in to them, and for three Sabbath days reasoned with them from the Scriptures.

Acts 17:17
So he reasoned in the synagogue with the Jews and the devout persons, and in the marketplace every day with those who met him.

John 3:2
The same came to him by night, and said to him, "Rabbi, we know that you are a teacher come from God, for no one can do these signs that you do, unless God is with him."

Acts 22:3
I am indeed a Jew, born in Tarsus of Cilicia, but brought up in this city at the feet of Gamaliel, instructed according to the strict tradition of the law of our fathers, being zealous for God, even as you all are today.

Peter's strategy is described in Acts 3:9-10. Peter simply healed and preached. He was not a rabbi and did not go into the synagogues. Why was Peter the one who preached to the multitudes that gathered at Pentecost (Acts 2:14), after the healing of the lame man (Acts 3:12), and to the Sanhedrin (Acts 4:8) just to name a few? There were other apostles with him. Peter was the spiritual head of the group, but he was also a powerful speaker. Since Stephen and Philip were both Hellenistic Jews (Jews living in the Greek culture), they were able to minister to the Greek speaking peoples.

Acts 3:9-10
All the people saw him walking and praising God. They recognized him, that it was he who used to sit begging for gifts for the needy at the Beautiful Gate of the temple. They were filled with wonder and amazement at what had happened to him.

Acts 2:14
But Peter, standing up with the eleven, lifted up his voice and spoke out to them, "You men of Judea, and all you who dwell at Jerusalem, let this be known to you, and listen to my words.

Acts 3:12
When Peter saw it, he responded to the people, "You men of Israel, why do you marvel at this man? Why do you fasten your eyes on us, as though by our own power or godliness we had made him walk?

Acts 4:8
Then Peter, filled with the Holy Spirit, said to them, "You rulers of the people, and elders of Israel."

Stephen preached the gospel to his people group while Philip proclaimed the gospel to the Samaritans, a similar group which were half-Jew and half-Greek. Since they both possessed supernatural abilities, they performed mighty miracles before they shared the gospel. They differed in that Stephen had a more public ministry (refuting the Jews in public and speaking before the Sanhedrin) and Philip had a much more private and personal ministry which involved the sharing of the gospel with Simon the Magician and the eunuch from Ethiopia.

Apollos had a gifted intellect, was a powerful orator, and was mighty in the Scriptures. Since he was unafraid of large crowds, he frequently debated the Jews in public. He was able to refute their arguments for all to see (Acts 18:24-25). As one can see from these examples, they all had strategies, but the strategies could be different. These approaches were based upon their language, backgrounds, gifts, and abilities. The Church should equip the saints to share the gospel. The saints can then develop their own strategies to proclaim this amazingly good news. Perhaps those who are orphans may share the gospel and minister to orphans. Maybe those who may have experienced pregnancy as teens might be the best people to bring the gospel to teens who are pregnant.

Acts 18:24-25
Now a certain Jew named Apollos, an Alexandrian by race, an eloquent man, came to Ephesus. He was mighty in the Scriptures...being fervent in spirit ...taught...the things concerning Jesus...he knew only the baptism of John.

Those in various professions could use their achievements as opportunities to give God glory and then share the good news. An actor, musician, athlete, physician, or entrepreneur might share they're gratefulness for God's help when they achieve something. As they stand before an audience or are asked by others, the gospel could be shared. Some think if they mention God that this is sufficient, but it is not. The Lord Jesus is the central focus of the good news. To simply mention God, they may bring to people's minds the god they believe in, which may or may not be the true God. Instead, it could be a deity of their false religion or some deity of their own making (Romans 1:23), essentially an idol. This does not bring God glory.

Romans 1:23
And traded the glory of the incorruptible God for the likeness of an image of corruptible man, and of birds, four-footed animals, and creeping things.

Not only can believers act individually in their numerous evangelistic strategies but together. Some members in a local church who possess the same language, ethnicities, trials, backgrounds, interests, gifts, or abilities could come together and build a powerful team. Add to this, people with the gift of leadership to lead, the gift of administration to manage, and the gift of teaching to train in biblical principles and here is a team who can be used by the Holy Spirit.

A Potential Evangelistic Encounter

The apostles viewed almost every situation as a potential evangelistic encounter. Sometimes, these men would create opportunities to share the gospel. Other times, they took the opportunities when they came from the Spirit. In Acts 2, the day of Pentecost arrived, and the disciples were in the upper room praying. Suddenly, the Spirit came. There was the sound of a violent wind and a manifestation of tongues of fire rested above each one. This drew a big crowd. What did the apostles do? Peter and the others took this opportunity that God had presented and shared the gospel. They took the opportunity when it came.

In Acts 3, Peter and John encountered a crippled man as they went into the temple to pray. When he asked for alms, they instead healed him. It isn't too difficult to assume that a lame man now walking would draw a large crowd. Once the crowd had gathered around this amazing event, the apostle preached the gospel. He made the opportunity to share the gospel. Previously, we saw that the miracles of the Lord Jesus drew numerous crowds which created many of the opportunities they had to preach the gospel.

In Acts 4, the apostle Peter was arrested and then brought before the Sanhedrin. Peter took the opportunity that was given to him and preached the gospel. In Acts 6-7, Stephen was arrested and dragged in before the Sanhedrin because he preached the gospel. This gave him another opportunity to preach it again to his accusers which he took. In Acts 10, the Lord told Cornelius to send for Peter. Peter was given an opportunity from the Lord, and he took it. He traveled to Caesarea and proclaimed the good news of Jesus Christ to Cornelius and his entire household. Then the Spirit came upon them confirming their salvation.

In Acts 16, Paul was arrested and imprisoned in Philippi. When an Earthquake occurred, rather than escaping for his life, he utilized the situation to win the jailer and his whole household to Christ. This was not an opportunity that he planned. It was an opportunity he took. It is interesting that Paul allowed himself to be beaten and imprisoned, though He was a Roman which made this illegal. Perhaps, he sensed God was at work and let the situation play itself out. In Acts 21, the Jews claimed that Paul had allowed a Gentile to enter the holy temple, and he was arrested. Consequently, Paul took the opportunity to share the good news with the crowd. From there, he preached the gospel to a series of prominent people: the High Priest, the Sanhedrin (Acts 23), Felix (Acts 24), Festus (Acts 25), and Herod Agrippa (Acts 26).

Before Festus in Acts 25:9-11, Paul invoked his right as a Roman citizen to appeal to Caesar and speak directly to the emperor. Every Roman citizen had this right, and Paul knew it. He obviously wanted to save this appeal for an opportune moment, if necessary. The apostle's subsequent journey to Rome had been previously prophesied to him on the road to Damascus by Jesus Himself (Acts 23:11). After Festus asked Paul if he would be willing to go to Jerusalem to be judged, he knew the time had come. He was not only cognizant of this prophesy but had been informed that the Jews would attempt to ambush and kill him on the way. How else could the Lord have gotten His gospel to the courts of the most powerful man on Earth? The apostle had just made a critical opportunity to share the gospel.

Acts 25:9-11
But Festus, desiring to gain favor with the Jews, answered Paul and said, "Are you willing to go up to Jerusalem, and be judged by me there concerning these things?" But Paul said, "I am standing before Caesar's judgment seat, where I ought to be tried. I have done no wrong to the Jews, as you also know very well. For if I have done wrong and have committed anything worthy of death, I don't

refuse to die; but if none of those things is true that they accuse me of, no one can give me up to them. I appeal to Caesar!"

Acts 23:11
The following night, the Lord stood by him and said, "Cheer up, Paul, for as you have testified about me at Jerusalem, so you must testify also at Rome."

When Paul arrived in Rome, once again, he proclaimed the gospel with anyone who would listen. Every situation became a potential evangelistic encounter. He anticipated an opportunity in every negative situation. God could and did work anywhere Paul found himself. The apostle wrote to the church at Philippi that the gospel of Christ was advancing in this desperate and dark situation. In Philippians 1:12-13, he explains, "Now I desire to have you know, brothers, that the things which happened to me have turned out rather to the progress of the Good News; so that it became evident to the whole palace guard, and to all the rest, that my bonds are in Christ."

Philippians 1:12-13
Now I desire to have you know, brothers, that the things which happened to me have turned out rather to the progress of the Good News, so that it became evident to the whole palace guard, and to all the rest, that my bonds are in Christ.

The apostle describes how some of the emperor's guards had heard the gospel and believed. Later, he closes his letter with a greeting from the actual household of Caesar himself (Philippians 4:22). There were those in the emperor's own palace that had received Christ. So, Christians should be ready to accept the many opportunities the Lord provides to proclaim the plan.

Philippians 4:22
All the saints greet you, especially those who are of Caesar's household.

How can believers make or take these many opportunities when they arrive? First, they should pray and then watch for open doors. Paul requested that the Colossians pray that God would open up a door for the Word in Colossians 4:3. Second, they must be alert and aware of circumstances that suddenly arise where the gospel can be proclaimed. These have been mentioned earlier in the examples of Peter.

Colossians 4:3
Praying together for us also, that God may open to us a door for the word, to speak the mystery of Christ, for which I am also in bonds.

Third, the apostles expected the Lord God at any time to place them into situations in which they could make or take an opportunity. They were not caught off guard. Jesus told them that they would be His witnesses (Acts 1:8), and they expected the Spirit to be at work. Christians should expect and experience the same.

Acts 1:8
But you will receive power when the Holy Spirit has come upon you. You will be witnesses to me in Jerusalem, in all Judea and Samaria, and to the uttermost parts of the Earth.

Fourth, evangelism was a way of life. Paul declared to the Corinthians that he did all things for the sake of the good news so he could become a fellow-partaker of the gospel (1 Corinthians 9:23). As the saints were persecuted in the city of Jerusalem, they fled. Everywhere these saints traveled, they preached the gospel (Acts 8: 4).

1 Corinthians 9:23
Now I do this for the sake of the Good News, that I may be a joint partaker of it.

Acts 8:4
Therefore those who were scattered...went...preaching the word.

A Manifestation of Spiritual Gifts

When believers are sharing the gospel, they need spiritual power to see souls saved which comes from the Holy Spirit. The Holy Spirit works through His Word and prayer, but He also empowers through spiritual gifts. As Christians develop personal evangelistic strategies and make or take the many opportunities to share the gospel, they should be ministering in the area of their spiritual gifts. The main biblical passages discussing gifts of the Spirit are 1 Corinthians 12-14, Romans 12:4-8, 1 Peter 4:10-11, and Ephesians 4:11-16. Every single Christian is given a spiritual gift in order to minister to the Body of Christ (the church). These important spiritual gifts are supernatural abilities which should be employed in both bringing people into Christ's church (evangelism) and also ministering to them (edification). Believers should consider using their gifts both inside and outside the church.

Romans 12:4-8
For even as we have many members in one body, and all the members don't have the same function, so we, who are many, are one body in Christ, and individually members of one another, having gifts differing according to the grace that was given to us: if prophecy, let's prophesy according to the proportion of our faith; or service, let's give ourselves to service; or he who teaches, to his teaching; or he who exhorts, to his exhorting; he who gives, let him do it with generosity; he who rules, with diligence; he who shows mercy, with cheerfulness.

1 Peter 4:10-11
As each has received a gift, employ it in serving one another, as good managers of the grace of God in its various forms. If anyone speaks, let it be as it were the very words of God. If anyone serves, let it be as of the strength which God supplies, that in all things God may be glorified through Jesus Christ, to whom belong the glory and the dominion forever and ever. Amen.

Ephesians 4:11-16
He gave some to be apostles; and some, prophets; and some, evangelists; and some, shepherds and teachers; for the perfecting of the saints, to the work of serving, to the building up of the body of Christ, until we all attain to the unity of the faith and of the knowledge of the Son of God, to a full grown man, to the

measure of the stature of the fullness of Christ, that we may no longer be children, tossed back and forth and carried about with every wind of doctrine, by the trickery of men, in craftiness, after the wiles of error; but speaking truth in love, we may grow up in all things into him who is the head, Christ, from whom all the body, being fitted and knit together through that which every joint supplies, according to the working in measure of each individual part, makes the body increase to the building up of itself in love.

At salvation, individual believers are given at least one of the spiritual gifts for the common good. This would include saving and maturing. These gifts may or may not be tied to one's ability or personality. Gifts are given to every believer by the Spirit according to God's divine will. Paul indicates that these gifts are manifestations of God's Holy Spirit. In 1 Corinthians 12:4-7, the apostle asserts this fact in these words, "Now there are various kinds of gifts, but the same Spirit. There are various kinds of service, and the same Lord. There are various kinds of workings, but the same God, who works all things in all. But to each one is given the manifestation of the Spirit for the profit of all." Here Paul asserts that there are a variety of gifts used in a wide variety of ministries having a variety of effects. These are real manifestations of the Spirit. When the saints are exercising their different gifts, everyone will be viewing the Holy Spirit at work in a powerful way.

1 Corinthians 12:4-7
Now there are various kinds of gifts, but the same Spirit. There are various kinds of service, and the same Lord. There are various kinds of workings, but the same God, who works all things in all. But to each one is given the manifestation of the Spirit for the profit of all.

As mentioned earlier, similarly gifted people may desire to develop a true gospel ministry together. At other times, a ministry demands a variety of gifts to function. If the saints are ministering the good news to older folks in a retirement center, they will need Christians with the gifts of mercy, service, or helps. If the church desires to feed those in need and share the gospel, they will need the gifts of leadership and administration to organize the event, the gifts of service to feed those in need, the gift of giving to provide the food and other expenses, and the gifts of teaching or exhortation to share the gospel with the crowd altogether. Identifying the spiritual gifts of all the members of a local church is absolutely essential for developing evangelistic ministries needed to reach many of the unsaved. They should not have to outsource its evangelism to non-profit organizations.

How can the saints determine their spiritual gifts? Within the life of Spirit-filled righteousness, believers should begin examining their spiritual capabilities as they explore their use in a variety of ministries. These saints should consider their competency in expressing the gifts (Acts 6:3-4; 18:24-25) and the kinds of fruit that are produced (2 Corinthians 3:1-3; Romans 1:13). Their gifts should align with the desires, concerns, and burdens of their own hearts (Romans 10:1; 1 Corinthians 9:16). Their specific gifts should be confirmed by the saints who have similar giftedness (1 Corinthians 14:29), spiritual and biblical wisdom (Proverbs 1:5; 15:22), and those who are in authority (1 Peter 5:1-3; Hebrews 13:17).

Acts 6:3-4
Therefore select from among you, brothers, seven men of good report, full of the Holy Spirit and of wisdom, whom we may appoint over this business. But we will continue steadfastly in prayer and in the ministry of the word."

Acts 18:24-25
Now a certain Jew named Apollos, an Alexandrian by race, an eloquent man, came to Ephesus. He was mighty in the Scriptures. This man had been instructed in the way of the Lord; and being fervent in spirit, he spoke and taught accurately the things concerning Jesus, although he knew only the baptism of John.

LEADING THE WAY

2 Corinthians 3:1-3
Are we beginning again to commend ourselves? Or do we need, as do some, letters of commendation to you or from you? You are our letter, written in our hearts, known and read by all men, being revealed that you are a letter of Christ, served by us, written not with ink, but with the Spirit of the living God; not in tablets of stone, but in tablets that are hearts of flesh.

Romans 1:13
Now I don't desire to have you unaware, brothers, that I often planned to come to you, and was hindered so far, that I might have some fruit among you also, even as among the rest of the Gentiles.

Romans 10:1
Brothers, my heart's desire and my prayer to God is for Israel, that they may be saved.

1 Corinthians 9:16
For if I preach the Good News, I have nothing to boast about; for necessity is laid on me; but woe is to me if I don't preach the Good News.

1 Corinthians 14:29
Let the prophets speak, two or three, and let the others discern.

Proverbs 1:5
That the wise man may hear, and increase in learning; that the man of understanding may attain to sound counsel.

Proverbs 15:22
Where there is no counsel, plans fail; but in a multitude of counselors they are established.

1 Peter 5:1-3
Therefore I exhort the elders among you, as a fellow elder, and a witness of the sufferings of Christ, and who will also share in the glory that will be revealed: Shepherd the flock of God which is among you, exercising the oversight, not under compulsion, but voluntarily, not for dishonest gain, but willingly; not as lording it over those entrusted to you, but making yourselves examples to the flock.

Hebrews 13:17
Obey your leaders and submit to them, for they watch on behalf of your souls, as those who will give account, that they may do this with joy, and not with groaning, for that would be unprofitable for you.

A Contact with the Unsaved

One must their spend time with unbelievers to share the good news. Jesus interacted quite often with unbelievers and treated them with compassion (Matthew 9:35-38) and love (Mark 10:21-22). The Lord ate with them (Luke 5:29), had discussions with them (Matthew 9:3-6), taught them (Mark 4:1-2), met their personal needs (Luke 17:12-14), attended their weddings (John 2:1-4) and funerals (Matthew 9:23-26), and even served them (Matthew 15:32). He spent time with them on a regular basis and they desired the same. This does not mean the Lord was ever "bound together" with them (1 Corinthians 6:14). Christ spent time with them to preach the kingdom, but none were his close friends. The closest an unbeliever ever came to Jesus was Judas who pretended to believe. Christians should spend their time with unbelievers to share the gospel and with other believers for fellowship.

Matthew 9:35-38
Jesus went about all the cities and the villages, teaching in their synagogues and preaching the Good News of the Kingdom, and healing every disease and every sickness among the people. But when he saw the multitudes, he was moved with compassion for them because they were harassed and scattered, like sheep without a shepherd. Then he said to his disciples, "The harvest indeed is plentiful, but the laborers are few. Pray therefore that the Lord of the harvest will send out laborers into his harvest."

Mark 10:21-22
He said to him, "Teacher, I have observed all these things from my youth." Jesus looking at him loved him, and said to him, "One thing you lack. Go, sell whatever you have, and give to the poor, and you will have treasure in heaven; and come, follow me, taking up the cross."

Luke 5:29
Levi made a great feast for him in his house. There was a great crowd of tax collectors and others who were reclining with them.

LEADING THE WAY

Matthew 9:3-6
Behold, some...scribes said to themselves, "This man blasphemes." Jesus, knowing their thoughts, said, "Why do you think evil in your hearts? For which is easier, to say, 'Your sins are forgiven;' or to say, 'Get up, and walk?' But that you may know that the Son of Man has authority on Earth to forgive sins – " (then he said to the paralytic), "Get up, and take up your mat, and go to your house."

Mark 4:1-2
Again he began to teach by the seaside. A great multitude was gathered to him, so that he entered into a boat in the sea, and sat down. All the multitude were on the land by the sea. He taught them many things in parables, and told them in his teaching.

Luke 17:12-14
As he entered into a certain village, ten men who were lepers met him, who stood at a distance. They lifted up their voices, saying, "Jesus, Master, have mercy on us!" When he saw them, he said to them, "Go and show yourselves to the priests." As they went, they were cleansed.

John 2:1-4
The third day, there was a wedding in Cana of Galilee. Jesus' mother was there. Jesus also was invited, with his disciples, to the wedding. When the wine ran out, Jesus' mother said to him, "They have no wine." Jesus said to her, "Woman, what does that have to do with you and me? My hour has not yet come."

Matthew 9:23-26
When Jesus came into the ruler's house and saw the flute players and the crowd in noisy disorder, he said to them, "Make room, because the girl isn't dead, but sleeping." They were ridiculing him. But when the crowd was sent out, he entered in, took her by the hand, and the girl arose. The report of this went out into all that land.

Matthew 15:32
Jesus summoned his disciples and said, "I have compassion on the multitude, because they have continued with me now three days and have nothing to eat. I don't want to send them away fasting, or they might faint on the way."

1 Corinthians 6:14
Now God raised up the Lord, and will also raise us up by his power.

Matthew, who was a scorned tax-gatherer, invited many of his friends and acquaintances to his house to hear Christ.

In Matthew 9:10-12, the apostle records it in these words, "It happened as he sat in the house, behold, many tax collectors and sinners came and sat down with Jesus and his disciples. When the Pharisees saw it, they said to his disciples, 'Why does your teacher eat with tax collectors and sinners?' When Jesus heard it, he said to them, 'Those who are healthy have no need for a physician, but those who are sick do.'" The Lord went to share the good news with them. The Pharisees rebuked Him for eating with sinners and Jesus responded. He told them that the righteous do not need Him, but sinners do. Jesus dined with a man named Zacchaeus in Luke 19:10. Once again, He was rebuked, but Jesus told them that He had come to seek and save the lost.

Matthew 9:10-12
As he sat in the house...many tax collectors and sinners came and sat down with Jesus and his disciples. When the Pharisees saw it, they said to his disciples, "Why does your teacher eat with tax collectors and sinners?" When Jesus heard it, he said to them, "Those who are healthy have no need for a physician, but those who are sick do.

Luke 19:10
For the Son of Man came to seek and to save that which was lost.

Those who do not know and love the Lord Jesus Christ have to be sought out. We cannot expect them to come to us for the gospel. Most will never come to a church to hear the pastor preach the gospel. Christians will have to depart from their churches and venture out into the world to tell them. In Matthew 4:23, the apostle describes Jesus preaching the gospel all throughout Galilee. He went where they lived! Throughout the book of Acts, Paul traveled to numerous regions where the unsaved lived to share the gospel with them. He found unbelievers in the many different marketplaces buying, selling, and socializing. Paul entered into the midst of them and began to share the Word. What better place to go? This was where the unbelievers were frequently gathered. This was where life was being lived.

Matthew 4:23
Jesus went about in all Galilee, teaching in their synagogues, preaching the Good News of the Kingdom, and healing every disease and every sickness among the people.

Christians must seek the unsaved in their neighborhoods, clubs, associations, and other organizations to which they belong and share the gospel. Christians may inadvertently become isolated from the unsaved world as they spend more and more time with family members and church friends. They lose the opportunity of sharing the good news because they no longer know any unsaved people. It is important for Christians to seek out their own kind but must also seek out unbelievers to win them to Christ.

An Individually Tailored Presentation

In the New Testament, the same essential saving elements are found in every presentation of the gospel. Yet, they were all very different. One will not find in the Scriptures any two gospel presentations which were exactly the same. In John 3:1-5, Nicodemus, an important teacher in Israel, came to Jesus to speak with Him. Jesus presented the gospel as being born again with both water and the Spirit. Jesus expected Nicodemus to know the passage he was referring to (Ezekiel 36:25-27). In this passage, God says He will cleanse His holy people with water and the Spirit to give them a new heart.

John 3:1-5
Now there was a man of the Pharisees named Nicodemus, a ruler of the Jews. The same came to him by night, and said to him, "Rabbi, we know that you are a teacher come from God, for no one can do these signs that you do, unless God is with him." Jesus answered him, "Most certainly, I tell you, unless one is born anew, he can't see God's Kingdom." Nicodemus said to him, "How can a man be born when he is old? Can he enter a second time into his mother's womb, and be born?" Jesus answered, "Most certainly I tell you, unless one is born of water and spirit, he can't enter into God's Kingdom.

Ezekiel 36:25-27
I will sprinkle clean water on you, and you will be clean. I will cleanse you from all your filthiness, and from all your idols. I will also give you a new heart, and I will put a new spirit within you. I will take away the stony heart out of your flesh, and I will give you a heart of flesh. I will put my Spirit within you, and cause you to walk in my statutes. You will keep my ordinances and do them.

In John 4:6-10, Jesus was sitting at a well and proclaimed the gospel to a Samaritan woman who had come to draw some water. Christ described Himself as having living water (the gospel) which sprang into eternal life. The Samaritan woman was poor and ignorant of the Scriptures. He was sitting in front of a well. She had come to draw water. This became the perfect opportunity to utilize the situation to His advantage. He simply began to speak of a different kind of water that He could offer her.

John 4:6-10
Jacob's well was there. Jesus therefore, being tired from his journey, sat down by the well. It was about the sixth hour. A woman of Samaria came to draw water. Jesus said to her, "Give me a drink." For his disciples had gone away into the city to buy food. The Samaritan woman therefore said to him, "How is it that you, being a Jew, ask for a drink from me, a Samaritan woman?" (For Jews have no dealings with Samaritans.) Jesus answered her, "If you knew the gift of God, and who it is who says to you, 'Give me a drink,' you would have asked him, and he would have given you living water."

Peter had a completely different situation occur. On the day of Pentecost, there was a loud noise like a wind, and those in the upper room who were praying came pouring out into the street below. They began speaking in the many different languages of the people present that day. This was the fulfillment of a prophecy by the Holy Spirit and Peter knew it. In Acts 2:14-16, Luke describes this amazing scene, "But Peter, standing up with the eleven, lifted up his voice, and spoke out to them, 'You men of Judea, and all you who dwell at Jerusalem, let this be known to you, and listen to my words.'" The apostle calls them to attention. Then adds,

"For these aren't drunken, as you suppose, seeing it is only the third hour of the day. But this is what has been spoken through the prophet Joel." Peter began his presentation with what was happening at that moment. His listeners, who had gathered, were devout Jews and would have known the prophecy which was being fulfilled right before their eyes.

Acts 2:14-16
But Peter, standing up with the eleven, lifted up his voice and spoke out to them, "You men of Judea, and all you who dwell at Jerusalem, let this be known to you, and listen to my words. For these aren't drunken, as you suppose, seeing it is only the third hour of the day. But this is what has been spoken through the prophet Joel.

Sometime later, another very different encounter occurs. In Acts 3:12, Peter preached the gospel beginning with the power and name of Jesus. He had been put to death and rose again. It was His power that healed the lame man who was now walking before their eyes. There had been only a very short time since Christ's crucifixion. They would have been very familiar with the death of Christ. In Acts 8:29-35, Philip met the Ethiopian eunuch who was reading from Isaiah; he began his presentation in that passage. The eunuch was a God-fearing Gentile, so he was familiar the Scriptures.

Acts 3:12
When Peter saw it, he responded to the people, "You men of Israel, why do you marvel at this man? Why do you fasten your eyes on us, as though by our own power or godliness we had made him walk?"

Acts 8:29-35
The Spirit said to Philip, "Go near...join yourself to this chariot." Philip ran to him, and heard him reading Isaiah the prophet, and said, "Do you understand what you are reading?" He said, "How can I, unless someone explains it to me?" He begged Philip to come up and sit with him. Now the passage of the Scripture which he was reading was this," He was led as a sheep to the slaughter. As a lamb before his shearer is silent, so he doesn't open his mouth. In his humiliation, his judgment was taken away. Who will declare His generation? For his life is taken from the Earth. "The eunuch answered Philip, "Who is the prophet talking about? About himself, or about someone else?" Philip opened his mouth, and beginning from this Scripture, preached...Jesus.

In Acts 13:15-23, Paul entered a synagogue on the Sabbath in Pisidian Antioch and spoke from the Old Testament and its prophecies in the scrolls in front of him. He proclaimed God's deliverance of Israel from Egypt, in the wilderness, in Canaan through the times of the judges, all throughout the entire era of the kings, and through the promised Messiah. In Nazareth, the Lord also read from the Holy Scriptures, and He proclaimed that He was the fulfillment of the many prophecies of the Old Testament (Luke 4:21). In both cases, His audience would have been devout Jews who understood all these things. This was an excellent starting point for His proclamation of the Kingdom of God. They would know all of the Messianic prophecies.

Acts 13:16-23
Paul stood up, and beckoning with his hand said, "Men of Israel, and you who fear God, listen. The God of this people chose our fathers, and exalted the people when they stayed as aliens in the land of Egypt, and with an uplifted arm, he led them out of it....When he...destroyed seven nations in the land of Canaan....he raised up David to be their king, to whom he also testified, 'I have found David the son of Jesse, a man after my heart, who will do all my will.' From this man's offspring, God has brought salvation to Israel according to his promise,

Luke 4:21
He began to tell them, "Today, this Scripture has been fulfilled in your hearing."

In Acts 14:8-15, Paul arrives in Lystra and heals a crippled man. A crowd gathers and declares them to be two gods to which Paul preached the gospel using creation as a starting point. Paul was speaking to polytheistic heathens on the street, so he began with the God of creation. In Acts 17:23-25, Paul enters Athens and notices the statue dedicated to an unknown god among many statutes of false deities. He then proclaimed to the people that he had come to reveal to them the identity of this unknown god. Paul realized that these intellectuals did not want to offend any god they may have forgotten and began his presentation there.

Acts 14:8-15
At Lystra a certain man sat, impotent in his feet, a cripple from his mother's womb, who never had walked. He was listening to Paul speaking, who, fastening eyes on him, and seeing that he had faith to be made whole, said with a loud voice, "Stand upright on your feet!" He leaped up and walked...But when the apostles, Barnabas and Paul, heard of it, they tore their clothes, and sprang into the multitude, crying out, "Men, why are you doing these things? We also are men of like passions with you, and bring you good news, that you should turn from these vain things to the living God, who made the sky...earth...sea...."

Acts 17:23-25
For as I passed along and observed the objects of your worship, I also found an altar with this inscription: 'TO AN UNKNOWN GOD.' What therefore you worship in ignorance, I announce to you. The God who made the world and all things in it, he, being Lord of heaven and Earth, doesn't dwell in temples made with hands. He isn't served by men's hands, as though he needed anything, seeing he himself gives to all life and breath, and all things.

In Acts 22:1-3, when Paul was arrested in Jerusalem for supposedly bringing a Gentile into the temple, Paul stood before a large crowd of Jews and began with his personal testimony and how he had come to Christ as a Jew in their Hebrew language. He personalized his approach to people who were listening to him. This is a critical understanding. The good news is best proclaimed in response to a given situation and given context utilizing the essential elements of the gospel message. The presentation was weaved around the preacher, the one who was to hear it, and the situation in which they found themselves. Then, the essential gospel message was proclaimed. This does not mean that Christians do not have the right to simply begin with heralding the message of salvation. As an ancient messenger would have done with a proclamation from the king, so shall we do.

Acts 22:1-3
"Brothers and fathers, listen to the defense which I now make to you." When they heard that he spoke to them in the Hebrew language, they were even more quiet. He said, "I am indeed a Jew, born in Tarsus of Cilicia, but brought up in this city at the feet of Gamaliel, instructed according to the strict tradition of the law of our fathers, being zealous for God, even as you all are today.

A Lack of Hindrance to the Gospel

Paul was extremely sensitive to people. He did not want to offend them so they would refuse to listen to the gospel. In 1 Corinthians 8-10, Paul discusses Christian liberty. Then in 1 Corinthians 10:32-33, Paul summarizes his teaching on this important truth, "Give no occasions for stumbling, either to Jews, or to Greeks, or to the assembly of God; even as I also please all men in all things, not seeking my own profit, but the profit of the many, that they may be saved." God's people are to give no opportunity for stumbling to believers or unbelievers. He desired to please all men in all things, seeking the profit of the many to be saved, not his own.

1 Corinthians 10:32-33
Give no occasion for stumbling, whether to Jews, or to Greeks, or to the assembly of God; even as I also please all men in all things, not seeking my own profit, but the profit of the many, that they may be saved.

In 1 Corinthians 9:12, the apostle declares that he could have asked for remuneration from them for his preaching, but he didn't. He did not want to cause a hindrance to the gospel. The context for these key passages is our Christian liberty. It is in the area of Christian liberty that believers do not want to offend those who will be hearing the gospel.

1 Corinthians 9:12
If others partake of this right over you, don't we yet more? Nevertheless we didn't use this right, but we bear all things, that we may cause no hindrance to the Good News of Christ.

Not a Lack of Offense

This hindrance has nothing to do with the offense of the good news. A gospel of sin and judgment will offend. A Son of God who dies and rises from the dead will offend. In 1

Peter 2:8, Peter declares that the Lord Jesus Christ is a stone that people will stumble over and a rock that will offend them. In 1 Corinthians 1:23, the apostle proclaimed that the continual preaching of the crucifixion and person of Jesus Christ was a stumbling block to Jews and foolishness to Gentiles. When Christians preach the good news, it will offend some; to the ones who are being saved, it is the power of God (verse 18). Therefore, they should not water down the gospel.

1 Peter 2:8
And, "a stumbling stone and a rock of offense." For they stumble at the word, being disobedient, to which also they were appointed.

1 Corinthians 1:23
But we preach Christ crucified: a stumbling block to Jews, and foolishness to Greeks.

1 Corinthians 1:18
For the word of the cross is foolishness to those who are dying, but to us who are being saved it is the power of God.

Not an Issue of Holiness

This offense has nothing to do with personal holiness. Christians are not to compromise their holiness in order to keep the gospel from offending someone. They cannot sin in order to fit in. They cannot participate in evil, so the good news is then welcomed by unbelievers. Paul describes his behavior among the unsaved and the saved as being pure, holy, and with godly sincerity. His conscience testified of this, and it resulted in a real confidence (2 Corinthians 1:12). Paul never in any way compromised his holiness to share the gospel with the Jews and Gentiles. In fact, he went out of his way to make sure no one could accuse him of any kind of wrongdoing or evil.

2 Corinthians 1:12
For our boasting is this: the testimony of our conscience, that in holiness and sincerity of God, not in fleshly wisdom but in the grace of God we behaved ourselves in the world, and more abundantly toward you.

Christians cannot compromise their righteousness to adhere to some sinful custom or cultural activity. Jesus was accused of being a drunkard and a glutton, but these were lies. Jesus associated with the lost in order to share the good news with them (Matthew 11:19), but He did not sin with them. Christ merely associated with them. That is all. This is an important and critical distinction.

Not a Problem of Doctrine

This hindrance has nothing to do with sound doctrine. A group of false teachers had unknowingly crept into Galatia and demanded that all Gentile believers become God-fearing Jews first, then believers. All these false teachers promoted circumcision, legalism, and ritual among the Christians. In Galatians 2:4-5, Paul stands against these false teachers who wanted to bring them into bondage. In Acts 15:1-2, at the end of his first missionary journey, Paul settled into Antioch, and these kinds of teachers came into their congregation. So, Paul stood against them and was unwilling to compromise. When it comes to doctrine, Christians cannot compromise doctrine in order to prevent an offense of the gospel. Some doctrines can appear intolerant but ignoring them will not remove the offense.

Galatians 2:4-5
This was because of the false brothers secretly brought in, who stole in to spy out our liberty which we have in Christ Jesus, that they might bring us into bondage, to whom we gave no place in the way of subjection, not for an hour, that the truth of the Good News might continue with you.

Acts 15:1-2
Some men came down from Judea and taught the brothers, "Unless you are circumcised after the custom of Moses, you can't be saved." Therefore when Paul and Barnabas had no small discord and discussion with them, they appointed Paul and Barnabas, and some others of them, to go up to Jerusalem to the apostles and elders about this question.

A Removal of Christian Liberty

Finally, the hindrance to which Paul is speaking does not involve the offense of the gospel, personal holiness, or sound doctrine. Instead, it involves the area of Christian liberty. Paul defined Christian liberty in 1 Corinthians 8:8-9, when he discussed the eating of meat that had been sacrificed to idols and then sold in the marketplace. In verses 4-7, Paul disclosed that there were some who lacked knowledge and would not ever eat meat sacrificed to idols because they thought it defiled them. He explains that there was no defilement due to the idol being nothing. Then in verses 8-9, he makes an important general statement when he asserts that eating any particular food did not commend Christians to their God. Their relationship to the Lord is not better or worse for it. Caution should be taken because this liberty might be a stumbling block to the weak. Christian liberty involves things that are basically spiritually neutral. They will not spiritually help nor hinder believers, such as food.

1 Corinthians 8:8-9
But food will not commend us to God. For neither, if we don't eat, are we the worse; nor, if we eat, are we the better. But be careful that by no means does this liberty of yours become a stumbling block to the weak.

1 Corinthians 8:4-7
Therefore concerning the eating of things sacrificed to idols, we know that no idol is anything in the world, and that there is no other God but one. For though there are things that are called "gods", whether in the heavens or on Earth; as there are many "gods" and many "lords"; yet to us there is one God, the Father, of whom are all things, and we for him; and one Lord, Jesus Christ, through

whom are all things, and we live through him. However, that knowledge isn't in all men. But some, with consciousness of the idol until now, eat as of a thing sacrificed to an idol, and their conscience, being weak, is defiled.

One more important thought. Christians may not show "solidarity" to another religion by engaging in one of their idolatrous practices. In 1 Corinthians 10:14, Paul commands the saints to flee from idolatry. John utters almost the exact same exhortation in 1 John 5:21. Here, he indicates that they should guard themselves from idolatry. In fact, idolatry is listed as one of the deeds of the flesh (sins) in Galatians 5:20. Believers cannot participate in false religious rituals because these are from the doctrines of demons (1 Timothy 4:1). They would be a part of demonic worship. Also, this is completely unacceptable to God. Paul continued this important thought in Romans 14:23. He exhorted the Romans not to eat any kind of food if they had doubts. This eating would not come from faith. What does not come from faith is sin for them. According to 1 Corinthians 2:9-12, if Christians know that something within their Christian liberty is seen as a sin to another person, they should not do it. This encourages that weaker one to act against their conscience. For this person, it would be sin.

1 Corinthians 10:14
Therefore, my beloved, flee from idolatry.

1 John 5:21
Little children, keep yourselves from idols.

Galatians 5:20
Idolatry, sorcery, hatred, strife, jealousies, outbursts of anger, rivalries, divisions, heresies.

1 Timothy 4:1
But the Spirit says expressly that in later times some will fall away from the faith, paying attention to seducing spirits and doctrines of demons.

Romans 14:23
But he who doubts is condemned if he eats, because it isn't of faith; and whatever is not of faith is sin.

1 Corinthians 2:9-12
But as it is written, Things which an eye didn't see, and an ear didn't hear, which didn't enter into the heart of man, these God has prepared for those who love him." But to us, God revealed them through the Spirit. For the Spirit searches all things, yes, the deep things of God. For who among men knows the things of a man, except the spirit of the man, which is in him? Even so, no one knows the things of God, except God's Spirit. But we received not the spirit of the world, but the Spirit which is from God, that we might know the things that were freely given to us by God.

Another area of Christian liberty involves the rights saints have that could be set aside so the spread of the gospel is not hindered. The example Paul used in 1 Corinthians 9, was his right to earn a living from his proclaiming of the gospel. Many false teachers were preaching among the churches for the purpose of peddling God's Word and attempting to gain money from the gospel (2 Corinthians 2:17). Paul refused to be accused of this sinful behavior, so Paul worked with his own hands to support himself. In verses 13-15, he set aside that right. Now there would be no offense and no hindrance.

2 Corinthians 2:17
For we are not as so many, peddling the word of God. But as of sincerity, but as of God, in the sight of God, we speak in Christ.

1 Corinthians 9:13-15
Don't you know that those who serve around sacred things eat from the things of the temple, and those who wait on the altar have their portion with the altar? Even so the Lord ordained that those who proclaim the Good News should live from the Good News. But I have used none of these things, and I don't write these things that it may be done so in my case; for I would rather die, than that anyone should make my boasting void.

Another area of the believer's liberty involves man-made customs, manners, and social etiquette. Christians are not bound by these practices. In Romans 12:17, Paul discloses that Christians are to respect what is right in the sight of all men. Men deem certain things as respectable, and they are to respect those things for the sake of the gospel.

Romans 12:17
Repay no one evil for evil. Respect what is honorable in the sight of all men.

In 1 Corinthians 9:19-22, the apostle Paul summarized his personal evangelistic strategy in this area. He explains, "For though I was free from all, I brought myself under bondage to all, that I might gain the more. To the Jews I became a Jew [behaved like a Jew], that I might gain Jews; to those who are under the law, [behaved] as under the law, that I might gain those who are under the law; to those who are without law [Gentiles], as [behaving] without law (not being without law toward God [commandments], but under law toward Christ), that I might win those who are without law. To the weak I became as weak [spiritually], that I might gain the weak. I have become [in behavior] all things to all men, that I may by all means save some."

1 Corinthians 9:19-22
For though I was free from all, I brought myself under bondage to all, that I might gain the more. To the Jews I became as a Jew, that I might gain Jews; to those who are under the law, as under the law, that I might gain those who are under the law; to those who are without law, as without law (not being without law toward God, but under law toward Christ), that I might win those who are without law. To the weak I became as weak, that I might gain the weak. I have become all things to all men, that I may by all means save some.

He told the church at Corinth that though he was free from everything, he brought himself under bondage to win some for Christ. To the Jews, he gave up rights or took on customs that they respected. Then, he did the same for the Gentiles. To the weak, he became weak not eating certain food. Paul became all things to all men, so some would be won to the gospel. Then the apostle describes the utter self-control that was needed to accomplish this by comparing the Christian life to a race.

In 1 Corinthians 10:32-33, Paul told his readers he did not want to offend or give an opportunity for their stumbling. Paul, the apostle, meant he would not offend others with spiritually neutral objects given significance by them. This also included rights that he had which others had abused, or practices, customs, or social etiquette that were meaningful to others. Once again, becoming "all things to all men" will never involve the offense of the gospel, the holiness of Christians, or the true doctrines of the faith. Christians are to be careful that in their lives in the community, they do not bring some hindrance to the gospel. Christians are not to offend those who are unsaved or saved in their Christian liberty. These saints must be careful because they cannot know whether someone that they may have offended, was to be brought to Christ through them.

1 Corinthians 10:32-33
Give no occasion for stumbling, whether to Jews...Greeks...even as I also please all men in all things, not seeking my own profit, but the profit of the many, that they may be saved.

A Love Relationship in Christ

Christians are to portray Christ to the world by the way they interact with each other. The Lord has placed Christians into a very unique relationship with each other. Saints are called into one flock (John 10:7-11), one vine (John 15:1-2), one kingdom (Colossians 1:13), one body (1 Corinthians 12:12-14), one citizenship and family (Ephesians 2:19), one bride betrothed to one groom (Ephesians 5:22-24), and one temple (Ephesians 2:20-22). Regardless of their ethnicities, backgrounds, social status, and gender, they are called into one body by the Spirit. Paul declares in 1 Corinthians 12:13 that all Christians are baptized into and made to drink of one Spirit. How believers interact with one another is to be a testimony to the world. They demonstrate that Christ is alive and is at work among them. This unity can only be achieved supernaturally, and the world knows it.

John 10:7-11
Jesus therefore said to them again, "Most certainly, I tell you, I am the sheep's door. All who came before me are thieves and robbers, but the sheep didn't listen to them. I am the door. If anyone enters in by me, he will be saved, and will go in and go out, and will find pasture. The thief only comes to steal, kill, and destroy. I came that they may have life, and may have it abundantly. I am the good shepherd.

John 15:1-2
I am the true vine, and my Father is the farmer. Every branch in me that doesn't bear fruit, he takes away. Every branch that bears fruit, he prunes, that it may bear more fruit.

Colossians 1:13
Who delivered us out of the power of darkness, and translated us into the Kingdom of the Son of his love.

1 Corinthians 12:12-14
For as the body is one, and has many members, and all the members of the body, being many, are one body; so also is Christ. For in one Spirit we were all baptized into one body, whether Jews or Greeks, whether bond or free; and were all given to drink into one Spirit. For the body is not one member, but many.

Ephesians 2:19
So then you are no longer strangers and foreigners, but you are fellow citizens with the saints and of the household of God.

Ephesians 5:22-24
Wives, be subject to your own husbands, as to the Lord. For the husband is the head of the wife, as Christ also is the head of the assembly, being himself the savior of the body. But as the assembly is subject to Christ, so let the wives also be to their own husbands in everything.

Ephesians 2:20-22
Being built on the foundation of the apostles and prophets, Christ Jesus himself being the chief cornerstone; in whom the whole building, fitted together, grows into a holy temple in the Lord; in whom you also are built together for a habitation of God in the Spirit.

1 Corinthians 12:13
For in one Spirit we were all baptized into one body, whether Jews or Greeks, whether bond or free; and were all given to drink into one Spirit.

In the New Testament, this important corporate witness of the early church involved the amazing fellowship that Christians were having with one another. One simply has to trace these two words with a concordance and will see the importance of these "one another" commands. Besides these commands, it involved teaching, prayer, and communion. In Acts 2:40-41, Peter standing with the others from the upper room preached a sermon and about 3,000 came to Christ.

Acts 2:40-41
With many other words he testified, and exhorted them, saying, "Save yourselves from this crooked generation!" Then those who gladly received his word were baptized. There were added that day about three thousand souls.

In Acts 2:42-46, Luke describes their interaction when he writes, "They continued steadfastly in the apostles' teaching and fellowship, in the breaking of bread, and prayer. Fear came on every soul, and many wonders and signs were done through the apostles. All who believed were together and had all things in common. They sold their possessions and goods, and distributed them to all, according as anyone had need. Day by day, continuing steadfastly with one accord in the temple, and breaking bread at home, they took their food with gladness and singleness of heart."

Acts 2:40-41
With many other words he testified, and exhorted them, saying, "Save yourselves from this crooked generation!" Then those who gladly received his word were baptized. There were added that day about three thousand souls.

It involved fellowship (ministry), the breaking of bread (communion), prayer, and devotion to the teaching given by the apostles. Every day they were meeting in the temple and each other's homes with joy and sincerity. They took care of any person having need. This was all done in public view with a powerful impact. In verse 47, Luke concludes that the saints had favor with the people and increased in number. It is seen again in Acts 4:32-36. Peter had completed his second sermon and about 5,000 were saved. This brought the size of the church to over 10,000 counting the woman and children who were saved. This assembly was of one heart and soul. They met the needs of others through the mutual sharing of of material possessions in common.

Acts 2:47
Praising God, and having favor with all the people. The Lord added to the assembly day by day those who were being saved.

Acts 2:42-46
They continued steadfastly in the apostles' teaching and fellowship, in the breaking of bread, and prayer. Fear came on every soul, and many wonders and signs were done through the apostles. All who believed were together, and had all things in common. They sold their possessions and goods, and distributed them to all, according as anyone had need. Day by day, continuing steadfastly with one accord in the temple, and breaking bread at home, they took their food with gladness and singleness of hear.

In Acts 5:1-5, Ananias and Sapphira fell dead from God's hand because the two of them had deceived the church. Yet, more importantly, they had lied to God about the profits of the land they sold for an offering. This had quite an impact on the community around them. In verses 11-13, the author recounts that some people were too afraid to join, but others were coming to Jesus Christ. Great fear came upon everyone who heard, but all the people honored them. These actions among the saints were having a huge impact. The gospel, which Christians preach, may cause some to call them foolish (1 Corinthians 1:23) and others to claim they are mad

(Acts 26:24). Some people will criticize and revile them for the gospel's sake (Matthew 5:11), but the unsaved world cannot criticize the true fellowship believers have together in love, sacrifice, sharing, and unity. They will be compelled to stand in awe and respond with deep respect for what they have in Christ.

Acts 5:1-5
But a certain man named Ananias, with Sapphira, his wife, sold a possession, and kept back part of the price, his wife also being aware of it, then brought a certain part and laid it at the apostles' feet. But Peter said, "Ananias, why has Satan filled your heart to lie to the Holy Spirit and to keep back part of the price of the land? While you kept it, didn't it remain your own? After it was sold, wasn't it in your power? How is it that you have conceived this thing in your heart? You haven't lied to men, but to God." Ananias, hearing these words, fell down and died. Great fear came on all who heard these things.

Acts 5:11-13
Great fear came on the whole assembly, and on all who heard these things. By the hands of the apostles many signs and wonders were done among the people. They were all with one accord in Solomon's porch. None of the rest dared to join them, however the people honored them.

1 Corinthians 1:23
But we preach Christ crucified: a stumbling block to Jews, and foolishness to Greeks,

Acts 26:24
As he thus made his defense, Festus said with a loud voice, "Paul, you are crazy! Your great learning is driving you insane!"

Matthew 5:11
Blessed are you when people reproach you, persecute you, and say all kinds of evil against you falsely, for my sake.

The world longs for what Christians are able to produce in Christ. This can only be produced through the power of the Holy Spirit. In fact, Paul lists the fruits of the Holy Spirit in Galatians 5:22-23 and most have to do with interaction with others: love, joy, peace, patience, kindness, goodness, faith, gentleness, and self-control. The evil deeds of the flesh in verses 19-21 have to do with a believer's interaction with others: hate, strife, adultery, sexual immorality, uncleanness, lusting, idolatry, sorcery, jealousy, anger, rivalries, divisions, heresies, being envious, murders, orgies, and drunkenness. Which of these will be a testimony to the world? None. Both Jesus and Paul portray Christians as lights to the world that should shine brightly (Matthew 5:15, Philippians 2:15). As a body, the saved must portray their light in the fruits of the Spirit to all. James accused believers of arguing and fighting among themselves due to the desires and lusts of the flesh and friendship with the world (James 4:1-6). Paul accused saints of grumbling against one another (Philippians 2:14).

Galatians 5:22-23
But the fruit of the Spirit is love, joy, peace, patience, kindness, goodness, faith, gentleness, and self-control. Against such things there is no law.

Galatians 5:19-21
Now the deeds of the flesh are obvious, which are: adultery, sexual immorality, uncleanness, lustfulness, idolatry, sorcery, hatred, strife, jealousies, outbursts of anger, rivalries, divisions, heresies, envy, murders, drunkenness, orgies, and things like these; of which I forewarn you, even as I also forewarned you, that those who practice such things will not inherit God's Kingdom.

Matthew 5:15
Neither do you light a lamp and put it under a measuring basket, but on a stand; and it shines to all who are in the house.

Philippians 2:15
That you may become blameless and harmless, children of God without defect in the middle of a crooked and perverse generation, among whom you are seen as lights in the world.

James 4:1-6
Where do wars and fightings among you come from? Don't they come from your pleasures that war in your members? You lust, and don't have. You murder and covet, and can't obtain. You fight and make war. You don't have, because you don't ask. You ask, and don't receive, because you ask with wrong motives, so that you may spend it on your pleasures. You adulterers and adulteresses, don't you know that friendship with the world is hostility toward

God? Whoever therefore wants to be a friend of the world makes himself an enemy of God. But he gives more grace. Therefore it says, "God resists the proud, but gives grace to the humble."

Philippians 2:14
Do all things without complaining and arguing.

The apostle Paul accused the saints in Corinth of having too many divisive and contentious groups. These different groups were organized according to the teachers that they followed. There was Paul, Peter, Apollos, and Jesus Christ (1 Corinthians 1:10-12). They were not displaying the fruits of the Spirit for all to see. Jesus sums up this concept in John 13: 14-17 in the upper room at the last supper.

1 Corinthians 1:10-12
Now I beg you, brothers, through the name of our Lord, Jesus Christ, that you all speak the same thing, and that there be no divisions among you, but that you be perfected together in the same mind and in the same judgment. For it has been reported to me concerning you, my brothers, by those who are from Chloe's household, that there are contentions among you. Now I mean this, that each one of you says, "I follow Paul," "I follow Apollos," "I follow Cephas," and, "I follow Christ."

John 13:14-17
If I then, the Lord and the Teacher, have washed your feet, you also ought to wash one another's feet. For I have given you an example, that you should also do as I have done to you. Most certainly I tell you, a servant is not greater than his lord, neither is one who is sent greater than he who sent him. If you know these things, blessed are you if you do them.

In Luke 22:24-30, the author discloses that there grew a dispute among the apostles as to who was the greatest. This dispute demonstrated the lack of a servant attitude and love. Jesus began the supper by washing the apostles' feet and then gave them a new commandment. They were to love one another as Christ had loved them. By this, the world would know that they were His disciples. Christians are to be a part of a local congregation. How they interact with each other will testify of the authenticity of their relationship to Christ.

This love should have a huge impact but so may strife and divisions. The local church will be a witness for good or bad depending on their interactions with each other.

Luke 22:24-27
A dispute also arose among them, which of them was considered to be greatest. He said to them, "The kings of the nations lord it over them, and those who have authority over them are called 'benefactors.' But not so with you. But one who is the greater among you, let him become as the younger, and one who is governing, as one who serves. For who is greater, one who sits at the table, or one who serves? Isn't it he who sits at the table? But I am among you as one who serves."

An Ancient Portrait

In John 4:1-30, the apostle John records an extraordinary incident between Jesus and a Samaritan woman. On his way to Galilee, Jesus and His disciples stopped at a Samaritan village called Sychar. Wearied from His journey, Jesus sat down at a well and asked His disciples to go into town about one half of a mile away and retrieve some food. Around six in the evening, a Samaritan woman came to fetch water from the well. Though current Jewish custom did not allow men or rabbis to speak to any women in public, Jesus decided to speak to the woman. Though there was animosity between the Jews (pure race) and the Samaritans (unclean half-Jew, half Gentile), Jesus began an interaction with the woman.

He did not wait for His disciples to return so they could preach; instead, Jesus took His own individual responsibility to do it. The Lord lived among the unsaved, not cloistered with only believers around Him, and He saw this moment with this woman as a potential evangelistic encounter. So, Jesus Christ began a conversation about water. He tailored His presentation of the gospel around the well and water she was fetching. He simply asked her for a drink of water. The

Samaritan woman was stunned and inquired as to why a Jewish man would even speak to her let alone ask her for something.

The Messiah followed one of His evangelistic strategies which was to utilize physical questions which had spiritual meanings attached to them. So, he replied that if she knew the gift of God that was sitting before her, she would request of Him living water (He was a well providing the water of eternal life). Of course, at first, she explained to Him that she did not understand how He could give her water when He did not have a physical bucket. She was baffled by now and asked Him how He could be greater than Jacob who dug the well.

He had no access to water of any kind except the well and had no bucket. This did not make sense. Jesus challenged her to think about His words and drew her attention completely to Him. Then the Lord explained His analogy. Jesus was offering her water that was spiritual flowing out of His well (Himself) that sprang up into eternal life. From His living water, she would never thirst again because it was forever and ever. She could still not understand the spiritual intent of His words, so she begs Him for this never-ending water. She did not want to keep traveling the half mile every day.

We know historically that there was water closer, but it is obvious she was not allowed to partake of it because of her sinful deeds. She was a shunned woman and was probably turned away by the other women in Sychar. He knew this because He knew what was in all people. Jesus then indicted her for the sinful life she has been leading with a loaded statement. He requested that she go and return to Him with her husband. Jesus did not worry about the offense of sin. She could not find salvation by repentance if her sin was not confronted. Jesus was giving her an opportunity to repent before Him in order to be saved.

The woman responded with a safe answer that would not expose her sinful life for what it was. She replied that she did not have a husband. He glared at her and stated the true sinful facts. She had five husbands and the man she was currently living with was not one of them. Immediately, she knew she had been exposed by someone who must at least be a prophet. Yet, she does not repent. After a discussion about true worship, she declares that the Messiah will come and explain all things. Then Jesus identifies Himself as that Messiah. Here the Lord Jesus Christ clearly states that He is the Anointed One. Rather than repent and receive Him as Savior and Lord, the woman left her water pot and ran into the city to tell people about this man at the well. She asked if they thought He could possibly be the Messiah. Many came to meet Him and entreated him to stay in the city and speak with them. The Lord Jesus remained there two days and proclaimed the good news. Though John does not record whether the Samaritan woman came to Christ, he wrote that many believed. Here Jesus utilized His own interests and skills to bring many to Himself.

A Modern Anecdote

When I came to Christ, I wanted the tools necessary to prove my faith. I was on a prestigious college campus where the students were debating many philosophies and ways of looking at life, and I wanted to get into the game. I loved the intellectual stimulation of deep investigation, research, and discussion. I had joined a campus group of Christians who were extremely evangelistic. They had set a table up in the center of our campus and many of us manned the table and discussed Jesus with those passing by.

We had heard that a new book had been published with the proofs for the veracity of the Bible and the Sonship of Jesus Christ. It explained in detail the fulfilled prophecies, miracles, and proofs for the resurrection of Jesus Christ. This was exactly where my interests were. I was so thrilled and desirous of this book that I drove up to the speaker's office to get one of the first copies. With that in hand, as soon as the new semester registration began, I registered for my first speech class. I did not know how I would work it in, but I was going to utilize this book and share the proofs for the plan of redemption every chance I got.

I thought a speech class would be a "captive" audience to share the gospel and they were. Not wanting to overdo it, I tried to share the gospel in every other speech. When we had a speech where we had to use visuals, I developed a series of slides on the proofs for the resurrection. Every slide took them progressively through the verification of Jesus Christ's death on the cross. I had slides which discussed the blood and water pouring out of His side, the lack of need to break His legs to suffocate him, the ritualistic Jewish burial with the oils, perfumes, and tightly wound bandages, the known location of the tomb, the massive rock that was placed in front of it, the sealing of it with the insignia of the Roman emperor, and the placing of the guards before it.

Then I discussed the empty tomb of Jesus, the bandages lying flat with the headpiece rolled up, the removal of the stone, the breaking of the official seal, the passing out of the guards, and the angelic presence when the first witnesses came. After this, I shared with the class the testimony of each and every witness to the resurrected Christ. I was so excited, enthusiastic, and committed. I wanted everyone to believe and receive Jesus Christ as Savior and Lord. I even gave an invitation to invite Christ into their lives after class with me or even ask some questions or have a dialogue.

After the presentation, the instructor complemented me on my skills and preparation as a speaker. Then he casually mentioned that he probably would have considered picking a different topic, but it was certainly my choice. Everyone just sat there in silence. After several more speeches the class was finally over. As I was walking out of the room figuring that nothing had happened, I felt a tap on my right shoulder. This young man behind me quietly mumbled, "Can I talk to you?" I agreed, so Dennis and I went for coffee at one of the college cafes. I admit that I was nervous, but I knew the Lord would work His will in this situation.

He began to describe how depressed he had been since he started college. Everything seemed simple and clear in high school, but everything he valued was now questioned and he felt there was no place to land. He knew that if he landed on some man-made philosophy, it would crumble. When I shared the Lord Jesus Christ and the solid evidence and power of his death and resurrection, he told himself, "This Jesus was more than a man and this book was more than a philosophy book. This was the truth." Then he asked me to help him receive Christ as Savior and Lord. Right there, in that cafe at a major university I had the privilege of bringing him to Christ. I utilized my interests and skills to share the gospel. Then I made an opportunity to share the gospel with my fellow students. Finally, I had to allow God to do the rest in their lives because He has the ultimate power to save.

A Personal Response

Dear Heavenly Father,

Please help me to share the gospel with the right motives and methods. Fill me with Your Holy Spirit so I will take my individual responsibility for sharing the gospel with (add names) and others I know and meet. Give me the desire and burden and then guide me as I develop my own personal evangelistic strategy to share the good news. Please open up my eyes to view every situation as a potential evangelistic encounter.

Assist me as I discover the spiritual gifts you have given to me and the specific interests and abilities that I might use to present Your plan of redemption to the world. Help me to spend time with the unsaved and show your love and share Your Word. Give me wisdom to tailor my presentation to the situation at hand without compromising the essential tenets of the gospel. Put in my heart a willingness to sacrifice my Christian liberty so that I do not offend them. Help me to love the other Christians in my life so we will be a bright light and powerful example to the world. I pray this in the name of Jesus. Amen.

Chapter 8

Utilize Your Interests and Skills

Christians should develop evangelistic strategies which are performed alone or with other believers. They should be created around their particular interests, skills, and gifts.

In the section, "A Typical Scenario," the author portrays the ways Christians can share the gospel while participating in their favorite activities.

What is the scenario about?

A Christian wanted to share the gospel and decided to join a golf club and share the gospel with people he met.

What held the believer back from sharing the gospel?

He did not have a strategy to share the gospel, so he simply put it off.

What finally led the Christian to share the good news and how did it occur?

He asked to pray for or meet the needs of other golfers and was kind and courteous with the staff preparing for opportunities to share.

Have you had a similar experience?

(Various answers should be shared including yours.)

LEADING THE WAY

In the section, "A Scriptural Principle" the author presents an important biblical principle in evangelism which concerns the development of personal evangelistic strategies.

How would you express this principle in your own words?

This eighth principle is "we must utilize our interests and skills."

(Various answers should be shared including yours.)

How would you rewrite this principle to make it even more personal to your life (using your name and situation)?

(Various answers should be shared including yours.)

Why do you think this principle might be important in your life right now as you share the gospel?

(Various answers should be shared including yours.)

How would you rate yourself on the percentage of times you followed this principle in the past as a believer?

(Various answers should be shared including yours.)

Directions: Put a horizontal mark and your name where you see yourself on the percentage line.

| 0%   25%   50%   75%   100% |

In the section, "A Biblical Explanation," the author explains the building of personal evangelistic strategies around our background, interests, abilities, and gifts and its importance in sharing the gospel effectively.

What are three biblical examples of those who used personal evangelistic strategies and describe them?

John went about in the wilderness of Judea dressed in camel's hair eating locusts and honey. Why? John was a prophet and took a Nazarite vow to live a life of purity and devotion to God (Matthew 11:9; Luke 1:13-15). This did not allow for the drinking of wine or the cutting of hair. He lived an austere life in the wilderness wearing the uncomfortable clothing made of camel's hair. This contrasted his humble lifestyle with the overindulgent religious leaders of the day. Then he preached repentance in preparation for the coming Messiah near a populated river where water was available for baptism. This was his method.

As a Rabbi, Jesus could speak in the synagogues, and he healed and preached. Paul was a Rabbi and spoke in the synagogues and then to the Gentiles in the marketplaces. Peter's strategy was to simply heal and preach in the marketplace. Stephen and Philip were both Hellenistic Jews (Jews living in the Greek culture), they were able to minister to the Greek speaking peoples. Apollos had a gifted intellect, was a powerful orator, and was mighty in the Scriptures, so he debated the Jews in public.

How do spiritual gifts pertain to proclaiming the gospel?

When believers are sharing the gospel, they need spiritual power to see souls saved which comes from the Holy Spirit. The Holy Spirit works through His Word and prayer, but He also empowers through spiritual gifts.

What is an example of an individually tailored presentation of the gospel in the books of Acts?

Peter began his presentation with what was happening at that moment.

Prophecy was being fulfilled as the believers were speaking in different languages.

In Acts 3:12, Peter preached the gospel beginning with the power and name of Jesus. He had been put to death and rose again. It was His power that healed the lame man who was now walking before their eyes.

In Acts 13:15-23, Paul entered a synagogue on the Sabbath in Pisidian Antioch and spoke from the Old Testament and its prophecies in the scrolls in front of him.

In Acts 14:8-15, Paul arrives in Lystra and heals a crippled man.

In Acts 17:23-25, Paul enters Athens and notices the statue dedicated to an unknown god among many statutes of false deities. He then proclaimed to the people that he had come to reveal to them the identity of this unknown god.

In Acts 22:1-3, when Paul was arrested in Jerusalem for supposedly bringing a Gentile into the temple, Paul stood before a large crowd of Jews and began with his personal testimony and how he had come to Christ as a Jew in their Hebrew language.

What did Paul mean when he said he did not want to offend people as he shared the gospel? What did he not mean?

He did not want to offend them so they would refuse to listen to the gospel. Finally, the hindrance to which Paul is speaking does not involve the offense of the gospel, personal holiness, or sound doctrine. Instead, it involves the area of Christian liberty.

Christian liberty involves things that are basically spiritually neutral. They will not spiritually help nor hinder believers, such as food.

How do the members of the church as a whole testify to the world that they have a relationship with Christ?

Christians are to portray Christ to the world by the way they interact with each other.

In what ways might these truths impact your life?

(Various answers should be shared including yours.)

LEADING THE WAY

In the section, "An Ancient Portrait," the author provides a unique portrayal of the Lord Jesus and His encounter with a Samaritan woman.

Can you briefly describe the setting of this real-life ancient drama?

Wearied from His journey, Jesus sat down at a well and asked His disciples to go into town about one half of a mile away and retrieve some food.

Can you describe the major characters involved?

The major characters are Jesus and the Samaritan woman.

How did the evangelist initiate the gospel presentation?

He tailored His presentation of the gospel around the well and water she was fetching. He simply asked her for a drink of water. The Samaritan woman was stunned and inquired as to why a Jewish man would even speak to her let alone ask her for something.

So, he replied that if she knew the gift of God that was sitting before her, she would request of Him living water (He was a well providing the water of eternal life). Of course, at first, she explained to Him that she did not understand how He could give her water when He did not have a physical bucket.

He requested that she go and return to Him with her husband. Jesus did not worry about the offense of sin. She could not find salvation by repentance if her sin was not confronted.

What was result of this evangelistic presentation?

Rather than repent and receive Him as Savior and Lord, the woman left her water pot and ran into the city to tell people about this man at the well. She asked if they thought He could possibly be the Messiah. Many came to meet Him and entreated him to stay in the city and speak with them. The Lord Jesus remained there two days and proclaimed the good news.

How was the principle explained in this chapter applied to the situation?

Though John does not record whether the Samaritan woman came to Christ, he wrote that many believed. Here Jesus utilized His own interests and skills to bring many to Himself.

Based on the truths learned in this chapter, what would you have done differently if you were the evangelist or how would you have responded if you were the recipient?

(Various answers should be shared including yours.)

In the section, "A Modern Anecdote," the author discusses a situation in which he decided to present the gospel during his college speech classes.

Can you briefly describe the setting of this real-life modern drama?

The setting is a college speech class. I thought a speech class would be a "captive" audience to share the gospel and they were. Not wanting to overdo it, I tried to share the gospel in every other speech. When we had a speech where we had to use visuals, I developed a series of slides on the proofs for the resurrection. Every slide took them progressively through the verification of Jesus Christ's death on the cross. I had slides which discussed the blood and water pouring out of His side, the lack of need to break His legs to suffocate him, the ritualistic Jewish burial with the oils, perfumes, and tightly wound bandages, the known location of the tomb, the massive rock that was placed in front of it, the sealing of it with the insignia of the Roman emperor, and the placing of the guards before it.

Can you describe the major characters involved?

The major characters are the author, teacher, and David.

How did the author initiate the gospel presentation?

Then I discussed the empty tomb of Jesus, the bandages lying flat with the headpiece rolled up, the removal of the stone, the breaking of the official seal, the passing out of the guards, and the angelic presence when the first witnesses came. After this, I shared with the class the testimony of each and every witness to the resurrected Christ. I was so excited, enthusiastic, and committed. I wanted everyone to believe and receive Jesus Christ as Savior and Lord. I

AN INSTRUCTOR'S MANUAL

even gave an invitation to invite Christ into their lives after class with me or even ask some questions or have a dialogue.

What was result of this evangelistic presentation?

Then he casually mentioned that he probably would have considered picking a different topic, but it was certainly my choice. Everyone just sat there in silence. After several more speeches the class was finally over.

This young man behind me quietly mumbled, "Can I talk to you?" I agreed, so Dennis and I went for coffee at one of the college cafes. I admit that I was nervous, but I knew the Lord would work His will in this situation.

How was the principle explained in this chapter applied to the situation?

When I shared the Lord Jesus Christ and the solid evidence and power of his death and resurrection, he told himself, "This Jesus was more than a man and this book was more than a philosophy book. This was the truth." Then he asked me to help him receive Christ as Savior and Lord. Right there, in that cafe at a major university I had the privilege of bringing him to Christ. I utilized my interests and skills to share the gospel.

Based on the truths learned in this chapter, what would you have done differently if you were the author or how would you have responded if you were the recipient?

(Various answers should be shared including yours.)

In the section, "A Personal Response," the author provides a model you may use for prayer if you find it necessary after discovering the truths in this chapter.

Are you presently attempting to present the gospel of Jesus to someone? If not, are there some who may be among your acquaintances who may not know Jesus Christ and may need prayer for an opportunity for you to share with them and open hearts to receive Him?

(Various answers should be shared including yours.)

Based on the truths you have just learned, what will you continue to do in your current evangelistic efforts and what might you do differently?

(Various answers should be shared including yours.)

What additional thoughts would you like to share with the others?

(Various answers should be shared including yours.)

Chapter 9

Welcome an Initial Response

When Christians proceed out into the world to share the amazingly good news of Jesus Christ, they must realize that moving from unbelief to belief may require some people to make various initial steps toward the gospel without fully receiving Christ at the moment that His redemptive plan is presented. God's people should become familiar with these initial responses (steps), view them as positive, and rejoice in the progress that unbeliever may be making in their journey to the cross. In this chapter, we concern ourselves with these steps or positive reactions before actual belief.

A Typical Scenario

Have you ever been in a situation that was something like the following? You have a brother who you would like to see receive Jesus Christ as Savior and Lord. For some time, you have been concerned about your brother and his unhealthy lifestyle. He drinks too much alcohol and eats too much fatty foods. He is well known at every fast-food restaurant in his area. He never exercises and spends too much time watching television and playing video games. You are concerned also because your brother is completely self-centered. He is only interested in one thing: himself. He has zero ambition and makes no contributions to anyone or anything. You worry about him often but have no clue as to how to approach him for Christ. You are fearful that he will not only die early but, in his sins, condemning him to hell for all eternity. What a terrible tragedy this would be! You know something must be said but are not sure exactly what it should be.

In this chapter, you will learn that you should be sharing the good news of Jesus Christ regularly but not necessarily expect an immediate salvation response. Sometimes, people will response positively in a variety of ways and then receive Jesus Christ later. They may initially respond with a deep conviction but require more time, be ignorant of God's truth and need more information, perhaps have a searching heart and desire more learning, possess an honest confusion and want more discussion, desire more convincing and need more thought, want more time to consider Scripture and require more biblical proof, be open minded and desire to compare the various religions, possess a fearful concern and be afraid to continue further investigation, have people who are opposing them becoming Christians and may need to deal with this, may need a continual presentation desiring to hear the gospel in more detail, or could suddenly realize the truth and want to come immediately to Christ. After you learn these critical truths perhaps this same situation could like quite different.

Now, rather than sharing the gospel outright, which you have the right to do as God's herald, you decide to take your brother down a path toward Christ by spending some time with him. Then, you will work the gospel in here and there. First, you ask your brother if he could help you purchase a new laptop. During that time, you ask him if he remembers the church's club program you both attended as children. He responds by sharing some funny memories of you, him, and the other kids in your group. Then, you challenge him to quote just one Scripture verse that he could remember from those days of Scripture memory.

He quotes John 3:16 and you ask him if he ever believed in that verse. He shrugs his shoulders and says that he took that stuff more seriously as a kid but wasn't much interested in it now. You explain to him that Jesus is not just for kids, but as a fully mature adult you believe in Him and rely on Him in everyday life. You leave the conversation there. He does not tell you to stop talking about it, so you rejoice in his positive response.

John 3:16
For God so loved the world, that he gave his one and only Son, that whoever believes in him should not perish, but have eternal life.

Second, you invite him to a small comic convention. You loved superheroes as kids and so he went. During that time, you talk constantly about a variety of subjects, but you want to turn the conversation toward the Bible. So, you tell him that you have been studying some of the great superheroes of the Bible. He looks at you with confusion on his face. You tell him that you could start your own super group with the likes of Samson (super strength), David (mighty warrior), Peter (healing and invulnerability), Joshua (control of time); Moses (control of nature); Paul (could raise the dead); Philip (teleportation) even Jesus Christ (invisibility, invulnerability, flight, etc.), and others. As you explain each real person from the Bible, he finally becomes interested.

He blurts out, "You believe in all those stories?" You nod your head, and he shakes his. Then he responds, "Okay, I'm coming over this week and you are going to show me these powers they had." This was a positive reaction and makes you happy. When he arrives, you have made a superhero chart with some drawings of Bible characters with their powers and the Bible verses that confirmed these truths. As you study the Bible together, you focus on the power saints now have. This power is for spiritual living rather than physical battles or authenticating the Scripture. You explain that he does not have to rely on alcohol or anything else to cope with his difficulties; instead, he should depend upon the Lord. He could become involved in something far more powerful than fighting the foes of imaginary comic heroes which is the advancement of God's Kingdom on Earth. Later, with more time and discussions, your brother receives Jesus as Savior and Lord. Finally, you both will be in heaven.

Though this is an imaginary scenario, it is quite typical of the kinds of situations we find ourselves in where the gospel could be shared yet it is not. Why? Often times, it is due to the fact that Christians think every time they share the good news people should with respond with a desperate plea to receive Christ. If they don't, it is not a positive response, when it could be one. Understanding the variety of different positive responses may encourage us to respond positively in return as we continue the discussion of salvation. We now proceed to the ninth principle which involves a description of these positive responses.

A Scriptural Principle

When people consider the positive reactions others could make to Christ and His gospel, many think of the moment of salvation. Yet, the Scriptures teach and describe a variety of positive reactions different people may have on their way to receiving Jesus Christ as Savior and Lord. Some people may immediately believe in the gospel when they first hear, but others may need additional time. Though receiving the Lord will occur in a moment of time, it also may be the result of a series of one or more positive steps (reactions) some might take in their pilgrimage to the cross. These positive reactions should be anticipated and encouraged by those sharing the gospel. So, the ninth principle is "we must welcome an initial response."

A Biblical Explanation

We see this journey throughout the New Testament. The disciples struggled for a long time in their pilgrimage to full belief in Christ. In Matthew 8:27, after Jesus had calmed a turbulent sea, the disciples responded by questioning each other. The disciples wanted to know what kind of a man could the wind and seas obey. They had seen many miracles, heard much teaching, and yet still questioned. In Matthew 14:33, Christ's doubting disciples saw the Lord walk on the water and pull a doubting, disturbed Peter from the deep. Yet, they still declared in amazement that Jesus truly was the Son of God! It was finally beginning to dawn on them that Jesus was the Messiah and divine.

Matthew 8:27
The men marveled, saying, "What kind of man is this, that even the wind and the sea obey him?"

Matthew 14:33
Those who were in the boat came and worshiped him, saying, "You are truly the Son of God!"

Even after the resurrection, Thomas would not believe. He stipulated that he would not believe unless he saw the resurrected Jesus Christ with his own eyes and touched His wounds with his own hands. This was such a bold assertion considering that after him others would have to believe without seeing. In John 20:24-28, the apostle records these words, "Then he said to Thomas, 'Reach here your finger, and see my hands. Reach here your hand, and put it into my side. Don't be unbelieving, but believing.' Thomas answered him, 'My Lord and My God.'"

John 20:24-28
But Thomas, one of the twelve, called Didymus, wasn't with them when Jesus came. The other disciples therefore said to him, "We have seen the Lord!" But he

said to them, "Unless I see in his hands the print of the nails, put my finger into the print of the nails, and put my hand into his side, I will not believe."

So, when this disciple met Christ, he declared that Jesus was His Lord and God! Finally, Thomas fully believed. When the Lord's disciples received the Great Commission from the risen Jesus, Matthew disclosed that some of the eleven still doubted (Matthew 28:16-17). In Acts 1:3, Jesus spent forty days convincing the apostles of His resurrection, deity, and mission.

Matthew 28:16-17
But the eleven disciples went into Galilee, to the mountain where Jesus had sent them. 17 When they saw him, they bowed down to him; but some doubted.

Acts 1:3
To these he also showed himself alive after he suffered, by many proofs, appearing to them over a period of forty days, and speaking about God's Kingdom.

In Acts 8, the Ethiopian eunuch had been a God-fearing Gentile for some time before he was saved on the road from Jerusalem to Gaza. In Acts 10, Cornelius had been a devout God-fearing Gentile for some time before he had a divine vision to send for Peter to hear the gospel. In Thessalonica, it took over three Sabbath's of preaching before many believed (Acts 17:2-3). In Acts 17:10-12, it took many days of Scripture examination before many of the Bereans in that city would come to Christ. They wanted to be certain that what Paul was saying about this resurrected Savior named Jesus was true before they believed.

Acts 17:2-3
Paul, as was his custom, went in to them, and for three Sabbath days reasoned with them from the Scriptures, explaining and demonstrating that the Christ had to suffer and rise again from the dead, and saying, "This Jesus, whom I proclaim to you, is the Christ."

Acts 17:10-12
The brothers immediately sent Paul and Silas away by night to Beroea. When they arrived, they went into the Jewish synagogue. Now these were more noble than those in Thessalonica, in that they received the word with all readiness of mind, examining the Scriptures daily to see whether these things were so. Many of them therefore believed; also of the prominent Greek women... not a few men.

As has been seen, the Holy Spirit convicts the world of sin, righteousness, and judgment (John 16:8). This may take time as He opens up the eyes of the blind (2 Corinthians 4:4) and plants the seed of the gospel in the hearts of the unsaved (1 Peter 2:22-23). The point is clear, some may come to Jesus Christ immediately after a presentation of the good news, but others may not. Christians should understand the variety of positive responses people make as they journey to the cross. We should not be discouraged if the unsaved do not initially come to Jesus Christ.

John 16:8
When he has come, he will convict the world about sin, about righteousness, and about judgment.

2 Corinthians 4:4
In whom the god of this world has blinded the minds of the unbelieving, that the light of the Good News of the glory of Christ, who is the image of God, should not dawn on them.

1 Peter 2:22-23
Seeing you have purified your souls in your obedience to the truth through the Spirit in sincere brotherly affection, love one another from the heart fervently, having been born again, not of corruptible seed, but of incorruptible, through the word of God, which lives and remains forever.

Yet, Christians must also acknowledge that people may have initial positive reactions to the gospel but never come to saving faith. This becomes confusing to believers. They see these positive reactions and cannot understand how they could fall away.

In Matthew 13:20-22, Jesus describes seeds that fall on the rocky places and others which fall among the thorns. Both of these represent people who may make positive reactions to the gospel initially but simply walk away. They may have tasted of the things of the kingdom of God but did not fully receive it into their hearts and minds (Hebrews 6:4-5).

Matthew 13:20-22
What was sown on the rocky places, this is he who hears the word and immediately with joy receives it; yet he has no root in himself, but endures for a while. When oppression or persecution arises because of the word, immediately he stumbles. What was sown among the thorns, this is he who hears the word, but the cares of this age and the deceitfulness of riches choke the word, and he becomes unfruitful.

Hebrews 6:4-5
For concerning those who were once enlightened and tasted of the heavenly gift, and were made partakers of the Holy Spirit, and tasted the good word of God and the powers of the age to come.

One will fall away because the seed is not firmly rooted, and persecution uproots it. The other will fall away because the worry of the world or the deceitfulness of riches chokes the Word in their hearts. In 1 John 2:19, the apostle John explains that they left the body of Christ because they never were really a true member of His church. Why? So, it could be demonstrated that they were not true believers. They had not really received Jesus Christ.

1 John 2:19
They went out from us, but they didn't belong to us; for if they had belonged to us, they would have continued with us. But they left, that they might be revealed that none of them belong to us.

A Deep Conviction

Some might respond with a deep conviction. In Luke 3:1-17, John the Baptist came preaching repentance for sin as he prepared the way for the coming of the Lord. The people responded with a deep conviction of their own sin. This led them to an important inquiry. They asked John what should be done differently as they prepared for the coming of the Messiah. In Acts 2:37, Luke testifies, "Now when they heard this, they were cut to the heart, and said to Peter and the rest of the apostles, 'Brothers, what shall we do?'" Peter preached the resurrection of the Lord Jesus Christ and the Jerusalem crowd demanded to know how they might be saved. Luke described their hearts as having been pierced. This is a deep conviction. Yet, Peter continues to preach with many other words and kept on exhorting them for some time to be saved (verse 40). They might have been convicted of their sins, but Peter felt they needed to hear more before they believed.

Mark 1:4-5
John came baptizing in the wilderness and preaching the baptism of repentance for forgiveness of sins. All the country of Judea and all those of Jerusalem went out to him. They were baptized by him in the Jordan river, confessing their sins.

Acts 2:37
Now when they heard this, they were cut to the heart, and said to Peter and the rest of the apostles, "Brothers, what shall we do?"

Acts 2:40
With many other words he testified, and exhorted them, saying, "Save yourselves from this crooked generation!"

Conviction is not enough. They must understand the good news and believe. This may require additional explanation. Some people may want or need to hear much more than even the essential gospel to believe. Yet, others may need some additional time to think through what is being said. Christians should see this as a solid positive response and give unbelievers all the information or time they may need to understand and believe.

A True Ignorance

Some might respond with true ignorance. There are some people who don't necessarily have a hardened heart toward God but are simply awaiting God's message about His Son. They simply do not know enough about the coming of the Messiah and His gospel. In Romans 1:20, Paul asserts that God the Father has revealed Himself clearly through His creation. Everyone begins life knowing that there is a God through the natural world that He created. In Romans 2:14-16, the author remarks that every person has another witness to the knowledge of God besides just His creation. Inside all human beings is His law (conscience) constantly convicting them of sin and indicating a coming judgment. To come to Christ, men must respond to creation and to the conscience. They must recognize there is a God, honor Him, thank Him, and sorrow over their numerous sins (Romans 1:21). Then in God's timetable, the gospel will be delivered to them.

Romans 1:20
For the invisible things of him since the creation of the world are clearly seen, being perceived through the things that are made, even his everlasting power and divinity, that they may be without excuse.

Romans 2:14-16
(For when Gentiles who don't have the law do by nature the things of the law, these, not having the law, are a law to themselves, in that they show the work of the law written in their hearts, their conscience testifying with them, and their thoughts among themselves accusing or else excusing them) in the day when God will judge the secrets of men, according to my Good News, by Jesus Christ.

Romans 1:21
Because knowing God, they didn't glorify him as God, and didn't give thanks, but became vain in their reasoning, and their senseless heart was darkened.

Between the time of the presentation of the good news and their response, they may experience true ignorance as they are on their journey toward Christ. This is a positive reaction in their preparation to be saved. Paul claims he experienced this true ignorance. In Acts 22:3-5, Paul speaks to the Jews in Jerusalem of his previous zeal for God. Paul explains that he genuinely thought he was serving the true God in his faith by persecuting any and all Christians. He was genuine and ignorant. The ignorance had led to a great and powerful persecution at his hands.

Acts 22:3-10
I am indeed a Jew, born in Tarsus of Cilicia, but brought up in this city at the feet of Gamaliel, instructed according to the strict tradition of the law of our fathers, being zealous for God, even as you all are today. I persecuted this Way to the death, binding and delivering into prisons both men and women, as also the high priest and all the council of the elders testify, from whom also I received letters to the brothers, and traveled to Damascus to bring them also who were there to Jerusalem in bonds to be punished.

In 1 Timothy 1:12, Paul discusses the abundant mercy of God in calling him to salvation. He says, "And I thank him who enabled me, Christ Jesus our Lord, because he counted me faithful, appointing me to service." Here, the apostle speaks of his deep gratitude for God putting him into ministry for Him even though he had a violent past with believers. He continues with a portrayal of his viciousness, "Although I was…a blasphemer, a persecutor, and insolent."

1 Timothy 1:12
I thank him who enabled me, Christ Jesus our Lord, because he counted me faithful, appointing me to service.

Though he had been so cruel to the followers of Jesus, he adds these words, "However, I obtained mercy, because I did it ignorantly in unbelief." He explained that he did not know or understand the true gospel at that time. He thought he was serving God. He was not like the Pharisees who had fully understood the gospel and rejected it. Instead, the true knowledge of the good news did not fully come to him until the Damascus road (Acts 9). Paul was not saved before this.

In Acts 19:1-7, Paul traveled to Ephesus and met several disciples of John the Baptist. These men had heard about the coming Messiah. Yet, they had not been present when John baptized the Lord Jesus as the Lamb of God. They were truly ignorant. When they heard the good news from Paul, they immediately believed. Christians may meet some who are ready but ignorant. Their genuine ignorance is a positive response to the gospel. They are on the right path, and they simply need real saving knowledge. This will require a fuller picture of Jesus than others who may have grown up with His teachings.

Acts 19:1-7
While Apollos was at Corinth, Paul, having passed through the upper country, came to Ephesus and found certain disciples. He [Paul] said to them, "Did you receive the Holy Spirit when you believed?" They said to him, "No, we haven't even heard that there is a Holy Spirit." He said, "Into what then were you baptized?" They said, "Into John's baptism." Paul said, "John indeed baptized with the baptism of repentance, saying to the people that they should believe in the one who would come after him, that is, in Jesus." When they heard this, they were baptized in the name of the Lord Jesus. When Paul had laid his hands on them, the Holy Spirit came on them and they spoke with other languages and prophesied. They were about twelve men in all.

Still others, who may have false understandings of Jesus, will need correction concerning who Jesus really is. As Paul thought that he was truly serving God, there may be those in the cults who are on a journey to the cross. These "ignorant" souls may require the correction of many misunderstandings about Christ to be saved.

A Searching Heart

Some might respond with a true searching heart. This is distinct from the last point. This kind of person is not only genuinely ignorant but is really searching for the truth. Paul was not searching because he had thought that he had found the truth. This person is honestly and truly seeking a true relationship with God. Though they may not know it, they are genuinely waiting for someone to present the good news to them and them to Christ as Savior and Lord.

Sergius Paulus, who resided on the island of Paphos, sent for Paul to hear the Word of God. When the apostle arrived on the island during his first missionary journey, Elymas, the magician, thwarted his attempts. Elymas was strongly opposed to the proconsul hearing the good news of Jesus (Acts 13:6-7). Sometimes, unbelievers will come to Christians seeking answers for their hopelessness and despair.

Acts 13:6-7
When they had gone through the island to Paphos, they found a certain sorcerer, a false prophet, a Jew, whose name was Bar Jesus, who was with the proconsul, Sergius Paulus, a man of understanding. This man summoned Barnabas and Saul, and sought to hear the word of God.

This is evidenced in the story of the God-fearing Gentile Cornelius, who was searching for the truth. In Acts 10:1-2, Luke recounts, "Now there was a certain man in Caesarea, Cornelius by name, a centurion [military commander] of what was called the Italian Regiment, a devout man, and one who feared God with all his house, who gave gifts for the needy generously to the people, and always prayed to God."

Acts 10:1-2
Now there was a certain man in Caesarea, Cornelius by name, a centurion of what was called the Italian Regiment, a devout man, and one who feared God with all his house, who gave gifts for the needy generously to the people, and always prayed to God.

This man was constantly seeking after God, serving Him, and praying to Him. This soldier had not even heard about Jesus Christ. In verses 3-5, God addresses him through an angel in a vision and directs him to send for Peter. Peter did not search for him, he found Peter. This took some time because Peter was not ready to preach the good news to the Gentiles. God had to prepare Peter through a vision. When Peter arrived, Cornelius fell down before him (Acts 10:24-33). This is a searching heart.

Acts 10:3-5
At about the ninth hour of the day, he clearly saw in a vision an angel of God coming to him, and saying to him, "Cornelius!" He, fastening his eyes on him, and being frightened, said, "What is it, Lord?" He said to him, "Your prayers and your gifts to the needy have gone up for a memorial before God. Now send men to Joppa, and get Simon, who is also called Peter.

Acts 10:24-26
On the next day they entered into Caesarea. Cornelius was waiting for them, having called together his relatives and his near friends. When Peter entered, Cornelius met him, fell down at his feet, and worshiped him. But Peter raised him up, saying, "Stand up! I myself am also a man."

In Acts 28:24-26, Paul had been chained in Rome waiting to stand before Caesar. Luke testified that Paul preached the gospel of the kingdom to all who came to him. Sometimes, we may not need to go to unbelievers, but they may come to us to find out about our Savior and Lord. The true seekers who came would have received Christ. God will bring those who are truly searching for Him into our lives to present His redemptive plan to them. We must be spiritually awake and aware so when the time comes, we will see the opportunity clearly and then take it.

Acts 28:30-31
Paul stayed two whole years in his own rented house and received all who were coming to him, preaching God's Kingdom, and teaching the things concerning the Lord Jesus Christ with all boldness, without hindrance.

An Honest Confusion

Some might respond with honest confusion. There may be those who may not accept Christ right away because they may be honestly confused. This was the exact predicament of the Ethiopian eunuch. As has been seen, this official was a God-fearing Gentile reading a portion of Isaiah traveling on the road from Jerusalem to Gaza. Unfortunately, the man could not understand the passage he was reading. In Acts 8:30, it is stated, "Philip ran to him, and heard him reading Isaiah the prophet, and said, 'Do you understand what you are reading?'" The evangelist jogs alongside of the eunuch's chariot and asks if he is confused. Luke continues in verse 31, "He said, 'How can I, unless someone explains it to me?' He begged Philip to come up and sit with him." Next, Philip shares the gospel with him, and he receives Christ. The Spirit of God supernaturally transported Philip to that very road in order for him to explain the passage and bring the eunuch to Christ. His heart was right, but his mind was confused.

Acts 8:30
Philip ran to him, and heard him reading Isaiah the prophet, and said, "Do you understand what you are reading?"

Acts 8:31
He said, "How can I, unless someone explains it to me?" He begged Philip to come up and sit with him.

Even the disciples spent much of their earlier time with Jesus honestly ignorant, not always understanding His many teachings and actions. One example is found in John 6:48-69. When Jesus told His followers that they must eat his body and drink His blood to be saved, Peter did not comprehend what he meant. This was an analogy of a full relationship with Him to be saved.

Many followers fell away, but Peter absolutely refused to leave. Why? He knew Jesus spoke the words of eternal life. Though he was ignorant of what the Lord meant, he knew with more time and explanation he would eventually come to understand. When Christians share the gospel, it might take some more time for the Spirit to open the minds of the unsaved (John 15:26; Acts 16:14). They must be patient as the Holy Spirit works in their lives.

John 15:26
When the Counselor has come, whom I will send to you from the Father, the Spirit of truth, who proceeds from the Father, he will testify about me.

Acts 16:14
A certain woman named Lydia, a seller of purple, of the city of Thyatira, one who worshiped God, heard us. The Lord opened her heart to listen to the things which were spoken by Paul.

A Continued Persuasion

Some may respond by requiring a more persuasion. This persuasion might include more biblical explanations and proofs, not the persuasion of a sales pitch. Some unbelievers will honestly listen to a presentation of the gospel but need some additional facts or proofs from the Scripture. Or they may require more time to carefully ponder what they heard. In Acts 17:2, Luke recounts what happened in the city of Thessalonica when the apostle entered the synagogue that was located there, "Paul, as was his custom, went in to them, and for three Sabbath days reasoned with them from the scriptures." Here, Paul spends three different days reasoning with these citizens, before they began to commit themselves to the Savior.

Acts 17:2
Paul, as was his custom, went into them, and for three Sabbath days reasoned with them from the Scriptures.

He was asking the Gentiles among them to give up the idol worship that the entire population believed their whole lives (1 Thessalonians 1:9). He was asking the Jewish people among them to believe that Jesus was their long-awaited Jewish Messiah. This would require the Jews to believe that Jesus had not blasphemed, though the Lord was murdered for it. Instead, He actually was the Son of God (Acts 17:4-5).

1 Thessalonians 1:9
For they themselves report concerning us what kind of a reception we had from you, and how you turned to God from idols, to serve a living and true God.

Acts 17:4-5
Some of them were persuaded and joined Paul and Silas, of the devout Greeks a great multitude, and not a few of the chief women. But the unpersuaded Jews took along[a] some wicked men from the marketplace, and gathering a crowd, set the city in an uproar. Assaulting the house of Jason, they sought to bring them out to the people.

Once they were saved, they were fervently spreading this good news throughout the regions of Macedonia and Achaia (1 Thessalonians 1:6-7). Christians might have to take much more time to biblically convince some in order to bring them to Jesus Christ. They should see this as a positive response.

1 Thessalonians 1:6-7
You became imitators of us and of the Lord, having received the word in much affliction, with joy of the Holy Spirit, so that you became an example to all who believe in Macedonia and in Achaia.

A Scriptural Consideration

Some might respond with a scriptural consideration. One, who is from a Judeo-Christian background, may desire to legitimately search the Scriptures for themselves. They will commit themselves to Christ after a careful examination. The unsaved citizens of Berea are an example of this scriptural consideration. After the apostle fled from Thessalonica, Paul entered the city of Berea and preached the gospel. This was a more noble-minded people, and they would not just listen and believe.

In Acts 17:11, Luke records, "Now these were more noble than those in Thessalonica." He begins his description with a comment about their more noble character because of how they handled the Old Testament Scriptures when the apostle Paul proclaimed the gospel from them. Then, he adds this, "In that they received the word with all readiness of the mind examining the scriptures daily to see whether these things were so."

Acts 17:11
Now these were more noble than those in Thessalonica, in that they received the word with all readiness of mind, examining the Scriptures daily to see whether these things were so.

As the apostle presented the gospel to the people using the Old Testament, they were meticulously searching the scrolls for themselves. They knew these books and desired to determine the veracity of Paul's claims for themselves. The Bereans were awaiting the coming Messiah. Their hearts were open to God, but they demanded to see the proofs that demonstrated that Jesus was the Messiah. The result was the belief of many (verse 12). These people were considered much nobler because they took the time to verify the truths that Paul had come to them to proclaim.

Acts 17:12
Many of them therefore believed...the prominent Greek women...not a few men.

When the Lord identified Himself as the Messiah to the woman at the well, she went and told many in the city. They all came out to meet Jesus for themselves, then they believed (John 4:39-42). Sometimes, it will be necessary to allow some people time to meet Jesus for themselves. We may need to provide a Bible for them and even some other resources. We must realize that questioning the Scriptures, studying them, and pondering these spiritual things on their own according to their own time frame.

John 4:39-42
From that city many of the Samaritans believed in him because of the word of the woman, who testified, "He told me everything that I did." So when the Samaritans came to him, they begged him to stay with them. He stayed there two days. Many more believed because of his word. They said to the woman, "Now we believe, not because of your speaking; for we have heard for ourselves, and know that this is indeed the Christ, the Savior of the world."

An Open Mind

Some may respond with open minds. There may be those who are willing to listen to the gospel because they have an open mind. They might not have settled on one particular belief system or religion and are willing to discuss religious things. In Acts 17:17-18, Paul met a group of these people in Athens. The Areopagus (a religious council) screened every new teaching to determine whether or not it was from their gods. In Acts 17:33-34, Paul finished preaching the gospel, and Luke records the reactions. He writes, "Thus Paul went out from among them. But certain men joined with him, and believed, among who also was Dionysius the Areopagite, and a woman named Damaris, and others with them. Some did mock him, but others wanted to hear more. These people including Dionysius and Damaris came to the Lord. They came for a second hearing because they were more open-minded.

Acts 17:17-18
So he reasoned in the synagogue with the Jews and the devout persons, and in the marketplace every day with those who met him. Some of the Epicurean and Stoic philosophers also were conversing with him. Some said, "What does this babbler want to say?" Others said, "He seems to be advocating foreign deities," because he preached Jesus and the resurrection.

Acts 17:33-34
Thus Paul went out from among them. But certain men joined with him and believed, among whom also was Dionysius the Areopagite, and a woman named Damaris, and others with them.

Another example is King Herod Agrippa, who heard the apostle's defense of the good news in Acts 26. This man was open-minded enough to not rely on the testimony of Festus but to hear Paul himself (Acts 26:28). Though Festus thought Paul was "out of his mind," King Agrippa determined that Paul was about to persuade Him and was listening intently.

Acts 26:28
Agrippa said...,"With a little persuasion are you trying to make me a Christian?"

In Acts 16, Paul entered the city of Philippi and found no synagogue. When Paul heard there was a place of prayer down by the river, he went to share the gospel to whomever he encountered. One of these people was a woman named Lydia. When the apostle proclaimed the good news to all these Jewish women, Lydia did not storm off. She heard the gospel with an open mind, and the Lord opened her heart.
In Acts 18, when Paul had been sharing the good news in the synagogue in Corinth, many resisted him. So, Paul went to the house of Titius Justus, a worshiper of God, who resided next-door to that synagogue and preached there.... Many had open minds enough to come and hear him preach.

As a result, Crispus, the official of the synagogue, and his household with many Corinthians believed. As Christians share the gospel, they will encounter unbelievers with open minds and are willing to listen to the truth. This should be seen as a positive step in the direction of the good news of the Lord Jesus Christ. The open mind may very well be the initial work of the Spirit.

A Fearful Awakening

Some might respond with a fearful spiritual awakening. There may be those who encounter a fearful situation or serious crisis from the Lord in their preparation to accept the gospel. Something frightens them and they begin to open up to God. Occasionally, the Father will have to do something dramatic and eventful in people's lives to turn them finally to Him.

This is what happened in the life of the jailer in Philippi. In Acts 16, Paul removed a demon from a servant girl and destroyed her fortune telling abilities. After they lost their business, her masters had Paul and Silas beaten and thrown into the local jail. Yet, Paul and Silas were just singing and praying which the prisoners and their jailer must have heard. Suddenly an Earthquake occurred causing the jailer to think the prisoners had escaped. The jailer would have been killed for allowing this to happen, so he decided to take his own life right there on the spot. Paul cried out for the jailer to stop because everyone had remained there. No one had escaped. The jailer fell at Paul's feet in fear and trembling begging him to be saved. In Acts 16:29-31, Paul describes it in these words, "He called for lights and sprang in, and, fell down trembling before Paul and Silas, and brought them out and said, 'Sirs, what must I do to be saved?' They said, 'Believe in the Lord Jesus Christ, and you will be saved, you and your household.'" Paul brought him and his entire household to Christ. It required a powerful Earthquake to prepare that man for salvation.

Acts 16:29-31
He called for lights, sprang in, fell down trembling before Paul and Silas, brought them out, and said, "Sirs, what must I do to be saved?" They said, "Believe in the Lord Jesus Christ, and you will be saved, you and your household."

God may use a fearful awakening to bring those who are called to His Beloved Son. In Luke 15, in the story of the prodigal son, the Lord brought a terrible famine in the land which brought fear and desperation. This finally drove the son back to his loving father. As he longed for the food of the pigs, the son had a spiritual awakening and realized that he needed his father.

Saul was diametrically opposed to the gospel. In Acts 8-9, he went about persecuting Christians everywhere they fled. Then on the road to Damascus, Paul encountered the risen Lord Jesus in a dramatic way. Paul witnessed a blazing light from heaven brighter than the sun, heard the voice of Christ speak to Him, and was struck with blindness for three days. This was a terribly fearful conversion experience (Acts 9:8-9). At these times of crises, the Lord begins to awaken people spiritually because of fear which provides a great chance to share the gospel.

Acts 9:8-9
Saul arose from the ground, and when his eyes were opened, he saw no one. They led him by the hand, and brought him into Damascus. He was without sight for three days, and neither ate nor drank.

A Difficult Opposition

Some might respond with a struggle against opposition. There are people who recognize that there is a true God of creation and a real lawgiver from their conscience. They are moving in their spiritual journey toward the Lord but are opposed by someone. Satan has raised someone up to stop them from coming to Jesus Christ. This produces a difficult struggle. Some may have to deal with this opposition before they receive the Lord Jesus Christ. This may be a friend who takes up their time or a spouse who does not allow contact by the evangelist.

A clear example of this is found in Acts 13:6-8, when Paul traveled to Cyprus. Luke describes the scene, "Who was with the proconsul, Sergius Paulus, a man of understanding. This man summoned Barnabas and Saul and sought to hear the word of God. But Elymas the sorcerer (for so is his name by interpretation) withstood them, seeking to turn aside the proconsul from the faith." Sergius Paulus, the proconsul of the island, sent for Paul because this official wanted to hear the Word of Paul's God. Elymas, a sorcerer, who was an advisor in his court, opposed the apostle. Elymas did not want the proconsul to come to Christ. Finally, Paul struck him with blindness for a season. As Paul rebuked him, he called Elymas a son of the Devil. Paul knew who was behind his opposition. When Sergius saw this and heard Paul's gospel, he believed.

Acts 13:6-8
When they had gone through the island to Paphos, they found a certain sorcerer, a false prophet, a Jew, whose name was Bar Jesus, who was with the proconsul, Sergius Paulus, a man of understanding. This man summoned Barnabas and Saul, and sought to hear the word of God. But Elymas the sorcerer (for so is his name by interpretation) withstood them, seeking to turn the proconsul away from the faith.

Christians should be aware that there might be people in their lives who may attempt to keep them from coming to Christ as they share the good news with them. These people might even be in their own family. Not everyone walks into the kingdom unopposed. Jesus warned his disciples of this in Matthew 10:33-34. Jesus proclaimed that He would not bring peace but a sword between a man and his father, and a daughter and her mother, and among the members of their own household. Family members, children, friends, fellow students, or co-workers who oppose the unsaved may have to be dealt with first. There may be a spiritual battle for some time for them to even get the opportunity to hear the good news. Whole families may face the destruction of all familial relationships, or their lives may be threatened if the person even considers another religion. This must be overcome.

Matthew 10:33-34
But whoever denies me before men, I will also deny him before my Father who is in heaven. Don't think that I came to send peace on the Earth. I didn't come to send peace, but a sword.

An Additional Presentation

Some might respond with a desire to hear the good news again. Sometimes people may need to hear the gospel more than once before they receive Jesus Christ. In Acts 19:8, Paul arrived in Ephesus and taught in the synagogue for three months reasoning from the Scriptures. Over and over again, the members of the Jewish synagogue were hearing Christ's gospel. He taught two years in the school of Tyrannus and many in the whole region came to hear about Christ.

Acts 19:8
He entered into the synagogue and spoke boldly for a period of three months, reasoning and persuading about the things concerning God's Kingdom.

In Acts 19:18-20, Luke recounts that many were forsaking their magic practices in Ephesus and then burned all their demonic books. The Word of God was growing rapidly and prevailing against evil. With their continual sharing of the gospel, many would have heard the gospel multiple times before coming to Christ.

Acts 19:18-20
Many also of those who had believed came, confessing, and declaring their deeds. Many of those who practiced magical arts brought their books together and burned them in the sight of all. They counted their price, and found it to be fifty thousand pieces of silver. So the word of the Lord was growing and becoming mighty.

Previously, in Acts 13:42-44, Luke records that the people of Antioch begged Paul to return the next Sabbath and speak to them again. The historian portrays the encounter in these key words, "So when the Jews went out of the synagogue, the Gentiles begged that these words might be preached to them the next Sabbath. When the synagogue broke up, many of the Jews and of the devout proselytes followed Paul and Barnabas, who, speaking to them, urged them to continue in the grace of God. The next Sabbath almost the whole city was gathered together to hear the word of God."

Acts 13:42-44
So when the Jews went out of the synagogue, the Gentiles begged that these words might be preached to them the next Sabbath. Now when the synagogue broke up, many of the Jews and of the devout proselytes followed Paul and Barnabas, who, speaking to them, urged them to continue in the grace of God. The next Sabbath, almost the whole city was gathered together to hear the word of God.

The ones who had originally heard his words went and told others to come and hear also. In their sharing, the saints might be required to share the good news to some people more than once to bring them to Christ. The person may almost be ready but need one more presentation. The saints must be prepared to take that next step. One presentation may simply not be enough.

A Sudden Realization

Some might respond with a sudden realization that Christ is the Son of God, and they must be saved. God may work quickly when the good news is preached. Unbelievers may immediately and dramatically realize that Christ is indeed God, place their faith in Him, and never turn back. This is true concerning the powerful conversion of the apostle Paul. In 1 Timothy 1:13 and Acts 26:10, he describes exactly how he vehemently pursued Christians from Jerusalem to every region in order to persecute them even unto death.

1 Timothy 1:13
Although I used to be a blasphemer, a persecutor, and insolent. However, I obtained mercy, because I did it ignorantly in unbelief.

Acts 26:10
I also did this in Jerusalem. I both shut up many of the saints in prisons, having received authority from the chief priests, and when they were put to death I gave my vote against them.

Then the supernatural miracle on the road to Damascus occurred. Suddenly, the apostle was now pursuing people everywhere to win them to Christ (Acts 22:15-16). What a sudden realization he must have had! In fact, so sudden was His conversion that he frightened the saints. In Acts 9:26, the inspired writer depicts this way, "When Saul had come to Jerusalem, he tried to join himself to the disciples; but they were all afraid of him, not believing that he was a disciple."

Acts 22:15-16
For you will be a witness for him to all men of what you have seen and heard. Now why do you wait? Arise, be baptized, and wash away your sins, calling on the name of the Lord.'

When the apostle went to Jerusalem, many Christians were hesitant to associate with him, not fully believing that this could happen. Christians should always be prepared for an unbeliever's sudden and dramatic conversion to the Lord Jesus Christ. Though this does not happen every time, it certainly happens some of the time. What a sight!

An Ancient Portrait

In Luke 7:36-50, Jesus welcomes the initial response of a sinful woman seeking His forgiveness. When Jesus was in Galilee, the Lord was invited into the house of a Pharisee named Simon. While Jesus was at Simon's table, a woman, who had the reputation among the Jews of being a "sinner" (most likely a prostitute), entered the house with a jar of expensive oil. I am sure to everyone's amazement, she began to wet the feet of the Lord with her tears and wipe them with her hair. Then, she kissed Christ's feet and anointed Him with her oil. This woman came with a deep conviction and a searching heart and Jesus welcomed her.

Rather than being filled with empathy and compassion as they viewed this poor woman kneeling before Christ, these religious men of Israel were stunned that Jesus even allowed such a sinner to touch Him. They must have thought, "Why did He have anything to do with her?" These scoffers viewed the entire scene with disgust. They reasoned that if this Jesus was truly prophet He claimed to be, then He would know how wretched the woman before Him was. She was not welcome in Simon's home.

To open up the minds of Simon and his guests as to the significance of the moment, Jesus told them a story. This tale was about a lender who was owed money by two people. One owed him five hundred denarii (500 day's wages) and the other five denarii (5 day's wages). The gracious lender then forgave them both. One was forgiven a large amount and the other a smaller amount. Then Jesus asked Simon to pick the person who would love this lender more? Simon responded that it would be the one with the larger amount. The implication was obvious. This woman, who was such a sinner, was welcomed by Jesus because of her greater love.

Then the Lord turned the tables on his host. Though Jesus welcomed the woman, He was not welcomed by Simon. He compared Simon's prideful and cold treatment of Him with her humble and seeking conduct. Christ told Simon that he did not wash the Lord's feet when He entered his home (a custom due to the wearing of sandals), but this woman had washed them with her tears and wiped them dry with her hair. This Pharisee did not kiss the Lord when He arrived (a common greeting at that time), but the woman continually kissed His feet. The host did not anoint the head of the Lord with oil (a common custom to remove the smell of travel, like perfume), but she anointed His feet continually. This woman humbled herself before Jesus, but Simon had only contempt for Him.

They did not realize that she was in the middle of an act of deep conviction and repentance crying out for ultimate forgiveness. Simon had no interest in seeking forgiveness. Now her searching heart would be satisfied. So, the Lord pronounced His forgiveness of the many sins of the woman had committed. He acknowledged her great love for Him as Savior and Lord.

She loved Him much because she desperately needed so much forgiveness. Simon was rebuked for the little love he had for Jesus because this Pharisee had not experienced any forgiveness from Him. He had not sought it through a deep conviction and searching heart. Here, we see a wonderful example of the welcoming of an initial response.

A Modern Anecdote

One Saturday night, I was at a get together at a friend's house, and we were all sitting in the living room talking with one another. Suddenly, I realized it was getting late and checked my watch to discover that it was near 10:30pm. I stood up and thanked the host for a great evening. After this, I explained to the group that I had to get up early the next morning and so must depart. Suddenly a voice rang out, "What could you possibly be doing so early in the morning and so important that you have to leave now?" I glanced over in the direction of the voice, and it was a co-worker of mine; his name was Brian. I indicated that I had to go to church to teach a bible class the next morning that began at 8:00 am and wanted to get a decent night's sleep. I need at least eight hours to be at my best.

Brian responded with a chastising, "The Bible! You know, there are many other good religious books beside the Bible. I consider myself a seeker of truth and have studied all the major religions and picked out the best of each. I follow my own religion." Though I really desired a good night's sleep, I couldn't let this one go by. I asked him if he had actually read the Bible. Brian explained that he had not read the Bible or any other religious books.

I issued him this challenge, "If you are a real seeker of the truth, then I dare you to read the Bible and compare it to the other religious writings. Read them all. If you are a seeker of truth and your heart is open to it, then you will see that the Bible is the truth from the true God of the universe." He laughed uproariously. Then he declared, "Okay, I will take that challenge and return a challenge. You get me a Bible and be available to answer questions. I will read it first, then I will read the others."

I wrote down his address and took a Bible over to him the next day. I suggested that he begin with the Gospel of John. He agreed with my proposal, and I gave him my number telling him to call anytime with his questions. Over the next three months, he read, and I answered questions. He became enthralled with Jesus. After Brian read the Gospel of John, he proceeded through the other gospels. During those months, I shared the gospel with him several times and asked him if he desired to receive Jesus Christ. He responded with, "No, you said I should compare the books and that is what I am going to do. I want to see this through to the end."

Slowly he accumulated other religious writings including the Koran, the Book of Mormon, The Gospel of Thomas, the Lost Books of the Bible, the Catholic Catechism, the Talmud, and the numerous "holy writings" of Hinduism, Buddhism, Taoism, and Confucianism. Then he told me he thought I should read the writings with him and see if I was wrong. I took the challenge and we read and read.

It was a long and arduous journey, but I knew the Bible could measure up to any book. Finally, we finished, and he said to me, "Now, I am going to take some time to process of all of this in my mind because I really do want the truth." Two weeks later, Brian called me and asked me to come right over. When I arrived, he asked me to come in and sit down. He looked me straight in the eyes and said, "Thank you so much for taking this long and difficult journey with me." He held up the Bible and declared, "This book is true, and I am ready to receive Christ as my Savior and Lord." That day his eternity was changed forever. He now issues the very same challenge I issued to him to every unbeliever he meets. Through this experience, I discovered the power of welcoming an initial response from someone and then being extremely patient as they journey down the spiritual road to salvation in Jesus Christ. There are many different positive responses we shall see that are short of salvation.

A Personal Response

Dear Heavenly Father,

Please provide an opportunity for me to proclaim the plan of redemption to (add names) and others I know and meet. I ask that you fill me with your Holy Spirit as I share Your gospel with them. If their first response is to open their minds to Your Word, I yearn to be loving toward them and provide the time needed. If they suddenly realize that Jesus is Your Son, I want to be joyful. If they are truly ignorant, I desire much patience as You provide the knowledge, they need through me. If they have a fearful concern at first and avoid me or change the subject, help me respond in love.

If they have searching hearts and must have more time to consider Your gospel, let them sense my kindness as I wait. If they may require several presentations to come to Your Son, I want to show them the goodness You have given me as I interact with them. If they want additional proofs to be persuaded, may I be faithful in providing them. If they react with honest confusion, may I be gentle in my discussion.

If someone in their lives opposes them and attempts to stop them from becoming Christians, I will need self-control and wisdom. If they require a careful searching of the Scriptures to see if my words from Your gospel are true, I want to be persistent in my approach. If they develop a deep conviction of their sins, I would like to show them Your full forgiveness in Jesus. Most of all, Lord I want to demonstrate Your Son in my life as I share with them. Then I ask that You bring them fully to Christ. I pray this in the name of Jesus. Amen.

Instructor's Notes

AN INSTRUCTOR'S MANUAL

Chapter 9

Welcome an Initial Response

Moving from unbelief to belief may require some people to make initial steps toward the gospel without receiving Christ at the moment that His redemptive plan is presented.

In the section, "A Typical Scenario," the author provides an example for the saints to present the gospel by connecting to the individual interests of their immediate family members.

What is the scenario about?

A Christians spends time with his brother and eases him into a gospel presentation through a common interest in comic books.

What held the believer back from sharing the gospel?

He was not sure whether he should share the gospel up front with his brother or take some time to share different aspects of it.

What finally led the Christian to share the good news and how did it occur?

After spending time together, they began to discuss superheroes and he compared imaginary heroes with the real ones in the Bible.

Have you had a similar experience?

(Various answers should be shared including yours.)

In the section, "A Scriptural Principle" the author presents the numerous ways the people can positively respond to the gospel without making an immediate commitment to Christ.

How would you express this principle in your own words?

This ninth principle is "we must welcome an initial response."

(Various answers should be shared including yours.)

How would you rewrite this principle to make it even more personal to your life (using your name and situation)?

(Various answers should be shared including yours.)

Why do you think this principle might be important in your life right now as you share the gospel?

(Various answers should be shared including yours.)

How would you rate yourself on the percentage of times you followed this principle in the past as a believer?

(Various answers should be shared including yours.)

Directions: Put a horizontal mark and your name where you see yourself on the percentage line.

| 0% | 25% | 50% | 75% | 100% |

In the section, "A Biblical Explanation," the author explains the numerous initial positive responses to the gospel and their importance in sharing the good news effectively.

What are two biblical examples of those who made an initial response to Christ but did not yet believe in Him?

Some of the answers to choose from are the following.

In Matthew 8:27, after Jesus had calmed a turbulent sea, the disciples responded by questioning each other. The disciples wanted to know what kind of a man could the wind and seas obey. They had seen many miracles, heard much teaching, and yet still questioned. In Matthew 14:33, Christ's doubting disciples saw the Lord walk on the water and pull a doubting, disturbed Peter from the deep. Yet, they still declared in amazement that Jesus truly was the Son of God! It was finally beginning to dawn on them that Jesus was the Messiah and divine.

Even after the resurrection, Thomas would not believe.

So, when this disciple met Christ, he declared that Jesus was His Lord and God! Finally, Thomas fully believed.

When the Lord's disciples received the Great Commission from the risen Jesus, Matthew disclosed that some of the eleven still doubted (Matthew 28:16-20).

In Acts 8, the Ethiopian eunuch had been a God-fearing Gentile for some time before he was saved on the road from Jerusalem to Gaza. In Acts 10, Cornelius had been a devout God-fearing Gentile for some time before he had a divine vision to send for Peter to hear the gospel.

In Thessalonica, it took over three Sabbath's of preaching before many believed (Acts 17:2-3).

In Acts 17:10-12, it took many days of Scripture examination before many of the Bereans in that city would come to Christ.

What is the difference between responding to the good news with an honest confusion and an open mind?

Some might respond with honest confusion. There may be those who may not accept Christ right away because they may be honestly confused. This was the exact predicament of the Ethiopian eunuch.

Some may respond with open minds. There may be those who are willing to listen to the gospel because they have an open mind. They might not have settled on one particular belief system or religion and are willing to discuss religious things.

What is the difference between responding to the good news with a fearful awakening and a difficult opposition?

Some might respond with a fearful spiritual awakening. There may be those who encounter a fearful situation or serious crisis from the Lord in their preparation to accept the gospel. Something frightens them and they begin to open up to God. Occasionally, the Father will have to do something dramatic and eventful in people's lives to turn them finally to Him.

Some might respond with a struggle against opposition. There are people who recognize that there is a true God of creation and a real lawgiver from their conscience. They are moving in their spiritual journey toward the Lord but are opposed by someone.

Some may have to deal with this opposition before they receive the Lord Jesus Christ.

What is the difference between responding to the good news with a continued persuasion and an additional presentation?
Some might respond with a desire to hear the good news again. Sometimes people may need to hear the gospel more than once before they receive Jesus Christ.

Some might respond with a desire to hear the good news again. Sometimes people may need to hear the gospel more than once before they receive Jesus Christ.

What must Christians do when unbelievers respond to the gospel desiring a scriptural consideration?

Some might respond with a scriptural consideration. One, who is from a Judeo-Christian background, may desire to legitimately search the Scriptures for themselves. They will commit themselves to Christ after a careful examination.

In what ways might these truths impact your life?

(Various answers should be shared including yours.)

In the section, "An Ancient Portrait," the author provides a unique portrayal of a woman's tears at the feet on Jesus in the house of Simon.

Can you briefly describe the setting of this real-life ancient drama?

The setting is Simon the Pharisee's house. When Jesus was in Galilee, the Lord was invited into the house of a Pharisee named Simon. While Jesus was at Simon's table, a woman, who had the reputation among the Jews of being a "sinner" (most likely a prostitute), entered the house with a jar of expensive oil.

Can you describe the major characters involved?

The major characters are Jesus, the woman, Simon, and his guests.

How did the evangelist initiate the gospel presentation?

He allowed the woman to anoint him.

I am sure to everyone's amazement, she began to wet the feet of the Lord with her tears and wipe them with her hair. Then, she kissed Christ's feet and anointed Him with her oil. This woman came with a deep conviction and a searching heart and Jesus welcomed her.

What was result of this evangelistic presentation?

So, the Lord pronounced His forgiveness of the many sins of the woman had committed. He acknowledged her great love for Him as Savior and Lord.

She loved Him much because she desperately needed so much forgiveness. Simon was rebuked for the little love he had for Jesus because this Pharisee had not experienced any forgiveness from Him.

How was the principle explained in this chapter applied to the situation?

He had not sought it through a deep conviction and searching heart. Here, we see a wonderful example of the welcoming of an initial response.

Based on the truths learned in this chapter, what would you have done differently if you were the evangelist or how would you have responded if you were the recipient?

(Various answers should be shared including yours.)

In the section, "A Modern Anecdote," the author discusses a situation where he challenged a friend to seriously compare the Bible with all other religious writings.

Can you briefly describe the setting of this real-life modern drama?

The setting was the house of a friend of the author in a Saturday night.

Can you describe the major characters involved?

The major characters are the author and Brian.

How did the author initiate the gospel presentation?

I issued him this challenge, "If you are a real seeker of the truth, then I dare you to read the Bible and compare it to the other religious writings. Read them all. If you are a seeker of truth and your heart is open to it, then you will see that the Bible is the truth from the true God of the universe." He laughed uproariously. Then he declared, "Okay, I will take that challenge and return a challenge. You get me a Bible and be available to answer questions. I will read it first, then I will read the others."

Over the next three months, he read, and I answered questions. He became enthralled with Jesus. After Brian read the Gospel of John, he proceeded through the other gospels.

What was result of this evangelistic presentation?

It was a long and arduous journey, but I knew the Bible could measure up to any book. Finally, we finished, and he said to me, "Now, I am going to take some time to process of all of this in my mind because I really do want the truth."

He held up the Bible and declared, "This book is true, and I am ready to receive Christ as my Savior and Lord." That day his eternity was changed forever.

How was the principle explained in this chapter applied to the situation?

Through this experience, I discovered the power of welcoming an initial response from someone and then being extremely patient as they journey down the spiritual road to salvation in Jesus Christ.

Based on the truths learned in this chapter, what would you have done differently if you were the author or how would you have responded if you were the recipient?

(Various answers should be shared including yours.)

In the section, "A Personal Response," the author provides a model you may use for prayer if you find it necessary after discovering the truths in this chapter.

Are you presently attempting to present the gospel of Jesus to someone? If not, are there some among your teammates who may not know Jesus Christ and may need prayer for an opportunity for you to share with them and open hearts to receive Him?

(Various answers should be shared including yours.)

Based on the truths you have just learned, what will you continue to do in your current evangelistic efforts and what might you do differently?

(Various answers should be shared including yours.)

What additional thoughts would you like to share with the others?

(Various answers should be shared including yours.)

Chapter 10

Pursue a Saving Faith

In an earlier chapter, the essential elements of the gospel were presented. Each element will have a corresponding and appropriate response. These right responses will save the person and give them eternal life. Why does it have to be so precise? God is precise. God has determined exactly what people must believe and do to enter into His heaven. This is His plan and His redemption through His Son. People do not have a say in determining what needs to be believed or done. In Isaiah 55:8-9, God Himself explains that His ways are above our ways as the heavens are above the Earth. He does not think or act like man. He is not to be questioned. Period. It is His paradise, and the following discussion will entail how people can enter it.

Isaiah 55:8-9
"For my thoughts are not your thoughts, and your ways are not my ways," says Yahweh. "For as the heavens are higher than the Earth, so are my ways higher than your ways, and my thoughts than your thoughts."

A Typical Scenario

Have you ever been in a situation that was something like the following? Sometimes, people will claim to be Christians, but when you look at their words, actions, and lifestyles, you do not see Christ anywhere. You know that the Bible teaches that Christians are to marry other Christians (1 Corinthians 6:14-17; 7:39). This makes things difficult when dating. As you get to know the person, early on in the relationship you must inquire as to whether they claim Christ as Savior and

Lord and must discern if this is in fact true. No one can look into the heart of a person, but Jesus said that you will know His followers by their fruits (words and actions).

1 Corinthians 6:14-17
Now God raised up the Lord, and will also raise us up by his power. Don't you know that your bodies are members of Christ? Shall I then take the members of Christ and make them members of a prostitute? May it never be! Or don't you know that he who is joined to a prostitute is one body? For, "The two", he says, "will become one flesh." But he who is joined to the Lord is one spirit.

1 Corinthians 7:39
A wife is bound by law for as long as her husband lives; but if the husband is dead, she is free to be married to whomever she desires, only in the Lord.

Let us say you are a male and meet this young lady who you thought was very attractive who attended your church. You wanted to spend some time with her so you asked if she would like to meet for coffee. As you talk about a variety of things, you finally ask her, "So, how exactly did you become a Christian?" She responds by describing a moment when she was at a youth camp and suddenly felt Jesus come into her life. The person explains that it was a quiet moment of realization, and the wind was slightly whistling through the trees. She knew nature was from God, and Jesus was God's Son. Normally, you would say that sounds good and will from then on assume she is a believer when she may not be.

In this chapter we will learn that there is a specific set of beliefs and actions one must take to be saved. Everyone who declares that "Jesus is my personal Savior" is not necessarily a Christian. For you to be saved, you must repent of your sins, believe that Jesus is God that He died on the cross to pay the penalty for your sins, rose from the dead, and enter in a love relationship with Him. This is done by asking Him to be your Savior and submitting to Him as Lord. This is based on your faith alone, not works. Then you should be baptized in water for all of the world to see. This baptism is the first fruit of salvation. It does not save. After you learn these powerful truths, perhaps this same dating encounter could look quite different.

This time after the person's response, you do not leave. You inquire as to what the person actually believes about "receiving Jesus as Savior and Lord." She replies that Jesus is a friend and companion. He would help her when she was sad and talk to her throughout the day. You now know that this is not the gospel, nor is it what the Bible indicates a true believer's relationship with Christ is like. You ask the person if she believes people could get to heaven without Jesus. She then responds that there were many ways to heaven, and she certainly wasn't going to judge. You gently tell her that the Bible is clear on how to get into God's heaven.

You calmly and gently assert that you do not think that she has truly received Jesus Christ as Savior and Lord and ask if she would like the opportunity. After explaining all of the principles in this chapter, she receives Jesus Christ as Savior and Lord and now knows for sure that she has eternal life.

Though this is an imaginary scenario, it is so typical of the kinds of encounters we may have with people as we attempt to develop relationships with them. We may miss the critical opportunity to share the gospel with the misinformed due to our ignorance of exactly what one must truly belief to be saved. The comprehension of these truths can instigate us to share how to receive Christ more often. This brings us to the tenth principle which involves the beliefs pouring forth into necessary words and actions which must be taken to receive Christ as Savior and Lord.

A Scriptural Principle

Many people in churches today rely upon their church membership, birth into a Christian family, a life lived by the golden rule, a specific experience or encounter, good feelings about God, or even attendance at a particular church. These feelings, notions, actions, and experiences do not save. God has outlined very specific beliefs one must have and actions one must perform concerning His Son to enter into salvation. Principle ten is "we must pursue a saving faith."

This means that the saints must always pursue the proper salvation response when they are sharing the good news of Jesus Christ and should never be satisfied with some type of partial response which will not save them. This could be difficult because Christians would have to question claims of those who may seem sincere but may be mistaken.

A Biblical Explanation

Many people today, even the cults, will claim that they have "Jesus in their hearts" or that "Jesus is their personal Savior." Unfortunately, they are absolutely deceived. These terms are used frequently today. Yet, they obscure the real response one must make to be saved. It isn't as simple as just "believing in Jesus" or simply saying "Jesus is my Savior." True saving faith is more than an intellectual knowledge that "Jesus loves me." It is a firm belief and a trust that literally changes one's life. This "belief" requires an understanding of the true identity of Jesus Christ, His purpose for coming, His words and actions, and how to respond.

James argues this very point in James 2:19. The demons have the right knowledge about God. At least they shudder.

They have some kind of response. He contrasts that with those who claim to believe in Christ but produce no fruits or good works. They act the same as they did before belief. In Luke 8:28, the demons rightly exclaimed that He was the Son of the Most High God! They rightly believed, but this belief is not enough. Belief must pour forth into a transformed life.

James 2:19
You believe that God is one. You do well. The demons also believe, and shudder.

Luke 8:28
When he saw Jesus, he cried out, and fell down before him, and with a loud voice said, "What do I have to do with you, Jesus, you Son of the Most High God? I beg you, don't torment me!"

This same concept is displayed in Matthew 7:22-23. Jesus has just informed His disciples that numerous false prophets and deceitful teachers would arise after His ascension. These evil workers would claim a saving relationship with Him among His people and on judgment day. Yet, the Lord Jesus will send them away declaring that He never knew them.

Matthew 7:22-23
Many will tell me in that day, "Lord, Lord, didn't we prophesy in your name, in your name cast out demons, and in your name do many mighty works?" Then I will tell them, 'I never knew you. Depart from me, you who work iniquity.'

Many will have claimed to have prophesied in His name, cast out demons by His authority, and done miracles by His power, yet the Lord will deny having any relationship with them. Whatever they may have said or done in His name was not from Him. They had a right belief but no true saving faith that transformed them.

Then Jesus points to the crux of the issue: they were living lawlessly. He indicates that these wolves in sheep's clothing could easily be identified by their insufficient fruit or their lack of transformed lives. The pretenders will be people of unrighteousness (no change), though they will appear to do great feats in His name. Their lives will not demonstrate a divine relationship. Why? Their beliefs are not life changing!

This critical precept does not only apply to false prophets but anyone who claims the name of Jesus Christ. In verses 24-27, He broadens His claim by acknowledging two kinds of people. Some will hear His words and act upon them. These will build their houses upon rocks, and the storms of life will not wash them away. Others will hear but will not act upon His words. They will build their houses upon the sand, and the storms of life will wash them away.

Matthew 7:24-27
Everyone therefore who hears these words of mine and does them, I will liken him to a wise man who built his house on a rock. The rain came down, the floods came, and the winds blew and beat on that house; and it didn't fall, for it was founded on the rock. Everyone who hears these words of mine and doesn't do them will be like a foolish man who built his house on the sand. The rain came down, the floods came, and the winds blew and beat on that house; and it fell — and its fall was great."

This hearing and doing of Christ's Word involve hearing, believing, and acting upon those beliefs. In 1 John 3:10, John provides two criteria to determine if those who claim Christ are really saved. Real saints love the brethren and practice righteousness. These two actions do not produce salvation in one's life; they are merely the distinguishing marks of those who are saved. These true believers have transformed lives indicated by the love of their fellow Christians and righteous living. Believing in Jesus intellectually or knowing who He is will not be enough to produce these crucial signs of a true relationship with Christ.

1 John 3:10
In this the children of God are revealed, and the children of the devil. Whoever doesn't do righteousness is not of God, neither is he who doesn't love his brother.

Then, one might ask, "What about all the Bible passages that simply say believe? There are two reasons for this. First, the concept of "believe" utilized by the Lord has a much fuller meaning. It involves an understanding of Christ's true identity, His purpose for coming, His words and actions, and how one must respond. If one truly believes, he will respond appropriately. This is exactly what Jesus meant in Matthew 7:21, when He claimed that those who did the will of His Father, not those who cried, "Lord, Lord" would be saved. A complete understanding and belief in these things produce a godly response. True belief in Jesus Christ is life changing.

Matthew 7:21
Not everyone who says to me, "Lord, Lord," will enter into the Kingdom of Heaven, but he who does the will of my Father who is in heaven.

Second, Jesus, the apostles, and the other inspired writers of the New Testament described the process of becoming a Christian by emphasizing one or another of the beliefs and actions one must take to be saved during or after salvation. This did not imply in any way that all the components for saving faith was not necessary. All of them simply could not be spoken or recorded every time the gospel is mentioned.

Just one example should suffice. After Peter's sermon in Acts two, the crowd asked him how they might be saved. Peter responded that they needed to repent and be baptized. Here Peter is viewing saving faith from the initial action to the final reaction. They must repent to be saved and then respond to their saving faith through baptism.

It should be expected that the writers of Scripture could not possibly have recorded every word that was uttered in every presentation of the gospel. Often, they would have provided the most essential for their intended purpose for mentioning the incident. This is known by a comparison of the gospel accounts of a particular incident. Each writer will provide some similar details and some additional details, yet without contradiction.

Often, the writers indicated that they were not recording everything that was actually said. In fact, according to Acts 2:40, Peter testified and exhorted the crowd with many more words. These words Luke does not record, but they would have filled in the biblical portrait of a full saving response. John claims that if he had written every word and action of Jesus, the world couldn't hold the books that would contain them (John 21:25). The writers through the inspiration of the Holy Spirit revealed what the Father wanted revealed (John 14:26; 2 Peter 1:20-21).

Acts 2:40
With many other words he testified, and exhorted them, saying, "Save yourselves from this crooked generation!

John 21:25
There are also many other things which Jesus did, which if they would all be written, I suppose that even the world itself wouldn't have room for the books that would be written.

John 14:26
But the Counselor, the Holy Spirit, whom the Father will send in my name, will teach you all things, and will remind you of all that I said to you.

2 Peter 1:20-21
Knowing this first, that no prophecy of Scripture is of private interpretation. For no prophecy ever came by the will of man: but holy men of God spoke, being moved by the Holy Spirit.

The reading and understanding of all the passages that relate to the gospel through the New Testament sets forth a complete doctrine on the proclamation of God's plan of redemption. Christians do not understand all God's teaching on marriage by studying only one passage of Scripture. They must take into account every passage that mentions or alludes to marriage to view the full portrait of this blessed institution. It is the same with the good news. Therefore, all of the various Scriptures must be studied and interpreted receive a complete understanding.

The saving response described below embodies all of the teachings of the writers of the New Testament. These specific positive reactions or responses will spring forth into life eternal and the deeds that demonstrate this life. If one truly "believes in Jesus" then the following aspects of belief and saving responses will occur! How does one know? The Bible discusses all of these beliefs and responses in conjunction with salvation. All of these individual teachings must be collected and joined together to give someone a true picture of saving faith. These are the keys to eternal life.

The Seeking of His Kingdom

As Christians present God's plan of redemption and the offer of the kingdom of God and eternal life, the response of unbelievers will be a "seeking" of His kingdom. Essentially, this entails the acceptance of the offer. They will want to become a part of the kingdom of God. When the Lord was explaining to the people that in His kingdom they did not have to be concerned about clothing and food, He asserted that they should be seeking the kingdom of God instead. In Matthew 6:33, Jesus said, "But seek first God's Kingdom, and his righteousness; and all these things will be given to you as well."

This "seeking" is how people truly respond to the offer of the kingdom of God. This is why Jesus told them that if they seek His kingdom, they will find it (Matthew 7:7; Luke 11:9-10). In Luke 15:8, Jesus characterized true believers as those who sought His kingdom like one searching for a lost coin.

She lit a lamp, cleaned the house, and diligently sought to find the coin. The Greek word that is translated "seek" means "to crave, demand, strive after." These people will deeply desire to be in the kingdom and to live it out. This is why they repent of their sins and begin to seek His righteousness. They want to behave like children of the kingdom.

Matthew 7:7
Ask, and it will be given you. Seek, and you will find. Knock, and it will be opened for you.

Luke 11:9-10
I tell you, keep asking, and it will be given you. Keep seeking, and you will find. Keep knocking, and it will be opened to you. For everyone who asks receives. He who seeks finds. To him who knocks it will be opened.

Luke 15:8
Or what woman, if she had ten drachma coins, if she lost one drachma coin, wouldn't light a lamp, sweep the house, and seek diligently until she found it?

This sounds rather obvious but is really the first step in the salvation process when the kingdom of God, and eternal life is offered to them. They will not walk away or reject it. Instead, they will seek it. When a piece of fruit is ready to be picked on a tree, it will almost fall off into one's hand. In the same way, Christians will not have to argue people into the kingdom of God. They will "fall into one's hand" seeking it.

The Repentance of Sin

One's response to the proclamation of sin and judgment is the repentance of sin. This results from a real understanding of the absolute holiness of God, His Son, and Spirit. Once the unsaved realize who Christ is, they will understand how unworthy and sinful they are. This was the response of the centurion when he requested Jesus to heal his servant. In Luke 7:6-10, he asked Jesus to heal him from afar because the centurion felt he was not worthy to have Jesus come to his home. He was a sinner, and he knew it.

Luke 7:6-10
Jesus went with them. When he was now not far from the house, the centurion sent friends to him, saying to him, "Lord, don't trouble yourself, for I am not worthy for you to come under my roof. Therefore I didn't even think myself worthy to come to you; but say the word, and my servant will be healed. For I also am a man placed under authority, having under myself soldiers. I tell this one, 'Go!' and he goes; and to another, 'Come!' and he comes; and to my servant, 'Do this,' and he does it." When Jesus heard these things, he marveled at him, and turned and said to the multitude who followed him, "I tell you, I have not found such great faith, no, not in Israel." Those who were sent, returning to the house, found that the servant who had been sick was well.

No person can be saved without full repentance, which demonstrates true belief. In 2 Timothy 2:24-26, Paul exhorts Timothy, his son in the faith, to gently correct those who are opposing him. Why? Perhaps, God will cause them to repent and lead them into the knowledge of the truth. In Matthew 3:2, John the Baptist declared people should repent because the kingdom of God was at hand. In Matthew 4:17, the apostle reveals that the ministry of the Lord Jesus was also the preaching of repentance and the proclaiming of kingdom of God. One's repentance is an essential part of the salvation response.

2 Timothy 2:24-26
The Lord's servant must not quarrel, but be gentle toward all, able to teach, patient, in gentleness correcting those who oppose him: perhaps God may give them repentance leading to a full knowledge of the truth, and they may recover themselves out of the devil's snare, having been taken captive by him to his will.

Matthew 3:2
Repent, for the Kingdom of Heaven is at hand!

Matthew 4:17
From that time, Jesus began to preach, and to say, "Repent! For the Kingdom of Heaven is at hand."

There are three aspects to this concept of "repentance" in the Scripture. As in the concept of "belief," "repentance" has a fuller meaning. It involves three aspects which are presented in various places by different writers in the New Testament. Repentance involves Christians admitting that they have sinned, sorrowing over their evil doing, and turning away from that sin toward righteousness.

The first is the admission of sin. People must admit that they have sinned. John discloses this important aspect as he deals with some in the church that had decided they had matured past sin. He begins in 1 John 1:8 and 10 by saying these people are liars and deceivers of themselves. Some said they never sinned, and others said they had matured past sinning and John stands against both of these falsehoods. In verse 9, he provides a characteristic of Christians. The saints confess their sins and find forgiveness. The Greek word translated "confess" literally means to say the same thing. Confession is "to say the same thing about sin" that God says. We are to acknowledge our sins before the Lord God and admit they are wrong before Him.

1 John 1:8
If we say that we have no sin, we deceive ourselves, and the truth is not in us.

1 John 1:10
If we say that we haven't sinned, we make him a liar, and his word is not in us.

1 John 1:9
If we confess our sins, he is faithful and righteous to forgive us the sins, and to cleanse us from all unrighteousness.

When Jesus encountered a rich young ruler, he claimed to have kept all the law from his youth up. Could that be true? No, he simply refused to admit his sin. Paul described this wretched condition in Romans 1:18; he was suppressing the truth in unrighteousness. Perhaps, so much so that he had convinced himself he was able to keep the whole law. So, Jesus told him to sell all he had which he refused to do.

This manifested the real sin in his heart (greed) which the rich man had not displayed outwardly (Mark 10:21-23; Matthew 19:21-24; Luke 18:22-25). He had to come to Christ admitting he was a sinner, which he refused to do. Instead, this rich young ruler left Jesus with his self-righteousness intact but not saved.

Romans 1:18
For the wrath [anger] of God is revealed from heaven against all ungodliness and unrighteousness of men who suppress the truth in unrighteousness.

Mark 10:21-23
Jesus looking at him loved him, and said to him, "One thing you lack. Go, sell whatever you have, and give to the poor, and you will have treasure in heaven; and come, follow me, taking up the cross."
But his face fell at that saying, and he went away sorrowful, for he was one who had great possessions. Jesus looked around, and said to his disciples, "How difficult it is for those who have riches to enter into God's Kingdom!"

Matthew 19:21-24
Jesus said to him, "If you want to be perfect, go, sell what you have, and give to the poor, and you will have treasure in heaven; and come, follow me." But when the young man heard this, he went away sad, for he was one who had great possessions. Jesus said to his disciples, "Most certainly I say to you, a rich man will enter into the Kingdom of Heaven with difficulty. Again I tell you, it is easier for a camel to go through a needle's eye than for a rich man to enter into God's Kingdom."

Luke 18:22-25
When Jesus heard these things, he said to him, "You still lack one thing. Sell all that you have, and distribute it to the poor. Then you will have treasure in heaven; then come, follow me." But when he heard these things, he became very sad, for he was very rich. Jesus, seeing that he became very sad, said, "How hard it is for those who have riches to enter into God's Kingdom! For it is easier for a camel to enter in through a needle's eye than for a rich man to enter into God's Kingdom."

The second is to mourn over sins. In the Beatitudes, Jesus says that a characteristic of those in the kingdom of God is mourning. This word speaks of mourning over the dead. In that passage, it has a spiritual application. The word implies mourning over sins and their consequence of spiritual death. When someone receives the Lord, they admit their sin and mourn, grieve, and sorrow over it. This is not necessarily a big emotional experience but a true sorrow.

In 1 Corinthians, Paul describes the sins and difficulties this church encountered because they had been prideful and rebellious. Paul was terribly hurt because the church had taken a stand against him. False prophets had risen up and found a leader in the church. This leader with most of the church stood against Paul and his ministry. So, he sent the difficult and confrontational letter of 1 Corinthians. When he visited, they did not respond well so he shortened his visit and departed. Later, Paul sent Titus to discover their final response to him and his many words of rebuke. When Titus returned, he brought good news of the church's repentance for standing against the apostle Paul.

In 2 Corinthians 7:9-10, Paul describes how much sorrow the church had over their sin. He says, "I now rejoice, not that you were made sorry, but that you were made sorry to repentance. For you were made sorry in a godly way that you might suffer loss by us in nothing. For godly sorrow works repentance to salvation which brings no regret. But the sorrow of the world works death."

2 Corinthians 7:9-10
I now rejoice, not that you were grieved, but that you were grieved to repentance. For you [saints] were grieved in a godly way, that you might suffer loss by us in nothing. For godly sorrow produces repentance to salvation, which brings no regret. But the sorrow of the world produces death.

This sorrow was a godly sorrow which produced a real repentance leading to salvation. This is the sorrow that Christians have when they come to Christ. This is the sorrow Christians have when they live for Christ. The first leads to initial salvation and the other to final eternal salvation. This is the true sorrow over sin that eternally saves. This is the sorrow that produces real repentance.

This is the sorrow that was expressed by the woman who came to Jesus in Luke 7:37-39. This grieving woman washed His feet with her tears and wiped them with her hair. What sorrow over sin! The repentant woman kissed His feet and anointed them with expensive perfume. What humility and mourning over wrongdoing!

Luke 7:37-39
Behold, a woman in the city who was a sinner, when she knew that he was reclining in the Pharisee's house, brought an alabaster jar of ointment. Standing behind at his feet weeping, she began to wet his feet with her tears, and she wiped them with the hair of her head, kissed his feet, and anointed them with the ointment. Now when the Pharisee who had invited him saw it, he said to himself, "This man, if he were a prophet, would have perceived who and what kind of woman this is who touches him, that she is a sinner."

Also, in the Corinthian passage, Paul describes a sorrow that only leads to death. This sorrow is one that produces bitterness, despair, anger, and pride. This sorrow lashes out at the other person for hurting them, rebuking them, or interrupting their sin. It vents at oneself in punishment and self-hatred. It will not plead for forgiveness.

Third is the repentance of sins. Though this word is used with a fuller meaning in defining the entire concept, it also has a unique meaning of its own. The Greek word translated repent means to turn around in the other direction or change one's mind or behavior. One must turn around from sin and go in the opposite direction.

Luke records Peter's denial of knowing Christ in Luke 22:62 and how the apostle wept in great sorrow and remorse afterward. Later, Luke records in Acts chapter two, three, and other passages the many sermons that Peter preached in great boldness for Christ. Peter demonstrated that he had turned in the opposite direction from that sin. Of course, the Holy Spirit will provide the strength needed to accomplish this supernatural feat (Acts 2:4; Romans 8:13).

Luke 22:62
He went out, and wept bitterly.

Acts 2:4
They were all filled with the Holy Spirit, and began to speak with other languages, as the Spirit gave them the ability to speak.

Romans 8:13
For if you live after the flesh, you must die; but if by the Spirit you put to death the deeds of the body, you will live.

Contrast that with Judas. In Matthew 27:3-5, he would not repent before the Lord Jesus, nor would he humble himself before Jesus. Judas refused to request any forgiveness, thus removing the guilt and sorrow. Instead, he killed himself to alleviate them from his life. This is the sorrow unto death. At times, the saints might not want to offend their unsaved acquaintances, neighbors, and friends so they will leave out this important saving step in their presentations. Instead, they will replace it with the hurt or sorrow these unbelievers may feel over their unmet needs, trials, or difficulties. They offer Jesus as the great healer, who will save them from their unfulfilled lives.

Matthew 27:3-5
Then Judas, who betrayed him, when he saw that Jesus was condemned, felt remorse, and brought back the thirty pieces of silver to the chief priests and elders, saying, "I have sinned in that I betrayed innocent blood." But they said, "What is that to us? You see to it." He threw down the pieces of silver in the sanctuary and departed. Then he went away and hanged himself.

This is not the true gospel. This "concept" will not allow those hearing the message to view Jesus Christ as He truly is - the righteous judge and Holy One. The Lord will save them from their punishment for unrighteousness and bring them safely to an eternal, supernatural life not a temporal life of comfort, prosperity, and success. These are terrible lies propagated by false teachers who desire to fool people in order to grow massive churches or ministries producing fame, and fortune for themselves. Their false messages come in a constant stream of positivity and inspiration. Yet, sin is the issue. People must be confronted about their sins to see their desperate need for salvation in Jesus Christ. Their saving response will be their admission of their wrongs, sorrow over their sin, and a turning toward righteousness.

The Belief in Christ as God

One's response to the proclamation of Christ as God must be belief in Christ's deity. No one can be saved unless that person believes Jesus Christ is God, one with the Father as His Son (John 8:58-59; 10:30). In 1 John 2, the author John is dealing with those who call themselves Christians but don't believe in the deity of Jesus, only His humanity. In verse 22, John calls them liars. If they do not confess the Son, they do not confess the Father. In 1 John 3:23, John explains to his readers that God's key commandment is to believe in the name of His Son, Jesus Christ. The apostle writes these words, "This is his commandment, that we should believe in the name of his Son, Jesus Christ, and love one another, even as he commanded." Then, in chapter 5, verses 9-13, John explains that the Lord has testified concerning His Son, Jesus Christ. If one does not believe in the Son, he calls God a liar and does not have eternal life.

John 8:58-59
Jesus said to them, "Most certainly, I tell you, before Abraham came into existence, I AM. Therefore they took up stones to throw at him, but Jesus was hidden, and went out of the temple, having gone through the middle of them, and so passed by."

John 10:30
I and the Father are one.

1 John 2:22
Who is the liar but he who denies that Jesus is the Christ? This is the Antichrist, he who denies the Father and the Son.

1 John 3:23
This is his commandment, that we should believe in the name of his Son, Jesus Christ, and love one another, even as he commanded.

1 John 5:9-13
If we receive the witness of men, the witness of God is greater; for this is God's testimony which he has testified concerning his Son. He who believes in the Son of God has the testimony in himself. He who doesn't believe God has made him a liar, because he has not believed in the testimony that God has given concerning his Son. The testimony is this, that God gave to us eternal life, and this life is in his Son. He who has the Son has the life. He who doesn't have God's Son doesn't have the life. These things I have written to you who believe in the name of the Son of God, that you may know that you have eternal life, and that you may continue to believe in the name of the Son of God.

This doctrine must be fully believed. This full belief issues forth in all the other aspects. A classic passage which verifies this truth is John 3:16 where Jesus declares that God loved the world so much that He gave His only begotten Son, so that everyone who believes in Him should not perish but will have eternal life. John finishes his proclamation of the good news in his book by declaring Jesus had performed many other signs that were not written in the gospel, but the ones that were written were to prove Jesus is the Christ, the Son of God (John 20:30-31). Eternal life comes from believing that Jesus Christ is the Son. This is the "belief" that Jesus is referring to when he declared over and over that one must "believe in Him" to be saved. It is important to note that the cults do not believe in the full divinity of Christ; instead, they believe He was an angel, a created god, or someone less than fully divine. So, Christians must include this important truth. This may mean exposing a cult's false beliefs.

John 3:16
For God so loved the world, that he gave his one and only Son, that whoever believes in him should not perish, but have eternal life.

John 20:30-31
Therefore Jesus did many other signs in the presence of his disciples, which are not written in this book; but these are written, that you may believe that Jesus is the Christ, the Son of God, and that believing you may have life in his name.

The Reception of Christ as Savior

One's response to the proclamation of Jesus Christ as only Savior of the world is to receive Him as Savior. The unsaved must believe that Christ died on the cross to pay the penalty for their sins and accept His saving grace by receiving Him. Jesus was crucified between two thieves. One of the thieves came to realize who Jesus was. Hanging on a cross that thief asked Christ to be His Savior. In Luke 23:42, he cried out to Jesus asking Him to remember him when He came into His kingdom. Jesus assured him that very day he would be in paradise. This dying man received Christ that day.

Luke 23:42
He said to Jesus, "Lord, remember me when you come into your Kingdom."

In 2 Timothy 1:10, Paul declares to Timothy that the one who has abolished death and brought life and immortality through the gospel was "our Savior Jesus Christ." Notice, he uses the possessive pronoun "our" to refer to the Lord being ours. That is a relationship word. The same phrase can be found in 2 Peter 1:1. In that passage, Peter refers to Jesus as "our God and Savior." The acceptance of His saving work is implied in the term "our Savior." This is why in recent years Christians speak of "accepting Christ as Savior."

2 Timothy 1:10
But has now been revealed by the appearing of our Savior, Christ Jesus, who abolished death, and brought life and immortality to light through the Good News.

2 Peter 1:1
Simon Peter, a servant and apostle of Jesus Christ, to those who have obtained a like precious faith with us in the righteousness of our God and Savior, Jesus Christ.

John clarifies this concept using the term "received." The proper biblical term for one's relationship with Jesus Christ is "received." Christians should be identifying themselves as having "received Jesus Christ as Savior and Lord." In John 1:12, the apostle refers to our relationship with Jesus Christ in this way, "But as many as received him, to them he gave the right to become God's children, to those who believe in his name." The Greek word translated "receive" means "to take." In the context of a person, it refers to taking with the hand, laying hold of any person or thing in order to use it, to make it one's own, or to give a person access to oneself in a person-to-person relationship. It is a word that denotes more much than just knowledge.

John 1:12
But as many as received him, to them he gave the right to become God's children, to those who believe in his name.

In John 6:21, this key term was used physically when John described the disciples allowing Christ to enter their boat. They saw the Lord Jesus walking upon the water and were frightened because they thought He was a ghost. When He had convinced them otherwise, they received Jesus into the boat. When He entered, they were immediately at the shore.

The Greek word is used spiritually of receiving Christ into people's lives and allowing Him to do His work through His Spirit. As they received Him into the boat, unbelievers are to receive Him into their lives.

John 6:21
They were willing...to receive him into the boat. Immediately the boat was at the land where they were going.

In John 19:27, while on the cross, Jesus asked John to care for His mother. John records that she was received into his household from that day forward. Mary became a part of his family. She entered into an intimate, familial relationship with him. In the same way, when Christ is received by one, he enters into a familial relationship (children of God) with Him. In John 20:22, when the Lord foretold the coming of His Spirit to the disciples, He portrayed it as "receiving" the Holy Spirit. When the Holy Spirit comes into the life of believers at salvation, He is literally received into their bodies (1 John 2:27). They become temples of the Holy Spirit (1 Corinthians 3:16; 6:19). Christ in His Spirit becomes the most important person in their lives and changes them (2 Corinthians 5:17).

John 19:27
Then he said to the disciple, "Behold, your mother!" From that hour, the disciple took her to his own home.

John 20:22
When he had said this, he breathed on them, and said to them, "Receive the Holy Spirit!"

1 John 2:27
As for you, the anointing which you received from him remains in you, and you don't need for anyone to teach you. But as his anointing teaches you concerning all things, and is true, and is no lie, and even as it taught you, you will remain in him.

1 Corinthians 3:16
Don't you know that you are a temple of God, and that God's Spirit lives in you?

1 Corinthians 6:19
Or don't you know that your body is a temple of the Holy Spirit who is in you, whom you have from God? You are not your own.

2 Corinthians 5:17
Therefore if anyone is in Christ, he is a new creation. The old things have passed away. Behold, all things have become new.

This also means trusting Christ for one's eternal salvation as the absolute, only way to heaven. One must believe that Christ is the only way to heaven to be truly saved. This is a core belief. It was Jesus who stated in John 14:6, "I am the way, the truth, and the life. No one comes to the Father, except through me." Then in Acts 4:12, Peter said, "There is salvation in none other, for neither is there any other name under heaven, that is given among men, by which we must be saved!" If some say that they have received Jesus Christ but believe He is not the "only way", it is the wrong Jesus.

John 14:6
Jesus said to him, "I am the way, the truth, and the life. No one comes to the Father, except through me.

Acts 4:12
There is salvation in no one else, for there is no other name under heaven that is given among men, by which we must be saved!

The Corinthians were questioning the resurrection of the dead. In 1 Corinthians 15:13-21, Paul claims that they were rejecting the very foundation of the Christian faith. If there is no resurrection, Jesus Christ was not raised. Without Him, believers have no real faith, so they are dead in their sins. Yet, Jesus has been raised and so shall they. Christians trust in Him and Him alone for their resurrection from the dead. When Christ is proclaimed as the only Savior, unbelievers must come to Him, recognize His saving work on the cross for them, acknowledge that He is the only way, and receive Him as the Savior accepting His free gift of eternal life.

1 Corinthians 15:13-21
But if there is no resurrection of the dead, neither has Christ been raised. If Christ has not been raised, then our preaching is in vain, and your faith also is in vain. Yes, we are also found false witnesses of God, because we testified about God that he raised up Christ, whom he didn't raise up, if it is so that the dead are not raised. For if the dead aren't raised, neither has Christ been raised. If Christ has not been raised, your faith is vain; you are still in your sins. Then they also who are fallen asleep in Christ have perished. If we have only hoped in Christ in this life, we are of all men most pitiable. But now Christ has been raised from the dead. He became the first fruit of those who are asleep. For since death came by man, the resurrection of the dead also came by man.

The Submission to Christ as Lord

One's response to the proclamation of Christ as Lord is the recognition of His Lordship producing in the Christian the appropriate response: submission and obedience to Him as Master. This is not complete and absolute obedience, for this is impossible in this life. In Romans 8:22, Paul describes the groaning that all Christians have within themselves for redemption. In the redemption of their bodies, Christians will find true and absolute submission and obedience. It will not be fully experienced in this life.

Romans 8:22
For we know that the whole creation groans and travails in pain together until now.

Paul calls his body "the body of death" because within it is contained "the flesh." This "old man" battles us day after day (Romans 7:22-25; Ephesians 4:22-23). As long as it is not redeemed, we would not be fully able to finally overcome it. Instead, we should desire, strive, and pursue the submission and obedience that is found in Romans 12:1-2. Christians strive after presenting their bodies every single day as living sacrifices, holy, and acceptable to God in service to Him. True believers refuse to be conformed to this world reach for being transformed by the renewing of their minds in order to be pleasing to their God. This results in what John calls practicing righteousness in his first letter (1 John 2:29). This quality distinguishes believers from non-believers.

Romans 7:22-25
For I delight in God's law after the inward person, but I see a different law in my members, warring against the law of my mind, and bringing me into captivity under the law of sin which is in my members. What a wretched man I am! Who will deliver me out of the body of this death? I thank God through Jesus Christ, our Lord! So then with the mind, I myself serve God's law, but with the flesh, sin's law.

Ephesians 4:22-23
That you put away, as concerning your former way of life, the old man that grows corrupt after the lusts of deceit, and that you be renewed in the spirit of your mind.

Romans 12:1-2
Therefore I urge you, brothers, by the mercies of God, to present your bodies a living sacrifice, holy, acceptable to God, which is your spiritual service. Don't be conformed to this world, but be transformed by the renewing of your mind, so that you may prove what is the good, well-pleasing, and perfect will of God.

1 John 2:29
If you know that he is righteous, you know that everyone who practices righteousness has been born of him.

In 1 John 3:5-10, he goes further by stating that one who is born of God, does not continually commit sin. The verb is in the present tense which signals continuous action in present time. One who commits sins (continuous action in present time) is of the Devil. The key concept is continuous action as a pattern of life. Christians sin as individual acts but do not practice sin. They may have difficulty obeying their Lord on some occasions, but as a pattern of life obedience is present.

1 John 3:5-10
You know that he was revealed to take away our sins, and no sin is in him. Whoever remains in him doesn't sin. Whoever sins hasn't seen him and doesn't know him. Little children, let no one lead you astray. He who does righteousness is righteous, even as he is righteous. He who sins is of the devil, for the devil has been sinning from the beginning. To this end the Son of God was revealed: that he might destroy the works of the devil. Whoever is born of God doesn't commit sin, because his seed remains in him, and he can't sin, because he is born of God. In this the children of God are revealed, and the children of the devil. Whoever doesn't do righteousness is not of God, neither is he who doesn't love his brother.

True Christians recognize that Jesus Christ is their Lord. This will pour forth into obedience to His commandments. In Matthew 16:24, Jesus indicated to His disciples that they needed to deny themselves, take up their crosses, and follow Him, if they wanted to come after Him. When Paul recounts his personal testimony in Acts 22:8-10, he was struck down and asked, "What shall I do, Lord?" This was the recognition that Jesus Christ, to whom he was speaking, was Lord and demanded obedience from that moment onward. When we receive Christ, the submission and intent to obey pours forth into salvation. If that submission and intent is real, then the fruit of obedience and good works will demonstrate our true faith. Faith will be shown by works (James 2:14).

Matthew 16:24
Then Jesus said to his disciples, "If anyone desires to come after me, let him deny himself, take up his cross, and follow me.

Acts 22:8-10
I answered, "Who are you, Lord?" He said to me, "I am Jesus of Nazareth, whom you persecute." Those who were with me indeed saw the light and were afraid, but they didn't understand the voice of him....I said, "What shall I do, Lord?" The Lord said to me, "Arise, and go into Damascus....

James 2:14
What good is it, my brothers, if a man says he has faith, but has no works? Can faith save him?

In Acts 16:25, Paul and Silas were singing and praising the Lord Jesus in prison. A powerful Earthquake occurred, and the jailer thought everyone had escaped. Since the jailer would have been murdered for this, he prepared to commit suicide. Luke describes, "And brought them out and said, 'Sirs, what must I do to be saved?' They said, 'Believe in the Lord Jesus...you will be saved, you and your household.'" Paul shouted for the jailor to stop, and all the prisoners were still in the jail. The jailor must have been awestruck by this. Now, he knew Paul was from God and asks to be saved.

Acts 16:25
But about midnight Paul and Silas were praying and singing hymns to God, and the prisoners were listening to them.

Paul's answer in verse 31 was clear; he needed to believe in the Lord Jesus Christ. The jailer must believe in the Master Jesus Christ. This implies both submission and obedience. In Romans 10:9, Paul told the Romans that if they confessed with their mouths that Jesus is Lord and believed in their hearts that He had risen from the dead they would be saved. His Lordship is essential. It must never be omitted from presentations. Obedience is required from the first days of following Christ.

Acts 16:31
They said, "Believe in the Lord Jesus Christ, and you will be saved, you and your household."

Romans 10:9
That if you will confess with your mouth that Jesus is Lord, and believe in your heart that God raised him from the dead, you will be saved.

Some would like to separate the Lordship of Christ from His saving work. This is impossible. Can one be saved and produce no fruits? Some want this to be because a loved one they know claimed to know Jesus but never lived for Him. Unfortunately, there is not one example of this in the New

Testament. The thief on the cross never had an opportunity to live for Christ.

Yet, in the moments the thief did have, he declared that Jesus was sinless and rebuked the other thief for taunting Him! This was the only good work he could do, and he did it. Recognizing Jesus as the Lord demands submission and obedience issuing forth in good works, even on a cross.

Those saved on their death bed will experience the same, even if only for moments or hours. Anyone who has truly repented of sin, turned the other way, and now has the opportunity to live for Christ will produce fruits. Why? They understand that He is the Lord! In Matthew 20:8-10, the Lord told a parable about day laborers who were hired to work in the field at different times of the day, and each received the same wage.

Matthew 20:8-10
When evening had come, the lord of the vineyard said to his manager, "Call the laborers and pay them their wages, beginning from the last to the first." When those who were hired at about the eleventh hour came, they each received a denarius. When the first came, they supposed that they would receive more; and they likewise each received a denarius.

Every one of them, including the ones hired just before the day was over, worked in the field. This was a picture of salvation. All produced works, once hired, some more, some less. The full understanding of who Jesus is issues forth in submission to Him as Lord. When people encounter His majesty, they will fall on their face before Him.

The Affirmation of Christ's Resurrection

One's response to the defense of the deity of Jesus Christ is the firm belief that He is the Son of God from the miracles, fulfilled prophecies, and His resurrection from the dead. The biblical response to this is an affirmation of the resurrection. In Romans 10:9, Paul explains, "That if you will confess with your mouth that Jesus is Lord, and believe in your heart that God raised him from the dead, you will be saved."

Romans 10:9
That if you will confess with your mouth that Jesus is Lord, and believe in your heart that God raised him from the dead, you will be saved.

Paul said that if one confesses that Jesus is Lord with His mouth and believes He rose from the dead in his heart, he will be saved. In 1 Corinthians 15, Paul gives the essence of the gospel which is Christ died, was buried, and rose again according to the Scriptures (verses 3-4).

1 Corinthians 15:3-4
For I delivered to you first of all that which I also received: that Christ died for our sins according to the Scriptures, that he was buried, that he was raised on the third day according to the Scriptures.

In John 20:24-28, Thomas, His disciple, refused to believe in the resurrection of Christ until he witnessed the wounds on His hands and put his finger in His side. Eight days later, Jesus appeared and allowed Thomas to verify this miracle with His own senses. Immediately, he declared that Jesus was "my Lord and my God." Notice the possessive pronoun. He was declaring his own salvation from the recognition of Christ's resurrection which proved His deity.

John 20:24-28
But Thomas, one of the twelve, called Didymus, wasn't with them when Jesus came. The other disciples therefore said to him, "We have seen the Lord!" But he said to them, "Unless I see in his hands the print of the nails, put my finger into the print of the nails, and put my hand into his side, I will not believe." After eight days again his disciples were inside and Thomas was with them. Jesus came, the doors being locked, and stood in the middle, and said, "Peace be to you." Then he said to Thomas, "Reach here your finger, and see my hands.

Reach here your hand, and put it into my side. Don't be unbelieving, but believing." Thomas answered him, "My Lord and my God!"

Then Jesus paints a portrait of believers in the future, who will never witness the wounds. These beloved saints will be blessed because though they will not have seen, yet they will believe in His resurrection. This describes all those who have come to Jesus Christ after His ascension, except Paul. In their gospel presentations, the saints should include the defenses of Christ's deity and request an affirmation of His resurrection to demonstrate their newfound belief in His deity. This belief comes through the Holy Spirit working in their hearts as the evidence are presented and accepted. It is through these proofs that He has chosen to work.

The Relationship to Christ in Love

One's response to the proclamation of a relationship with Christ is to love Him. The word love used of Christ in the Greek in its most basic understanding is to value or to prize. It does not convey the feelings implied by the English word. Feelings may be part of it but does not compose the central aspect. The key is this valuing and prizing of someone or something which issues forth in a variety of loving words and actions. It also has to do with the right understanding of the person or object loved.

John delineates these critical fundamental elements when he describes exactly how to love the brethren in 1 John 3:18. He asserts that they are to love in deed and in truth as well as in their words and language. To love someone must by its nature be expressed. Those expressions are found in both verbal and physical actions with loving language and deeds according to the truth. The truth here refers to the Scripture. Loving someone is always according to God's Word.

1 John 3:18
My little children, let's not love in word…tongue only, but in deed and truth.

In the case of Christ, those who come to Him believe that He is the God of the universe, has died for them, forgiven their sins, submitted to Him as Lord, and love Him for it. They then spend their lives learning about Him through His Word, talking to Him through their prayers, and loving Him through obedience and good deeds. They love Him the way the Scriptures tell them to love Him. The way He desires to be loved. This love then grows and grows.

In John 14:15, Jesus declares that if someone loves Him, he will keep His commandments. Then in verse 24, the Lord pronounced that someone who does not love Him does not keep His commandments. Obedience flows out of love. In John 14:23, just before this declaration, John recorded this statement from the Lord, "Jesus answered him, 'If a man loves me, he will keep my word. My Father will love him, and we will come to him, and make our home with him.'" After this, the Lord Jesus makes an amazing statement that if someone loves Him, the Father will love them. Also, if one loves the Son, then one loves His Father, the true God. In John 17:26, Christ professes that the love that a Christian has for Him (Jesus) is in reality the love of the Father for Jesus in them. When He was asked which commandment was the greatest, Jesus said that it was to love the Lord with all one's heart, mind, soul, strength, and understanding. Every true believer also loves the Son in the exact same way. This is a love relationship.

John 14:15
If you love me, keep my commandments.

John 14:24
He who doesn't love me doesn't keep my words. The word which you hear isn't mine, but the Father's who sent me.

John 14:23
Jesus answered him, "If a man loves me, he will keep my word. My Father will love him, and we will come to him, and make our home with him."

John 17:26
I made known to them your name, and will make it known; that the love with which you loved me may be in them, and I in them.

Over and over, the writers of the New Testament describe Christians as those who love Jesus Christ. In Ephesians 6:24, Paul closes his letter with a blessing of grace that addresses all his believing readers as those who love the Lord Jesus Christ. In 1 Corinthians 16:22, Paul concludes his letter by pronouncing a curse on all who will not love the Lord Jesus Christ. Here, he is speaking generally of all unbelievers but also alluding to the false prophets that were disrupting the Corinthian church and were standing against him. They will spend an eternity in hell without God.

Ephesians 6:24
Grace be with all those who love our Lord Jesus Christ with incorruptible love. Amen.

1 Corinthians 16:22
If any man doesn't love the Lord Jesus Christ, let him be cursed. Come, Lord!

In James 1:12, the half-brother of Jesus promises a reward to all the Christians who persevere under trial. He addresses them as "those who love Him." Later in chapter 2, verse 5, the head of the Jerusalem church contrasts the poor of this world with the rich. He discloses a promise to the poor who are believers. The Lord promised that those who love Him will be rich in faith and heirs of the kingdom. Once again, he addresses believers as the ones who love the Lord.

James 1:12
Blessed is a person who endures temptation, for when he has been approved, he will receive the crown of life, which the Lord promised to those who love him.

James 2:5
Listen, my beloved brothers. Didn't God choose those who are poor in this world to be rich in faith, and heirs of the Kingdom which he promised to those who love him?

In 1 Peter 1:8, Peter complements his readers concerning their love for Christ. He characterizes them as those who are filled with joy. Why? Though they have not seen Him, they love Him! He portrays true believers as those who believe in Jesus Christ as God and love their Lord. This was a lesson that the apostle learned the hard way! When Jesus restored Peter to ministry, Jesus questioned his love for Him (John 21:16-17). Why? Love for Christ is the core of one's salvation.

1 Peter 1:8
Whom, not having known, you love. In him, though now you don't see him, yet believing, you rejoice greatly with joy that is unspeakable and full of glory.

John 21:16-17
He said to him again a second time, "Simon, son of Jonah, do you love me?" He said to him, "Yes, Lord; you know that I have affection for you." He said to him, "Tend my sheep." He said to him the third time, "Simon, son of Jonah, do you have affection for me?" Peter was grieved because he asked him the third time, "Do you have affection for me?" He said to him, "Lord, you know everything. You know that I have affection for you." Jesus said to him, "Feed my sheep."

This love for Christ will be in direct opposition to the love of the world. When an unbeliever repents, he forsakes the love of the world and replaces it with a love for Christ. The world would be the society of unbelievers with everything that is evil within it. John describes it in 1 John 2:15-16. The world is comprised of the lust of the eyes, the flesh, and pride of living. This would be whatever the eyes and flesh passionately desire and whatever causes unbelievers to boast concerning the way in which they live.

1 John 2:15-16
Don't love the world or the things that are in the world. If anyone loves the world, the Father's love isn't in him. For all that is in the world, the lust of the flesh, the lust of the eyes, and the pride of life, isn't the Father's, but is the world's.

In James 4:1-4, James stands against all those who seek their own pleasure above God among his readers. This led to fighting and quarreling among themselves. He exclaims that friendship with the world is enmity against their God. These seekers of pleasure wanted all that the world offered, and James identifies them as spiritual adulterers. He uses the Old Testament concept of Israel's idolatry as adulterating their love relationship with God (Ezekiel 16:15-19, 30; Hosea 1:2). Their love of the world and its pleasures was the same kind of adultery. Christians view the Hebrew people as sinning in a way they would never do; yet often do the same thing.

James 4:1-4
Where do wars and fightings among you come from? Don't they come from your pleasures that war in your members? You lust, and don't have. You murder and covet, and can't obtain. You fight and make war. You don't have, because you don't ask. You ask, and don't receive, because you ask with wrong motives, so that you may spend it on your pleasures. You adulterers and adulteresses, don't you know that friendship with the world is hostility toward God? Whoever therefore wants to be a friend of the world makes himself an enemy of God.

Ezekiel 16:15-19
But you trusted in your beauty, and played the prostitute because of your renown, and poured out your prostitution on everyone who passed by. It was his. You took some of your garments, and made for yourselves high places decked with various colors, and played the prostitute on them. This shall not happen, neither shall it be. You also took your beautiful jewels of my gold and of my silver, which I had given you, and made for yourself images of men, and played the prostitute with them. You took your embroidered garments, covered them, and set my oil and my incense before them. My bread also which I gave you, fine flour, oil, and honey, with which I fed you, you even set it before them for a pleasant aroma; and so it was," says the Lord Yahweh.

Ezekiel 16:30
"How weak is your heart," says the Lord Yahweh, "since you do all these things, the work of an impudent prostitute."

Hosea 1:2
When Yahweh spoke at first by Hosea, Yahweh said to Hosea, "Go, take for yourself a wife of prostitution and children of unfaithfulness; for the land commits great adultery, forsaking Yahweh."

This adulterous love can take a variety of forms. It can be the love of men's approval (John 12:43), the love of money (1 Timothy 6:10), the love of self (2 Timothy 3:2), the love of pleasure (2 Timothy 3:4), the love of this present world (2 Timothy 4:10), the love of the wages of unrighteousness (2 Peter 2:15), and the love of preeminence (3 John 1:9). Then add the many permutations and combinations of this sinful love and it can express itself endlessly.

John 12:43
For they loved men's praise more than God's praise.

1 Timothy 6:10
For the love of money is a root of all kinds of evil. Some have been led astray from...faith in their greed, and have pierced themselves through with many sorrows.

2 Timothy 3:2
For men will be lovers of self, lovers of money, boastful, arrogant, blasphemers, disobedient to parents, unthankful, unholy.

2 Timothy 3:4
Traitors, headstrong...lovers of pleasure rather than lovers of God.

2 Timothy 4:10
For Demas left me, having loved this present world, and went to Thessalonica; Crescens to Galatia; and Titus to Dalmatia.

2 Peter 2:15
Forsaking the right way, they went astray, having followed the way of Balaam...son of Beor, who loved the wages of wrongdoing.

3 John 1:9
I wrote to the assembly [church], but Diotrephes, who loves to be first among them, doesn't accept what we say.

Why? Why must someone turn from loving this world to loving God instead? The answer comes from the parable of the seed thrown among the thorns in Matthew 13:22. The love of the world (the deceitfulness of riches and its worries) choke the Word and they fall away, never allowing the seed of faith to take root. Jesus clarifies this struggle between two loves when He speaks of those that are serving two masters in Matthew 6:24. Either they will love one and hate the other or be devoted to one or despise the other. People cannot love God and love money (the essence of the world system). They are naturally and supernaturally opposed to each other.

Matthew 13:22
What was sown among the thorns, this is he who hears the word, but the cares of this age and the deceitfulness of riches choke the word, and he becomes unfruitful.

Matthew 6:24
No one can serve two masters, for either he will hate the one and love the other, or else he will be devoted to one and despise the other. You can't serve both God and Mammon.

This does not mean that true believers will not struggle with the flesh. They will, but they will also regularly win the battle. In Romans 7:18-20, the apostle claims he desires good, but sometimes does evil. He battles his flesh (sin principle in the body) within his mind. In Galatians 5:17, Paul indicates that the Spirit in Christians will oppose the flesh in them so they will not do what they want. Here lies the key point. A true believer will desire to be righteous through the Spirit in Him, but his body will desire to be evil. As the daily battles are fought, the believer will regularly choose good, but the unbeliever will choose evil.

Romans 7:18-20
For I know that in me, that is, in my flesh, dwells no good thing. For desire is present with me, but I don't find it doing that which is good. For the good which I desire, I don't do; but the evil which I don't desire, that I practice. But if what I don't desire, that I do, it is no more I that do it, but sin which dwells in me.

Galatians 5:17
For the flesh lusts against the Spirit, and the Spirit against the flesh; and these are contrary to one another, that you may not do the things that you desire.

The Dependence on Faith Alone

To be saved, unbelievers must believe that faith alone will save them. They must trust in Christ's saving work on the cross alone rather than the accumulation of good works or personal righteousness. In Roman 3:28, Paul declares that Christians are justified by faith apart from the works of the Law. Once again, in Romans 5:1, he asserts that believers are justified by faith alone. When false teachers fooled the Galatians into thinking that Gentiles had to be circumcised, Paul explained to them that the works of the law could not justify but only hearing by faith (Galatians 2:16). Men can only be justified (declared righteous) by faith in what Christ did for them on the cross.

Romans 3:28
We maintain therefore that a man is justified by faith apart from the works of the law.

Romans 5:1
Being therefore justified by faith, we have peace with God through our Lord Jesus Chris.

Galatians 2:16
Yet knowing that a man is not justified by the works of the law but through faith in Jesus Christ, even we believed in Christ Jesus, that we might be justified by faith in Christ, and not by the works of the law, because no flesh will be justified by the works of the law.

In Ephesians 2:8, Paul clearly explains that salvation is a result of faith, not works. Why? So, no man can boast before God. No one will ever be able to claim that he worked his way into heaven. Instead, as has been seen, good works pour forth from a life of faith. In Ephesians 2:10, Paul continues his discussion by indicating that once faith comes Christians are to walk in good works.

Ephesians 2:8
For by grace you have been saved through faith, and that not of yourselves; it is the gift of God.

Ephesians 2:10
For we are his workmanship, created in Christ Jesus for good works, which God prepared before that we would walk in them.

In Colossians 1:10, Paul prays that the church would walk in a worthy manner that pleased the Lord in everything and produced fruit in every good work. In 2 Timothy 6:18, Paul encourages Timothy to instruct the saints, who are well-to-do financially, to be rich in good works instead. Righteous works flow supernaturally from true faith, but they do not save. This is an important distinction.

Colossians 1:10
That you may walk worthily of the Lord, to please him in all respects, bearing fruit in every good work and increasing in the knowledge of God.

1 Timothy 6:18
That they do good, that they be rich in good works, that they be ready to distribute, willing to share.

The Response of Water Baptism

In Matthew 28:18-20, the risen Lord Jesus commanded His followers to make disciples by going, baptizing, and teaching. Notice the marvelous framework for evangelism and edification. They were to make many disciples by going, baptizing (evangelism), and teaching (edification). This is the sequence used in producing followers of Christ.

Matthew 28:18-20
Jesus came to them and spoke to them, saying, "All authority has been given to me in heaven and on Earth. Go and make disciples of all nations, baptizing them in the name of the Father and of the Son and of the Holy Spirit, teaching them to observe all things that I commanded you. Behold, I am with you always, even to the end of the age." Amen.

This was also the pattern of Jesus Christ and the apostles in their proclamation of the gospel. In John 3:22, the apostle John records that Jesus was in the land of Judea baptizing. Obviously, this occurred after the preaching of the kingdom which is always described by the gospel writers as Christ's message of redemption (Matthew 4:17; Mark 1:15; Luke 8:1). They believed then were baptized. In actuality, Jesus was doing the preaching of the kingdom, but His disciples were baptizing those who were receiving Him (John 4:2).

John 3:22
After these things, Jesus came with his disciples into the land of Judea. He stayed there with them and baptized.

Matthew 4:17
From that time, Jesus began to preach, and to say, "Repent! For the Kingdom of Heaven is at hand."

Mark 1:15
And saying, "The time is fulfilled, and God's Kingdom is at hand! Repent, and believe in the Good News."

Luke 8:1
Soon afterwards, he went about through cities and villages, preaching and bringing the good news of God's Kingdom. With him were the twelve,

John 4:2
Although Jesus himself didn't baptize, but his disciple.

In Acts 2:41, after the people received Peter's word (the gospel), then they were baptized. They received Jesus Christ (John 1:12), and then were baptized. This would have been a momentous undertaking because at least three thousand people were saved that day. Yet, they baptized all of them. Why? Baptism after salvation was God's desired pattern. Christ went about proclaiming the kingdom, and everyone who received Him was baptized.

Acts 2:41
Then those who gladly received his word were baptized. There were added that day about three thousand souls.

John 1:12
But as many as received him, to them he gave the right to become God's children, to those who believe in his name.

In Acts 8:12-13, Luke clearly records that after the citizens of Samaria believed in the good news of the kingdom and Jesus Christ preached by Philip, they were being baptized. In his ministry Paul evangelized the lost in the same way. In Acts 16:15, Lydia and her household believed and were baptized. Then a few verses later in Acts 16:33, the jailer and his household believed and were baptized. In Acts 18:8, Luke described the salvation of Crispus, his household, and many Corinthians. Paul proclaimed the Word, they believed, and were baptized. Their baptism came immediately after salvation, and it was always a baptism of true believers. No babies were ever baptized. Baptism was invariably by full immersion in physical water. Baptism was never seen as something one does in the church many years later because they finally are living for Jesus Christ. Baptism was always performed in front of unbelievers as a testimony of faith to them, not exclusively before believers.

Acts 8:12-13
But when they believed Philip preaching good news concerning God's Kingdom and the name of Jesus Christ, they were baptized, both men and women. Simon himself also believed. Being baptized, he continued with Philip. Seeing signs and great miracles occurring, he was amazed.

Acts 16:15
When she and her household were baptized, she begged us, saying, "If you have judged me to be faithful to the Lord, come into my house and stay." So she persuaded us.

Acts 16:33
He took them the same hour of the night and washed their stripes, and was immediately baptized, he and all his household.

Acts 18:8
Crispus, the ruler of the synagogue, believed in the Lord with all his house. Many of the Corinthians, when they heard, believed and were baptized.

An Ancient Portrait

In Acts 19:1-41, we pick up the record of Paul's ministry in Ephesus. As was his custom he immediately entered the synagogue so that as a traveling rabbi he would be allowed to provide a word of encouragement to the congregation of Jews and God-fearing Gentiles. This Word was always the sharing of the gospel and the pursuit of a saving faith. For three months Paul addressed, reasoned, and discussed the truths of the good news with these people. As he pursued saving faith, many came to Christ.

When he received resistance from the others, he simply moved next-door to the school of Tyrannus. He kept doing his part in the gospel and he relied on God to do His. For two years he proclaimed, taught, and delivered the whole council of God. Eventually, almost all who lived in Asia heard God's Word of redemption and the truths of the New Covenant established in Christ. While he pursued a saving faith among them, the Lord God authenticated their message by doing mighty miracles by Paul's hand. These signs and wonders were so powerful that even a handkerchief or an apron that the apostle had touched brought relief. People found total and complete healing.

There were seven sons of a Jewish priest named Sceva who attempted to imitate Paul's great power that God had given him. While they were attempting to cast out a demon, he cried out that he knew both Jesus and Paul but did not know them. This demon declared that he did not have to obey these unbelieving men. Then the evil angel within the man jumped on them and beat them. They were left naked and wounded fleeing from the man's house. This is God's work given to His believing people and not to those who have rejected Him. When those in Ephesus had heard what this demon had done and how powerful Paul was, the fear of God fell upon all of its citizens. The name of Jesus became magnified before the apostle's eminent arrival. The gospel he would preach had already been confirmed in the minds of those who would believe, and they would find saving faith.

After Paul's arrival, many came to Christ. Among them were those who were practitioners of black magic. These new believers brought the books of their dark magic arts and threw them into a huge pile in the center of their city and burned them for all to see. The cost of the books came to fifty thousand pieces of silver. This was a staggering amount at that time. What a witness to the saving power of Jesus! Luke records that the Word of God was growing and prevailing against the forces of darkness in that whole area. Then, there was a great uproar in the city by those who were merchants selling silver idols of Artemis, whose temple was located there. Demetrius, the leader, gathered together all the merchants of similar trades in order to put a stop to God's mighty work through Paul. A riot almost ensued but was curtailed by one of the administrators of the city.

In Acts 20:17-38, Paul arrived in Miletus and sent for the elders from Ephesus. He could not go into the city again. There he spent time encouraging and exhorting them. Then, it was time for Paul to leave for the region of Macedonia. He bid them farewell and was off to his next location. He was continually preaching and proclaiming the gospel. Then, he would pursue saving faith among his listeners and watched many come to Jesus Christ. The point is that the apostle Paul would not change his gospel presentation to appease anyone in the city of Ephesus or anywhere else. The apostle always pursued a saving faith by giving a true gospel presentation. He never added any concept, opinion, or cultural norm that would appeal culturally to his audience. Also, He did not leave out an element of the gospel in order to appease his audience or be relevant at the time.

A Modern Anecdote

When an opportunity came to run a vacation bible school for my church (a week-long event of two hours each day for children), I jumped at this opportunity with one stipulation. I asked them to allow me to design the camp around a fresh, current, and biblical theme. For this theme, I decided to use Paul's analogy of Christians as soldiers at war with the forces of evil. I picked this because the military or police theme was very popular in books, television shows, and movies at the time. I also had several police and highway patrol officers in our church whom I could recruit to help.

I borrowed a flight uniform from my brother who was a civilian mechanic on an air force base. The first day, we had a CHP officer ride his motorcycle around the parking lot as the children (3rd to 6th graders) arrived. There was a large sign in front of the church that read, "Welcome to SWAT CAMP." Below it in smaller letters were written, "**S**piritual **W**eapons **A**nd **T**actics for Growth in Christ (Ephesians 6:10-19)." It was very exciting for the children.

The day was broken up into four periods. The first was a large group teaching time (Meeting with Our Commander God), the second had a small group application and prayer time (Battle Strategy Session), the third involved a fun game time (Training and Obstacle Course), and the fourth time encouraged a positive interaction with law enforcement personnel who attended our church and were believers (Law Enforcement Interaction). One of our officers always brought a vehicle or some equipment that he could also demonstrate. The children loved the hands-on experience.

The teaching time explained each piece of the armor of God with one element of the gospel message taught at the end of each session. The application time involved how they could take each spiritual principle and apply it to their own lives. Then they prayed for themselves, their friends, family members, fellow students, teachers, and the government and its officers. It was a powerful time.

The game time encompassed an obstacle course where the kids could run through old worn tires, climb walls, and play a variety of simulation games. In the law enforcement time, we discussed Romans 13:1-4 and the importance of obeying the governing authorities and their laws. Different officers from a variety of governmental agencies demonstrated some of their equipment and shared their personal testimony.

Each day, I shared an element of the good news and on the last day gave an invitation to receive Christ as Savior and Lord. It was very low key, gentle, and optional. I wanted the

Spirit to work in their hearts and minds not my cleverness, intimidation, or persuasive ability. During the course of the week, there were two sisters who were continually fooling around and then getting into trouble. I spent much time with Emily and Emma discussing their poor behavior. I felt as if they had been forced to come and were not interested.

Several children came forward while the girls sat silent in the back. After the program was completed the two girls walked up to me and said that they had decided to receive Christ. They were too embarrassed to come forward because of their poor behavior during the week. They told me how sorry they were and wanted to know what they should do. I pursued a saving faith with them on the spot. They repented of their sins and affirmed their belief in Jesus as the Son of

God and only Savior of the world. Emily and Emma told me that they believed that He died on the cross for their sins, resurrected from the dead, and now wanted a spiritual love relationship with Jesus Christ as Savior and Lord. So, they received Christ. Then, I explained that I wanted to inform their mother and baptize them. Mom was delighted she had been a Christian for quite a while, but she was not sure how to lead her girls to Christ. Some months after their baptism, they were forced to move away due to financial reasons.

I did not hear from them for many years. Then one of the girls contacted me in her late twenties to let me know they were still in love Jesus. They thanked me for the time I took with them. Of course, I gave the glory to God who did much of the work in their lives. I learned through this experience the importance of pursuing a true saving faith and not just settling for a quick response that doesn't save (Acts 2:37-41).

Acts 2:37-41

Now when they heard this, they were cut to the heart, and said to Peter and the rest of the apostles, "Brothers, what shall we do?" Peter said to them, "Repent, and be baptized, every one of you, in the name of Jesus Christ for the forgiveness of sins, and you will receive the gift of the Holy Spirit. For the promise is to you, and to your children, and to all who are far off, even as many as the Lord our God will call to himself." With many other words he testified, and exhorted them, saying, "Save yourselves from this crooked generation!" Then those who gladly received his word were baptized. There were added that day about three thousand souls.

A Personal Response

Dear Heavenly Father,

I ask that you give me the burden and the desire I need to share the gospel with (add names) and others I know and meet. Provide for me the wisdom to present each aspect of Your gospel to them clearly and completely. Then I request that You do a powerful work in their hearts to make the proper responses. Humble them in their hearts, so they will admit their sin before You. I ask that You help them to fully understand that Jesus is Your Son, and they will believe in Him. Please affirm in their hearts that He resurrected from the dead. As a result, lead them into receiving Your Son as Savior and submitting to Him as Lord of their lives. Guide them as they commit themselves to a love relationship with Jesus Christ and that salvation comes through Him and Him alone. Help them to see that the first step of obedience is to be water baptized and proclaim their new faith in Him before their families, friends, the church, and the world. I pray this in the name of Jesus. Amen.

LEADING THE WAY

Instructor's Notes

AN INSTRUCTOR'S MANUAL

Chapter 10

Pursue a Saving Faith

In evangelism, Christians must pursue a true saving faith as a response to the gospel. This is not merely words but a belief and a trust that literally changes people's lives.

In the section, "A Typical Scenario," the author identifies how Christians might determine if the people they might want to date may be believers.

What is the scenario about?

A Christian is dating someone and desires to know whether the person is a believer and if not share the gospel.

What held the believer back from sharing the gospel?

He was nervous about bringing up the person's salvation on the first date but did not want to date an unbeliever.

What finally led the Christian to share the good news and how did it occur?

He asked the person how she became a believer and she was unclear about her salvation, so he shared the gospel with her.

Have you had a similar experience?

(Various answers should be shared including yours.)

LEADING THE WAY

In the section, "A Scriptural Principle" the author presents an important biblical principle in evangelism which concerns the true response that saves.

How would you express this principle in your own words?

Principle ten is "we must pursue a saving faith."

(Various answers should be shared including yours.)

How would you rewrite this principle to make it even more personal to your life (using your name and situation)?

(Various answers should be shared including yours.)

Why do you think this principle might be important in your life right now as you share the gospel?

(Various answers should be shared including yours.)

How would you rate yourself on the percentage of times you followed this principle in the past when you did something wrong in a relationship?

(Various answers should be shared including yours.)

Directions: Put a horizontal mark and your name where you see yourself on the percentage line.

0%   25%   50%   75%   100%

In the section, "A Biblical Explanation," the author explains the elements of the proper response to the gospel and their importance in sharing the gospel effectively.

What are the three aspects involved in one truly repenting of his or her sin to receive Christ?

There are three aspects to this concept of "repentance" in the Scripture. As in the concept of "belief," "repentance" has a fuller meaning. It involves three aspects which are presented in various places by different writers in the New Testament. Repentance involves Christians admitting that they have sinned, sorrowing over their evil doing, and turning away from that sin toward righteousness.

What does it really mean "to believe" in Jesus?

Eternal life comes from believing that Jesus Christ is the Son. This is the "belief" that Jesus is referring to when he declared over and over that one must "believe in Him" to be saved.

What does it really mean "to receive" Jesus as Savior?

John clarifies this concept using the term "received." The proper biblical term for one's relationship with Jesus Christ is "received."

The Greek word translated "receive" means "to take." In the context of a person, it refers to taking with the hand, laying hold of any person or thing in order to use it, to make it one's own, or to give a person access to oneself in a person-to-person relationship.

When He entered, they were immediately at the shore. The Greek word is used spiritually of receiving Christ into people's lives and allowing Him to do His work through His Spirit. As they received Him into the boat, unbelievers are to receive Him into their lives.

John records that she was received into his household from that day forward. Mary became a part of his family. She entered into an intimate, familial relationship with him. In the same way, when Christ is received by one, he enters into a familial relationship (children of God) with Him.

In John 20:22, when the Lord foretold the coming of His Spirit to the disciples, He portrayed it as "receiving" the Holy Spirit.

How does one's initial "submission" to Christ as Lord impact his or her future life?

One's response to the proclamation of Christ as Lord is the recognition of His Lordship producing in the Christian the appropriate response: submission and obedience to Him as Master. This is not complete and absolute obedience, for this is impossible in this life.

Though water baptism does not save, why is participating in it important immediately after receiving Christ?

To be saved, unbelievers must believe that faith alone will save them. They must trust in Christ's saving work on the cross alone rather than the accumulation of good works or personal righteousness.

Instead, as has been seen, good works pour forth from a life of faith. In Ephesians 2:10, Paul continues his discussion by indicating that once faith comes Christians are to walk in good works.

In what ways might these truths impact your life?

(Various answers should be shared including yours.)

In the section, "An Ancient Portrait," the author provides a unique portrayal of Paul's ministry among the many people of Ephesus.

Can you briefly describe the setting of this real-life ancient drama?

The setting is the city of Ephesus and Paul's ministry there.

Can you describe the major characters involved?

The major characters are Paul, his companions, and the Ephesians.

How did the evangelist initiate the gospel presentation?

In Acts 19:1-41, we pick up the record of Paul's ministry in Ephesus. As was his custom he immediately entered the synagogue so that as a traveling rabbi he would be allowed to provide a word of encouragement to the congregation of Jews and God-fearing Gentiles. This Word was always the sharing of the gospel and the pursuit of a saving faith. For three months Paul addressed, reasoned, and discussed the truths of the good news with these people. As he pursued saving faith, many came to Christ.

When he received resistance from the others, he simply moved next- door to the school of Tyrannus. He kept doing his part in the gospel and he relied on God to do His.

What was result of this evangelistic presentation?

After Paul's arrival, many came to Christ. Among them were those who were practitioners of black magic. These new believers brought the books of their dark magic arts and threw them into a huge pile in the center of their city and burned them for all to see. The cost of the books came to fifty thousand pieces of silver. This was a staggering amount at that time. What a witness to the saving power of Jesus! Luke records that the Word of God was growing and prevailing against the forces of darkness in that whole area. Then, there was a great uproar in the city by those who were merchants selling silver idols of Artemis, whose temple was located there. Demetrius, the leader, gathered together all the merchants of similar trades in order to put a stop to God's mighty work through Paul. A riot almost ensued but was curtailed by one of the administrators of the city.

How was the principle explained in this chapter applied to the situation?

The point is that the apostle Paul would not change his gospel presentation to appease anyone in the city of Ephesus or anywhere else. The apostle always pursued a saving faith by giving a true gospel presentation. He never added any concept, opinion, or cultural norm that would appeal culturally to his audience. Also, He did not leave out an element of the gospel in order to appease his audience or be relevant at the time.

Based on the truths learned in this chapter, what would you have done differently if you were the evangelist or how would you have responded if you were the recipient?

(Various answers should be shared including yours.)

AN INSTRUCTOR'S MANUAL

In the section, "A Modern Anecdote," the author discusses a situation concerning the response of the good news by two young ladies at a vacation bible school.

Can you briefly describe the setting of this real-life modern drama?

When an opportunity came to run a vacation bible school for my church (a week-long event of two hours each day for children), I jumped at this opportunity with one stipulation. I asked them to allow me to design the camp around a fresh, current, and biblical theme.

Can you describe the major characters involved?

The major characters are the author, Emily, and Emma.

How did the author initiate the gospel presentation?

There was a large sign in front of the church that read, "Welcome to SWAT CAMP." Below it in smaller letters were written, "Spiritual Weapons And Tactics For Growth in Christ (Ephesians 6:10-19)." It was very exciting for the children.

Each day, I shared an element of the good news and on the last day gave an invitation to receive Christ as Savior and Lord. It was very low key, gentle, and optional. I wanted the Spirit to work in their hearts and minds not my cleverness, intimidation, or persuasive ability. During the course of the week, there were two sisters who were continually fooling around and then getting into trouble.

What was result of this evangelistic presentation?

Several children came forward while the girls sat silent in the back. After the program was completed the two girls walked up to me and said that they had decided to receive Christ. They were too embarrassed to come forward because of their poor behavior during the week. They told me how sorry they were and wanted to know what they should do.

How was the principle explained in this chapter applied to the situation?

So, they received Christ. Then, I explained that I wanted to inform their mother and baptize them.

I learned through this experience the importance of pursuing a saving faith in people's lives and not settling for a quick response that does not save.

Based on the truths learned in this chapter, what would you have done differently if you were the author or how would you have responded if you were the recipient?

(*Various answers should be shared including yours.*)

AN INSTRUCTOR'S MANUAL

In the section, "A Personal Response," the author provides a model you may use for prayer if you find it necessary after discovering the truths in this chapter.

Are you presently attempting to present the gospel of Jesus to someone? If not, are there some who may be members of a local club you belong to who may not know Jesus Christ and may need prayer for an opportunity for you to share with them and open hearts to receive Him?

(Various answers should be shared including yours.)

Based on the truths you have just learned, what will you continue to do in your current evangelistic efforts and what might you do differently?

(Various answers should be shared including yours.)

What additional thoughts would you like to share with the others?

Chapter 11

Expect a Dramatic Reaction

As people receive Jesus Christ as Savior and Lord, their temporal lives on Earth and supernatural lives in eternity are forever changed. Nothing is the same. They will begin to think differently, feel differently, and act differently. Some will start this process immediately and dramatically while others will proceed slowly and meticulously. Others will find themselves somewhere in between. Often, if there is a very dramatic response it will make people suspicious or wonder why they haven't had the same experience. Instead, the saints should expect dramatic reactions to occur as many different types of people come to Christ. They do not have to fear this or necessarily be suspicious.

A Typical Scenario

Have you ever been in a situation that was something like the following? Your sister just got back from college, and she is filled with excitement and joy. She was approached on her college campus by a Christian group whom she claims led her to the Lord. She begins to describe to you the amazing experience she had. She started attending a church near the college. In a month's time, she was already going on her first two-week mission's trip to a foreign country. She started singing in the Christian praise band and is volunteering in the children's ministry on Wednesday night. Suddenly, all your red flags go up. Questions begin to arise in your mind, "Who is this Christian group? How did she exactly get saved? What kind of church is this? Why hasn't she taken her time to get to know people? Could this be just a fad?"

In this chapter, you will learn that some Christians have a powerful and dramatic reaction to receiving Jesus Christ as Savior and Lord. It is real, dynamic, and long-lasting. It can involve a tremendous sense of blessing and joy. It might include an overwhelming desire to evangelize, and they may desire to serve the Lord immediately. It could incorporate a dramatic removal of things from their old sinful lives and the complete embracing of their new lives. They might even develop such a deep respect and devotion to the proclaimer that it may lead them to support the person in some way. If some suffering or rejection comes, they might gladly accept it. After you learn these important truths, perhaps this same situation might look very different.

Knowing these truths, you take a different approach. You begin by rejoicing with her. At the same time, you ease into inquiring exactly what she actually said and did to become a Christian. You are so excited that you want to hear all about it. You discover that everything you have learned that one needs to say and do to become a believer occurred. You are so happy for her. She is now both your sister and your sister in Christ also. You ask her the names of the organization on campus and the church she is now attending. Later, you do some research and determine that both are credible and true Christian groups. You tell her that you would love to join her for church one Sunday to support her new life in Christ.

At another time, you discuss all the ministries she is now participating in. Then you ask her how you can encourage and support her in her ministry to the Lord. You now realize that you were really observing a supernatural, vibrant, and spiritual reaction to a person fully and completely turning from the darkness into the light. This is simply a new saint who has put her whole heart into Jesus. What a blessing! You expect that years later, she will still be in that praise band, going on mission trips, and working with kids.

Though this is an imaginary scenario, it describes clearly the sometimes dynamic responses of believers when they receive Jesus Christ as Savior and Lord. Though this does not necessarily mean that every person who comes to Christ has this dramatic experience, we should embrace those who do. We should not miss the opportunity to share in their joy. This can also provide an additional incentive for us to share the gospel more often. This leads us to an eleventh principle which involves a description of the many dramatic reactions some may have when giving their lives to Christ.

A Scriptural Principle

Salvation is the critically important moment of a person's physical life upon this Earth. It is dramatic and life-altering in every possible way. In Ephesians 2:1-5, Paul declared that all unbelievers are dead in their trespasses and sins. In this condition, they follow after the prince of the power of the air, are sons of disobedience, live in the passions of the flesh, carry out the desires of the body, and are by nature children of wrath! They have no spiritual life in them. When they receive Christ, they become fully alive in Jesus Christ! They reject the Devil, no longer follow after the passions and lusts of the flesh and are by nature children of blessing as sons and daughters of God. Everything is different. These new believers were spiritually dead but now are spiritually and supernaturally alive. What a momentous event! Therefore, principle eleven is "we must expect a dramatic reaction."

Ephesians 2:1-5
You were made alive when you were dead in transgressions and sins, in which you once walked according to the course of this world, according to the prince of the power of the air, the spirit who now works in the children of disobedience. We also all once lived among them in the lusts of our flesh, doing the desires of the flesh and of the mind, and were by nature children of wrath, even as the rest.

But God, being rich in mercy, for his great love with which he loved us...when we were dead through our trespasses, made us alive together with Christ — by grace you have been saved.

A Biblical Explanation

In 2 Corinthians 5:17, Paul indicates that all individuals who come to saving faith in the Lord immediately become brand-new people, new creations. Paul portrays believers in in this way, "Therefore if anyone is in Christ, he is a new creation. The old things have passed away. Behold, all things have become new." The word translated "new" in the Greek means "brand-new of a different kind." To become a brand-new creation is such a powerful event that it may elicit a variety of positive responses. The Christian, who shares the gospel, needs to be prepared for the kinds of responses after salvation that a person may have. All Christians will react positively to their new belief in Christ in a wide variety of ways, some more intensely than others. The New Testament provides many examples of these reactions.

2 Corinthians 5:17
Therefore if anyone is in Christ, he is a [brand] new creation. The old things have passed away. Behold, all things have become new.

A Tremendous Sense of Blessing

When some become new Christians, they might become filled with an overwhelming sense of blessing. The mercy and grace of God issuing forth in the forgiveness of all their sins becomes almost too much to bear. They feel a sense of wonder. They are awestruck by God's patience and love for them. His mercy astounds them.

The apostle describes this real sense of blessing to young Timothy in 1 Timothy 1:16-17. He jubilantly expresses to his son in the faith the incredible blessing of the grace, mercy, and patience that God had showed toward him at salvation. He writes, "However, for this cause I obtained mercy, that in me first, Jesus Christ might display all his patience, for an example of those who were going to believe in him for eternal life. Now to the King eternal, immortal, invisible, to God who alone is wise, be honor and glory forever and ever." Then, as if he is overwhelmed by it all, Paul breaks into a great doxology of praise for God's blessing upon him and cries out for the Lord God's honor and glory forever and ever. Paul always had this great sense of blessing as he ministered to people and served the Lord.

1 Timothy 1:16-17
However, for this cause I obtained mercy, that in me first, Jesus Christ might display all his patience for an example of those who were going to believe in him for eternal life. Now to the King eternal, immortal, invisible, to God who alone is wise, be honor and glory forever and ever. Amen.

In Galatians 4:12-15, Paul dealt with a group of churches who had been deceived by many false prophets attempting to bring them back under the bondage of the law to save them. Paul reminded them of the tremendous good fortune (blessings) they felt when the weight of the law was lifted.

Galatians 4:12-15
I beg you, brothers, become as I am, for I also have become as you are. You did me no wrong, but you know that because of weakness in the flesh I preached the Good News to you the first time. That which was a temptation to you in my flesh, you didn't despise nor reject; but you received me as an angel of God, even as Christ Jesus. What was the blessing you enjoyed? For I testify to you that, if possible, you would have plucked out your eyes and given them to me.

A Great Feeling of Joy

When some become new Christians, they may experience a flood of joy when they receive Jesus Christ. In Acts 8:8, when Philip preached the good news in Samaria and healed many people, Luke wrote that there was rejoicing in the city. In verses 38-39, after the Ethiopian eunuch heard the gospel and came to Christ, Luke described him as traveling down the road rejoicing. When Paul brought the good news into the household of the Philippian jailer and they believed, there was great rejoicing in that home (Acts 16:30-34). His household had entered into the kingdom of God and eternal life. Is this not something that is worth rejoicing over?

Acts 8:8
There was great joy in that city.

Acts 8:38-39
He commanded the chariot to stand still, and they both went down into the water, both Philip and the eunuch, and he baptized him. When they came up out of the water, the Spirit of the Lord caught Philip away, and the eunuch didn't see him any more, for he went on his way rejoicing.

The Thessalonians had experienced this same kind of joy and gladness upon their salvation. In 1 Thessalonians 1:6-7, Paul explains it this way, "You became imitators of us, and of the Lord, having received the word in much affliction, with joy of the Holy Spirit, so that you became an example to all who believe in Macedonia and in Achaia." Paul explained how the believers in the city had found Christ in the midst of intense persecution and still had great joy.

1 Thessalonians 1:6-7
You became imitators of us and of the Lord, having received the word in much affliction, with joy of the Holy Spirit, so that you became an example to all who believe in Macedonia and in Achaia.

Some saints may experience the opening of the floodgates of happiness and joy when they receive Jesus Christ as their new Savior and Lord. This will be a joy that is not Earthly but supernatural. It will be beyond human comprehension because it will involve something deeply spiritual. All new Christians will not experience it.

An Overwhelming Desire to Evangelize

When some people become new Christians, they might immediately begin to share the good news with their friends and acquaintances. They now have something amazing that has happened to them and want to share it with the world all the time. This is precisely what occurred in the opening seven chapters of Acts. The saints were declaring the good news of Jesus everywhere they traveled to everyone they encountered. Christ was adding to their number daily.

Then persecution instigated by Saul broke out. Would the Christians be silenced and go into hiding? No, they did the opposite. In Acts 8:4, Luke wrote, "Therefore those who were scattered abroad went around preaching the word." When persecution broke out due to Stephen's preaching and Saul's rise, the saints were scattered and kept sharing the gospel. They had all recently come to Christ. After Paul was saved, he went immediately out to share the gospel. This frightened the believers in the church because they had never seen such a transformation (Acts 9:26).

Acts 8:4
Therefore those who were scattered abroad went around preaching the word.

Acts 9:26
When Saul had come to Jerusalem, he tried to join himself to the disciples; but they were all afraid of him, not believing that he was a disciple.

In the rest of the physician Luke's historical account in Acts, Paul essentially shared the good news everywhere he traveled. As people receive the gospel and trust in Christ, some may want to respond immediately by sharing the good news everywhere they go to everyone they meet. This may frighten some people who might not be used to this kind of boldness in the church. The Spirit decides how He works.

A Wonderful Willingness to Suffer

When some become new Christians, they might become extremely enraptured and captivated by Christ. Their minds might be so completely set on Him that they are willing to pay any price for Him at the very next moment. This is what the Thessalonians experienced. In 1 Thessalonians 1:6-7, Paul praises his readers for receiving the Word in much affliction with the joy of the Holy Spirit. What examples!

1 Thessalonians 1:6-7
You became imitators of us and of the Lord, having received the word in much affliction, with joy of the Holy Spirit, so that you became an example to all who believe in Macedonia and in Achaia.

In Hebrews 10:32-33, the author acknowledged that his readers were drifting from the faith due to persecution. He reminds them of their past willingness to suffer persecution for their faith. He asserts, "But remember the former days, in which, after you were enlightened." He calls the members of the church to remember the wonderful days after their initial commitment. Then adds, "You endured a great struggle with sufferings; partly, being exposed to both reproaches and oppressions; and partly, becoming partakers with those who were treated so."

Hebrews 10:32-33
But remember the former days...after you were enlightened, you endured a great struggle with sufferings; partly, being exposed to both reproaches and oppressions; and partly, becoming partakers with those who were treated so.

He prompts them to really reflect upon their earlier days of salvation when they were willing to suffer for the name of Christ. When they first came to Christ, they were willing to be mocked and laughed at publicly, to lose their property, and even be thrown in jail. Why? They had a better eternal possession which could not be taken away from them. Some who receive Christ may be persecuted and accept it with great joy. They will wear the suffering like a badge of honor.

A Strong Devotion to the Proclaimer

When some become new Christians, they may become so grateful, they may develop a strong devotion to the one who proclaimed Christ to them. This is recorded throughout the New Testament. Paul's devoted churches supported him prayerfully (Ephesians 6:18-20) and financially (Philippians 4:15). When he was taking a collection for needy saints, they supported him (1 Corinthians 16:1-5). Many other churches also supported Paul in various ways. He spoke often of these various churches that he so depended upon for his financial, spiritual, and emotional well-being as he ministered.

Ephesians 6:18-20
With all prayer and requests, praying at all times in the Spirit, and being watchful to this end in all perseverance and requests for all the saints: on my behalf, that utterance may be given to me in opening my mouth, to make known with boldness the mystery of the Good News, for which I am an ambassador in chains; that in it I may speak boldly, as I ought to speak.

Philippians 4:15
You yourselves also know, you Philippians, that in the beginning of the Good News, when I departed from Macedonia, no assembly shared with me in the matter of giving and receiving but you only.

1 Corinthians 16:1-5
Now concerning the collection for the saints, as I commanded the assemblies of Galatia, you do likewise. On the first day of every week, let each one of you save, as he may prosper, that no collections are made when I come. When I arrive, I will send whoever you approve with letters to carry your gracious gift to Jerusalem. If it is appropriate for me to go also, they will go with me. But I will come to you when I have passed through Macedonia, for I am passing through Macedonia.

As has been seen previously, the Galatians received Paul as if he were an angel of God. In Galatians 4:14-15, Paul says, "That which was a temptation to you in my flesh, you didn't despise nor reject; but you received me as an angel of God, even as Christ Jesus. What was the blessing you enjoyed? For I testify to you that, if possible, you would have plucked out your eyes and given them to me." They were so grateful that these saints were willing to pluck out their own eyes to help him (Galatians 4:14-15). This may have been a reference to his poor eyesight. A Christian may experience a great sense of gratefulness and attachment from those they win to Christ through their ministry.

Galatians 4:14-15
That which was a temptation to you in my flesh, you didn't despise nor reject; but you received me as an angel of God, even as Christ Jesus. What was the blessing you enjoyed? For I testify to you that, if possible, you would have plucked out your eyes and given them to me.

An Immediate Participation in Ministry

When some become new Christians, they might want to begin to serve their Lord almost instantaneously. In Acts 16, Paul came into Philippi on his second missionary journey and apparently did not find a Jewish synagogue. He went down to the river which was a very common place for Jews and the God-fearing Gentiles to meet. In verses 13-15, Paul encountered Lydia who came to Christ. Immediately, she invited him into her home. After Paul had been released from jail, they returned to Lydia's home where the church met. Lydia became immediately involved in ministry.

Acts 16:13-15
On the Sabbath day we went outside of the city by a riverside, where we supposed there was a place of prayer, and we sat down and spoke to the women who had come together. A certain woman named Lydia, a seller of purple, of the city of Thyatira, one who worshiped God, heard us. The Lord opened her heart to listen to the things which were spoken by Paul. When she and her household were baptized, she begged us, saying, "If you have judged me to be faithful to the Lord, come into my house and stay." So she persuaded us.

In Philippians 4:15-16, while Paul was in Rome awaiting trial, he received a generous gift from the Philippians. He declares, "You yourselves also know, you Philippians, that in the beginning of the Good News, when I departed from Macedonia, no assembly [church] shared with me [Paul] in the matter of giving and receiving but you only. For even in Thessalonica you sent once and again to my need. He then recounted all of their past support in his letter. Their support was from the very beginning of their faith. Some new saints may immediately desire to become involved in ministry.

Philippians 4:15-16
You yourselves also know, you Philippians, that in the beginning of the Good News, when I departed from Macedonia, no assembly shared with me in the matter of giving and receiving but you only. For even in Thessalonica you sent once and again to my need.

A Removal of Things from the Old Life

When some become new Christians, these saints might have accumulated evil or demonic objects from their former lives and desire to immediately remove them. Their new life in Christ is now so incompatible with these "old life" objects, they must be removed soon afterward (2 Corinthians 5:17). This may involve different kinds of objects: Ouija boards, magical stones, tarot cards, crystal balls, magazines, sexual or drug paraphernalia, technology, alcohol, drugs, or even anything that kept them from Christ and deep in sin. Many will desire to remove these demonic or sinful, evil objects in some kind of ceremony or moment of cleansing.

2 Corinthians 5:17
Therefore if anyone is in Christ, he is a [brand] new creation. The old things have passed away. Behold, all things have become new.

In Acts 19:18-19, Paul ministers in Ephesus bringing many people out of the magical arts (occult practices). Luke, the historian, asserts this, "Many also of those who had believed came, confessing, and declaring their deeds. Many of those who practiced magical arts brought their books together and burned them in the sight of all. They counted their price, and found it to be fifty thousand pieces of silver."

Acts 19:18-19
Many also of those who had believed came, confessing, and declaring their deeds. 19 Many of those who practiced magical arts brought their books together and burned them in the sight of all. They counted their price, and found it to be fifty thousand pieces of silver.

Immediately, these newborn Christians collected all of their many books of magic and burned them in the sight of all. As people are brought to Jesus Christ, they may become so incredibly passionate about their repentance from their sins that they will almost immediately destroy all objects from their old lives. What an amazing testimony to the world of their new faith! From this everyone would know that Christ had made them into new creations.

A Dramatic Transformation

When some become new Christians, they might change dramatically in their outward behavior. Perhaps, one day they were involved in drugs, illicit sex, alcoholism, or other sins. The next day without any apparent struggle, these sins were gone from their lives. As has been previously seen, Paul went through a startling change. He was transformed from a staunch, fully committed persecutor of Christians to a firmly committed proclaimer of Christ (1 Timothy 1:13-15).

1 Timothy 1:13-15
Although I used to be a blasphemer, a persecutor, and insolent. However, I obtained mercy, because I did it ignorantly in unbelief. The grace of our Lord abounded exceedingly with faith and love which is in Christ Jesus. The saying is faithful and worthy of all acceptance, that Christ Jesus came into the world to save sinners, of whom I am chief.

As Paul experienced a dramatic change, so did the church at Thessalonica. The apostle had only been in Thessalonica a few weeks and wrote a letter a short time later. They already had a working faith, a laboring love, and an enduring hope. Their powerful message had gone out to many places in the surrounding regions (1 Thessalonians 1:2-3, 8-10). Everyone had knowledge of all the dramatic changes the Holy Spirit was achieving in their midst.

1 Thessalonians 1:2-3
We always give thanks to God for all of you, mentioning you in our prayers, remembering without ceasing your work of faith and labor of love and perseverance of hope in our Lord Jesus Christ, before our God and Father.

1 Thessalonians 1:8-10
For from you the word of the Lord has been declared, not only in Macedonia and Achaia, but also in every place your faith toward God has gone out, so that we need not to say anything. For they themselves report concerning us what kind of a reception we had from you, and how you turned to God from idols, to serve a living and true God, and to wait for his Son from heaven, whom he raised from the dead: Jesus, who delivers us from the wrath to come.

The Christians in the church in the city of Colossae had a similar sensational transformation. In Colossians 1:5-6, Paul pens, "Because of the hope which is laid up for you in the Heavens, of which you heard before in the word of the truth of the Good News, which has come to you; even as it is in all the world and is bearing fruit and growing, as it does in you also, since the day you heard and knew the grace of God in truth." From the day these new saints had heard the good news, they demonstrated true faith, exhibited love toward one another, produced abounding spiritual fruit, and it was constantly increasing. Sometimes, people become Christians and make startling and dramatic changes in their life by the power of the Spirit. This does not always happen to every Christian, but it does to some of them. This is result of the power, work, and will of a sovereign, gracious, and merciful God who loves His people.

Colossians 1:5-6
Because of the hope which is laid up for you in the heavens, of which you heard before in the word of the truth of the Good News which has come to you, even as it is in all the world and is bearing fruit and growing, as it does in you also, since the day you heard and knew the grace of God in truth.

An Ancient Portrait

A classic biblical example of a dramatic reaction after one comes to Christ is the tax-collector Zacchaeus when he meets Jesus, repents, and receives the Lord. The story of Zacchaeus is found in Luke 19:1-10. Jesus entered the town of Jericho on His way to Jerusalem for the yearly Passover with a large crowd. This important city was on the route to Jerusalem and all the pilgrims would be traveling through this town also. The citizens of Jericho would have heard that Jesus had raised Lazarus from the dead and would have come out to see Him. The town would have been teeming with people.

Amid this crowd, a rich and powerful tax collector named Zacchaeus entered the scene. It was the law that once these officials charged the people what Rome had designated, they could then charge any fee they desired. As a result, these men gouged the people and became rich. If they did not pay, the tax collectors would try and intimidate them into paying through threats or physical force. Since Zacchaeus was one of the "chief" tax collectors, he would receive a percentage of the amount of taxes collected by every tax collector under his charge. As chief, he too would need to use intimidation to accomplish his determined extortion.

These men were hated by the Jews because they were constantly extorting the people and working for the Romans. The Hebrews called them "sinners." This was the lowest class of people in their country. They were unclean, defiled, and outcasts. These evil people were to be avoided and not allowed to enter a Jewish home or synagogue. Zacchaeus was a member.

He had heard that Jesus was in town and wanted to see him. Why? We can discern this from what happened. This man was honestly seeking true salvation as the Holy Spirit was working in his heart. The Spirit was convicting Him of His sin and leading Him to the Jesus, the Savior. He had one "big" problem. He was small, a little man vying for a place to see in a large crowd. So, Zacchaeus decided to run ahead of Jesus and find himself a place to see this extraordinary man.

He climbed up into a sycamore or perhaps a mulberry tree because these had short trunks and long branches which made them easy to climb. When the Messiah came to the place where Zacchaeus was located, something remarkable happened. The Lord stopped, looked him straight in the eyes, and called him by his name. Jesus knew Zacchaeus, who he was and all that he had done. He said, "Come down,

I will stay with you today." Jesus decided to lodge with him overnight. This tax collector hurried down and received the Lord Jesus joyfully into his home. Zacchaeus stood before Jesus and repented saying, "Behold, Lord, half of my goods I will give to the poor."

The Lord's recognition of Zacchaeus was miraculous and obviously the final action that convinced this searching, but scorned man, that Jesus was the true Messiah. It obviously led to his act of repentance. In his repentance, we see a very dramatic reaction to receiving Christ as Savior and Lord. Zacchaeus first declares he will give half of his money away. Why? Money had been his idol and god. Now, Jesus was His God and Master, and he wouldn't serve money any longer.

Then Zacchaeus committed himself to making restitution. This tax collector had essentially stolen and cheated so many people out of so much money that he declared, "If I have wrongfully exacted anything of anyone, I restore four times as much." He saw the awfulness of his greed which had led him to oppress many innocent people and absolutely had to compensate them. The Lord saw this dramatic response, and He declared, "Today, salvation has come to this house." This was a true son of Abraham in the Spirit now not one of the flesh alone. Jesus welcomed dramatic reactions to salvation from people, and we should do the same.

A Modern Anecdote

After I received Jesus as Savior and Lord, I went through a time of great evangelistic fervor. I wanted to share Christ with everyone I knew. I had gotten a job during the summer at an amusement park while I attended college. Of course, I began developing relationships with the many employees and witnessing for Christ. As I shared Christ with a young lady, she began to discuss what she was learning with her store manager. When she mentioned my name, Shannon, the manager, realized we had been old drama club buddies from high school.

On her next break, she came looking for me. She found me in the employee's cafeteria having lunch with two others. Shannon walked up, stood in front of me, and interrupted us. Then Shannon smiled and declared, "Hey, Jones, when did you become religious?" I turned, looked at her, and then responded, "Six months ago when I became a Christian." We grinned at each other and set a time to catch up the next day. When we got together it was like we had never been apart. We became once again close friends.

As we caught up, it was like we had chosen completely opposite paths in life. I applied to college, and she went out and got a job. While I was studying, she was partying. While I was seeking the answers to the fundamental philosophical questions of life, she was seeking the fundamental sensory pleasures of this life. One day, I walked Shannon to her car and saw a large painting of a snake on the back of it. When I asked her about it, she told me that everybody called her the "Serpent Lady." Since I wanted to start a conversation about the gospel, I made the casual comment, "You know, one of the names of Satan in the Bible is the Serpent of Old."

She immediately made a humorous remark and changed the subject, but I knew that it bothered her. She responded by telling me she had grown up reading the Bible and knew the story of Satan tempting Adam and Eve in the garden, but she explained that she was not interested in that "religious mumbo jumbo" anymore. After this remark, Shannon and I began an ongoing, almost daily conversation about the Bible and whether it was mumbo jumbo. Every chance I got, I would provide her with the various proofs for the validity of the Scriptures and share the gospel with her. I tried not to be overbearing but to have a gentle, casual conversation.

Then one night, a female friend of mine and I offered her a ride home. The serpent car was out of commission. As we were discussing the events of the day, she suddenly stopped. Shannon looked at me and admitted how utterly miserable she was. Though she looked outwardly like she was happy and had everything together, inwardly she felt completely empty. Shannon compared her partying to the roller coasters at the park. She complained that as long as she partied, she would go up on that coaster and fly high. The next morning, when she came down off the high, the emptiness returned. I again shared the gospel with her and asked her if she would like to end the emptiness by receiving Jesus Christ.

She looked me right in the eyes and replied, "Yes, I finally am. I am ready to receive Jesus as Savior and Lord. I am ready to get rid of this ridiculous emptiness." In a traveling car on the freeways of Southern California, I led her in the prayer and commitment that allowed her to enter into eternal life and the purpose for which God created her. The next day, she was in the employee's cafeteria and called to me and said, "Hey Don, come over and talk to my friend, she feels empty like I did." She became an amazing witness for Christ at that park and in her party crowd. Everybody she knew saw the amazing transformation in her life and everywhere she went she shared the gospel. Shannon went on to marry a pastor and live a life dedicated to the Lord. Through this and other similar experiences, I learned that sometimes I should expect a dramatic transformation such as Paul experienced (Acts 1:20-21).

LEADING THE WAY

Acts 1:20-21
Immediately in the synagogues he proclaimed the Christ, that he is the Son of God. All who heard him were amazed, and said, "Isn't this he who in Jerusalem made havoc of those who called on this name? And he had come here intending to bring them bound before the chief priests!"

A Personal Response

Dear Heavenly Father,

I thank you for the privilege of sharing Your gospel with a world that is desperate for Your Son. Please provide the motivation and courage I need to present Your good news of salvation with (add names) and others I know and meet. Bring them to Christ as Savior and Lord. Please allow me to have the opportunity to see the great feeling of joy they may have when they receive Your Son and rejoice with them. If they possess an overwhelming desire to evangelize, give me wisdom and boldness to assist them in this supernatural endeavor. If they develop a strong attachment to me as the proclaimer and desire to support my ministry, please help me to direct them to the best way to do this. If they desire an immediate participation in ministry, provide me with the wisdom I need to direct them to an appropriate place to serve. If they have a dramatic transformation, help me to encourage them in their rapid growth process. If they may experience some kind of persecution in the early days of their conversion, show me how I can support them and keep them strong. I pray this in the name of Jesus. Amen.

AN INSTRUCTOR'S MANUAL

Chapter 11

Expect a Dramatic Reaction

When people receive Jesus as Savior and Lord, some will respond immediately and dramatically while others may react slowly and meticulously.

In the section, "A Typical Scenario," the author depicts the support a Christian gives his sister when she has a dramatic reaction to receiving Christ.

What is the scenario about?

A sister comes home from college joyfully claiming she is a believer and becomes immediately involved in several ministries.

What held the believer back from sharing the gospel?

The brother is suspicious of such a dramatic reaction and his sister getting involved so quickly.

What finally led the Christian to share the good news and how did it occur?

The brother took some time to listen to his sister and investigate the various ministries and embrace her dramatic reaction.

Have you had a similar experience?

(Various answers should be shared including yours.)

In the section, "A Scriptural Principle" the author presents an important biblical principle in evangelism which concerns the dramatic reactions of some who receive Christ.

How would you express this principle in your own words?

Therefore, principle eleven is "we must expect a dramatic reaction."

(*Various answers should be shared including yours.*)

How would you rewrite this principle to make it even more personal to your life (using your name and situation)?

(*Various answers should be shared including yours.*)

Why do you think this principle might be important in your life right now as you share the gospel?

(*Various answers should be shared including yours.*)

How would you rate yourself on the percentage of times you followed this principle in the past as a believer?

(*Various answers should be shared including yours.*)

Directions: Put a horizontal mark and your name where you see yourself on the percentage line.

0%   25%   50%   75%   100%

In the section, "A Biblical Explanation," the author explains the ways in which new believers may demonstrate their new faith and its importance in sharing the gospel effectively.

Do all people who receive Christ as Savior and Lord have a dramatic reaction? Why or why not?

As people receive Jesus Christ as Savior and Lord, their temporal lives on Earth and supernatural lives in eternity are forever changed. Nothing is the same. They will begin to think differently, feel differently, and act differently. Some will start this process immediately and dramatically while others will proceed slowly and meticulously. Others will find themselves somewhere in between.

What is the difference between the responses of tremendous sense of blessing and a great feeling of joy?

When some become new Christians, they might become filled with an overwhelming sense of blessing. The mercy and grace of God issuing forth in the forgiveness of all their sins becomes almost too much to bear. They feel a sense of wonder. They are awestruck by God's patience and love for them. His mercy astounds them.

When some become new Christians, they may experience a flood of joy when they receive Jesus Christ.

How can the response of a wonderful willingness to suffer be related to an overwhelming desire to evangelize?

When some people become new Christians, they might immediately begin to share the good news with their friends and acquaintances. They now have something amazing that has happened to them and want to share it with the world all the time.

When some become new Christians, they might become extremely enraptured and captivated by Christ. Their minds might be so completely set on Him that they are willing to pay any price for Him at the very next moment.

How might a strong devotion to the proclaimer relate to an immediate participation in ministry?

When some become new Christians, they may become so grateful, they may develop a strong devotion to the one who proclaimed Christ to them.

When some become new Christians, they might want to begin to serve their Lord almost instantaneously [perhaps, with the proclaimer].

What is the relationship between a removal of things from the old life and a dramatic transformation?

When some become new Christians, these saints might have accumulated evil or demonic objects from their former lives and desire to immediately remove them. Their new life in Christ is now so incompatible with these "old life" objects, they must be removed soon afterward (2 Corinthians 5:17).

In what ways might these truths impact your life?

(Various answers should be shared including yours.)

In the section, "An Ancient Portrait," the author provides a unique portrayal of the dramatic reaction of the chief tax-collector Zacchaeus when he came to Christ.

Can you briefly describe the setting of this real-life ancient drama?

The setting of this story is the entrance of Jesus into the town of Jericho on His way to Jerusalem for the yearly Passover with a large crowd. This important city was on the route to Jerusalem and all the pilgrims would be traveling through this town also.

Can you describe the major characters involved?

The major characters are Jesus and Zacchaeus.

How did the evangelist initiate the gospel presentation?

He climbed up into a sycamore or perhaps a mulberry tree because these had short trunks and long branches which made them easy to climb. When the Messiah came to the place where Zacchaeus was located, something remarkable happened. The Lord stopped, looked him straight in the eyes, and called him by his name. Jesus knew Zacchaeus, who he was and all that he had done. He said, "Come down, I will stay with you today." Jesus decided to lodge with him overnight.

What was result of this evangelistic presentation?

This tax collector hurried down and received the Lord Jesus joyfully into his home. Zacchaeus stood before Jesus and repented saying, "Behold, Lord, half of my goods I will give to the poor."

How was the principle explained in this chapter applied to the situation?

This was a true son of Abraham in the Spirit now not one of the flesh alone. Jesus welcomed dramatic reactions to salvation from people, and we should do the same.

Based on the truths learned in this chapter, what would you have done differently if you were the evangelist or how would you have responded if you were the recipient?

(Various answers should be shared including yours.)

In the section, "A Modern Anecdote," the author discusses a situation in which he was able to present the good news of Jesus Christ to an old high school friend from drama club.

Can you briefly describe the setting of this real-life modern drama?

The setting is an amusement park. I wanted to share Christ with everyone I knew. I had gotten a job during the summer at an amusement park while I attended college.

Can you describe the major characters involved?

The major characters are the author and Shannon.

How did the author initiate the gospel presentation?

When I asked her about it, she told me that everybody called her the "Serpent Lady." Since I wanted to start a conversation about the gospel, I made the casual comment, "You know, one of the names of Satan in the Bible is the Serpent of Old."

What was result of this evangelistic presentation?

After this remark, Shannon and I began an ongoing, almost daily conversation about the Bible and whether it was mumbo jumbo. Every chance I got, I would provide her with the various proofs for the validity of the Scriptures and share the gospel with her. I tried not to be overbearing but to have a gentle, casual conversation.

How was the principle explained in this chapter applied to the situation?

She looked me right in the eyes and replied, "Yes, I finally am. I am ready to receive Jesus as Savior and Lord. I am ready to get rid of this ridiculous emptiness." In a traveling car on the freeways of Southern California, I led her in the prayer and commitment that allowed her to enter into eternal life and the purpose for which God created her.

The next day, she was in the employee's cafeteria and called to me and said, "Hey Don, come over and talk to my friend, she feels empty like I did." She became an amazing witness for Christ at that park and in her party crowd.

Based on the truths learned in this chapter, what would you have done differently if you were the author or how would you have responded if you were the recipient?

(Various answers should be shared including yours.)

In the section, "A Personal Response," the author provides a model you may use for prayer if you find it necessary after discovering the truths in this chapter.

Are you presently attempting to present the gospel of Jesus to someone? If not, are there some who frequent a favorite place of yours who may not know Jesus Christ and may need prayer for an opportunity for you to share with them and open hearts to receive Him?

(Various answers should be shared including yours.)

Based on the truths you have just learned, what will you continue to do in your current evangelistic efforts and what might you do differently?

(Various answers should be shared including yours.)

What additional thoughts would you like to share with the others?

(Various answers should be shared including yours.)

LEADING THE WAY

Instructor's Notes

AN INSTRUCTOR'S MANUAL

Chapter 12

Counter with a Loving Attitude

In a perfect world, every person a Christian shares the good news with will receive Jesus as his or her Savior and Lord immediately and with great fervor. This is not a perfect world and most people whether the saints like it or not will never come to Christ. Often, they might even respond quite negatively to their presentation. What are Christians to do? Do they get angry and retaliate? Do they stay silent and take the abuse? Do they respond with certain words and actions? These questions will be partially answered in this chapter as we consider the attitudes the saints should have toward persecutors. Other more detailed responses should be found in my book on persecution. This book deals primarily with the sharing the gospel not all the ramifications of suffering.

A Typical Scenario

Have you ever been in a situation that was something like the following? You have driven by people in distress on the roadway many times, you almost never think about it. When you do, as soon as they are out of view, they are out of your mind. When you do see them, you think to yourself, "It is too dangerous. I don't really know anything about cars, and they might try and kidnap me. Also, I will look foolish if I stop and cannot help them." Then you think, "Maybe someday, I will stop and help someone and share the gospel with them." You put this out of your mind purely out of fear. Sharing the gospel with a stranger stranded on the road sounds like it could be dangerous and frightening to say the least. Then you think, "Well, people will probably think that I helped them just to put a notch on my evangelism belt. I am not going to do it."

In this chapter you will learn that whenever you share the gospel most will not come to Christ. The road is narrow to life, but you will have given them a chance to believe. Also, though someone may reject your message, you ought to still show them love and kindness. You might meet their need, give them a blessing, offer to prayer for them, and if needed, even forgive them in the name of Christ your Savior and Lord. You do not have to get angry or annoyed. You must merely share the gospel and in their rejection be an example of Christ and move on. In the past, you have learned that heralds can share the gospel with strangers. You do not have to make any excuses for your behavior in the name of the Lord as a messenger did not in the name of his king. After you learn these important truths, perhaps something like this may happen.

Today, you have been thinking that you should interact more with unsaved people. You realize that a biblical way is to meet their needs and share the gospel. You are driving down the street and see a woman stranded in the middle of the roadway with her flashers on. You know that this could be very dangerous because a driver of another car could not be paying attention and ram into her. So, you pull your car over to the side and get out. You walk over and motion her to roll down her window. Then, you tell her that you will get some people to help push her car out of the roadway.

You flag down a couple of passing cars and a couple of men get out of their cars. You help push her car over to the side of the street and out of danger's way. The others leave, and she calls a tow truck. Then she thanks you profusely. You tell her it might be better if you stayed until the truck came so she will be safe. She agrees. Silently you pray for boldness and wisdom. You start a simple conversation about why you stopped to help her. You probably explain that you have been studying Acts in the Bible and wanted to follow the apostle Peter's approach. He healed a lame man in the name of the Lord and then preached the gospel to him in Acts chapter three. So, you indicate that you stopped to help her in the name of your Savior and Lord Jesus Christ." She looks at you stunned. She sternly says that she appreciates your help but does not believe in Jesus Christ at all and did not want to hear about it. In fact, she demanded you leave. Rather, than getting upset, you hand her your business card and encourage her to give you a call if she ever changed her mind. You tell her that you and your wife would love to talk to her about the Lord Jesus. You leave her with these simple the words, "God bless you."

Though this is an imaginary scenario, it is typical of the many kinds of encounters we have every day with those who do not know Christ. We might not share the gospel because we do not know what to do when we are rejected. Though this chapter does not discuss every verbal response believers are to have regarding a rejection of the gospel, it does describe the main attitudes we should have. Knowing how to handle rejection may provide the very catalyst we may need to share the gospel on a regular basis. This brings us to the twelfth principle which involves handling negative responses to the gospel.

A Scriptural Principle

It is important to understand that the majority of people will react negatively to the gospel. If the road is narrow that proceeds to life, most people will not follow it. Instead, they will respond with one or more negative reactions. For every person who comes to Christ, many others will not. Though all men are called, few are chosen (Matthew 14:22). Once Christians realize this, they can prepare their response to these opposers of the gospel. Believers should respond to these negative reactions in a manner that will save the lives of men, not destroy them. So, principle twelve is "we must counter with a loving attitude." God has carefully articulated the various responses Christians are to have through His Son and the apostles.

Matthew 14:22
Immediately Jesus made the disciples get into the boat and go ahead of him to the other side, while he sent the multitudes away.

A Biblical Explanation

Why do many people negatively react to the gospel? Why do they persecute Christians? Why would they reject eternal life? The answers to these critical questions are found in the sinful nature of man. People are born with a propensity to commit sin (Romans 7:21-23; Romans 5:12,19; Ephesians 2:2). They are spiritually dead (Ephesians 2:1-5; Colossians 2:13-14; Romans 5:15; 6:4-7), hardened in their hearts (Romans 2:5; Acts 7:51; Ephesians 4:18-19), ignorant of spiritual things (1 Corinthians 1:18, 23; 2:14; Romans 1:21-22), prideful (Mark 7:21-22; Romans 1:30; 1 Corinthians 1:18-21), controlled by their lustful desires (Romans 1:28-32; 6:17-18; Ephesians 2:3), and blinded by Satan (2 Corinthians 4:4; Colossians 1:13; 1 John 2:11). They continually refuse to give up their beloved sin to humble themselves before Jesus Christ (Romans 1:18-21). With this desperate condition of unbelievers, what else should the saints expect from them but negative reactions leading to persecution?

Romans 7:21-23
I find then the law that, to me, while I desire to do good, evil is present. For I delight in God's law after the inward person, but I see a different law in my members, warring against the law of my mind, and bringing me into captivity under the law of sin which is in my members.

Romans 5:12
Therefore as sin entered into the world through one man, and death through sin; so death passed to all men, because all sinned.

Romans 5:19
For as through the one man's disobedience many were made sinners, even so through the obedience of the one, many will be made righteous.

Ephesians 2:2
In which you once walked according to the course of this world, according to the prince of the power of the air, the spirit who now works in the children of disobedience.

Ephesians 2:1-5
You were made alive when you were dead in transgressions and sins, in which you once walked according to the course of this world, according to the prince of the power of the air, the spirit who now works in the children of disobedience. We also all once lived among them in the lusts of our flesh, doing the desires of the flesh and of the mind, and were by nature children of wrath, even as the rest. But God, being rich in mercy, for his great love with which he loved us, even when we were dead through our trespasses, made us alive together with Christ – by grace you have been saved.

Colossians 2:13-14
You were dead through your trespasses and the uncircumcision of your flesh. He made you alive together with him, having forgiven us all our trespasses, wiping out the handwriting in ordinances which was against us. He has taken it out of the way, nailing it to the cross.

Romans 5:15
But the free gift isn't like the trespass. For if by the trespass of the one the many died, much more did the grace of God, and the gift by the grace of the one man, Jesus Christ, abound to the many.

Romans 6:4-7
We were buried therefore with him through baptism into death, that just as Christ was raised from the dead through the glory of the Father, so we also might walk in newness of life. For if we have become united with him in the

likeness of his death, we will also be part of his resurrection; knowing this, that our old man was crucified with him, that the body of sin might be done away with, so that we would no longer be in bondage to sin. 7 For he who has died has been freed from sin.

Romans 2:5
But according to your hardness and unrepentant heart you are treasuring up for yourself wrath in the day of wrath, revelation, and of the righteous judgment of God.

Acts 7:51
You stiff-necked and uncircumcised in heart and ears, you always resist the Holy Spirit! As your fathers did, so you do.

Ephesians 4:18-19
Being darkened in their understanding, alienated from the life of God because of the ignorance...in them, because of the hardening of their hearts. They, having become callous, gave themselves up to lust, to work all uncleanness with greediness.

1 Corinthians 1:18
For the word of the cross is foolishness to those who are dying, but to us who are being saved it is the power of God.

1 Corinthians 1:23
But we preach Christ crucified: a stumbling block to Jews, and foolishness to Greeks.

1 Corinthians 2:14
Now the natural man doesn't receive the things of God's Spirit, for they are foolishness to him, and he can't know them, because they are spiritually discerned.

Romans 1:21-22
Because knowing God, they didn't glorify him as God, and didn't give thanks, but became vain in their reasoning, and their senseless heart was darkened. Professing themselves to be wise, they became fools,

Mark 7:21-22
For from within, out of hearts [minds and bodies] of men, proceed evil thoughts, adulteries, sexual sins, murders, thefts, covetings, wickedness, deceit, lustful desires, an evil eye, blasphemy, pride, and foolishness.

Romans 1:30
Backbiters, hateful to God, insolent, arrogant, boastful, inventors of evil things, disobedient to parents.

1 Corinthians 1:18-21
For the word of the cross is foolishness to those who are dying, but to us who are being saved it is the power of God. For it is written, "I will destroy the wisdom of the wise. I will bring the discernment of the discerning to nothing." Where is the wise? Where is the scribe? Where is the lawyer of this world? Hasn't God made foolish the wisdom of this world? For seeing that in the wisdom of God, the world through its wisdom didn't know God, it was God's good pleasure through the foolishness of the preaching to save those who believe.

Romans 1:28-32
Even as they refused to have God in their knowledge, God gave them up to a reprobate mind, to do those things which are not fitting; being filled with all unrighteousness, sexual immorality, wickedness, covetousness, malice; full of envy, murder, strife, deceit, evil habits, secret slanderers, backbiters, hateful to God, insolent, arrogant, boastful, inventors of evil things, disobedient to parents, without understanding, covenant breakers, without natural affection, unforgiving, unmerciful; who, knowing the ordinance of God, that those who practice such things are worthy of death, not only do the same, but also approve of those who practice them.

Romans 6:17-18
But thanks be to God, that, whereas you were bondservants of sin, you became obedient from the heart to that form of teaching to which you were delivered. Being made free from sin, you became bondservants of righteousness.

Ephesians 2:3
We also all once lived among them in the lusts of our flesh, doing the desires of the flesh and of the mind, and were by nature children of wrath, even as the rest.

2 Corinthians 4:4
In whom the god of this world [Satan] has blinded the minds of the unbelieving, that the light of the Good News of the glory of Christ, who is the image of God, should not dawn on them.

Colossians 1:13
Who delivered us out of the power of darkness, and translated us into the Kingdom of the Son of his love.

1 John 2:11
But he who hates his brother is in the darkness, and walks in the darkness, and doesn't know where he is going...the darkness has blinded his eyes.

Romans 1:18-21
For the wrath [anger] of God is revealed from heaven against all ungodliness and unrighteousness of men who suppress the truth in unrighteousness, because that which is known of God is revealed in them, for God revealed it to them. For the invisible things of him since the creation of the world are clearly seen, being perceived through the things that are made, even his everlasting power and divinity, that they may be without excuse. Because knowing God, they didn't glorify him as God, and didn't give thanks, but became vain in their reasoning, and their senseless heart was darkened.

How should all Christians respond? James and John, the apostles, thought Christians should respond with wrath. In Luke 9, the Lord sent messengers into a Samaritan village to make advanced preparations to lodge there. The messengers returned with a rejection from the villagers. They would not accommodate Him because He was traveling to Jerusalem. The Samaritans hated the Jews and their temple. Theirs had been destroyed a long time ago and they were jealous of the magnificent Herodian temple of the Jews. In Luke 9:54, Luke writes, "When his disciples, James and John, saw this, they said, 'Lord, do you want us to command fire to come down from the sky, and destroy them, just as Elijah did?'" When James and John witnessed this refusal on the part of the Samaritans, they were livid. The two brothers immediately asked if they could command fire to come from heaven and consume these inconsiderate rude people. The Lord rebuked them. He explained that He had not come to destroy men's lives but to save them.

Luke 9:54
When his disciples, James and John, saw this, they said, "Lord, do you want us to command fire to come down from the sky and destroy them, just as Elijah did?"

The Proper Response Explained

The response of Christians to their persecutors is the same as the reaction of believers to their enemies. Essentially, they comprise the same group. Enemies persecute Christians and those who persecute Christians are their enemies. The Lord Jesus taught that God's people are to love, bless, do good to, pray for, not resist, and forgive their enemies. This critical discussion will explain how these responses were the true intent of God's law but were circumvented by God's nation Israel. The reasons for these supernatural responses lie in the person, purpose, and power of God that must be displayed in His people for the unsaved to see.

The True Intent of the Law

One of the purposes of the instruction of the Lord was to present God's true intent behind the divine law to Israel. God's offspring completely misunderstood His intent in the law because they had over time reinterpreted and added so many additional mandates to His righteous commandments. Then, they attempted daily to meticulously obey these man-made decrees or ordinances. This produced in them a false sense of righteousness. Their intent and motives could be evil as long as their outward actions appeared devout. He intended to correct this false notion by properly interpreting the law from God's point of view which had been lost. This required preaching God's true commandments and then to properly interpret them.

In Matthew 5:38-45 and Luke 6:27-36, Jesus challenges two of the decrees. One decree was "Take an eye for and eye, and a tooth for a tooth." Another of the decrees was "Love your neighbor and hate your enemies." All of the first saying and the first part of the second saying came directly from the Old Testament. The second part of the second saying was added essentially through human logic. In the first saying, the Jews misinterpreted God's law and His intent behind the law. In the second, the Jews added a part, He did not intend.

Once properly interpreted by Jesus, God's people were given the appropriate reactions they should take when any persecution comes their way. In them, Jesus describes the relationship that believers in Christ should maintain amid their persecutors, enemies, and unbelievers in general. This concept of "an eye for an eye" comes from three critical Old Testament passages: Exodus 21:23, Leviticus 24:19-20, and Deuteronomy 19:21. These were judicial laws set up for the nation of Israel to govern its people. They were not moral precepts for individuals to follow.

Exodus 21:23
But if any harm follows, then you must take life for life.

Leviticus 24:19-20
If anyone injures his neighbor, it shall be done to him as he has done: fracture for fracture, eye for eye, tooth for tooth. It shall be done to him as he has injured someone.

Deuteronomy 19:21
Your eyes shall not pity: life for life, eye for eye, tooth for tooth, hand for hand, foot for foot.

The context of each of these passages involves dispensing justice by society. The moral precepts involved dispensing love by individuals. In Leviticus 19:18, the law stated, "You shall not take vengeance, nor bear any grudge against the children of your people; but you shall love your neighbor as yourself. I am Yahweh."

Leviticus 19:18
You shall not take vengeance, nor bear any grudge against the children of your people; but you shall love your neighbor as yourself. I am Yahweh.

The concept of "love your neighbor" is found in the Old Testament but without the second part. That second part was added later by Jewish religious leaders. God commands believers to not act in vengeance; instead, they should love their neighbors. These religious scholars disregarded the first portion and added instead "hate your enemies" as the logical conclusion. This allowed them to hate any individual against them. This authorized them to hate in God's name.

The True Demonstration of God's Person

To love, bless, do good to, pray for, meet the needs of, and forgive someone's enemies are difficult tasks, something opposite to how the world would respond. Just before Jesus uttered these commandments in Matthew 5:19-20, He made a powerful statement to the Jewish people. He declared that unless their righteousness exceeded the Scribes and the Pharisees, they could not inherit the kingdom of heaven. God's standards are higher than man's, in fact higher than the highest of his man-made standards. Jesus explained in Matthew 5:45 and Luke 6:31-35 the five critical reasons why Christians need to take the higher path of righteousness, even towards enemies.

Matthew 5:19-20
Therefore, whoever shall break one of these least commandments and teach others to do so, shall be called least in the Kingdom of Heaven; but whoever shall do and teach them shall be called great in the Kingdom of Heaven. For I tell you that unless your righteousness exceeds that of the scribes and Pharisees, there is no way you will enter into the Kingdom of Heaven.

Matthew 5:45
That you may be children of your Father who is in heaven. For he makes his sun to rise on the evil and the good, and sends rain on the just and the unjust.

Luke 6:31-35
As you would like people to do to you, do exactly so to them. If you love those who love you, what credit is that to you? For even sinners love those who love

them. If you do good to those who do good to you, what credit is that to you? For even sinners do the same. If you lend to those from whom you hope to receive, what credit is that to you? Even sinners lend to sinners, to receive back as much. But love your enemies, and do good, and lend, expecting nothing back; and your reward will be great, and you will be children of the Most High; for he is kind toward the unthankful and evil.

First, Jesus explained to believers that loving their enemies constantly demonstrates that they are children of God. In Matthew 5:45, He asserts believers do these things that they may be children of their heavenly Father. Second, loving enemies is a quality or characteristic of God Himself. Jesus goes on to present in the same verse that God makes the sun rise and rain fall to bless all people both the just and unjust.

Matthew 5:45
That you may be children of your Father who is in heaven. For he makes his sun to rise on the evil and the good, and sends rain on the just and the unjust.

Third, saints should be holier than unbelievers. In verses 46-47, the Lord Jesus explains that even the tax-gatherers (a hated, heathen group) love people who love them and greet their friends. In Luke 6:34, Jesus says, "If you lend to those from whom you hope to receive, what credit is that to you? Even sinners lend to sinners, to receive back as much." The Lord extends this doing good even to lending. Even sinners lend to those who they know will return the money. The love of Christians for enemies requires love at a supernatural level.

Matthew 5:46-47
For if you love those who love you, what reward do you have? Don't even the tax collectors do the same? If you only greet your friends, what more do you do than others? Don't even the tax collectors do the same?

Luke 6:34
If you lend to those from whom you hope to receive, what credit is that to you? Even sinners lend to sinners, to receive back as much.

Fourth, a believer's reward for loving his enemies will be great. Jesus implies in Matthew 5:46 that there is not much reward in Christians loving those who love them. In Luke 6:35, He says that if the saints love their enemies, do good to them, and lend expecting nothing in return, then great will be their reward. Fifth, the children of God are to imitate their Father. In Matthew 5:48, Jesus says they are to be perfect as their Father is perfect and in Luke 6:36, believers should be merciful as their Father is merciful.

Luke 6:35
But love your enemies, and do good, and lend, expecting nothing back; and your reward will be great, and you will be children of the Most High; for he is kind toward the unthankful and evil.

Matthew 5:48
Therefore you shall be perfect... as your Father in heaven is perfect.

Even before these incredible words, Jesus explains that God's children are to be salt and shining lights in the world (Matthew 5:13-16). From these five reasons and elsewhere, it can be seen that shining lights and savory salt manifest God's person, purpose, and power to the world. Christians exhibit His person in that these are His characteristics, not man's. They portray His purpose since men can see clearly that He exists and loves all men. Since the unsaved will see His person, purpose, and power in their Christian lives, they will know that these believers are from the true God. When they see their loving words and actions, this prepares them to hear His loving and saving message.

Matthew 5:13-16
You are the salt of the Earth, but if the salt has lost its flavor, with what will it be salted? It is then good for nothing, but to be cast out and trodden under the feet of men. You are the light of the world. A city located on a hill can't be hidden. Neither do you light a lamp and put it under a measuring basket, but on a stand; and it shines to all who are in the house. 16 Even so, let your light shine before men, that they may see your good works and glorify your Father who is in heaven.

These lights must continually shine even in the face of persecution and enemy attack. This salt must continually remain tasty even in the midst of mistreatment and enemy opposition. When Christians are tormented, harassed, and violently assailed, they are not to respond with revenge and retaliation, which is a human approach. Instead, they are to react in love, blessing, good works, prayer, meeting needs (not resisting), and forgiveness. In this, God is manifested, the good news can be presented, and God's power to save lives will be unleashed. Unbelievers will be able to identify Christians as the ones who have the true God in their lives.

To love, bless, do good to, pray for, not resist, and forgive one's enemies are characteristics of God's person. In Exodus 34:6-7, Moses was allowed to see the backside of God's glory. As God passed by, He proclaimed that He was gracious, merciful, forgiving, slow to anger, and full of kindness and truth. These attributes comprise His character. Even though men are in total rebellion to Him, God's character does not change. Whether men are enemies or children of God, they will experience all of His attributes though not always in the same way.

Exodus 34:6-7
Yahweh passed by before him, and proclaimed, "Yahweh! Yahweh, a merciful and gracious God, slow to anger, and abundant in loving kindness and truth, keeping loving kindness for thousands, forgiving iniquity and disobedience and sin; and who will by no means clear the guilty, visiting the iniquity of the fathers on the children, and on the children's children, on the third and on the fourth generation."

In Romans 1:19-20, Paul declared that God's deity, power, and attributes are clearly seen through his creation. In Acts 14:17, Paul proclaims that God's creation also displays to the world His grace and mercy since the rains from the heavens brings fruitful seasons, which satisfies their hearts with food and with gladness. His blessing upon them in creation will prepare them for the gospel.

Romans 1:19-20
Because that which is known of God is revealed in them, for God revealed it to them. 20 For the invisible things of him since the creation of the world are clearly seen, being perceived through the things that are made, even his everlasting power and divinity, that they may be without excuse.

Acts 14:17
Yet he didn't leave himself without witness, in that he did good and gave you rains from the sky and fruitful seasons, filling our hearts with food and gladness.

Christians are growing more and more into the image of Christ. This means that their thinking, speaking, feeling, and behaving are becoming progressively more and more like Jesus their Savior and Lord. Paul discloses to the Corinthians that believers are beholding the glory of the Lord in a mirror and being transformed into the same image of Christ from glory to glory (2 Corinthians 3:18).

2 Corinthians 3:18
But we all, with unveiled face seeing the glory of the Lord as in a mirror, are transformed into the same image from glory to glory, even as from the Lord, the Spirit.

As they grow in Christ, they are being transformed into His image. John has a similar thought regarding a believer's behavior as he lives for Christ. In 1 John 2:6, John declares, "He who says he remains in him ought himself also to walk just like he walked." John tells his readers that if Christians abide in Him, they ought to walk exactly as He walked. True believers will obey this command (John 14:15, 23). They will walk as their Savior and Lord walked. These true believers will demonstrate God's holy character and behave like Him.

1 John 2:6
He who says he remains in him ought himself also to walk just like he walked.

John 14:15
If you love me, keep my commandments.

John 14:23
Jesus answered him, "If a man loves me, he will keep my word. My Father will love him, and we will come to him, and make our home with him."

When His children come to share the good news, then unbelievers will know them. Christians will behave like the God they know from His creation and blessing. Even if they persecute them, the character of God's grace, mercy, love, and blessing will manifest itself through the words and actions of His children. Again, they will know that those who proclaim the gospel of salvation are truly from God.

To accomplish this, God reveals His judgment upon sin through His creation from outside man (Romans 1:18-20) and the conscience from within man (Romans 2:14-16). Men reject the knowledge of God because they suppress the truth in their wickedness (Romans 1:18). Instead of honoring or thanking God for His grace, man created his own gods to worship and venerate (Romans 1:21-23). God's response was the abandonment of man to every sexual sin (Romans 1:24, 26, 28). In this, His wrath is revealed. When men see this, they know wrath and judgment are coming.

Romans 1:18-20
For the wrath [anger] of God is revealed from heaven against all ungodliness and unrighteousness of men who suppress the truth in unrighteousness, because that which is known of God is revealed in them, for God revealed it to them. For the invisible things of him since the creation of the world are clearly seen, being perceived through the things that are made, even his everlasting power and divinity, that they may be without excuse.

Romans 2:14-16
(For when Gentiles who don't have the law do by nature the things of the law, these, not having the law, are a law to themselves, in that they show the work of the law written in their hearts, their conscience testifying with them, and their thoughts among themselves accusing or else excusing them) in the day when God will judge the secrets of men, according to my Good News, by Jesus Christ.

Romans 1:18
For the wrath [anger] of God is revealed from heaven against all ungodliness and unrighteousness of men who suppress the truth in unrighteousness.

Romans 1:21-23
Because knowing God, they didn't glorify him as God, and didn't give thanks, but became vain in their reasoning, and their senseless heart was darkened. Professing themselves to be wise, they became fools, and traded the glory of the incorruptible God for the likeness of an image of corruptible man, and of birds, four-footed animals, and creeping things.

Romans 1:24
Therefore God also gave them up in the lusts of their hearts to uncleanness, that their bodies should be dishonored among themselves.

Romans 1:26
For this reason, God gave them up to vile passions. For their women changed the natural function into that which is against nature.

Romans 1:28
Even as they refused to have God in their knowledge, God gave them up to a reprobate mind, to do those things which are not fitting.

When God's children come to present their message of judgment and Christ's deliverance, these sinful unbelievers will know them. Christians will be like their Father, who the unsaved know from His creation and blessing. Even if they persecute the Lord God's children, His grace, mercy, love, and blessing will come through their words and actions. Again, they will know that their message of judgment and salvation is truly from God. When they see hate and scorn in the eyes of those sharing the gospel, they will not recognize them. Why? They cannot see the God that they have come to know from His creation.

God's eternal power is exhibited throughout His creation and, more importantly, is clearly seen (Romans 1:20). Notice, Paul describes His power as eternal. It is divine power that has no limit. It extends from eternity past to eternity future. It comes from a Greek root word that means "perpetually, incessantly, or invariably." The root is translated "always" or "constantly." This power of God will always and forever be powerful. It will never cease!

Romans 1:20
For the invisible things of him since the creation of the world are clearly seen, being perceived through the things that are made, even his everlasting power and divinity, that they may be without excuse.

The book of Romans is all about eternal judgment and salvation. This requires eternal power to eternally save or eternally condemn. Unbelievers clearly observe this power in creation, and they know it is eternal. Therefore, when they understand that their judgment is coming, they also know that God has the ability to make their condemnation eternal. Why? His power is eternal. They also understand that if they honor and thank God, He possesses the ability to make that salvation eternal because His power is eternal.

When God's children proclaim the message of judgment and salvation, these unbelievers will know them. Christians will be like their Father, who they know from His creation and blessing. Even if they persecute God's children, His grace, mercy, love, and blessing would shine through their words and actions.

The unsaved will know Christians have the gospel with the eternal power to save because they will see it displayed in their lives under persecution. This is a powerful testimony and witness to them whether they acknowledge it at the time or not. If they do, then they will be saved. If they don't, then they will have been given a true testimony of the good news of Jesus Christ, the Savior and Lord.

The Proper Response Described

For Christians to display God's divine character to their enemies in love, blessing, good works, prayer, and meeting their needs (not resisting them), it may require a battle with the supernatural forces of evil. Why? These responses are diametrically opposed to how human beings, society, or the Devil naturally think or feel toward enemies.

This battle will be against the flesh (James 1:14-15), the world (1 John 2:15-17), and the Devil (2 Corinthians 2:11). The flesh enjoys many natural impulses to hate, curse, and retaliate against enemies. Society has a long history of hate, cursing, and retaliating against national, cultural, racial, familial, and individual enemies. The Serpent has invested thousands of years of hating, cursing, and retaliating against God, His angels, and His people upon the Earth. This battle may require real effort and time to find victory (Mark 14:38; Romans 7:23; 1 Corinthians 9:25-26; Hebrews 12:4).

James 1:14-15
But each one is tempted when he is drawn away by his own lust and enticed. 15 Then the lust, when it has conceived, bears sin. The sin, when it is full grown, produces death.

1 John 2:15-17
Don't love the world or the things that are in the world. If anyone loves the world, the Father's love isn't in him. For all that is in the world, the lust of the flesh, the lust of the eyes, and the pride of life, isn't the Father's, but is the world's. The world is passing away with its lusts, but he who does God's will remains forever.

2 Corinthians 2:11
That no advantage may be gained over us by Satan, for we are not ignorant of his schemes.

Mark 14:38
Watch and pray, that you may not enter into temptation. The spirit indeed is willing, but the flesh is weak.

Romans 7:23
But I see a different law in my members, warring against the law of my mind, and bringing me into captivity under the law of sin which is in my members.

1 Corinthians 9:25-26
Every man who strives in the games exercises self-control in all things. Now they do it to receive a corruptible crown, but we an incorruptible. I therefore run like that, not aimlessly. I fight like that, not beating the air.

Hebrews 12:4
You have not yet resisted to blood, striving against sin.

For believers to stand against these antagonists, they will need supernatural strength. This strength must come from the Holy Spirit as Christians rely on divine power (Galatians 5:17-18; Ephesians 6:10-11; 1 Peter 5:6-7). Not only is this the childlike dependence of trust in God (the way a small child trusts in his dad for protection), it will require growing up in all aspects of Him (Ephesians 4:14-15; 1 Corinthians 13:11; 1 John 2:12-14).

Galatians 5:17-18
For the flesh lusts against the Spirit, and the Spirit against the flesh; and these are contrary to one another, that you may not do the things that you desire. But if you are led by the Spirit, you are not under the law.

Ephesians 6:10-11
Finally, be strong in the Lord, and in the strength of his might. Put on the whole armor of God, that you may be able to stand against the wiles of the devil.

1 Peter 5:6-7
Humble yourselves therefore under the mighty hand of God, that he may exalt you in due time, casting all your worries on him, because he cares for you.

Ephesians 4:14-15
That we may no longer be children, tossed back and forth and carried about with every wind of doctrine, by the trickery of men, in craftiness, after the wiles of error; but speaking truth in love, we may grow up in all things into him who is the head, Christ.

1 Corinthians 13:11
When I was a child, I spoke as a child, I felt as a child, I thought as a child. Now that I have become a man...put away childish things.

1 John 2:12-14
I write to you, little children, because your sins are forgiven you for his name's sake. I write to you, fathers, because you know him who is from the beginning. I write to you, young men, because you have overcome the evil one. I write to you, little children, because you know the Father. I have written to you, fathers, because you know him who is from the beginning. I have written to you, young men, because you are strong, and the word of God remains in you, and you have overcome the evil one.

As Christians grow up in Christ, the power necessary to battle these spiritual adversaries will be released (2 Peter 1:3-4; Philippians 2:12-13; 1 Thessalonians 1:5). First, the saints need to grow in the word (1 Peter 2:2; 1 Thessalonians 2:13; Ephesians 4:11-12). Second, believers need to pray with other believers for strength (Ephesians 6:18-19; Philippians 1:19; Matthew 26:41). Third, the saints need to be building up and edifying one another in fellowship together (Romans 14:19; 15:14; 1 Corinthians 14:12). As Christians spend time with each other, they should be helping the other grow in Christ. Fourth, those that love the Lord Jesus, must be living a life of obedience (1 Corinthians 3:1-3; Romans 6:19; Galatians 5:7) constantly submitting themselves to their Master (Romans 12:1-2; James 4:7; Ephesians 6:6). Fifth, His people must put on the armor of light (Romans 13:12; Ephesians 6:11; 1 John 1:7). Sixth, Christians must resist all these adversaries (2 Corinthians 7:1; James 4:7; 1 Peter 5:9).

2 Peter 1:3-4
Seeing that his divine power has granted to us all things that pertain to life and godliness, through the knowledge of him who called us by his own glory and virtue, by which he has granted to us his precious and exceedingly great promises; that through these you may become partakers of the divine nature, having escaped from the corruption that is in the world by lust.

LEADING THE WAY

Philippians 2:12-13
So then, my beloved, even as you have always obeyed, not only in my presence, but now much more in my absence, work out your own salvation with fear and trembling. For it is God who works in you both to will and to work, for his good pleasure.

1 Thessalonians 1:5
And that our Good News came to you not in word only, but also in power, and in the Holy Spirit, and with much assurance. You know what kind of men we showed ourselves to be among you for your sake.

1 Peter 2:2
As newborn babies, long for the pure milk of the Word, that with it you may grow.

1 Thessalonians 2:13
For this cause we also thank God without ceasing, that when you received from us the word of the message of God, you accepted it not as the word of men, but as it is in truth, the word of God, which also works in you who believe.

Ephesians 4:11-12
He gave some to be apostles; and some, prophets; and some, evangelists; and some, shepherds[a] and teachers; for the perfecting of the saints, to the work of serving, to the building up of the body of Christ.

Ephesians 6:18-19
With all prayer and requests, praying at all times in the Spirit, and being watchful to this end in all perseverance and requests for all the saints: 19 on my behalf, that utterance may be given to me in opening my mouth, to make known with boldness the mystery of the Good News.

Philippians 1:19
For I know that this will turn out to my salvation, through your prayers and the supply of the Spirit of Jesus Christ,

Matthew 26:41
Watch and pray, that you don't enter into temptation. The spirit indeed is willing, but the flesh is weak.

Romans 14:19
So then, let's follow after things which make for peace, and things by which we may build one another up.

Romans 15:14
I myself am also persuaded about you, my brothers, that you yourselves are full of goodness, filled with all knowledge, able also to admonish others.

1 Corinthians 14:12
So also you, since you are zealous for spiritual gifts, seek that you may abound to the building up of the assembly.

1 Corinthians 3:1-3
Brothers, I couldn't speak to you as to spiritual, but as to fleshly, as to babies in Christ. I fed you with milk, not with meat; for you weren't yet ready. Indeed, you aren't ready even now, for you are still fleshly. For insofar as there is jealousy, strife, and factions among you, aren't you fleshly, and don't you walk in the ways of men?

Romans 6:19
I speak in human terms because of the weakness of your flesh, for as you presented your members as servants to uncleanness and to wickedness upon wickedness, even so now present your members as servants to righteousness for sanctification.

Galatians 5:7
You were running well! Who interfered with you that you should not obey the truth?

Romans 12:1-2
Therefore I urge you, brothers, by the mercies of God, to present your bodies a living sacrifice, holy, acceptable to God, which is your spiritual service. Don't be conformed to this world, but be transformed by the renewing of your mind, so that you may prove what is the good, well-pleasing, and perfect will of God.

James 4:7
Be subject therefore to God. Resist the devil, and he will flee from you.

Ephesians 6:6
Not in the way of service only when eyes are on you, as men pleasers, but as servants of Christ, doing the will of God from the heart.

Romans 13:12
The night is far gone, and the day is near. Let's therefore throw off the deeds of darkness, and let's put on the armor of light.

Ephesians 6:6
Not in the way of service only when eyes are on you, as men pleasers, but as servants of Christ, doing the will of God from the heart.

Romans 13:12
The night is far gone, and the day is near. Let's therefore throw off the deeds of darkness, and let's put on the armor of light.

Ephesians 6:11
Put on the whole armor of God, that you may be able to stand against the wiles of the devil.

1 John 1:7
But if we walk in the light, as he is in the light, we have fellowship with one another, and the blood of Jesus Christ, his Son, cleanses us from all sin.

2 Corinthians 7:1
Having therefore these promises, beloved, let's cleanse ourselves from all defilement of flesh and spirit, perfecting holiness in the fear of God.

James 4:7
Be subject therefore to God. Resist the devil, and he will flee from you.

1 Peter 5:9
Withstand him steadfast in your faith, knowing that your brothers who are in the world are undergoing the same sufferings.

The Leaving of Vengeance to God

In Matthew 5:44 and Luke 6:27, Jesus states that the saints are to love their enemies. In Romans 13:1-4, Paul states that it is the responsibility of governing authorities to be avengers of God. Christians are to show love to their enemies, but the government is to prosecute those enemies for harming them, violating their rights, and breaking the law. One is personal and the other is judicial. The personal precepts involve love. The judicial precepts involve justice. Saints do not avenge, nor bear any grudge but love their neighbors as themselves. Vengeance comes from God and through the government.

Matthew 5:44
But I tell you, love your enemies, bless those who curse you, do good to those who hate you, and pray for those who mistreat you and persecute you.

Luke 6:27
But I tell you who hear: love your enemies, do good to those who hate you.

Romans 13:1-4
Let every soul be in subjection to the higher authorities, for there is no authority except from God, and those who exist are ordained by God. Therefore he who resists the authority withstands the ordinance of God; and those who withstand will receive to themselves judgment. For rulers are not a terror to the good work, but to the evil. Do you desire to have no fear of the authority? Do that which is good, and you will have praise from the authority, for he is a servant of God to you for good. But if you do that which is evil, be afraid, for he doesn't bear the sword in vain; for he is a servant of God, an avenger for wrath to him who does evil.

This is not only seen in the Old Testament in Leviticus 19:18 but also in the New Testament. In Romans 12:19, Paul quotes Moses in Deuteronomy 32:35 and fully reiterates the importance of not taking vengeance upon others but letting the Lord do His judicial work. In Romans 12:19, Paul writes, "Don't seek revenge yourselves, beloved, but give place to God's wrath. For it is written, 'Vengeance belongs to me; I will repay, says the Lord.'" In this passage, Paul explains that vengeance belongs to God. That is His responsibility. In 2 Thessalonians 1:4-5, the apostle Paul praises the members of the church at Thessalonica for their patient endurance of the suffering of persecution, which is a sign of the righteous judgment of God. He will repay their affliction. The Lord God will avenge His people either in this life or the life to come. This is part of what their judgment will encompass.

Leviticus 19:18
You shall not take vengeance, nor bear any grudge against the children of your people; but you shall love your neighbor as yourself. I am Yahweh.

Romans 12:19
Don't seek revenge yourselves, beloved, but give place to God's wrath. For it is written, "Vengeance belongs to me; I will repay, says the Lord."

Deuteronomy 32:35
Vengeance is mine, and recompense, at the time when their foot slides; for the day of their calamity is at hand. Their doom rushes at them."

Romans 12:19
Don't seek revenge yourselves, beloved, but give place to God's wrath. For it is written, "Vengeance belongs to me; I will repay, says the Lord."

2 Thessalonians 1:4-5
So that we ourselves boast about you in the assemblies of God for your perseverance and faith in all your persecutions and in the afflictions which you endure. This is an obvious sign of the righteous judgment of God, to the end that you may be counted worthy of God's Kingdom, for which you also suffer.

When persecution comes, Christians should be concerned with spiritual matters first. How the saints treat unbelievers in the ways that have been discussed is critical. Christians may seek justice from their government and pray for justice (Psalm 94:1-2; Revelation 6:9-10). This does not imply that believers cannot defend themselves as the law allows.

Psalm 94:1-2
Yahweh, you God to whom vengeance belongs, you God to whom vengeance belongs, shine out. Rise up, you judge of the Earth. Pay back the proud what they deserve.

Revelation 6:9-10
When he opened the fifth seal, I saw underneath the altar the souls of those who had been killed for the Word of God, and for the testimony of the Lamb which they had. They cried with a loud voice, saying, "How long, Master, the holy and true, until you judge and avenge our blood on those who dwell on the Earth?"

The Showing of Love to Persecutors

Jesus Christ explains in Matthew 5:44 and Luke 6:27 that Christians are to love their enemies, the ones who persecute them. The word "love" is this passage in not the concept of romantic love but something much deeper. The Greek word essentially means to value or prize someone or something.

This word was utilized by Jesus and His disciples to speak of valuing to the point of sacrifice. The classic use of the word is found in John 3:16, where Jesus asserts that God so loved the world that He gave His Son. God so valued the world that He gave, even though it was hostile to Him. Like our God, Christians are to love the world that they also give, even though it is hostile to them. Sacrificial giving is crucial in demonstrating this love to the world and distinguishing the true people of God from the false people of God. This also distinguishes the true gospel from the false gospel.

Matthew 5:44
But I tell you, love your enemies, bless those who curse you, do good to those who hate you, and pray for those who mistreat you and persecute you.

Luke 6:27
But I tell you who hear: love your enemies, do good to those who hate you.

John 3:16
For God so loved the world, that he gave his one and only Son, that whoever believes in him should not perish, but have eternal life.

This coincides with the great commandments that Jesus acknowledged in Luke 10:27. Men are to love God and love their neighbors as themselves. When a lawyer asked Him who was this neighbor, he referred to, Jesus told the story of the Good Samaritan in verses 30-36. This story indicated that his neighbor went beyond all races, genders, and creeds to anyone in need. Even enemies of saints may be in need and would obviously be their neighbor. In the story, the Jewish man, who was robbed and beaten, was aided by a Samaritan man. The Samaritans and Jews hated each other and were enemies. However, as God's people love themselves, they are to love their enemies.

Luke 10:27
He answered, "You shall love the Lord your God with all your heart, with all your soul, with all your strength, and with all your mind; and your neighbor as yourself."

Luke 10:30-36
Jesus answered, "A certain man was going down from Jerusalem to Jericho, and he fell among robbers, who both stripped him and beat him, and departed, leaving him half dead. By chance a certain priest was going down that way. When he saw him, he passed by on the other side. In the same way a Levite also, when he came to the place, and saw him, passed by on the other side. But a certain Samaritan, as he traveled, came where he was. When he saw him, he was moved with compassion, came to him, and bound up his wounds, pouring on oil and wine. He set him on his own animal, brought him to an inn, and took care of him. On the next day, when he departed, he took out two denarii, gave them to the host, and said to him, 'Take care of him. Whatever you spend beyond that, I will repay you when I return.' Now which of these three do you think seemed to be a neighbor to him who fell among the robbers?"

This is found in the Old Testament as well. In Proverbs 11:12, Solomon declares that the despising of one's neighbor displays a lack of wisdom. Later in Proverbs 14:21, he calls it sin. In the New Testament, Paul, the apostle, states this very same principle in a very straightforward manner. The loving of one's neighbor is an essential in the Christian life. Romans 13:8 clearly states, "Owe no one anything, except to love one another; for he who loves his neighbor has fulfilled the law."

Proverbs 11:12
One who despises his neighbor is void of wisdom, but a man of understanding holds his peace.

Proverbs 14:21
He who despises his neighbor sins, but he who has pity on the poor is blessed.

Romans 13:8
Owe no one anything, except to love one another; for he who loves his neighbor has fulfilled the law.

Here, Paul writes again that Christians are to owe nothing to anyone except to love one another. Believers are to have only one debt toward their neighbors. This debt is to love them. This love fulfilled the law. If someone summed up all God's commandments toward others, it would be to love one's neighbor, whether they are enemies or not. So much more could be said. A good concordance study of the word "love" would reveal much more. No matter what kind of negative reactions Christians may receive from the world, unbelievers are to be loved by those saints, especially ones who become their enemies.

The Giving of a Blessing to Persecutors

Not only are Christians to love their enemies but are also to give a blessing to them. In the passages of Matthew 5:44 and Luke 6:28, believers are commanded to bless everyone who curses them. Providing a blessing was a very familiar concept in the Old Testament. A typical kind of blessing is found in Ruth 2:3-5 when Boaz went out into his own fields. When he found his reapers, he greeted them with, "May the Lord be with you!" Then they returned his blessing with a similar one, "May the Lord bless you!" This general blessing was extremely meaningful. This expressed the genuine and heartfelt desire that the other person would find safety and protection in God. In Numbers 6:22-27, the Lord told Moses to have Aaron bless the people of Israel with the words the Lord gave him to speak. He was to request that the Lord bless them, keep them, make His face shine on them, be gracious to them, lift up His countenance on them, and give them peace. This was a manifold blessing as God poured out His grace upon them.

Matthew 5:44
But I tell you, love your enemies, bless those who curse you, do good to those who hate you, and pray for those who mistreat you and persecute you.

Luke 6:28
Bless those who curse you, and pray for those who mistreat you.

Ruth 2:3-5
She went, and came and gleaned in the field after the reapers; and she happened to come to the portion of the field belonging to Boaz, who was of the family of Elimelech. Behold, Boaz came from Bethlehem, and said to the reapers, "May Yahweh be with you." They answered him, "May Yahweh bless you." Then Boaz said to his servant who was set over the reapers, "Whose young lady is this?"

Numbers 6:22-27
Yahweh spoke to Moses, saying, "Speak to Aaron and to his sons, saying, 'This is how you shall bless the children of Israel.' You shall tell them, 'Yahweh bless you, and keep you. Yahweh make his face to shine on you, and be gracious to you. Yahweh lift up his face toward you, and give you peace.' So they shall put my name on the children of Israel; and I will bless them."

In Deuteronomy 7:13, God explained to Moses that if the Israelites kept His commandments, He would bless the fruit of their womb and multiply their offspring. God would pour out His grace upon them by blessing the fruit of the ground, multiplying all their grain, wine, oil, herds, and flocks. So, blessings can be general or very specific. This is the kind of blessing Paul encourages Christians to give to their enemies and persecutors. In Romans 12:14, Paul commands, "Bless those who persecute you; bless, and don't curse." The apostle desires the church at Rome to bless those who persecute them and not curse them. This would not be easy. The city of Rome was the seat of the Roman emperors. These despots were responsible for the persecution of many saints using horrific methods of terror. Martyrdom became a common way of life at many times; yet they were to bless.

Deuteronomy 7:13
He will love you, bless you, and multiply you. He will also bless the fruit of your body and the fruit of your ground, your grain and your new wine and your oil, the increase of your livestock and the young of your flock, in the land which he swore to your fathers to give you.

Romans 12:14
Bless those who persecute you; bless, and don't curse.

Paul endured many of these kinds of persecutions at the hand of the Jews and Gentiles. In 1 Corinthians 4:12, Paul describes his response to those who cursed him. He would give a blessing in return. He would wish God's grace upon those who railed against him. Though his words could have been unkind; instead, he blessed them. Believers who are persecuted should provide a blessing upon their persecutors or enemies, both in their hearts and from their mouths. Of course, God's ultimate blessing would be in their repentance from this evil and salvation.

1 Corinthians 4:12
We toil, working with our own hands. When people curse us, we bless. Being persecuted, we endure.

The Doing of Good to Persecutors

Not only are all Christians to love and bless their enemies, but they are to do good to them. In Matthew 5:44 and Luke 6:27, all believers are commanded by the Lord Jesus to do good to those who hate them. When His followers are seeking to do good works for the glory of God, perhaps they should consider their enemies or persecutors. These could be the recipients of their righteous deeds and aspirations.

Matthew 5:44
But I tell you, love your enemies, bless those who curse you, do good to those who hate you, and pray for those who mistreat you and persecute you.

Luke 6:27
But I tell you who hear: love your enemies, do good to those who hate you.

In Acts 14:8-18, both Paul and Barnabas entered Lystra and healed a man who had been lame from birth. Thinking they were gods (Hermes and Zeus), the people responded by worshiping and making sacrifices to them. Aghast by this inappropriate response, Paul and Barnabas tore their robes and declared to the crowd that they were mere men. Instead, they had come to proclaim the true God. It was time for the citizens of Lystra to turn toward the Lord God who had been testifying to these people throughout history. The true deity, whom they represented, had been sending rain from heaven and producing fruitful seasons to satisfy their hearts with food and gladness. In essence, His person, purpose, and power had been on display all along through His goodness. The point is that doing good to enemies is a characteristic of God and believers are to be the same way with theirs.

Acts 14:17
Yet he didn't leave himself without witness, in that he did good and gave you[a] rains from the sky and fruitful seasons, filling our hearts with food and gladness."

In John 5:29, Jesus pronounced that those who did good deeds would proceed to a resurrection of life. Paul teaches the same concept in Romans 2:10, when he wrote that glory and honor and peace will be for everyone who does good. In Matthew 5:16, Jesus declared, "Even so, let your light shine before men; that they may see your good works, and glorify your Father who is in Heaven." The Lord indicated that His people should let their light shine before men, so that all will see His goodness in them and glorify God. The term "men" includes enemies.

John 5:29
And will come...those who have done good, to the resurrection of life; and those who have done evil, to the resurrection of judgment.

Romans 2:10
But glory, honor, and peace go to every man who does good, to the Jew first, and also to the Greek.

Matthew 5:16
Even so, let your light shine before men, that they may see your good works and glorify your Father who is in heaven.

In Ephesians 2:10, Paul views God's church as His divine workmanship, created in Christ Jesus for good works (good deeds). Then, he encourages his readers to walk in them. These good works must extend to persecutors, enemies, and unbelievers in general. In 2 Peter 2:18-20, the apostle Peter commands Christian slaves with unruly and mean masters to be submissive with all respect. The apostle argues that when these slaves, who believe in Jesus, suffer unjustly, yet submit and respect their masters, this finds favor with God. Would that not be a good work toward a persecutor or an enemy?

Ephesians 2:10
For we are his workmanship, created in Christ...for good works, which God prepared before that we would walk in them.

2 Peter 2:18-20
For, uttering great swelling words of emptiness, they entice in the lusts of the flesh, by licentiousness, those who are indeed escaping from those who live in error; promising them liberty, while they themselves are bondservants of corruption; for a man is brought into bondage by whoever overcomes him. For if, after they have escaped the defilement of the world through the knowledge of the Lord and Savior Jesus Christ, they are again entangled in it and overcome, the last state has become worse for them than the first.

In Romans 15:1-3, Paul exhorts all believers to bear the weaknesses of those who are weak and not just seek their own pleasure. Then Paul provides a general principle. The saved are to please their neighbors (including enemies) for good and for their edification or building up. So, pleasing neighbors for their good is good works. In chapter 12, verse 21, Paul writes that Christians should overcome evil with good. This will include their enemies and persecutors. Why? Enemies and persecutors desire to bring evil upon believers; this should be overcome with good works. In 1 Corinthians

10:24, he reiterates this very command to the members of the church in Corinth. Again, he says that they are to seek their neighbor's good. Therefore, a characteristic of all believers is the doing of good works for the Lord. These are not just toward other Christians but toward all people (including persecutors and enemies).

Romans 15:1-3
Now we who are strong ought to bear the weaknesses of the weak, and not to please ourselves. Let each one of us please his neighbor for that which is good, to be building him up. For even Christ didn't please himself. But, as it is written, "The reproaches of those who reproached you fell on me."

Romans 12:21
Don't be overcome by evil, but overcome evil with good.

1 Corinthians 10:24
Let no one seek his own, but each one his neighbor's good.

In Galatians 6:10, Paul exhorted the Galatians to do good to all men, while they were given the opportunity, especially ones of the household of faith. So, the first priority of doing good is to other Christians and then to everyone. What do good deeds entail? John explains that loving the brethren will involve word, tongue, deed, and truth in 1 John 3:15. Would not good towards a neighbor involve both good words and good actions? This may seem humanly difficult to behave like this toward one's enemies, but it has always been the Lord God's way. If He had not sent His Son to offer salvation (good in word and tongue) and then die for men's sins (good in deed and truth), no one would ever have been saved. Wasn't mankind in rebellion and His enemy at the time? So, believers are to do good to those who oppose them because God did the same for them.

Galatians 6:10
So then, as we have opportunity, let's do what is good toward all men, and especially toward those who are of the household of the faith.

1 John 3:15
Whoever hates his brother is a murderer, and you know that no murderer has eternal life remaining in him

The Offering of Prayer for Persecutors

Not only are all Christians to bless their enemies but pray for them. In Matthew 5:44 and Luke 6:28, Christians are told to pray for those who mistreat them and persecute them. Before Christians believe in our Lord, they are unbelievers, who are reacting negatively to the gospel. The Scriptures are replete with accounts of many formerly hostile unbelievers who eventually receive Christ. These became illustrations of God's person, purpose, and power. Since He sometimes calls unsaved persecutors to His Son, Christians need to pray for their salvation.

Matthew 5:44
But I tell you, love your enemies, bless those who curse you, do good to those who hate you, and pray for those who mistreat you and persecute you.

Luke 6:28
Bless those who curse you, and pray for those who mistreat you.

Nicodemus, the teacher of the Jews, began in John 3 with negative reactions to Jesus and His gospel. He is not spoken of again until John 19:39-42 when he brought the spices to anoint the dead body of the Lord Jesus. Sometime between his conversation with Jesus in John 3 and His anointing of the body of Jesus in John 19, Nicodemus became a Christian.

John 19:39-42
Nicodemus, who at first came to Jesus by night, also came bringing a mixture of myrrh and aloes, about a hundred Roman pounds. So, they took Jesus' body, and bound it in linen cloths with the spices, as the custom of the Jews is to bury. Now in the place where he was crucified there was a garden. In the garden was a new tomb in which no man had ever yet been laid. Then because of the Jews' Preparation Day (for the tomb was near at hand) they laid Jesus there.

Before this, Nicodemus was an important member of the Sanhedrin. As a result, he must have participated in the variety of ways this Jewish council hounded, mocked, and discredited Jesus which ultimately led to the murder of the Lord Jesus. This teacher of Israel reacted negatively at first, later he believed. Perhaps, the Lord prayed for Nicodemus when He went off to pray though he was an enemy.

As has been noted, Paul was a vicious persecutor of the church. His negative reactions to the good news went to the furthest extremes against believers: tracking the newborn Christians, storming into their private homes, hauling off these innocent people, throwing these virtuous saints into prison, and eventually martyring them (Acts 8:1-3; 9:1-2). He began with negative reactions, lavishing in being both an enemy and persecutor of the church. Eventually, he came to Christ (Acts 9:5). Perhaps, those who were fleeing from Saul prayed for his salvation.

Acts 8:1-3
Saul was consenting to his death. A great persecution arose against the assembly which was in Jerusalem in that day. They were all scattered abroad throughout the regions of Judea and Samaria, except for the apostles. Devout men buried Stephen and lamented greatly.... But Saul ravaged the assembly, entering into every house and dragged both men and women off to prison.

Acts 9:1-2
But Saul, still breathing threats and slaughter against the disciples of the Lord, went to the high priest and asked for letters from him to the synagogues of Damascus, that if he found any who were of the Way...might bring them bound to Jerusalem.

Acts 9:5
He said, "Who are you, Lord [Master]?" The Lord said, "I am Jesus, whom you are persecuting.

Paul and the other apostles witnessed many enemies and persecutors of Christians transformed into supporters and proclaimers of the gospel. In Acts 16, Paul was thrown into prison in Philippi. It can be reasonably assumed the jailer did not give him a warm reception, since he was ordered to put Paul and Silas into stocks to secure them from escape. In verses 27-34, they did a good work in the life of the jailer by saving him from committing suicide. This gave Paul the opportunity to share the good news and he and his whole household came to the Savior. The jailer went from negative reactions to the gospel and being an enemy and persecutor to one of the original members of the newly founded church at Philippi. Perhaps, Paul and Silas were praying for the jailer even while their limbs were stretched out in the stocks.

Acts 16:27-34
The jailer, being roused out of sleep and seeing the prison doors open, drew his sword and was about to kill himself, supposing that the prisoners had escaped. But Paul cried with a loud voice, saying, "Don't harm yourself, for we are all here!" He called for lights, sprang in, fell down...before Paul and Silas, brought them out, and said, "Sirs, what must I do to be saved?" They said, "Believe in the Lord Jesus Christ, and you will be saved...." They spoke the word of the Lord to him, and to all who were in his house. He took them the same hour...and washed their stripes, and was immediately baptized, he and all his household. He brought them up into his house, and set food before them, and rejoiced greatly, with all his household, having believed in God.

In Acts 18:4-8, Paul was resisted, mocked, criticized, and eventually thrown out of the synagogue in Corinth. Would the leader of the synagogue be instrumental in this negative reaction? Yes. Yet, when Paul was instructing in the house next-door, owned by Titius Justus, Crispus, the leader of the synagogue, received Jesus Christ as Lord and Savior with all of His household. Crispus was transformed from being a persecutor of the church to being a staunch advocate and proclaimer of Jesus Christ.

Acts 18:4-8
He reasoned in the synagogue every Sabbath and persuaded Jews and Greeks. But when Silas and Timothy came down...Paul was compelled by the Spirit, testifying to the Jews that Jesus was the Christ. When they opposed him and blasphemed, he shook out his clothing and said to them, "Your blood be on your

own heads! I am clean. From now on, I will go to the Gentiles!" He departed there, and went into the house of a certain man named Justus, one who worshiped God...house was next-door to the synagogue. Crispus, the ruler of the synagogue, believed in the Lord with all his house. Many...Corinthians, when they heard, believed and were baptized.

In previous discussions of Paul's missionary journeys, it has been continually demonstrated that the hostile Jews and Gentiles, though they were the enemies and persecutors of Christians, ultimately became true saints. Could Paul have been praying for Crispus and these others? When Paul was imprisoned in Rome for the first time in Acts 28:30-31, the Philippian church was concerned about him and needed much encouragement.

Acts 28:30-31
Paul stayed two whole years in his own rented house and received all who were coming to him, preaching God's Kingdom, and teaching the things concerning the Lord Jesus Christ with all boldness, without hindrance.

In Philippians 1:12, he explained what God was doing in Rome. He asserted that there was a greater progress of the gospel. The Greek word translated "progress" refers to a pioneering work. It was used to describe the work of Roman soldiers when they had to cut through the thick habitation of an area. As a result, they would be able to build a decent road in order to transfer troops from one place to another.

Philippians 1:12
Now I desire to have you know, brothers, that the things which happened to me have turned out rather to the progress of the Good News.

God was building a road for the gospel into Rome. How? In verse 13, Paul says that the slumbering church in Rome had awakened because of his boldness. The saints were now out boldly preaching Christ. The whole Praetorian Guard had heard the gospel among many others who were coming to him. In Philippians 4:22, the letter closes with his final example of the pioneering work, when he sends a greeting from those who now believed from Caesar's own household. All of this was taking place right in the emperor's own city while Nero was a horrific persecutor of the church. Perhaps, Paul was praying for these guards and household members while imprisoned. Why wouldn't he be? This is a perfectly valid assumption. Why are all these examples important? God can and does bring the persecutors and enemies of the gospel to Christ. No man or woman is beyond the reach of the all-powerful, almighty, sovereign God. Consequently, salvation should be the first thing on the lips of believers as they are praying for their enemies and persecutors.

Philippians 1:13
So that it became evident to the whole palace guard, and to all the rest, that my bonds are in Christ.

Philippians 4:22
All the saints greet you, especially those who are of Caesar's household.

In the previous chapter, the role of prayer in evangelism was discussed. It was discovered that prayer is an essential part of evangelism. Likewise, evangelism is an essential part of prayer because it can move the hand of God. Christians must be praying for the souls of their unsaved enemies and persecutors. They should petition the Lord to open doors in the midst of their enemies, ask for His wisdom in how they ought to speak, and boldness to speak it amid persecution. Saints are to request that the Word spread rapidly among all of these lost people. Believers should request God to bring many additional workers into the harvest so as many as has been appointed to eternal life may be saved.

There is another appeal Christians should make to their Lord. It is found in Paul's first letter to Timothy. It involves those who are the governing authorities in their land. These important rulers are capable of legislating, administering, and then enforcing their laws which could protect Christians from persecution. This was displayed so clearly in the rise of Constantine the Great, who brought peace to Christendom. In fact, throughout history there have been many leaders and rulers who have supported Christianity and brought peace and freedom to believers.

In 1 Timothy 2:2, Paul urges young Timothy to pray for those who are in authority so these would allow Christians to live peaceful and quiet lives in godliness and dignity. He says, "For kings and all who are in high places; that we may lead a tranquil and quiet life in all godliness and reverence." This is a prayer that petitions God to soften the hearts of the unsaved rulers so they will look kindly upon Christians and not seek to persecute them. This was a request that believers be allowed to share the good news, worship their Lord, and walk in His holiness unencumbered by the government.

1 Timothy 2:2
For kings...all who are in high places, that we may lead a tranquil and quiet life in all godliness and reverence.

Christians should regularly bring the unsaved to God in prayer, especially those who respond negatively to the good news. They are to plead for the salvation of their persecutors and their proclamation of the gospel to them. They should pray that the governing authorities will allow them to live in peace.

The Unwillingness to Resist Persecutors

In Matthew 5:39-41 and Luke 6:29-30, Jesus declared that his followers should not "resist their enemies." The Greek word translated "resist" means to oppose or stand against. A careful reading of the context demonstrates that it has to do with enemies in need. In Matthew 5:42, after providing three examples of not resisting enemies, Jesus presents the general guiding principle. His followers are to give to every person who asks or wants to borrow from them. They should not oppose them because they are enemies. When people need something the saints have, they should generously provide it for them, even if they are enemies or persecutors.

Matthew 5:39-41
But I tell you, don't resist him who is evil; but whoever strikes you on your right cheek, turn to him the other also. If anyone sues you to take...your coat, let him have your cloak also. Whoever compels you to go one mile, go with him two.

Luke 6:29-30
To him who strikes you on the cheek, offer also the other; and from him who takes away your cloak, don't withhold your coat also. Give to everyone who asks you, and don't ask him who takes away your goods to give them back again.

Matthew 5:42
Give to him who asks you, and don't turn away him who desires to borrow from you.

He is contrasting this to their concept of "take an eye for an eye and a tooth for a tooth." This would dictate that when enemies ask, Christians should resist them or deprive them of what they need because they don't deserve it. This is not what God does; instead, He provides for the needs of all mankind. Therefore, the three examples the Lord provides has to do with someone who is in need. The first illustration involves the shaming and humiliating of believers who have offended their enemies.

In Matthew 5:39 and Luke 6:29, this enemy of the believer slaps him on the right cheek. Being hit or slapped on the right cheek indicates the believer was hit backhanded with their enemy's right hand. A straight slap would hit the person's left cheek. In ancient times, this slap was a serious challenge. It was a sign of humiliation to the offender by an offended person. Now, what is the context? An unbeliever becomes offended while he is in need.

Matthew 5:39
But I tell you, don't resist him who is evil; but whoever strikes you on your right cheek, turn to him the other also.

Luke 6:29
To him who strikes you on the cheek, offer also the other; and from him who takes away your cloak, don't withhold your coat also.

The Christian has absolutely no obligation to give him what he desires even though he may think he deserves it. When the believer refuses, he slaps him. The believer should let the enemy humiliate him. This is why Jesus said that His followers should just turn the other cheek. Let him humiliate the believer even more. Real Christians do not retaliate when humiliated. Yet, it would be better, if he had just provided it for him. Self-defense is not an issue here.

The second illustration involves an enemy who thinks a Christian possesses what he needs, so he sues the believer in court. In this example, the enemy needs the coat of the saint, so he sues the saint for it. People do not sue others unless they need or want something that the other possesses. The enemy decides that he deserves it, and the law will support him. This enemy needs this Christian's undergarment, his tunic. In some way, he thinks it is his, so he decides to sue. Jesus says, just give him the undergarment. While a believer is at it, let him give him his cloak also.

The Christian must not to retaliate or get angry. This saint should relinquish and give up his most essential garment, the cloak. This "cloak" was not only the undergarment that every person wore, but it also could be used for a blanket at night for warmth, if one needed it. Christians should go out of their way to reconcile with these enemies in need of what they have. This is what believers are to do.

The third illustration involved soldiers who were in need of help. These military men did not need objects from others but physical help. By law, soldiers could ask regular citizens to carry their pack for them for a distance. As an example, Simon the Cyrene was required to carry the cross of Jesus (Matthew 27:32). Roman soldiers were hated by the Jews and were considered enemies and persecutors. The implication was powerful. This hated Roman soldier asks a Jew to walk a mile with his pack. He is to take it two miles. So, when an enemy is in need of physical help, a believer should give him twice as much as he needs.

Matthew 27:32
As they came out, they found a man of Cyrene, Simon by name, and they compelled him to go with them, that he might carry his cross.

Paul discusses this same principle in the book of Romans. In Romans 12:17-20, Paul clearly states that Christians are to never repay evil for evil but to seek peace with men, if it is possible. In Romans 12:20, Paul clearly explains, "Therefore If your enemy is hungry, feed him. If he is thirsty, give him a drink; for in doing so, you will heap coals of fire on his head." In this verse, believers are given another aspect in the Lord's mandate to never seek vengeance. It can be very easy to withhold something an enemy needs out of vengeance. God will avenge, believers must feed their enemies. If they are cold, then give them a coat. These good deeds will heap hot coals upon their heads (a reference to humiliating them with good). Christians are to overcome evil with good.

Romans 12:17-20
Repay no one evil for evil. Respect what is honorable in the sight of all men. If it is possible, as much as it is up to you, be at peace with all men. Don't seek revenge yourselves, beloved, but give place to God's wrath. For it is written, "Vengeance belongs to me; I will repay, says the Lord." Therefore "If your enemy is hungry, feed him. If he is thirsty, give him a drink; for in doing so, you will heap coals of fire on his head."

Romans 12:20
Therefore "If your enemy is hungry, feed him. If he is thirsty, give him a drink; for in doing so, you will heap coals of fire on his head."

The point of the Lord is extremely clear. His followers are nothing like their unbelieving counterparts. They will go out of their way and beyond their comfort to meet the needs of people. Does someone need something a believer has and tries to humiliate him to get it? There is no need to challenge him because he can have it. Does someone sue a believer because he needs something the believer might be wearing? He should not bother because he will give him two articles of clothing. Does someone need a believer to help him carry something some distance? There is no problem because he will carry it twice as far. Believers are not like other people even their enemies will be helped.

The Willingness to Forgive Persecutors

Christians should forgive their persecutors and enemies. Though this concept is not seen in these Matthew and Luke passages which were mentioned earlier, nevertheless, it is an important consideration. There are several passages in the Bible that attest to the importance of this principle. In any discussion of how Christians should treat their enemies the examples of Jesus and Stephen must be examined.

In Luke 23:34, the Lord is hanging on the cross, dripping with blood from the crown of thorns and the nails in his hands and feet. In His excruciating pain from the tortures and violent beatings, agonizing in the slow dying process, humiliated from the mocking of the people, He cried to the Father to forgive these ignorant persecutors.

Luke 23:34
Jesus said, "Father, forgive them, for they don't know what they are doing." Dividing his garments among them, they cast lots.

The Romans, who were doing all the dirty work the Jews could not do, did not realize that they were really crucifying the ultimate King of Kings and Lord of Lords. The common Jews, who were standing around the cross throwing insults at the Lord, could not fully understand that their longed-for Messiah was hanging from that cursed tree.

The frightened disciples who were hiding from the mob could not comprehend that their great moment of victory in salvation had not been lost in that dying man. Instead, it was about to be completed when the price was paid, and Christ had risen from the dead. Even, many of the rulers, who were caught up in their self-righteous pride, could not perceive that the veil of the temple was about to be split into two. The lamb would be sacrificed, and the new eternal high priest would enter the Holy of Holies to represent them before the Father in heaven.

In the midst of his deep pain, Christ knowing all of this, looked down with great compassion, and cried out for the Father's forgiveness. Christians know through their study of the Scriptures that the prayer could only be fulfilled if all of these ignorant, hardhearted persecutors and enemies of the cross received the soon to be risen Son of God as Savior and Lord. Yet, implied in the merciful cry to His Father, is a God who became truly man, and as man forgave His persecutors, tormentors, and scoffers.

LEADING THE WAY

In Acts 7:54-59, Stephen preached before the Sanhedrin and indicted them for their sin. They responded by rushing him, dragging him out of the city, and stoning him to death. In Acts 7:60, Luke records Stephen's final words on Earth, "He kneeled down, and cried with a loud voice, 'Lord, don't hold this sin against them!' When he had said this, he fell asleep." Here, the disciple took up Christ's compassionate mantle and begged God for their forgiveness. I am sure for the same reasons.

Acts 7:54-59
Now when they heard these things, they were cut to the heart, and they gnashed at him with their teeth. But he, being full of the Holy Spirit, looked up steadfastly into heaven and saw the glory of God, and Jesus standing on the right hand of God, and said, "Behold, I see the heavens opened, and the Son of Man standing at the right hand of God!" But they cried out with a loud voice and stopped their ears, then rushed at him with one accord. They threw him out of the city and stoned him. The witnesses placed their garments at the feet of a young man named Saul. They stoned Stephen as he called out, saying, "Lord Jesus, receive my spirit!"

Acts 7:60
He kneeled down, and cried with a loud voice, "Lord, don't hold this sin against them!" When he had said this, he fell asleep.

Once again, true forgiveness from the Lord God must be obtained through and only through His Son. Once again, implicit in his compassionate words is his own forgiveness of these murderers. The question then arises, "Does the Bible explicitly teach that Christians are to forgive unbelieving enemies and persecutors?" Most all Christians acknowledge that they must forgive their fellow saints (Ephesians 4:32; Colossians 3:13). Yet, most of these are not so sure of the specific teaching concerning the forgiveness of those who have not turned to Christ. Are believers to forgive all? The answer proceeds from the mouth of the Lord Himself which is a resounding, "Yes!" As Christ told Peter they must forgive and forgive and then forgive again (Matthew 18:22).

Ephesians 4:32
And be kind to one another, tender hearted, forgiving each other, just as God also in Christ forgave you.

Colossians 3:13
Bearing with one another, and forgiving each other, if any man has a complaint against any; even as Christ forgave you, so you also do.

Matthew 18:22
Jesus said to him, "I don't tell you until seven times, but, until seventy times seven."

All Christians are compelled by their Lord and Savior to forgive anyone and everyone, believer or unbeliever, friend or foe, brother or acquaintance, and persecutor or supporter for any and all transgressions! This is a tall order. This is not human but a real supernatural phenomenon. In the gospels and epistles, it clearly states that saints are to forgive both other believers and unbelievers. Why? Saints are forgiven by God. Because they have experienced forgiveness, they must show forgiveness.

In Matthew 6:12, during the Sermon on the Mount, He declared that the prayers of God's people should end with "Forgive us our debts, as we also forgive our debtors." Also, in Mark 11:25, on His way to Jerusalem, Jesus explained to His disciples that whenever they stood praying, they should forgive, if they had anything against anyone. In Luke 11:4, when asked how to pray by His disciples, He delivered the Lord's Prayer a second time saying, "Forgive us our sins, for we ourselves also forgive everyone who is indebted to us."

Matthew 6:12
Forgive us our debts, as we also forgive our debtors.

Mark 11:25
Whenever you stand praying, forgive, if you have anything against anyone; so that your Father, who is in heaven, may also forgive you your transgressions.

Luke 11:4
Forgive us our sins, for we ourselves also forgive everyone who is indebted to us. Bring us not into temptation, but deliver us from the evil one.

There is no distinction between believers and unbelievers. Jesus utilizes the words "debtors," "anyone," and "everyone." So, forgiveness is extended to all. He makes no distinction in the kinds of transgressions that ought to be forgiven. They must all be forgiven. Therefore, Christians must forgive their enemies and persecutors for what they do against them, no matter how bad the persecution.

One might ask the question, "What about justice?" It is for the Lord to determine when He will administer His justice in this life (Luke 13:1-4; Acts 12:23). Christians know that His justice will be administered at the great white throne. This is where every single transgression anyone has committed against believers will be judged. Their names and specific sins against them will be presented to the unsaved to be judged and punished (Revelation 20:11-13). Christians must understand, if any of their enemies or persecutors receives Jesus Christ, they too will be forgiven of all their sins, including the persecution. These enemies of the cross, if they repent and believe in Jesus as Savior and Lord, they will be forgiven, as those they persecuted were forgiven of all their sins. Paul was God's classic example (1 Timothy 1:15-17).

Luke 13:1-4
Now there were some present at the same time who told him about the Galileans, whose blood Pilate had mixed with their sacrifices. Jesus answered them, "Do you think that these Galileans were worse sinners than all the other Galileans, because they suffered such things? I tell you, no...unless you repent, you will all perish in the same way. Or those eighteen, on whom the tower in Siloam fell and killed them; do you think that they were worse offenders than all the men who dwell in Jerusalem?

Acts 12:23
Immediately an angel of the Lord struck him, because he didn't give God the glory. Then he was eaten by worms and died.

Revelation 20:11-13
I saw a great white throne, and him who sat on it, from whose face the Earth and the heaven fled away. There was found no place for them. I saw the dead, the great and the small, standing before the throne, and they opened books. Another book was opened, which is the book of life. The dead were judged out of the things which were written in the books, according to their works.

1 Timothy 1:15-17
The saying is faithful and worthy of all acceptance, that Christ Jesus came into the world to save sinners, of whom I am chief. However, for this cause I obtained mercy, that in me first, Jesus Christ might display all his patience for an example of those who were going to believe in him for eternal life. Now to the King eternal, immortal, invisible, to God who alone is wise, be honor and glory forever and ever. Amen.

An Ancient Portrait

As Christians share the good news with people, they will come to discover that many do not necessarily want their good news. To them it is bad news. They essentially want to live in the deception that they are basically good and will somehow enter heaven (if there is one). When Christians are proclaiming sin and judgment, the unsaved may reject them in a wide variety of ways. One such person, who thought he was good and righteous, rejected the good news that the Lord Jesus presented to him. Yet, in spite of it, Jesus showed him love. This is the true story (not a parable) of the rich young ruler who encountered Jesus in the region of Perea which is east of the Jordan found in three of the four gospel accounts (Mark 10:17-31; Matthew 19:16-30; Luke 18:18-30).

As the Lord was walking down the road in His travels, He was seen by a rich young ruler. This man was probably a leader in the synagogue, rather than a government official. He was wealthy, respected, and had obtained a position of leadership in his Jewish religious circles that was extremely rare. In the Hebrew world, Paul had everything someone might desire as they are growing up. He had achieved the dream of every Jewish man. Unfortunately, he felt empty, unsatisfied, and lacked real fulfillment. When he saw Jesus, he knew he could finally get some answers to his perplexing condition.

So, he ran to the Lord and knelt before Him. What a scene that must have been! This Jewish synagogue leader would have been recognized by most people on that road. First, he ran to Jesus which in that culture was unacceptable for any reason. Respected Mediterranean men did not run because of the possible exposure of their legs as they lifted their long robes. This would be humiliating. Second, he had prostrated himself before a known blasphemer who was claiming to be God's Son. This too was humiliating. The ruler did not care; he was desperate to end his spiritual destitution.

As he knelt before the Lord, as a sign of respect, this ruler addressed Jesus as "Good Teacher." Here was his ultimate problem. He thought men could obtain a certain "goodness." This wise teacher before him was good and so was he. Jesus responds immediately with inquiring as why he thought Jesus (as a man) was good when only God is truly good. This rich ruler and leader of the people who had attained so much according to the world's wisdom was not good. Jesus would refer to this later. The man asked Jesus how he could attain eternal life. What an amazing question! The Jews believed eternal life was not the life that begins at death but the life that is lived on Earth and into eternity as a part of God's kingdom. He knew that he had no spiritual fulfillment here nor would he eventually have an eternity with God. Since Jesus had been preaching entrance into the kingdom of God, perhaps He had the answer.

Jesus responded that the ruler knew the law so should observe it. This was a loaded statement, since Jesus knew no man could observe the law perfectly; that's why He came. The man answered just as Jesus had expected. He explained that from his childhood up he had obeyed the law. Could that be true? No, the rich young ruler simply refused to admit his sin. So, Jesus told him to sell all he had and give it to the poor. His refusal would manifest his greed, idolatry, and pride which was the real sins in his heart which were not displayed outwardly. The gospel writers record that at His request the ruler silently left the Lord sad and sorrowful because he had many possessions. He could not give up this idol in his greed and pride. He was exposed and was not the "good man" that he thought he was. He could not give up his idol for Jesus as Savior or Lord.

During this critical discourse, in Mark 10:21, he mentions the attitude Jesus had toward this man even as the ruler was rejecting his message. Mark records, "Jesus looking at him loved him." Jesus loved this rich young ruler even though the ruler did not ultimately want to hear His message. This is the loving attitude we are discussing that pours forth in gracious words and sacrificial actions. This love counters the rejection of our gospel.

Mark 10:21
Jesus looking at him loved him, and said to him, "One thing you lack. Go, sell whatever you have, and give to the poor, and you will have treasure in heaven; and come, follow me, taking up the cross."

A Modern Anecdote

For a period of time, I was the director of a children's club program at my local church every Wednesday night. Each club night, parents would come and drop off their children for a fun night of games, Bible teaching, and small group time. Outside of the periodic "Hello," we would not see the parents at all. It dawned on me that many of these parents probably did not know the Lord. Even if we brought their children to Christ, we could be sending them back into a non-Christian home where Jesus is not honored. Since God's blueprint is to have parents raise their children in the Lord, it could not happen if the parents were unbelievers.

At the time, there was an evangelistic training program that was sweeping through the churches. Our church had recruited maybe thirty people to be trained in the program and share the gospel. I decided to see if I could weave the two programs together. So, I contacted the director of the evangelism program and asked him if he could provide me with five teams of two individuals. Each team could visit the homes of my club members and share the gospel with their parents. This called for the creation of a club handbook to explain the program and what their children were doing each night with photos. At the end of the handbook was a gospel message for the club evangelists to use under the heading, "What Your Children Are Learning."

I made each evangelist an official member of the club and gave them a club uniform. Then, they spent several nights assigned to a particular grade level in order to get to know the program and all the kids. When they felt like they were a real part of the club and were able to answer questions about the gospel and the actual program, they were sent out into the community of parents. Each team visited several parents of their assigned grade level weekly. I would meet with the teams for bible study and prayer once a month. Then, they would provide a report of all things God was doing. We discovered that many of the parents went to either our church or a bible church in the area and were true believers. Others were not and with them God did some incredible things that caused much rejoicing among all of us.

One night, one of our evangelistic teams comprised of a married couple, Ken and Jackie, were invited into a home where it was very obvious that the woman at the door was a single mom and had three toddlers in tow. They introduced themselves and she said her name was Sara. The couple began their presentation only to be interrupted by these very active toddlers.

So, Ken took the kids into the other room, still in view of mom, and watched them play, while Jackie discussed the handbook and the gospel with her. Sara said that she had been so busy in her life that she didn't have time to think about herself but wanted her kids to be brought up in a church. Jackie explained to her that care for the eternity of her children was admirable, but she needed it too. In that living room, while the kids were laughing and playing in the family room, Sara turned her life over to Jesus Christ as Savior and Lord. As she grew in her knowledge and walk with the Lord, she started bringing her kids to the nursery we provided. Then, she began working with other kids to share the Lord Jesus with them.

Though makes for a great story, there were many other parents who rejected the club evangelists or their message. Some were so grateful that we were helping their children but wanted no part of it. At times, parents listened quietly but responded with a polite, "No, thank you." At other times, they asked questions and seemed as if they were just about to come to Christ but pulled back at the last moment. Others complained about the "indoctrination," but they were more than willing to send their children anyway. Some were met at the door and turned away.

These evangelists attempted to counter every negative response with a loving attitude. Each time, the parents were asked how we could meet the needs of their children in a greater way. Afterward, as they shared with the larger team, we all rejoiced together (Acts 14:25-28).

Acts 14:25-27
When they had spoken the word in Perga, they went down to Attalia. From there they sailed to Antioch, from where they had been committed to the grace of God for the work which they had fulfilled. When they had arrived, and had gathered the assembly together, they reported all the things that God had done with them, and that he had opened a door of faith to the nations. They stayed there with the disciples for a long time.

A Personal Response

Dear Heavenly Father,

Please give me a great burden and boldness to share Your gospel with (add names) and others. I do know from the exhortations and examples of the Lord and His disciples in Your Word that (add names) and others I know and meet may not react positively to the good news. If they respond in a negative way, please let me show Your love to them through gracious words and sacrificial actions. If they reject Your salvation message with cruel words to me, let me respond with a gentle and kind blessing instead. If they are mean and punitive toward me, assist me in doing nothing but good to them. Make me diligent to pray for their souls to come to Your Son. If they want to break off the relationship, help me not resist meeting whatever needs they may have, so they will know Your Spirit is in me. Most of all, please make me diligent in my prayers for their souls. I ask that you assist me in being persistent yet sensitive in sharing the gospel again. Please provide numerous opportunities for me to do this. I pray this in the name of Jesus. Amen.

AN INSTRUCTOR'S MANUAL

Chapter 12

Counter with a Loving Attitude

As Christians share the good news, people may respond in a negative manner. Believers should be careful to react in a way that reflects the character of God.

In the section, "A Typical Scenario," the author depicts the loving reaction of a believer to the gospel presentation he gave to someone he helped on the road.

What is the scenario about?

A man attempts to help a woman with her car on the road and shares the gospel only to be rejected.

What held the believer back from sharing the gospel?

He was fearful that if he helped people and shared the gospel, they would think he had ulterior motives or would reject it.

What finally led the Christian to share the good news and how did it occur?

He learned people reject the gospel and he needed to show them love so he helped a woman on the road and that is what happened.

Have you had a similar experience?

(Various answers should be shared including yours.)

LEADING THE WAY

In the section, "A Scriptural Principle" the author presents an important biblical principle in evangelism which concerns the loving reactions of believers to rejections of the gospel.

How would you express this principle in your own words?

So, principle twelve is "we must counter with a loving attitude."

(Various answers should be shared including yours.)

How would you rewrite this principle to make it even more personal to your life (using your name and situation)?

(Various answers should be shared including yours.)

Why do you think this principle might be important in your life right now as you share the gospel?

(Various answers should be shared including yours.)

How would you rate yourself on the percentage of times you followed this principle in the past as a believer?

(Various answers should be shared including yours.)

Directions: Put a horizontal mark and your name where you see yourself on the percentage line.

0%   25%   50%   75%   100%

In the section, "A Biblical Explanation," the author explains the attitudes Christians should have to negative reactions to the gospel and its importance in sharing it effectively.

If the saints don't take revenge on those who persecute them, then who will?

In Romans 13:1-4, Paul states that it is the responsibility of governing authorities to be avengers of God. Christians are to show love to their enemies, but the government is to prosecute those enemies for harming them, violating their rights, and breaking the law. One is personal and the other is judicial....Vengeance comes from God and through the government.

What does it mean "to love" those who persecute us?

The Greek word essentially means to value or prize someone or something. This word was utilized by Jesus and His disciples to speak of valuing to the point of sacrifice. The classic use of the word is found in John 3:16, where Jesus asserts that God so loved the world that He gave His Son. God so valued the world that He gave, even though it was hostile to Him.

What kind of blessings do we give those who persecute us and why?

Then they returned his blessing with a similar one, "May the Lord bless you!" This general blessing was extremely meaningful. This expressed the genuine and heartfelt desire that the other person would find safety and protection in God.

What prayer requests should we offer to God for those who persecute us and why?

Christians must be praying for the souls of their unsaved enemies and persecutors. They should petition the Lord to open doors in the midst of their enemies, ask for His wisdom in how they ought to speak, and boldness to speak it amid persecution. Saints are to request that the Word spread rapidly among all of these lost people. Believers should request God to bring many additional workers into the harvest so as many as has been appointed to eternal life may be saved.

In 1 Timothy 2:2, Paul urges young Timothy to pray for those who are in authority so these would allow Christians to live peaceful and quiet lives in godliness and dignity.

Christians should regularly bring the unsaved to God in prayer, especially those who respond negatively to the good news.

If we are not to resist persecutors, then what circumstances would this encompass?

They should not oppose them because they are enemies. When people need something the saints have, they should generously provide it for them, even if they are enemies or persecutors.

This is not what God does; instead, He provides for the needs of all mankind. Therefore, the three examples the Lord provides has to do with someone who is in need. The first illustration involves the shaming and humiliating of believers who have offended their enemies.

In the gospels and epistles, it clearly states that saints are to forgive both other believers and unbelievers. Why? Saints are forgiven by God. Because they have experienced forgiveness, they must show forgiveness.

In what ways might these truths impact your life?

(Various answers should be shared including yours.)

In the section, "An Ancient Portrait," the author provides a unique portrayal of the encounter of the Lord Jesus with the rich young ruler.

Can you briefly describe the setting of this real-life ancient drama?

The setting is in the region of Perea. This is the true story (not a parable) of the rich young ruler who encountered Jesus in the region of Perea which is east of the Jordan found in three of the four gospel accounts (Mark 10:17-31; Matthew 19:16-30; Luke 18:18-30).

Can you describe the major characters involved?

The major characters are Jesus and the rich young ruler.

How did the evangelist initiate the gospel presentation?

First, he ran to Jesus which in that culture was unacceptable for any reason. Respected Mediterranean men did not run because of the possible exposure of their legs as they lifted their long robes. This would be humiliating. Second, he had prostrated himself before a known blasphemer who was claiming to be God's Son. This too was humiliating. The ruler did not care; he was desperate to end his spiritual destitution.

He knew that he had no spiritual fulfillment here nor would he eventually have an eternity with God. Since Jesus had been preaching entrance into the kingdom of God, perhaps He had the answer. Jesus responded that the ruler knew the law so should observe it. This was a loaded statement, since Jesus knew no man could observe the law perfectly; that's why He came.

He knew that he had no spiritual fulfillment here nor would he eventually have an eternity with God. Since Jesus had been preaching entrance into the kingdom of God, perhaps He had the answer.

Jesus responded that the ruler knew the law so should observe it. This was a loaded statement, since Jesus knew no man could observe the law perfectly; that's why He came.

The man answered just as Jesus had expected. He explained that from his childhood up he had obeyed the law. Could that be true? No, the rich young ruler simply refused to admit his sin. So, Jesus told him to sell all he had and give it to the poor.

What was result of this evangelistic presentation?

His refusal would manifest his greed, idolatry, and pride which was the real sins in his heart which were not displayed outwardly. The gospel writers record that at His request the ruler silently left the Lord sad and sorrowful because he had many possessions. He could not give up this idol in his greed and pride. He was exposed and was not the "good man" that he thought he was. He could not give up his idol for Jesus as Savior or Lord.

How was the principle explained in this chapter applied to the situation?

During this critical discourse, in Mark 10:21, he mentions the attitude Jesus had toward this man even as the ruler was rejecting his message. Mark records, "Jesus looking at him loved him." Jesus loved this rich young ruler even though the ruler did not ultimately want to hear His message. This is the loving attitude we are discussing that pours forth in gracious words and sacrificial actions. This love counters the rejection of our gospel.

Based on the truths learned in this chapter, what would you have done differently if you were the evangelist or how would you have responded if you were the recipient?

(Various answers should be shared including yours.)

In the section, "A Modern Anecdote," the author discusses a situation in which he recruited a group of Christians who were trained in evangelism to work with his club program.

Can you briefly describe the setting of this real-life modern drama?

The setting is a children's club program at the author's local church. For a period of time, I was the director of a children's club program at my local church every Wednesday night. Each club night, parents would come and drop off their children for a fun night of games, Bible teaching, and small group time.

Can you describe the major characters involved?

The major characters are the author, the evangelists, and parents.

How did the author initiate the gospel presentation?

At the time, there was an evangelistic training program that was sweeping through the churches. Our church had recruited maybe thirty people to be trained in the program and share the gospel.

I decided to see if I could weave the two programs together. So, I contacted the director of the evangelism program and asked him if he could provide me with five teams of two individuals.

Each team could visit the homes of my club members and share the gospel with their parents. This called for the creation of a club handbook to explain the program and what their children were doing each night with photos.

I made each evangelist an official member of the club and gave them a club uniform. Then, they spent several nights assigned to a particular grade level in order to get to know the program and all the kids.

Each team visited several parents of their assigned grade level weekly. I would meet with the teams for bible study and prayer once a month. Then, they would provide a report of all things God was doing.

They introduced themselves and she said her name was Sara. The couple began their presentation only to be interrupted by these very active toddlers.

What was result of this evangelistic presentation?

In that living room, while the kids were laughing and playing in the family room, Sara turned her life over to Jesus Christ as Savior and Lord.

As she grew in her knowledge and walk with the Lord, she started bringing her kids to the nursery we provided. Then, she began working with other kids to share the Lord Jesus with them.

How was the principle explained in this chapter applied to the situation?

These evangelists attempted to counter every negative response with a loving attitude. Each time, the parents were asked how we could meet the needs of their children in a greater way.

Based on the truths learned in this chapter, what would you have done differently if you were the author or how would you have responded if you were the recipient?

(Various answers should be shared including yours.)

In the section, "A Personal Response," the author provides a model you may use for prayer if you find it necessary after discovering the truths in this chapter.

Are you presently attempting to present the gospel of Jesus to someone? If not, are there some who might serve you regularly at a store who may not know Jesus Christ and may need prayer for an opportunity for you to share with them and open hearts to receive Him?

(Various answers should be shared including yours.)

Based on the truths you have just learned, what will you continue to do in your current evangelistic efforts and what might you do differently?

(Various answers should be shared including yours.)

What additional thoughts would you like to share with the others?

(Various answers should be shared including yours.)

Chapter 13

Disciple with a Serious Intent

Once unbelievers receive Jesus Christ as their Savior and Lord, it does not end there. Someone will have to help these new believers navigate their new lives. In Matthew 28:19, Jesus told His apostles to go out into all the world and make disciples. The making of disciples involves more than just bringing people to Christ. The Greek word that is translated "disciple" means learner and follower. The people must also learn to follow Christ. The Christians who had shared the gospel with these newly saved would be responsible for discipling them or at least introducing them to believers who can.

Matthew 28:19
Go and make disciples of all nations, baptizing them in the name of the Father and of the Son and of the Holy Spirit.

A Typical Scenario

Have you ever been in a situation that was something like the following? Perhaps, you are standing in the supermarket and someone is looking for an item. You know the store very well and decide to ask if you can help. As you walk toward the aisle that contains the item, you chat about a variety of minor subjects. You never ask the person's name, nor do you expect to see the person again. It never enters your mind to share the good news of Jesus with the person or even begin a conversation about Christ. If the person did actually receive Christ, you would not know what to do with them anyway. This had been holding you back from sharing the gospel for a long time. You simply would not know how to follow-up if someone received Christ.

In this chapter we will learn that we are not only to share Christ with people but assist them in growing in their faith, if they should come to Christ. You can do it yourself or help them find a believer who might be willing to disciple them. They should be encouraged to concentrate on their personal spiritual growth, study the Scriptures consistently, develop a persistent prayer life, establish a stable fellowship with some believers, find sound biblical and doctrinal instruction from a pastor-teacher, become involved in a ministry that utilizes their spiritual gifts, share the good news regularly, live a steadfast righteous lifestyle with an intentional walk, and if necessary be resolute in their endurance of trials. This is not done all at once but over a very long period of time. After you learn these critical truths, this same situation might look quite different.

You might say, "Can I help you find an item? I know this store pretty well." The person thanks you for the help and names the item. You walk with them over toward the item and pray that God would give you a chance to present the gospel. Since the item was a dip, you casually ask if she was having a party. She indicates that it was a going away party for her last child who was going off to college. The woman was feeling devastated because she was already missing her son terribly, and he wasn't even gone yet. You explain to her that you had the same feelings, but you were comforted by a verse from the Holy Bible. You look up Genesis 2:24 on your phone app and read it to her. It says, "Therefore a man will leave his father and his mother, and will join with his wife, and they will be one flesh." You explain that leaving parents is God's blueprint for living.

Genesis 2:24
Therefore a man will leave his father and his mother, and will join with his wife, and they will be one flesh.

You realized that you were now transitioning into a new role which was to be a greater companion to your husband, a wise counselor to your adult children, and an awesome grandparent to their children. You return to your phone and read Proverbs 17:6, "Children's children are the crown of old men; the glory of children are their parents." You share with her how you were already preparing for grandparenthood. You are dating your husband again and having a great time. You also mention the fact that though their childhood was over, when you do see your children, you can finally enjoy their company unencumbered by having to meet every need.

Proverbs 17:6
Children's children are the crown of old men; the glory of children are their parents.

She responds by telling you that she had never thought of it that way, and it was very comforting. Then, she asks, "All that is in the Bible?" From there you present the good news in simple form and ask if she would like to meet sometime for coffee and discuss these truths further. She indicates that she would. You meet about a week later and she receives Christ as Savior and Lord. From there you meet with her every week for six months and study the Bible together. You discuss the important truths in this chapter. You invite her to church, encourage her to be baptized, and begin the process of discovering her spiritual gift and searching for a ministry for her to become a part of. During this process, her husband becomes interested, and the wife leads him to Christ.

Though this is an imaginary scenario, it is a very common situation we may find ourselves in. We could share the good news but may be afraid of what to do if they actually come to Christ. So, we are reluctant to evangelize. The Scriptures explain precisely how believers are to grow in their faith and knowing these truths might incite us to announce the good news much more often. This now leads us to the thirteenth principle which involves the discipling of people once they have entered the Kingdom of God.

A Scriptural Principle

In 2 Timothy 2:2, Paul explains to Timothy, a pastor, a simple discipleship process used in the ministry. He writes, "The things which you have heard from me among many witnesses, commit the same to faithful men, who will be able to teach others also." Timothy was to learn from Paul and then was to teach others. Those others were to teach others and so forth and so forth. Often times, to evangelize and disciple people means that Christians invite people to their church, let the pastor win them to Christ, and the church handles them from there. Their involvement usually ends with a postcard of an Easter or Christmas service handed to people they know. This human approach has no scriptural basis. Why wouldn't someone desire to be used by God? If God wanted the pastor to share Christ with them, would He have not brought the pastor into their lives? Every believer has the privilege of helping someone grow in Jesus Christ. Principle thirteen is "we must disciple with a serious intent." The saints are to be involved in the discipleship process with a serious intent.

2 Timothy 2:2
The things which you have heard from me among many witnesses, commit the same things to faithful men, who will be able to teach others also.

A Biblical Explanation

When people truly receive Christ as Savior and Lord, they do not merely attach Jesus to their current lives and continue living the way they did previously. There is a fundamental change that occurs in them which affects every area of their lives. In 2 Corinthians 5:17, Paul describes it in these words, "Therefore if anyone is in Christ, he is a new creation." The Greek word translated "new" means something "new of a different kind" as opposed to "new of the same kind." Think of it as meaning "brand-new (different) holy (separate and sacred). They have become a brand-new creation in Christ Jesus.

2 Corinthians 5:17
Therefore if anyone is in Christ, he is a new creation. The old things have passed away. Behold, all things have become new.

What happens to their past lives? Paul continues, "The old things have passed away." This Greek word for "passed away" is utilized to speak of "passing by something, leaving something in the past, perishing, or even death." Their old lives have been passed by, are left in the past before Christ, have perished, and are dead. Paul adds, "Behold, all things have become new." Everything has changed involving their earthly life and eternal destiny. They are wholly (completely, fully) changed. They enter into a completely new life.

In Romans 6:4, the apostle explains this in more detail using the same Greek word, "We were buried therefore with him through baptism to death, that just as Christ was raised from the dead through the glory of the Father, so we also might walk in newness of life." The baptism here is the total immersion in Christ's death and our resurrection into a new life. This new life was described in the prophecy of Ezekiel 36:26. Here God declared to Israel, "I will also give you a new heart, and I will put a new spirit within you." We have a brand-new heart and a new spirit in this new life as the new creation of God.

Romans 6:4
We were buried therefore with him through baptism into death, that just as Christ was raised from the dead through the glory of the Father, so we also might walk in newness of life.

Ezekiel 36:26
I will also give you a new heart, and I will put a new spirit within you. I will take away the stony heart out of your flesh, and I will give you a heart of flesh.

This new life is not just a life of living any way people want and then attending a church to be inspired on Sunday. They listen to a praise band play, sing some songs, hear a short message, perhaps watch a video, say hello to someone, hand over some money, then have a cup of coffee in the cafe. They go home feeling good about themselves and perhaps even have a strategy for dealing with frustration, anxiety, or how to have better friendships.

This is not the Christian life! There is so much more that must go on in one's life to be a real Christian before the Lord. The true spiritual walk (way of living life) does not include simply adding Jesus to our lives and continuing to live any way we want; instead, it involves a radically different lifestyle. Why? We have a brand-new Master, and it is not ourselves; it is Jesus. This new lifestyle must be passed on to others after they come to Christ. This is called "discipleship." This entails a lifelong learning process of being Christ-like.

A Baptismal Confirmation

The first response in our discipleship of new Christians is to clearly confirm the beliefs and commitments they have just made to Christ. They should be able to explain that they received Christ by repenting of their sins and believing that Jesus is God, died on the cross to pay the penalty for their sins, and is the only Savior of the world. They must have understood that they entered into a love relationship with Christ in faith by asking Him to be their Savior and then fully committing themselves to following Him as their Lord. If there are any misunderstandings, they should be cleared up by referring back to chapter ten and the passages which were discussed.

Once their true faith has been confirmed, then they must be baptized as soon as it is possible. This will solidify their salvation commitment in their own eyes, to the family of God, and the world. This is best way to help them become involved in a local church, since this is what the local church does. The date that they received Christ should be noted. I encourage people to write down their "personal testimony" of how they came to Christ with the date. They can then share this as they present the gospel in future days. It also helps confirm what they did if doubts arise. The Scriptures indicate that one's current beliefs and fruits (James 2:14; 1 John 2:4-6; 3:10) and the testimony of his personal moment of salvation when he received the Lord (Acts 9:1-7; 22:7-11; 26:12-18) demonstrate one's faith.

James 2:14
What good is it, my brothers, if a man says he has faith, but has no works? Can faith save him?

1 John 2:4-6
One who says, "I know him," and doesn't keep...commandments is a liar, and the truth isn't in him. But God's love has most certainly been perfected in whoever keeps his word. This is how we know that we are in him: he who says he remains in him ought himself also to walk just like he walked.

1 John 3:10
In this the children of God are revealed, and the children of the devil. Whoever doesn't do righteousness is not of God, neither is he who doesn't love his brother.

Acts 9:1-7
But Saul, still breathing threats and slaughter against the disciples of the Lord, went to the high priest and asked for letters from him to the synagogues of Damascus, that if he found any who were of the Way, whether men or women, he might bring them bound to Jerusalem. As he traveled, he got close to Damascus, and suddenly a light from the sky shone around him. He fell on the Earth, and heard a voice saying to him, "Saul, Saul, why do you persecute me?" He said, "Who are you, Lord?" The Lord said, "I am Jesus, whom you are persecuting. But rise up and enter into the city, then you will be told what you must do." The men who traveled with him stood speechless, hearing the sound, but seeing no one.

Acts 22:7-11
I fell to the ground, and heard a voice saying to me, "Saul, Saul, why are you persecuting me?" I answered, "Who are you, Lord?" He said to me, "I am Jesus of Nazareth, whom you persecute." Those who were with me indeed saw the light and were afraid, but they didn't understand the voice of him who spoke to me. I said, "What shall I do, Lord?" The Lord said to me, "Arise, and go into Damascus. There you will be told about all things which are appointed for you to do." When I couldn't see for the glory of that light, being led by the hand of those who were with me, I came into Damascus.

Acts 26:12-18
Whereupon as I traveled to Damascus with the authority and commission from the chief priests, at noon, O king, I saw on the way a light from the sky, brighter than the sun, shining around me and those who traveled with me. When we had all fallen to the Earth, I heard a voice saying to me in the Hebrew language, "Saul, Saul, why are you persecuting me? It is hard for you to kick against the goads." I said, "Who are you, Lord?" He said, "I am Jesus, whom you are persecuting. But arise, and stand on your feet, for I have appeared to you for this purpose: to appoint you a servant and a witness both of the things which you have seen, and of the things which I will reveal to you; delivering you from the people, and from the Gentiles, to whom I send you, to open their eyes, that they may turn from darkness to light and from the power of Satan to God, that they may receive remission of sins and an inheritance among those who are sanctified by faith in me."

A Commitment to Faith over Feelings

As we disciple, we must emphasize that the Christian life is a walk of faith, not feelings. This is critical for new saints to understand. Often, they might think that the enthusiasm their newfound faith will last a lifetime, but feelings change frequently, especially in relationships. Christians should not allow feelings to dictate any aspect of their beliefs, words, and actions. In 2 Corinthians 5:7, Paul explains that we walk by faith not by sight. They will live by faith not by what they see, feel, or experience. Otherwise, dependence on feelings will bring disappointment as they attempt to continually generate those feelings.

2 Corinthians 5:7
For we walk by faith, not by sight.

Here is an important principle. When we live our lives in obedience to the Lord, the feelings will often follow. Feelings always follow words and actions. The Lord Jesus and the apostles always appealed to thinking, beliefs, and obedience, never to feelings. Jesus never said, "If you love me, you will get excited about me!" No, He declared that if we love Him, we will obey Him (John 14:15). People will often let their feelings dictate their attitudes and actions. I feel miserable, so I will be grumpy and mean. I feel happy, so I will be smiling and encouraging. I feel sad, so I will withdraw from people and be silent. Of course, our emotions are important, but they are never considered when developing attitudes or actions concerning our obedience to the Lord. Our mind decides what is right to do; then, our actions follow. Once the actions have commenced, the feelings will follow them.

John 14:15
If you love me, keep my commandments.

The letters of the apostle Paul always begin with how we are to think about something from God's perspective, and then he will ask us to obey God. He never adds the caveat, if we feel like it, nor does he deal with the feelings at all. Why?

Feelings will proceed from one's actions. Even if they don't, Christians are guided not by feelings but by submission and obedience to the Lord. Some may think, "If I do something that I don't feel like doing or may not want to do, isn't that hypocritical?" The answer is no. If we don't feel like obeying the Lord in something and we do it anyway that is one of the greatest forms of sacrifice and obedience one can display. Is it not? In Revelation 2:1-3, the Lord Jesus Christ did not ask the Ephesians to feel something different when they fell out of love with Him. He told them to do something different. If I don't particularly feel emotional love toward the Lord but continue to obey him, I am showing love to Him. It is the same in our human relationships.

Revelation 2:1-3
To the angel of the assembly in Ephesus write: He who holds the seven stars in his right hand, he who walks among the seven golden lamp stands says these things: "I know your works, and your toil and perseverance, and that you can't tolerate evil men, and have tested those who call themselves apostles, and they are not, and found them false. You have perseverance and have endured for my name's sake, and have not grown weary."

A Concentration on Spiritual Growth

In Philippians 2:12-13, Paul explains that believers are to work out their salvation as God is at work in them to do His will. This does not refer to doing good works to be saved. It refers to working out all the aspects of our salvation toward one important end which is our transformation into the likeness of Jesus Christ. God desires for His children to think, speak, and act like His Son in their lives on this Earth. This is called spiritual growth. We are growing into the very image of Christ. In Ephesians 4:13, Paul describes the goal of the church on Earth as attaining to the unity of the faith and of the knowledge of the Son of God.

Philippians 2:12-13
So then, my beloved, even as you have always obeyed, not only in my presence, but now much more in my absence, work out your own salvation with fear and trembling. For it is God who works in you both to will and to work, for his good pleasure.

Ephesians 4:13
Until we all attain to the unity of the faith and of the knowledge of the Son of God, to a full grown man, to the measure of the stature of the fullness of Christ.

We do this until all are full grown and mature in Christ both individually and corporately. This means we are to measure up to the "stature of the fullness of Christ." This would be like a brother standing next to his older brother attempting to grow into his image. He would be checking his height, weight, and build. We are standing next to our Lord and doing the very same thing spiritually.

What does this mean? If Christ was dependent on God, we learn to be dependent on God. If Christ was patient, we learn to be patient. If Christ obeyed God's commands, we learn to obey God's commands. This growth process into Christ's image involves numerous actions that are individual and also involve the participation of others.

A Consistent Scriptural Study

As we disciple new believers, we must impart to them the absolute importance of knowing and using the Word of God in their lives to transform into Christ's image. In 3 John 1:3, the apostle John calls it "walking in truth." We are to live according to the truth. This consists of knowing and obeying the truth. Unfortunately, we think that we can figure out how God wants us to live by using reason or asking the question, "What would Jesus do?" We have no idea how God reasons, and we certainly do not know what Jesus would do unless we read and study the Bible.

3 John 1:3
For I rejoiced greatly when brothers came and testified about your truth, even as you walk in truth.

Merely asking this question and then trying to think it through is grossly inadequate. Why? God is nothing like us in His thinking, speaking, or actions. In Isaiah 55:8-9, the Lord God speaks through Isaiah and says, "'For my thoughts are not your thoughts, and your ways are not my ways,' says Yahweh." We cannot begin to live the life presuming it is exactly the same as we would think He would want us to live it. We must discover what His ways are.

Isaiah 55:8-9
"For my thoughts are not your thoughts, and your ways are not my ways," says Yahweh. "For as the heavens are higher than the Earth, so are my ways higher than your ways, and my thoughts than your thoughts.

The Lord God continues, "For as the heavens are higher than the Earth, so are my ways higher than your ways, and my thoughts than your thoughts." This is a lifelong process as growing in His knowledge issuing into obedience.

How does this actually work? In Isaiah 55:10-11, the Lord God explains this process, "For as the rain comes down and the snow from the sky, and doesn't return there, but waters the Earth, and makes it bring forth and bud, and gives seed to the sower and bread to the eater." Here the Father makes a comparison to rain. Rain goes forth and does its work in nature. His Word does the same. He continues, "So shall my word be that goes forth out of my mouth: it shall not return to me void, but it shall accomplish that which I please, and it shall prosper in the thing I sent it to do." God sends forth his Word into our lives to accomplish His own purposes, it will not return empty.

Isaiah 55:10-11
For as the rain comes down and the snow from the sky, and doesn't return there, but waters the Earth, and makes it grow and bud, and gives seed to the sower and bread to the eater; so is my word that goes out of my mouth: it will not return to me void, but it will accomplish that which I please, and it will prosper in the thing I sent it to do.

In 1 Thessalonians 2:13, Paul explains how it worked in the lives of these new believers, "For this cause we also thank God without ceasing, that, when you received from us the word of the message of God, you accepted it not as the word of men, but, as it is in truth, the word of God, which also works in you who believe." This work that the Word performs in our lives is the changing of our old unrighteous thoughts and ways to God's righteous thoughts and ways. God requires us, as Christians, to live supernaturally upon this Earth, not naturally. He sometimes asks us to think and behave in ways that seem contrary to everything we hold true, such as loving our enemies (Matthew 5:44) or forgiving people over and over again (Matthew 18:22).

1 Thessalonians 2:13
For this cause we also thank God without ceasing, that when you received from us the word of the message of God, you accepted it not as the word of men, but as it is in truth, the word of God, which also works in you who believe.

Matthew 5:44
But I tell you, love your enemies, bless those who curse you, do good to those who hate you, and pray for those who mistreat you and persecute you.

Matthew 18:22
Jesus said to him, "I don't tell you until seven times, but, until seventy times seven."

Who can do that? The saints can do it as the Holy Spirit works through His Word as we read it and study it. This is a crucial understanding for believers. In 2 Peter 1:2-3, Peter explains that through the knowledge of God we have all the things we need that pertain to life and godliness. More importantly, with this knowledge we are also granted the divine power to live it. The question then arises, "Where do we find this knowledge of Him?" As we saw in Isaiah 55, we find it in His Word. As we read His Word and grow in our knowledge of Him and His divine ways, the power to follow those ways comes to us through His Spirit. God dispenses power through the knowledge of His Holy Word. To put it succinctly: with the knowledge of the Lord God found in His Word comes the actual spiritual power to act on it.

2 Peter 1:2-3
Grace to you and peace be multiplied in the knowledge of God and of Jesus our Lord, seeing that his divine power has granted to us all things that pertain to life and godliness, through the knowledge of him who called us by his own glory and virtue.

In 1 Thessalonians 1:5, Paul describes this supernatural phenomenon when he claims that the gospel came to them in power, the Spirit of God, and full assurance. When they heard God's Word, power was unleashed by the Holy Spirit to believe it and assure them of its truth. This will not occur unless we are consistently in the Word of God.

1 Thessalonians 1:5
And that our Good News came to you not in word only, but also in power, and in the Holy Spirit, and with much assurance. You know what kind of men we showed ourselves to be among you for your sake.

This is why the Word speaks to so many areas of life because so many areas have to change to become like Christ. And the Word provides everything we need for life and godliness. The Word can provide us with God's thoughts and ways concerning the knowledge of Him, His Son, and Spirit.

It provides God's blueprints with principles for Christian living showing us how to relate to each other (1 John 4:7-12), the world (James 4:4), our spouses (Colossians 3:18-21), our children (Ephesians 6:1-4), the governmental authorities (Romans 13:1-8), and the church (1 Timothy 3:15), to name just a few out of so many.

1 John 4:7-12
Beloved, let's love one another, for love is of God; and everyone who loves has been born of God, and knows God. He who doesn't love doesn't know God, for God is love. By this God's love was revealed in us, that God has sent his one and only Son into the world that we might live through him. In this is love, not that we loved God, but that he loved us, and sent his Son as the atoning sacrifice for our sins. Beloved, if God loved us in this way, we also ought to love one another. No one has seen God at any time. If we love one another, God remains in us, and his love has been perfected in us.

James 4:4
You adulterers and adulteresses, don't you know that friendship with the world is hostility toward God? Whoever therefore wants to be a friend of the world makes himself an enemy of God.

Colossians 3:18-21
Wives, be in subjection to your husbands, as is fitting in the Lord. Husbands, love your wives, and don't be bitter against them. Children, obey your parents in all things, for this pleases the Lord. Fathers, don't provoke your children, so that they won't be discouraged.

Ephesians 6:1-4
Children, obey your parents in the Lord, for this is right. "Honor your father and mother," which is the first commandment with a promise: "that it may be well with you, and you may live long on the Earth." You fathers, don't provoke your children to wrath, but nurture them in the discipline and instruction of the Lord.

Romans 13:1-4
Let every soul be in subjection to the higher authorities, for there is no authority except from God, and those who exist are ordained by God. Therefore he who resists...authority withstands the ordinance of God; and those who withstand will receive to themselves judgment. For rulers are not a terror to the good work, but to the evil. Do you desire to have no fear of the authority? Do that which is good, and you will have praise from the authority, for he is a servant of God to you for good. But if you do that which is evil, be afraid, for he doesn't bear the sword in vain; for he is a servant of God, an avenger for wrath to him who does evil.

1 Timothy 3:15
But if I wait long, that you may know how men ought to behave themselves in God's house, which is the assembly of the living God, the pillar and ground of the truth.

It will convict us of sin when we are not following His ways (Hebrews 4:12). The Word provides Christians comfort in time of trouble (Psalm 119:28, 50). It will provide hope as we trudge through some of the deep trenches along the road of life (Romans 15:4). So, we need to help them learn to read and study God's Word or provide them some resources to do it. This sounds like a daunting task, but today there are so many resources to choose from.

Hebrews 4:12
For the word of God is living and active, and sharper than any two-edged sword, piercing even to the dividing of soul and spirit, of both joints and marrow, and is able to discern the thoughts and intentions of the heart.

Psalm 119:28
My soul is weary with sorrow: strengthen me according to your word.

Psalm 119:50
This is my comfort in my affliction, for your word has revived me.

Romans 15:4
For whatever things were written before were written for our learning, that through perseverance and through encouragement of the Scriptures we might have hope.

A Persistent Intercessional Prayer

As we read the Word, God literally is speaking to us. As we pray, we are speaking to the Lord Almighty. Prayer is the most intimate kind of communion with God. Prayer and the Word is the process of communication between God and man. In 1 John 5:14, John describes prayer as boldly being "toward or before" Him. The Greek word connotes a face-to-face interaction with God which we boldly have as believers. We should instruct the disciple that prayer is coming to the throne of God and standing face to face before the Father.

1 John 5:14
This is the boldness which we have toward him, that if we ask anything according to his will, he listens to us.

In Psalm 62:8, David portrays it as pouring out one's heart before God as his refuge and strength. We should do this for our needs and the needs of others. Even a cursory reading of the Psalms demonstrates this (Psalm 5:2; 6:9; 17:1; 39:12; 54:2). In many of Paul's letters, he asks for prayer (Colossians 4:3-5) and requests that the saints pray for others (Ephesians 6:18). In fact, in 1 Thessalonians 5:17, the apostle encourages Christians to never stop praying. Praying is a critical part of the Christian life and assists us in our spiritual growth.

Psalm 62:8
Trust in him at all times, you people. Pour out your heart before him. God is a refuge for us. Selah.

Psalm 5:2
Listen to the voice of my cry, my King and my God; for I pray to you.

Psalm 6:9
Yahweh has heard my supplication. Yahweh accepts my prayer.

Psalm 17:1
Hear, Yahweh, my righteous plea. Give ear to my prayer that doesn't go out of deceitful lips.

Psalm 39:12
Hear my prayer, Yahweh, and give ear to my cry. Don't be silent at my tears. For I am a stranger with you, a foreigner, as all my fathers were.

Psalm 54:2
Hear my prayer, God. Listen to the words of my mouth.

Colossians 4:3-5
Praying together for us also, that God may open to us a door for the word, to speak the mystery of Christ, for which I am also in bonds, that I may reveal it as I ought to speak. Walk in wisdom toward those who are outside, redeeming the time.

Ephesians 6:18
With all prayer and requests, praying at all times in the Spirit, and being watchful to this end in all perseverance and requests for all the saints:

1 Thessalonians 5:17
Pray without ceasing.

Prayer teaches believers dependence upon God. In Psalm 4:1, David cries out, "Answer me when I call, God of my righteousness. Give me relief from my distress. Have mercy on me, and hear my prayer." When we pray, share our needs with Him, and ask for help, then we depend on Him. In 1 Peter 5:6-7, we are told to cast all our cares upon Him. This is done through prayer. Praying also causes spiritual growth because it brings about obedience.

Psalm 4:1
Answer me when I call, God of my righteousness. Give me relief from my distress. Have mercy on me, and hear my prayer.

1 Peter 5:6-7
Humble yourselves therefore under the mighty hand of God, that he may exalt you in due time, casting all your worries on him, because he cares for you.

In Psalm 119:34, it says, "Give me understanding, and I will keep your law. Yes, I will obey it with my whole heart." We ask God to help us to obey his law and He will answer us. We become obedient and that is growth. Prayer can provide relief from many sinful habits and patterns in our lives. In Psalm 119:133, the psalmist prays, "Establish my footsteps in your word. Don't let any iniquity have dominion over me." When we conquer sinful habits, we grow in Him.

Psalm 119:34
Give me understanding, and I will keep your law. Yes, I will obey it with my whole heart.

Psalm 119:133
Establish my footsteps in your word. Don't let any iniquity have dominion....

Another way in which prayer assists us in our spiritual growth is by keeping us from many temptations and trials. At Gethsemane, the Lord Jesus told His disciples in Matthew 26:41, "Watch and pray, that you don't enter into temptation. The spirit indeed is willing, but the flesh is weak." Though our flesh easily stumbles into sin, we can ask the Lord to help us watch for temptations to avoid or withstand them. Prayer can also bring spiritual renewal in confession. In Psalm 51:2, David cries out to the Lord and begged Him to wash his sin away. Believers are to constantly be confessing their sins and purifying their hearts through prayer. After this we can ask God for a renewed commitment.

Matthew 26:41
Watch and pray, that you don't enter into temptation. The spirit indeed is willing, but the flesh is weak.

Psalm 51:2
Wash me thoroughly from my iniquity. Cleanse me from my sin.

In Psalm 51:10, David declares, "Create in me a clean heart, O God. Renew a right spirit within me." This causes spiritual growth. Prayer can bring divine wisdom. In James 1:5, he exhorts, "But if any of you lacks wisdom, let him ask of God, who gives to all liberally and without reproach; and it will be given to him." Of course, it is provided through His Word. Prayer can bring real peace to our lives. In Philippians 4:6-7, Paul encourages the readers to put away their anxiety and worries. Instead, they should make requests to God in prayer and He will answer them. From this, peace will come. These many aspects of prayer produce growth.

Psalm 51:10
Create in me a clean heart, O God. Renew a right spirit within me.

James 1:5
But if any of you lacks wisdom, let him ask of God, who gives to all liberally and without reproach, and it will be given to him.

Philippians 4:6-7
In nothing be anxious, but in everything, by prayer and petition with thanksgiving, let your requests be made known to God. And the peace of God, which surpasses all understanding, will guard your hearts and your thoughts in Christ Jesus.

A Steady Interactive Fellowship

In Christianity, not only do we have a unique relationship with Christ but with each other. The one who disciples must emphasize the importance of fellowship involves interaction among the saints. This means that attendance at a worship service does not guarantee fellowship. The apostle John uses this word to describe the interaction of the saints. In 1 John 1:6-7, he speaks of our "fellowship" with one another. The Greek word connotes a "joint participation" in something. We are involved in a joint participation in the advancement of the Kingdom of God and the maturing of the saints. This is why the goal of the evangelists and pastor-teachers is "to equip the saints for service." Why? It is to build up the body of Christ. Our service is to the world in evangelism and to each other in ministry (Ephesians 4:11-12).

1 John 1:6-7
If we say that we have fellowship with him and walk in the darkness, we lie, and don't tell the truth. But if we walk in the light, as he is in the light, we have fellowship with one another, and the blood of Jesus Christ, his Son, cleanses us from all sin.

Ephesians 4:11-12
He gave some to be apostles; and some, prophets; and some, evangelists; and

some, shepherds[a] and teachers; 12 for the perfecting of the saints, to the work of serving, to the building up of the body of Christ.

The primary way we do this with believers is to interact with one another (using our giftedness) to encourage others to grow toward spiritual maturity in Christ. We come along side and support each other. In Hebrews 10:24-25, the author of the book entreats the individual saints in the church to continue attending the local assembly. Why? He explains, "Let us consider how to provoke one another to love and good works." As we live the Christian life, we need others to provoke us to love and good works. Then he continues with, "Not forsaking our own assembling together, as the custom of some is." We must always be interacting with the saints. We can never forsake this fellowship. Then he describes it a different way, "But exhorting one another; and so much the more, as you see the Day approaching." We must have the stimulation of others to encourage each other in every way.

Hebrews 10:24-25
Let's consider how to provoke one another to love and good works, not forsaking our own assembling together, as the custom of some is, but exhorting one another, and so much the more as you see the Day approaching.

This is the fellowship John says we have. This is best seen in what is called the biblical "one anothers." Throughout the New Testament, the writers exhort Christians to support one another using these two words. We are encouraged to love and honor one another (Romans 12:10), build up one another in the faith (Romans 14:19;), bear the burdens of one another (Galatians 6:2), forgive one another (Ephesians 4:32), teach and warn one another (Colossians 3:16), comfort one another (1 Thessalonians 4:18), exhort one another (1 Thessalonians 5:11), serve one another (1 Peter 4:10), and then pray for one another (James 5:16). This is just a few of the descriptions of our fellowship together. Notice, it is all involves interaction.

LEADING THE WAY

Romans 12:10
In love of the brothers be tenderly affectionate to one another; in honor preferring one another.

Romans 14:19
So then, let's follow after things which make for peace, and things by which we may build one another up.

Galatians 6:2
Bear one another's burdens, and so fulfill the law of Christ.

Ephesians 4:32
And be kind to one another, tender hearted, forgiving each other, just as God also in Christ forgave you.

Colossians 3:16
Let the word of Christ dwell in you richly; in all wisdom teaching and admonishing one another with psalms, hymns, and spiritual songs, singing with grace in your heart to the Lord.

1 Thessalonians 4:18
Therefore comfort one another with these words.

1 Thessalonians 5:11
Therefore exhort one another, and build each other up, even as you also do.

1 Peter 4:10
As each has received a gift, employ it in serving one another, as good managers of the grace of God in its various forms.

James 5:16
Confess your offenses to one another, and pray for one another, that you may be healed. The insistent prayer of a righteous person is powerfully effective.

When we attend a worship service and pray, sing, give an offering, and then listen to a sermon, we are participating in certain aspects of biblical fellowship. Yet, there is so much more involved. Fellowship centers around interaction with the saints in daily living, not just the worship service. The Holy Scriptures focus on the interactions we have with the saints as we live out our daily lives and serve in ministry to the church. This is critical.

A Sound Doctrinal Instruction

God has placed within the church evangelists and pastor-teachers. As we have seen previously, the responsibility of the evangelist is to equip the saints to share the gospel. This will build the body up numerically. The responsibility of the pastor-teacher is to instruct the saints in sound doctrine. This will build the church up spiritually. In Ephesians 4:11-12, Paul describes this principle, "He gave some to be apostles; and some, prophets; [these saints laid the foundation and have now passed away] and some, evangelists; and some, shepherds and teachers [these saints remain today]."

The term "shepherds and teachers" refers to one person. These saints shepherd the flock by teaching them. It is absolutely essential to spiritual growth. Paul continues, "For the perfecting of the saints, to the work of serving, to the building up of the body of Christ."

This critical perfecting and building are toward spiritual maturity. In verse 13, he explains that their goal is for the flock to become fully mature to the point that they measure up to Christ's stature. In verse 14, he contrasts this maturity to their immaturity or truly childlike behavior. The apostle describes spiritual children (those who are not shepherd-taught) as ones who are "tossed back and forth and carried about with every wind of doctrine, by the trickery of men, in craftiness, after the wiles of error." These children go from spiritual fad to spiritual fad. They cannot land on any one truth because they do not know the Lord's truth. The pastor-teacher's job is to study the Word diligently and to teach it to the flock of God by presenting it to them clearly and fully.

Ephesians 4:13
Until we all attain to the unity of the faith and of the knowledge of the Son of God, to a full grown man, to the measure of the stature of the fullness of Christ.

Ephesians 4:14
That we may no longer be children, tossed back and forth and carried about with every wind of doctrine, by the trickery of men, in craftiness, after the wiles of error.

Paul taught Timothy this important responsibility in his two letters to this pastor son in the faith. In 1 Timothy 4:11, Paul gives Timothy a series of injunctions and then writes, "Command and teach these things." Then, in verse 13, he adds, "Until I come, pay attention to reading, to exhortation, and to teaching." In verse 15, he continues, "Be diligent in these things." In 1 Timothy 6:2, again he encourages, "Teach and exhort these things." In 2 Timothy 1:13-14, the apostle Paul exhorts the pastor, "Hold the pattern of sound words which you have heard from me, in faith and love which is in Christ Jesus. That good thing, which was committed to you, guard through the Holy Spirit who dwells in us."

1 Timothy 4:11
Command and teach these things.

1 Timothy 4:13
Until I come, pay attention to reading...exhortation...teaching.

1 Timothy 4:15
Be diligent in these things. Give yourself wholly to them, that your progress may be revealed to all.

1 Timothy 6:2
Those who have believing masters, let them not despise them because they are brothers, but rather let them serve them, because those who partake of the benefit are believing and beloved. Teach and exhort these things.

2 Timothy 1:13-14
Hold the pattern of sound words which you have heard from me, in faith and love which is in Christ Jesus. That good thing which was committed to you, guard through the Holy Spirit who dwells in us.

In fact, in 2 Timothy 2:15, Paul exhorts Timothy, "Give diligence to present yourself approved by God, a workman who doesn't need to be ashamed, [instead he is] properly handling the Word of Truth [Bible}." Then in 2 Timothy 3:14-17, Paul describes the Scriptures as inspired and profitable with the ability to equip Christians for every good work. As a result, in 2 Timothy 4:2, the apostle commands this young pastor before God and Jesus to do the following, "Preach the word; be urgent in season and out of season [when they want it or not]; reprove, rebuke, and exhort, with all patience and teaching." So, it becomes critical that you encourage your young disciples in the Lord to find real shepherd-teachers to provide the sound doctrine they need for their growth.

2 Timothy 2:15
Give diligence to present yourself approved by God, a workman who doesn't need to be ashamed, properly handling the Word of Truth.

2 Timothy 3:14-17
But you remain in the things which you have learned and have been assured of, knowing from whom you have learned them. From infancy, you have known the holy Scriptures which are able to make you wise for salvation through faith, which is in Christ Jesus. Every Scripture is God-breathed and profitable for teaching, for reproof, for correction, and for instruction in righteousness, that each person who belongs to God may be complete, thoroughly equipped for every good work.

2 Timothy 4:2
Preach the word; be urgent in season and out of season; reprove, rebuke, and exhort with all patience and teaching.

How is this growth actually accomplished? It involves all the truth mentioned under "A Consistent Scriptural Study" with one additional caveat: he can provide the deeper and broader truths of Scripture and their powerful applications to individual lives. The deeper truth is crucial. This is why in 1 John 2:13-14, John calls the mature Christians "spiritual fathers." Why? They know "Him who is from the beginning." Spiritual fathers so understand the Word of God that they are beginning to truly know the Son of God described in the

Word. This is not done through intellectual reasoning about their faith or some divine infusion of mystical knowledge. It is accomplished through a diligent and deep study of God's speaking and acting in His Word. This will lead to a clear understanding of how He thinks.

1 John 2:13-14
I write to you, fathers, because you know him who is from the beginning. I write to you, young men, because you have overcome the evil one. I write to you, little children, because you know the Father. I have written to you, fathers, because you know him who is from the beginning. I have written to you, young men, because you are strong, and the word of God remains in you, and you have overcome the evil one.

In the human realm, this would be very similar to reading hundreds and hundreds of historical letters between two people and finally getting to know them intimately. Though in this case, the person writing is very much alive. Also, He is writing to someone else, He has us in His mind as well. One might ask this, "Why doesn't He simply speak to us directly? He is God, can't He do this?" Yes, He can, but He has chosen to no longer communicate with man individually as he once did in the garden.

Why? When Adam and Eve were cast out of the garden, man's direct communication with God was over. This is a specific consequence of the fall and our sin. God determined that He would now speak to us through specific emissaries. In Hebrews 1:1-2, they are the fathers and prophets (OT) and then His Son (NT). Then, the apostles and the prophets in the communicated what the Son of God revealed to them (Ephesians 2:20).

Hebrews 1:1-2
God, having in the past spoken to the fathers through the prophets at many times and in various ways, has at the end of these days spoken to us by his Son, whom he appointed heir of all things, through whom also he made the worlds.

Ephesians 2:20
Being built on the foundation of the apostles and prophets, Christ Jesus himself being the chief cornerstone.

Everything the Father desired revealed was written and delivered to the holy saints (Jude 1:3; Revelation 22:18-19). The Lord has nothing else to say to His people that He has not already said until the return of His Beloved Son. He desires that we study His Word to learn about Him and His ways. Our personal study and the instruction of shepherd-teachers will accomplish this. As we study and they teach us, we can be assured God is speaking to us (2 Peter 1:20-21).

Jude 1:3
Beloved, while I was very eager to write to you about our common salvation, I was constrained to write to you exhorting you to contend earnestly for the faith which was once for all delivered to the saints.

Revelation 22:18-19
I testify to everyone who hears the words of the prophecy of this book, if anyone adds to them, may God add to him the plagues which are written in this book. If anyone takes away from the words of the book of this prophecy, may God take away his part from the tree of life, and out of the holy city, which are written in this book.

2 Peter 1:20-21
Knowing this first, that no prophecy [text, verse] of Scripture is of private interpretation. For no prophecy ever came by the will of man: but holy men of God spoke, being moved by the Holy Spirit.

A Continual Gifted Ministry

When we received Christ as Savior and Lord, we were baptized into the Body of Christ (1 Corinthians 12:13). This term is an analogy of a human body whose parts are totally dependent on one another. In a previous chapter, we already discussed the basic concept of utilizing spiritual gifts. We have spoken about supporting one another in the scattering of the saints, now we focus on the ministering those gifts in the gathering of the saints. The church is not an organization of volunteers it is an assembly of gifted saints ministering to one another. We have seen in our study thus far, the two gifts to the church (evangelists and shepherd-teachers) are to equip the saints to serve the world in sharing the gospel and minister to the saints in building them up in the faith.

1 Corinthians 12:13
For in one Spirit we were all baptized into one body, whether Jews or Greeks, whether bond or free; and were all given to drink into one Spirit.

Often times, people will complain that they are too busy to volunteer. Other times, the individual church does not provide opportunities for ministry except as a life group leader, usher, or children's worker. Everyone in the church is to be involved in ministering their gifts. We must discover our gifts and then create a ministry in order to use them if needed. God has gifted each church differently and it must discover the gifts of its members and develop the church's ministries around them. This should be accomplished by studying the interests and gifts of the particular members of a local congregation. The church of Jesus Christ should not be "outsourcing" their ministries to "parachurch" groups. Believers must be given numerous opportunities to minister their spiritual gifts in the church.

How do they do this? Have them read 1 Peter 4:10 and decide if they have a speaking gift or serving gift. This is easily determined by the answer to this question, "Do they like to talk or do?" Then they should look at the various gift lists and decide if they have the ability (spiritual) and desire to participate or create a particular kind of ministry to fulfill a spiritual need. Physical needs can be utilized to provide opportunities for meeting spiritual needs. Jesus Christ and the apostles did not heal primarily out of compassion. They healed and did numerous miracles for the confirmation of the gospel (Hebrews 2:3-4). This is why the healing ministry slowly disappears in their gospel ministries as the truth was slowly being written done and confirmed (Philippians 2:27; 2 Timothy 4:20).

1 Peter 4:10
As each has received a gift, employ it in serving one another, as good managers of the grace of God in its various forms.

Hebrews 2:3-4
How will we escape if we neglect so great a salvation – which at the first having been spoken through the Lord, was confirmed to us by those who heard, God also testifying with them, both by signs and wonders, by various works of power and by gifts of the Holy Spirit, according to his own will?

Philippians 2:27
For indeed he was sick, nearly to death, but God had mercy on him, and not on him only, but on me also, that I might not have sorrow on sorrow.

2 Timothy 4:20
Erastus remained at Corinth, but I left Trophimus at Miletus sick.

A Constant Gospel Evangelism

Another aspect of the Christian life that should be shared with our disciples is the regular sharing of the gospel by God's people. This is not in any way related to inviting people to church. To invite people to church is not sharing the gospel. If the words of Jesus were meant only for those who heard, then the gospel would have died out when those who heard passed away. Yet, it has survived thousands of years. In Acts 1:8, Jesus left the disciples and us with these words, "But you will receive power when the Holy Spirit has come upon you. You will be witnesses to me in Jerusalem, in all Judea...Samaria, and to the uttermost parts of the Earth." This includes all of us.

Acts 1:8
But you will receive power when the Holy Spirit has come upon you. You will be witnesses to me in Jerusalem, in all Judea and Samaria, and to the uttermost parts of the Earth.

When the persecution of Saul erupted in full force, the saints were scattered. What did they do? In Acts 8:4, Luke writes, "Therefore those who were scattered abroad went around preaching the word." It doesn't sound like they went out inviting people to their church. Why am I mentioning this? There is nothing wrong with inviting people to church, but the Lord God intended for all His people to be involved in sharing His good news, not just the pastor. We are the lights to the world. The Greek word translated "light" in the New Testament is used in two different contexts. The first is in contrast to sin and the other is in contrast to error. Being "lights" means to be living righteously and presenting God's truth. This is in sharp contrast to living in sin and presenting false doctrines. The world needs to see our holy lives and hear our holy message.

Acts 8:4
Therefore those who were scattered abroad went around preaching the word.

In Philippians 2:15, Paul explains, "That you may become blameless and harmless, children of God without defect." This is the goal of the Christian life which is holy living." It is lived amid the world. He adds, "In the middle of a crooked and perverse generation. The society is filled with people who are crooked (believing lies) and perverse (sinning all the time). Then he continues, "Among whom you are seen as lights in the world." These people will see us as those who have the truth and are holy because we live holy and speak holy things including the good news of Jesus.

Philippians 2:15
That you may become blameless and harmless, children of God without defect in

the middle of a crooked and perverse generation, among whom you are seen as lights in the world.

In Matthew 5:14-16, Jesus describes how God's kingdom subjects act, "You are the light of the world. A city located on a hill can't be hidden." He portrays us as a lighted city on a hill for all to see. Then He asserts, "Neither do you light a lamp, and put it under a measuring basket, but on a stand; and it shines to all who are in the house." We cannot allow ourselves to be covered up by sinful behavior, silent lips (won't share the gospel), or an unwillingness to interact with the unsaved. Instead, Jesus demands, "Even so, let your light shine before men; that they may see your good works, and glorify your Father who is in heaven."

Matthew 5:14-16
You are the light of the world. A city located on a hill can't be hidden. Neither do you light a lamp and put it under a measuring basket, but on a stand; and it shines to all who are in the house. Even so, let your light shine before men, that they may see your good works and glorify your Father who is in heaven.

I would like to conclude this section with the words of Peter in 1 Peter 3:15, "But sanctify the Lord God in your hearts." The Greek word translated "sanctify" means "to set apart, make sacred." We need to teach our disciples to set Christ apart from everything else in our lives and make Him first and foremost. Then they need to prepare themselves to have an answer to everyone who asks about our hope. The apostle finishes, "And always be ready to give an answer to everyone who asks you a reason concerning the hope that is in you, with humility and fear." When we study the Bible to not only to learn it personally but to share it with others (believers and non-believers), it is much more motivating. Working out to run a marathon is much more motivating than just running. We receive all the benefits of learning God's Word and the added bonus of being used by Him regularly. This will bring a phenomenal experience...lives.

1 Peter 3:15
But sanctify the Lord God in your hearts. Always be ready to give an answer to everyone who asks you a reason concerning the hope that is in you, with humility and fear.

A Steadfast Righteous Life

We must impress upon those we disciple that God desires us to live righteously as His Son Jesus did. In 1 John 2:6, the apostle writes, "He who says he remains in him [a believer] ought himself also to walk just like he walked." Then, in Colossians 2:6, Paul says, "Therefore as you have received Christ Jesus the Lord, so walk in Him." Most people tend to compartmentalize their lives and merely add Christ to it. Eight hours a day, they may be workers, homemakers, or students and for six hours or so a day, they might be moms, dads, husbands, wives, sisters, brothers, sons or daughters.

1 John 2:6
He who says he remains in him ought himself also to walk just like he walked.

Colossians 2:6
As therefore you received Christ Jesus, the Lord, walk in him.

On Saturdays, they might be gardeners, golfers, football enthusiasts, crafters, tennis players, or whatever they enjoy doing. Then when Sunday arrives (or Saturday night if they want Sundays off), they live their Christian lives. They might add a weeknight for life group, a kid's club program, or youth groups, but this is not the true biblical view of our lifelong journey with Christ.

In Colossians 1:10, Paul describes our Christian lives in these words, "So that you will walk in a manner worthy of the Lord, to please Him in all respects, bearing fruit in every good work and increasing in the knowledge of God." We are to walk about in our lives moment by moment in a manner that is worthy of the Lord. We are to live to please Him in every area of our lives (in all respects). We are to bear fruits through doing good works and increase in our knowledge of Him. Over and over the apostle Paul describes the Christian life as a "walk." The word translated "walk" means simply to walk about in one's life. Notice, a walk involves one step at a time. Wherever we go, whatever we think, say, and do, we behave as Christians. We must conduct our lives completely as believers in the Lord Jesus Christ. This will require much growth in holiness and righteousness.

Colossians 1:10
That you may walk worthily of the Lord, to please him in all respects, bearing fruit in every good work and increasing in the knowledge of God.

In Ephesians 2:10, Paul explains that we were created to for this very purpose, "For we are his workmanship, created in Christ Jesus for good works, which God prepared before that we would walk in them." We are to walk about living righteously and doing good deeds as His workmanship. We display God's creative work in our lives as He transforms us into the image of His Son. In Ephesians 4:1, the apostle literally begs his readers to live for Christ. He cries out, "I therefore, the prisoner in the Lord, beg you to walk worthily of the calling with which you were called." We were called out of the world into eternal life and ought to walk worthy of that calling. Paul was in prison waiting for his trial before Caesar because of the persecution he experienced because he himself walked worthy of the Lord.

Ephesians 2:10
For we are his workmanship, created in Christ Jesus for good works, which God prepared before that we would walk in them.

Ephesians 4:1
I therefore, the prisoner in the Lord, beg you to walk worthily of the calling with which you were called.

In 1 Thessalonians 2:12, he instructs the new believers to live worthy of their Father God when he writes, "To the end that you should walk worthily of God, who calls you into his own Kingdom and glory." We are members of the kingdom of God and recipients of His glory manifested in all His blessings. As a result, we should walk worthy of this great honor. This is not the earning of salvation but the display of all that it is. In 1 John 1:7, John calls it "walking in the light." We should teach those we disciple that living righteously is a process in which we can grow. In 1 Thessalonians 4:1, Paul encourages the saints, "Finally then, brothers, we beg and exhort you in the Lord Jesus, that as you received from us how you ought to walk and to please God, that you abound more and more." Their goal is to grow in their righteousness.

1 Thessalonians 2:12
To the end that you should walk worthily of God, who calls you into his own Kingdom and glory.

1 John 1:7
But if we walk in the light, as he is in the light, we have fellowship with one another, and the blood of Jesus Christ, his Son, cleanses us from all sin.

1 Thessalonians 4:1
Finally then, brothers, we beg and exhort you in the Lord Jesus, that as you received from us how you ought to walk and to please God, that you abound more and more.

How do they do this? They learn the commandments of God in the Word and then practice obeying them. In 2 John 1:6, the beloved disciple writes, "This is love, that we should walk according to his commandments." In Philippians 4:9, Paul asserts, "The things you have learned and received and heard and seen in me, practice these things, and the God of peace will be with you." It takes practice to live righteously. It is not automatic and requires a battle with the flesh (the sin principle in our bodies). In 1 Corinthians 9:27, Paul uses a boxing term to explain how he handles his flesh, "But I discipline [box] my body and make it my slave, so that, after I have preached to others, I myself will not be disqualified." He was so concerned about sinning in such a grievous way that he would lose his ministry, so he boxed his flesh.

2 John 1:6
This is love, that we should walk according to his commandments. This is the commandment, even as you heard from the beginning, that you should walk in it.

Philippians 4:9
The things which you learned, received, heard, and saw in me: do these things, and the God of peace will be with you.

1 Corinthians 9:27
But I beat my body and bring it into submission, lest by any means, after I have preached to others, I myself should be rejected.

A Humble Repentant Confession

Yet, no matter how much we desire not to sin, we will. As a result, we must be prepared to stumble, fall, confess, and begin the walk again. This may occur many times a day at first. Then, as we grow in Christ, it decreases. As we disciple someone, we must teach them about confession of sin. True believers are constantly recognizing the sins that they are committing and asking God for forgiveness. This is not just an eternal issue, but this is a relational one. It affects God's relationship with us. It is true that all our past, present, and future sins are forgiven when we receive Jesus Christ as Savior and Lord (Colossians 2:13-14; Romans 8:1).

Colossians 2:13-14
You were dead through your trespasses and the uncircumcision of your flesh. He made you alive together with him, having forgiven us all our trespasses, wiping out the handwriting in ordinances which was against us. He has taken it out of the way, nailing it to the cross.

Romans 8:1
There is therefore now no condemnation to those who are in Christ Jesus, who don't walk according to the flesh, but according to the Spirit.

Yet, in our relationship with God upon this Earth in the flesh, we still confess our sins. This restores our relationship with God. It eliminates any barriers between us. John speaks to this very issue in his first letter. Some were saying in the church that they had matured to such a level that they no longer sinned in any way. John, the apostle, counters with a scathing response. In 1 John 1:8, the apostle emphatically states, "If we say that we have no sin, we deceive ourselves, and the truth is not in us." Then in verse 10, he declares, "If we say that we haven't sinned, we make him a liar, and his word is not in us." Those who claim that they have never sinned or no longer sin are deceiving themselves, to others, and to God. His truth and Word are not in them. Why? The truth in the Word convicts us of our sin.

1 John 1:8
If we say that we have no sin, we deceive ourselves, and the truth is not in us.

1 John 1:10
If we say that we haven't sinned, we make him a liar, and his word is not in us.

Then sandwiched between these two convicting passages is what believers do when they realize they have sinned. In verse 9, he proclaims, "If we confess our sins, He is faithful and righteous to forgive us the sins, and to cleanse us from all unrighteousness." The verbs "confess" and "forgive" are in the present tense which indicates continual action in present time. Believers are continually confessing their sins and God is continually forgiving them. Repentance and asking God to forgive us is a lifelong practice.

1 John 1:9
If we confess our sins, he is faithful and righteous to forgive us the sins, and to cleanse us from all unrighteousness.

This admission of sin is the first step in the confession process. Again in 1 John 1:9, the word which is translated "confess" means "to say the same thing" which indicates that we are to say the same thing about our sin that God says. We tell the Lord our words or actions were sinful and against His commands. The next component of repentance is to mourn over those sins. In the Beatitudes, the Lord speaks of the spiritual characteristics of His children. Though these qualities appear physical, they refer to spiritual aspects of his kingdom people. In Matthew 5:3, Jesus declares, "Blessed are the poor in spirit, for theirs is the kingdom of God."

Matthew 5:3
"Blessed are the poor in spirit, for theirs is the Kingdom of Heaven.

He was speaking of those poor in their spirit. The Greek word translated "poor" means "bankrupt" and refers to the acknowledgement that His people know they are spiritually bankrupt in sin. This is the first aspect, we just discussed. The Lord continues in verse 4, "Blessed are those who mourn, for they shall be comforted." This important remark speaks of mourning over one's bankrupt condition before God as one mourns over the dead. It refers to a deep sorrow over our sin and sinfulness. This is the second aspect.

Matthew 5:4
Blessed are those who mourn, for they shall be comforted.

The third aspect of confession of sin is repentance. The Greek word translated "repent" means "to turn around in the opposite direction or change one's mind or behavior." We must turn around from our confessed sins and move in the opposite direction. We must live differently. In His seven letters to the churches in Revelation chapters two and three, Jesus indicts them for sin and then urges them to repent. They had to confess what they did, mourn over it, and turn in the opposite direction (Revelation 2:5, 16; 3:3, 19).

Revelation 2:5
Remember therefore from where you have fallen, and repent and do the first works; or else I am coming to you swiftly, and will move your lamp stand out of its place, unless you repent.

Revelation 2:16
Repent therefore, or else I am coming to you quickly, and I will make war against them with the sword of my mouth.

Revelation 3:3
Remember therefore how you have received and heard. Keep it and repent. If therefore you won't watch, I will come as a thief, and you won't know what hour I will come upon you.

Revelation 3:19
As many as I love, I reprove and chasten. Be zealous therefore, and repent.

Luke records Peter's denial of even knowing Christ in Luke 22:62 and how the apostle wept in sorrow and remorse afterward. Later, Luke records in Acts chapter two, three, and other passages the many sermons that Peter preached in great boldness for Christ. Peter clearly demonstrated that he had turned in the opposite direction from that sin. Of course, the Holy Spirit will provide the strength needed in order to accomplish this supernatural feat (Acts 2:4; Romans 8:13). Now, consider the response of Judas. In Matthew 27:3-5, he would not repent nor humble himself before the Lord Jesus. Therefore. the guilt and sorrow that was tormenting him day and night remained. Had he done what Peter had done, he would have experienced the same sense of relief through his salvation. Instead, he simply killed himself to alleviate them from his life. This is the sorrow unto death.

Luke 22:62
He went out, and wept bitterly.

Acts 2:4
They were all filled with the Holy Spirit, and began to speak with other languages, as the Spirit gave them the ability to speak.

Romans 8:13
For if you live after the flesh, you must die; but if by the Spirit you put to death the deeds of the body, you will live.

Matthew 27:3-5
Then Judas, who betrayed him, when he saw that Jesus was condemned, felt remorse, and brought back the thirty pieces of silver to the chief priests and elders, saying, "I have sinned in that I betrayed innocent blood." But they said, "What is that to us? You see to it. "He threw down the pieces of silver in the sanctuary and departed. Then he went away and hanged himself.

As we interlace the three principles we have studied in these initial chapters, we clearly see how we are to reconcile our relationship with the Lord before we can reconcile with others. The response of all believers when they have sinned against another will be to turn toward God first and ask Him for forgiveness. This is accomplished through the admission of their wrongs, sorrow over their sin, and a turning toward righteousness while leaving no sin in the transgression out. This is how we are to reconcile with our Father. The pattern is stumbling, falling, confessing, and beginning once again. This is done hopefully less and less as we mature.

An Intentional Spiritual Walk

How can all of these things truly occur in our very busy lives? Everything may sound overwhelming to a brand-new believer, so of course, we will teach them these things over time. Yet, this can and must be accomplished through their intentional living. Christians cannot allow themselves to be victims of all of the burdens and issues of life. They must set goals and desire greatly to live for Christ. In Ephesians 5:15, Paul explained this intentional walk of Christians in these words, "Therefore watch carefully how you walk, not as unwise, but as wise." The unwise are not careful about how they live, especially in the aspect of time which is what Paul is referring to in this passage. In verse 16, the apostle writes, "Redeeming the time, because the days are evil."

Ephesians 5:15
Therefore watch carefully how you walk, not as unwise, but as wise.

Ephesians 5:16
Redeeming the time, because the days are evil.

When it comes to our time, we must not act like those who do not believe in the Lord God. In Psalm 14:1, King David describes how an unwise person will live, "The fool has said in his heart, 'There is no God.' They are corrupt. They have done abominable deeds. There is no one who does good." Those who are not saved will live corruptly for themselves and do whatever they desire. Why? They do not believe in our God. We are not to live like those who do not believe in God and live in any way that their desires take them. We must live every moment in the light of the Lord God's presence. Why? The days are evil. We will be tempted to waste our "saved lives" on sinful activities or worthless deeds.

Psalm 14:1
The fool has said in his heart, "There is no God." They are corrupt.
They have done abominable deeds. There is no one who does good.

Evil is all around us and always tempting us to become distracted. Paul calls the Christian life a race (1 Corinthians 9:27). Imagine a road throughout a town and countryside where there will be a marathon race. Before the race, many vendors from all over set up booths with each representing one of the delights or appetites of man whether wicked or just distracting. There are many food and beer stands, sports activities, hobby shops, travel agents, prostitutes, and the list can go on and on. The runners become distracted and stop to enjoy the activities. In fact, they decide they would spend their lives there; the time is foolishly wasted. Everyone else at those booths does not believe in the true God. They are living for themselves as pleasure seekers.

1 Corinthians 9:27
But I beat my body and bring it into submission, lest by any means, after I have preached to others, I myself should be rejected.

The Bible distinguishes between three kinds of activities on Earth: righteous, wicked, and wasteful. When we became Christians, God forgave all our wicked deeds past, present, and future (Colossians 2:13-14). Christians have passed out of condemnation for these wicked deeds (Romans 8:1). Yet, Christians will have a judgment day where their other deeds will be judged. What deeds? The other two he discussed.

Colossians 2:13-14
You were dead through your trespasses and the uncircumcision of your flesh. He made you alive together with him, having forgiven us all our trespasses, wiping out the handwriting in ordinances which was against us. He has taken it...nailing it to the cross.

Romans 8:1
There is therefore now no condemnation to those who are in Christ Jesus, who don't walk according to the flesh, but according to the Spirit.

In the apostle's treatment of our rewards in 2 Corinthians 5:10, he explains, "For we must all be revealed before the judgment seat of Christ; that each one may receive the things in the body, according to what he has done, whether good or bad." Here Paul distinguishes between the only two sets of deeds that will be judged: good (righteous, holy actions) and bad (wasteful, useless). The Greek word translated "bad" is not the usual word used in the New Testament for evil or sin; rather, it means "wasteful, worthless, of no account."

2 Corinthians 5:10
For we must all be revealed before the judgment seat of Christ that each one may receive the things in the body according to what he has done, whether good or bad.

We must keep this in mind as we redeem our time upon this Earth. In James 4:14, he describes our lives as but a vapor which is here now and quickly gone. If we aren't careful, we will find ourselves at the end of our lives wondering why we did not do more for the Lord. The answer will be that we did not walk intentionally; instead, we got caught up in the sins and useless activities of the world.

James 4:14
Whereas you don't know what your life will be like tomorrow. For what is your life? For you are a vapor that appears for a little time, and then vanishes away.

In 1 Peter 4:3, regarding sin, Peter exhorts believers, "For we have spent enough of our past time doing the desire of the Gentiles, and having walked in lewdness, lusts, drunken binges, orgies, carousings, and abominable idolatries." He is simply saying as unbelievers we already spent enough time in sin, we now have to live for Christ. We must put away these old familiar sinful activities of our former lives and embrace the new activities of our new lives in Christ. This will require supernatural strength from the Holy Spirit, and He will provide this for you.

1 Peter 4:3
For we have spent enough of our past time doing the desire of the Gentiles, and having walked in lewdness, lusts, drunken binges, orgies, carousings, and abominable idolatries.

A Resolute Endurance of Trials

Receiving Jesus Christ does not exempt believers from the problems of life. When I became a true Christian, one of the verses that was frequently shared with me wherever I went was John 10:10. In this verse, Jesus declared, "I came that they may have life, and may have it abundantly." Christians thought that this meant that the Lord Jesus would prevent many of the problems that others faced. He would in essence put a protective bubble all around us and we would always be happy, successful, and fulfilled every moment. When it does not happen, many I knew wondered what was going on. The "abundant life" Jesus promised was life lived with Him and into eternity. It is living a life of faith through the many problems we might face. It did not mean a problem free life. In fact, it is exactly the opposite.

John 10:10
The thief only comes to steal, kill, and destroy. I came that they may have life and may have it abundantly.

We must instruct those we are discipling that God does protect us from many trials (Philippians 1:19) but also allows others to occur (James 1:2). The first trial we may experience is a trial that comes with our own salvation which the Bible calls persecution. In John 15:20, Jesus warned, "Remember the word that I said to you: 'A servant is not greater than his lord.'" Jesus Christ is speaking to His disciples (His servants) and desires to prepare them for what is about to occur. He continues, "If they persecuted me, they will also persecute you. If they kept my word, they will keep yours also." These words are for us also today. People who love Christ will embrace us because we love Him. People who hate Christ, including friends and family members, may hate us because they hate Him.

LEADING THE WAY

Philippians 1:19
For I know that this will turn out to my salvation, through your prayers and the supply of the Spirit of Jesus Christ.

James 1:2
Count it all joy...brothers, when you fall into various temptations.

John 15:20
Remember the word that I said to you: "A servant is not greater than his lord." If they persecuted me, they will also persecute you. If they kept my word, they will also keep yours.

There may be a stiff cost to following Christ. In Matthew 10:34-38, Jesus describes it this way, "Don't think that I came to send peace on the Earth. I didn't come to send peace, but a sword. For I came to set a man at odds against his father, and a daughter against her mother, and a daughter-in-law against her mother-in-law. A man's foes will be those of his own household." Those whom we are discipling may have to take a stand for Christ against their own family members. The Lord adds, "He who loves father or mother more than me is not worthy of me; and he who loves son or daughter more than me isn't worthy of me. He who doesn't take his cross and follow after me, isn't worthy of me." Our cross is the persecution we may bear for His sake.

Matthew 10:34-38
Don't think that I came to send peace on the Earth. I didn't come to send peace, but a sword. For I came to set a man at odds against his father, and a daughter against her mother, and a daughter-in-law against her mother-in-law. A man's foes will be those of his own household. He who loves father or mother more than me is not worthy of me; and he who loves son or daughter more than me isn't worthy of me. He who doesn't take his cross and follow after me isn't worthy of me.

The Lord Jesus will allow trials in our lives to produce maturity. It is one of the ways we grow in Christ. In James 1:2-4, the Lord's brother encourages believers to be joyful when trials come because they make them mature. How does that happen? It occurs in various ways. First, we are placed in a situation where we can be tempted to behave badly, thereby providing us an opportunity to obey God. In Matthew chapter four, Satan tempted Christ to disobey God, and He chose instead to obey His Father.

James 1:2-4
Count it all joy...brothers, when you fall into various temptations, knowing that the testing of your faith produces endurance. Let endurance have its perfect work, that you may be perfect and complete, lacking in nothing.

Anyone can obey God when things are going great, but when things are difficult, we learn to obey Him. In Hebrews 5:8, it says, "Though he was a Son, yet learned obedience by the things which he suffered." In His humanity, the Lord learned to obey God in all things through suffering. Second, it puts us in a place where God's power must work and be displayed because our personal efforts become exhausted.

Hebrews 5:8
Though he was a Son, yet learned obedience by the things which he suffered.

In 2 Corinthians 12:9, Paul received a thorn in the flesh to keep him humble, "My grace is sufficient for you, for my power is made perfect in weakness." After this, the apostle declared, "Most gladly therefore I will rather glory in my weaknesses, that the power of Christ may rest on me." Third, when it is from the Lord God's loving discipline for our sin, it produces obedience. In Psalm 119:67, the author explains that through the Father's discipline and affliction, he learned obedience. He cries, "Before I was afflicted, I went astray; but now I observe your word."

2 Corinthians 12:9
He has said to me, "My grace is sufficient for you, for my power is made perfect in weakness." Most gladly therefore I will rather glory in my weaknesses, that the power of Christ may rest on me.

Psalm 119:67
Before I was afflicted, I went astray; but now I observe your word.

Fourth, trials and problems result in righteousness. The psalmist continues in verse 71, "It is good for me that I have been afflicted." He relishes his affliction from God for his sin. Though this seems odd, it is not with the correct perspective. The inspired writer continues with this righteous and holy view, "That I may learn your statutes." Fifth, it teaches us to empathize and comfort others. In 2 Corinthians 1:4, Paul explains how God comforts us in our trials, and then we can comfort others in theirs. He writes, "Who [God] comforts us in all our affliction, that we may be able to comfort those who are in any affliction." How do we do this? Paul goes on to add, "Through the comfort with which we ourselves are comforted by God." The last two are critical. When we experience trials and we remain faithful to the Lord, we demonstrate our true faith (that we are truly saved) to God (Genesis 22:15-18), ourselves (1 Peter 1:6-7), others (Mark 2:12), and to the angels and demons (Ephesians 3:10; Job 1-2). We also come to understand how strong our faith really is so we can make it grow in a much deeper way (Matthew 8:26).

Psalm 119:71
It is good for me that I have been afflicted, that I may learn your statutes.

2 Corinthians 1:4
Who comforts us in all our affliction, that we may be able to comfort those who are in any affliction, through the comfort...we ourselves are comforted by God.

Genesis 22:15-18
Yahweh's angel called to Abraham a second time out of the sky, and said, "I have sworn by myself," says Yahweh, "because you have done this thing, and have not withheld your son, your only son, that I will bless you greatly, and I will multiply your offspring greatly like the stars of the heavens, and like the sand which is on the seashore. Your offspring will possess the gate of his enemies. All the nations of the Earth will be blessed by your offspring, because you have obeyed my voice."

1 Peter 1:6-7
Wherein you greatly rejoice, though now for a little while, if need be, you have been grieved in various trials, that the proof of your faith, which is more precious than gold that perishes even though it is tested by fire, may be found to result in praise, glory, and honor at the revelation of Jesus Christ.

Mark 2:12
He arose, and immediately took up the mat and went out in front of them all, so that they were all amazed and glorified God, saying, "We never saw anything like this!"

Ephesians 3:10
To the intent that now through the assembly the manifold wisdom of God might be made known to the principalities and the powers in the heavenly places.

Job 1:9-12
Then Satan answered Yahweh, and said, "Does Job fear God for nothing? Haven't you made a hedge around him, and around his house, and around all that he has, on every side? You have blessed the work of his hands, and his substance is increased in the land. But stretch out your hand now, and touch all that he has, and he will renounce you to your face." Yahweh said to Satan, "Behold, all that he has is in your power. Only on himself don't stretch out your hand." So Satan went out from the presence of Yahweh.

Matthew 8:26
He said to them, "Why are you fearful, O you of little faith?" Then he got up, rebuked the wind and the sea, and there was a great calm.

An Ancient Portrait

A perfect portrait of discipleship is found in the apostle Paul's relationship with Onesimus whom he had brought to Christ. This is found in the letter to Philemon. When Paul arrived in Rome, he met a runaway slave named Onesimus. After Onesimus came to Christ, Paul discovered that his owner was a dear friend of his in the city of Colossae named Philemon. For a time, both Paul and Onesimus ministered together, but it came time to return him to his master so he could face his crime. This was a serious offense.

Rather than just let Onesimus return and face it alone, he decided to use the opportunity to teach both Onesimus and Philemon some important truths concerning forgiveness, the true fellowship between followers of Christ, and obeying the law. This was a great discipleship opportunity for the both of them. Paul was the right person to do it, since he was both the spiritual father of Onesimus and Philemon. He was also an apostle of Christ, who was well respected in the church. So, Paul sent a letter on behalf of this new believer which recommended that Philemon should forgive him. Then, he should be welcomed as a new brother in Christ rather than as a fugitive slave who deserved severe punishment.

The apostle began his letter complementing Philemon on some qualities he is now going to have to display with his newly returned slave. He lauds him for his love toward believers and his deep faith in Christ which he now wants him to show toward Onesimus. Then, Paul asserts that as an apostle he could command Philemon to embrace Onesimus, but he would rather entreat him as someone who loves him in Christ. He could ask him as his spiritual father to please forgive this slave, but he would rather entreat him as aged prisoner of the Lord. He could appeal to Philemon's true commitment to Christ, but he would rather implore him as someone who himself has made numerous sacrifices for the Lord. Philemon should do the same in this circumstance.

Paul asserts that God really had a purpose in this slave running away, and it was for his salvation. Philemon has Onesimus back as a beloved brother in the flesh and in the Lord. He is especially a beloved brother to Paul. Rather than punishing his new brother as a slave, he should be embraced as a spiritual sibling. Even though Philemon owes him his eternal life, Paul does not want to call in the favor. Even though Philemon could easily have afforded the loss, he did not want him to be forced to do it to protect his friendship.

He speaks of the joy and refreshment of his heart he is going to feel when he learns what Philemon has done. His holy joy and refreshment will result from Philemon not only obeying but even go beyond any of his suggestions. Then he indicates that he will be making a visit, so Philemon will face the apostle himself. This will definitely encourage Philemon to do what needed to be done. His companions also greeted him. This will encourage his right actions because they will know of Philemon's treatment of Onesimus also. There were several: Epaphras, Mark, Demas, and Luke, with his fellow workers. These were mighty men of faith. Two of them, Mark and Luke, wrote gospels.

Though we are not told specifically what happens, we can be assured that Philemon welcomed Onesimus into his own household and church at Colossae. Perhaps, once the letter was read, Philemon did the unthinkable to the unbelieving Roman world, he unchained and released Onesimus. Then Philemon reached out his hands and cried, "Welcome, my brother!" Here, Paul trains Philemon and Onesimus by using his own behavior and the truths from the Scriptures. This is true discipleship.

A Modern Anecdote

When I was a pastor, one Sunday morning a couple with four small children came to our church. They were so taken with the preaching of God's Word (all Him, not me) that they wanted to become members within weeks. I asked if I could come over and talk to them. Often times, churches will have people meet in a group or take a short class to become members of the church. I wasn't that way. The Scriptures indicate that one must be a true believer in Christ before he can become a member of a local church body (His kingdom on Earth). The church is made up of true believers in Christ. I wanted to do this privately so that I could ask the proper questions, and they could answer them honestly.

This is much more difficult in a group. If it turned out that they were not saved, then I could take the time needed to share the good news with them, no matter how long it took. When I arrived at Eric and Tonya's house, we chatted for a few minutes and discussed a variety of things. Then, I launched into the most important question that could be asked, "So how did you both receive Jesus Christ as Savior and Lord?" The wife went first and explained that she had grown up in a large denomination and always believed in Jesus Christ from the time she was small.

He claimed the exact same thing. In fact, they had met in the church's youth group, but they admitted that they had not been practicing their religion for quite some time. Now, they wanted to get back to it, especially for the kids. For some, this may have been enough, but that is not salvation. I asked them if there was ever a moment in their lives when they actually remember being convicted of sin and repenting before Christ. Did they ever remember declaring to the Father that they knew Jesus was His only Son, died on the cross for their sins, and asked Him to save them? Did they ever remember a time when they fully submitted their lives to Christ as Lord promising to obey Him as best as they could? They both looked at me in complete bewilderment. Almost in unison, they muttered, "No, I haven't." I asked them if either of them had ever consistently read the Scriptures, prayed, participated in a church ministry, shared the gospel, used their gifts, and lived righteously for the Lord. These do not save but are signs of salvation. I did not want them to think they were the keys to heaven when they were not. Eric looked at me and said, "I have never done any of those things, I thought you needed to be a member of a church to be a Christian." Tonya agreed.

I gently explained that they may have known about Jesus Christ like we know about a great historical figure. We admire the person, want to follow his values and teachings, even be like him in some ways. Yet, this is not a relationship with Jesus Christ, our Savior and Lord. They looked puzzled because they had never even considered this. I then shared the true gospel. I explained that they must receive Jesus Christ as Savior and place their lives in His hands as Lord. After this, I inquired, "Eric and Tonya, would you want to receive Jesus Christ as Savior and Lord right now? This would mean that you both would enter into a love relationship with Him by faith and enter the kingdom of heaven." Their response was in unison. They said, "Yes!" After coming to Christ, the very next Sunday they were baptized. Then I personally began meeting with them one evening a week. We studied the basics of the Christian life. I used a simple fill-in series of books which can be purchased at any Christian bookstore. We discussed the importance of faith over feelings.

They learned that the Christian life was a walk of faith involving a consistent time in the Word, intercessory prayer, fellowshipping with other Christians, discovering their gifts, and serving in ministry. They must pursue righteousness as they confess their sins daily. They had found a church that taught sound doctrine, and they should attend regularly. We studied these truths together as the Holy Spirit guided us. Herein lies the absolute importance of discipling any new believer with a serious intent.

A Personal Response

Dear Heavenly Father,

I pray that you will provide the motivation and courage I need to declare and announce Your plan of salvation to (add names) and others I know and meet. Please bring them to our Savior and Lord Jesus Christ. If they receive Christ, give me wisdom to disciple them and help them grow in the knowledge of You. Guide us as I encourage them to confirm their faith by being baptized in Your name. Assist me as I teach them the power of faith over feelings.

I do not want them to be trapped in an endless pursuit of feeling inspired and close to you. Help me show them that the Christian life is a walk of real faith. Please provoke them to concentrate on their spiritual growth and not become distracted by worldly pursuits. Assist them in developing a consistent time of study in Your Holy Word and intercessory prayer. Give them a desire to attend church, fellowship with other Christians, discover their gifts, and serve Your Son in ministry.

Help them to find a pastor that will teach them sound doctrine. Fill them with a motivation to live a righteous life and to walk intentionally so they will redeem their time on this Earth. Encourage them to continually confess their sins before You and ask for forgiveness as they forgive others. When trials come, guide them in their patient endurance as they trust You and put on display their faith before the You, themselves, the angels, the demons, the church, their family and friends, and all whom they meet in the unsaved world. I pray this in the name of Jesus. Amen.

AN INSTRUCTOR'S MANUAL

Chapter 13

Disciple with a Serious Intent

Once unbelievers receive Jesus Christ as their Savior and Lord, it does not end there. Someone will have to help these new believers navigate their new lives in Christ.

In the section, "A Typical Scenario," the author displays the ways Christians can follow up conversations that they may have begun with people they casually meet.

What is the scenario about?

A man assists a woman in finding an item in the supermarket and begins a conversation about kids going off to college.

What held the believer back from sharing the gospel?

He did not know how to follow-up if a person was interested in the gospel or actually received Jesus as savior and Lord.

What finally led the Christian to share the good news and how did it occur?

He learned how to follow-up, so he began a discussion of empty nests and invited the woman over to meet with him and his wife.

Have you had a similar experience?

(Various answers should be shared including yours.)

LEADING THE WAY

In the section, "A Scriptural Principle" the author presents an important biblical principle in evangelism which concerns how to disciple or build up new believers in their faith.

How would you express this principle in your own words?

Principle thirteen is "we must disciple with a serious intent."

(Various answers should be shared including yours.)

How would you rewrite this principle to make it even more personal to your life (using your name and situation)?

(Various answers should be shared including yours.)

Why do you think this principle might be important in your life right now as you share the gospel?

(Various answers should be shared including yours.)

How would you rate yourself on the percentage of times you followed this principle in the past as a believer?

(Various answers should be shared including yours.)

Directions: Put a horizontal mark and your name where you see yourself on the percentage line.

0%   25%   50%   75%   100%

In the section, "A Biblical Explanation," the author explains how we are to assist new believers in their growth in Christ and its importance in sharing the gospel effectively.

What are they to really concentrate on in their Christian lives and why?

In 2 Corinthians 5:7, Paul explains that we walk by faith not by sight. They will live by faith not by what they see, feel, or experience.

When we live our lives in obedience to the Lord, the feelings will often follow. Feelings always follow words and actions. The Lord Jesus and the apostles always appealed to thinking, beliefs, and obedience, never to feelings.

What are two ways they can individually grow in Christ and explain each briefly?

In Ephesians 4:13, Paul describes the goal of the church on Earth as attaining to the unity of the faith and of the knowledge of the Son of God.

We do this until all are full grown and mature in Christ both individually and corporately. This means we are to measure up to the "stature of the fullness of Christ." This would be like a brother standing next to his older brother attempting to grow into his image. He would be checking his height, weight, and build. We are standing next to our Lord and doing the very same thing spiritually.

Who can do that? The saints can do it as the Holy Spirit works through His Word as we read it and study it. This is a crucial understanding for believers.

As we read the Word, God literally is speaking to us. As we pray, we are speaking to the Lord Almighty. Prayer is the most intimate kind of communion with God. Prayer and the Word is the process of communication between God and man.

What are two ways they can grow in Christ that involves the saints in a local church?

The primary way we do this with believers is to interact with one another (using our giftedness) to encourage others to grow toward spiritual maturity in Christ. We come along side and support each other.

God has placed within the church evangelists and pastor-teachers. As we have seen previously, the responsibility of the evangelist is to equip the saints to share the gospel. This will build the body up numerically.

What are two ways they can grow in Christ that involves those who do not know Christ as Savior and Lord?

We must share the gospel. This will help us learn the Word, depend on prayer and God's Holy Spirit. We should use our giftedness in developing a strategy.

What must they commit themselves to do to live righteously and how do they deal with sins and trials that will come?

We must commit ourselves to walk as he walked.

Yet, no matter how much we desire not to sin, we will. As a result, we must be prepared to stumble, fall, confess, and begin the walk again. This may occur many times a day at first. Then, as we grow in Christ, it decreases.

Yet, this can and must be accomplished through their intentional living.

In what ways might these truths impact your life?

(Various answers should be shared including yours.)

LEADING THE WAY

In the section, "An Ancient Portrait," the author provides a unique portrayal of Paul's discipleship of a master and his runaway slave.

Can you briefly describe the setting of this real-life ancient drama?

The setting is Rome at the time of Paul's first imprisonment.

Can you describe the major characters involved?

The major characters are Paul, Onesimus (slave), and Philemon (master).

How did the evangelist initiate the gospel presentation?

When Paul, the apostle, arrived in Rome, he met a runaway slave named Onesimus and shared the gospel with him.

What was result of this evangelistic presentation?

Onesimus came to Christ and ministered alongside Paul.

How was the principle explained in this chapter applied to the situation?

Rather than just let Onesimus return and face it alone, he decided to use the opportunity to teach both Onesimus and Philemon some important truths concerning forgiveness, the true fellowship between followers of Christ, and obeying the law. This was a great discipleship opportunity for the both of them. Paul was the right person to do it, since he was both the spiritual father of Onesimus and Philemon.

Then Philemon reached out his hands and cried, "Welcome, my brother!" Here, Paul trains Philemon and Onesimus by using his own behavior and the truths from the Scriptures. This is true discipleship.

Based on the truths learned in this chapter, what would you have done differently if you were the evangelist or how would you have responded if you were the recipient?

(Various answers should be shared including yours.)

In the section, "A Modern Anecdote," the author discusses a situation where he visited a couple who desired to become new members of his church but were not saved.

Can you briefly describe the setting of this real-life modern drama?

When I was a pastor, one Sunday morning a couple with four small children came to our church. They were so taken with the preaching of God's Word (all Him, not me) that they wanted to become members within weeks.

Can you describe the major characters involved?

The major characters are the author, Eric, and Tonya.

How did the author initiate the gospel presentation?

The church is made up of true believers in Christ. I wanted to do this privately so that I could ask the proper questions, and they could answer them honestly.

This is much more difficult in a group. If it turned out that they were not saved, then I could take the time needed to share the good news with them, no matter how long it took. When I arrived at Eric and Tonya's house, we chatted for a few minutes and discussed a variety of things

I gently explained that they may have known about Jesus Christ like we know about a great historical figure. We admire the person, want to follow his values and teachings, even be like him in some ways. Yet, this is not a relationship with Jesus Christ, our Savior and Lord. They looked puzzled because they had never even considered this. I then shared the true gospel.

AN INSTRUCTOR'S MANUAL

What was result of this evangelistic presentation?

Their response was in unison. They said, "Yes!" After coming to Christ, the very next Sunday they were baptized. Then I personally began meeting with them one evening a week. We studied the basics of the Christian life. I used a simple fill-in series of books which can be purchased at any Christian bookstore. We discussed the importance of faith over feelings.

How was the principle explained in this chapter applied to the situation?

They learned that the Christian life was a walk of faith involving a consistent time in the Word, intercessory prayer, fellowshipping with other Christians, discovering their gifts, and serving in ministry. They must pursue righteousness as they confess their sins daily. They had found a church that taught sound doctrine, and they should attend regularly. We studied these truths together as the Holy Spirit guided us. Herein lies the absolute importance of discipling any new believer with a serious intent.

Based on the truths learned in this chapter, what would you have done differently if you were the author or how would you have responded if you were the recipient?

(Various answers should be shared including yours.)

LEADING THE WAY

In the section, "A Personal Response," the author provides a model you may use for prayer if you find it necessary after discovering the truths in this chapter.

Are you presently attempting to present the gospel of Jesus to someone? If not, are there some among those you may know from the past or on social media who may not know Jesus Christ and may need prayer for an opportunity for you to share with them and open hearts to receive Him?

(Various answers should be shared including yours.)

Based on the truths you have just learned, what will you continue to do in your current evangelistic efforts and what might you do differently?

(Various answers should be shared including yours.)

What additional thoughts would you like to share with the others?

(Various answers should be shared including yours.)

Conclusion to the Personal Study

I received Jesus Christ as Savior and Lord in 1972 on the campus of USC in my second year of college. I immediately became involved in an evangelistic organization on campus. I was seven weeks old in the Lord and was off evangelizing. My three years with these saints included a wide variety of evangelistic activities including sharing Christ with students on campus, taking surveys in the neighborhood, passing out brochures at football games, and even sharing Christ with audience members at the Rose Parade in Pasadena.

As I grew in the Lord, I became a youth director, associate pastor, then a senior pastor and once again participated in a variety of evangelistic activities. These included Christmas caroling, neighborhood barbecues and concerts, evangelism crusades, and sharing evangelistic messages at youth and family camps. As an individual, there was a host of sharing God's good news with those who walked in off the street, on their deathbed, and those considering suicide. I have shared the gospel with many people in my years of counseling as a Christian Pastoral Counselor.

While participating in all of these evangelistic activities, I have read many books on evangelism, participated in many evangelistic training seminars and classes, and have become acquainted with many evangelistic strategies. In most of the evangelistic materials I have read and encountered, I have found a lack of a biblical evangelism framework, an absence of key evangelistic concepts, and the priority of method over doctrine.

In recent years, something new in mainline Christianity has developed. The gospel has changed. Some elements of it have been removed and other elements have been added or reinterpreted. This puts many souls at risk. This has resulted in a large group of so-called Christians who cannot articulate how they received Christ or what it means to be saved. In the past, baptism services involved the many new believers sharing how they became Christians and what their new life in Jesus Christ meant to them. Today, baptism focuses on interesting facts about the new believers and how much impact the church has had on them, rather than Jesus Christ. The good news has become so foggy that people who even mention something positive about Jesus or attend church services is presumed to be saved. No one is allowed to ask about their salvation because it would be judging them.

Another dangerous trend in the church today is the false notion that if you believe Jesus is the Son of God and He is in your heart, then you can believe anything else. Also, you can live any way you like, and you will be saved on the Day of Judgment. This is terribly imaginative thinking, which is not true. It is from the liar of liars, the Devil.

This book is my solution to the great need for this biblical evangelism framework, these critical evangelistic concepts, appropriate applications, and a clear articulation of the true gospel of Jesus Christ. Therefore, all who have had "an encounter with Jesus" or "accepted Jesus as their personal Savior" should set aside everything they have heard, seen, felt, and experienced and peer solely into God's Word. This book clearly explains what the Bible says one must believe and do to be saved for all eternity.

This book concerns the Lord God's design and plan for how He will allow humans into His heaven. The heaven He created. It also discloses what happens to those who reject Him and their eternity in judgment. This includes the fire of hell, the place God originally created for the Devil and his evil demons. This book explains what the Holy Scriptures say concerning His kingdom of priests that was planned in eternity past and has been given as a gift to His Son.

I present to the church of Jesus Christ this simple, clear, and pure teaching of God's Word on evangelism. God, the Father, has given every Christian the amazing privilege and responsibility to share this incredibly good news. May this book excite and incite everyone who reads it to offer eternal life through the gospel to everyone they know and all they encounter. May this book help all who claim to know Christ determine that they are truly His and not a member of some fabrication of the true church with a man-made conception of a false, sentimental Jesus that cannot save them.

As my readers walk among the broken, the disturbed, the afflicted, and the weak, and offer them a glass of water may they also offer them a cup of living water. This will not only quench the thirst of their physical bodies but the eternal thirst of their spiritual souls. For those Christians who walk among the prominent, the famous, the strong, the beautiful, and the capable of this temporal world may they never be fooled by their outward prosperity. It is my hope that my readers will see the true darkness these prosperous ones are in. May they be reminded of the many deaths from overdose and suicides that have resulted when they have achieved all that man can offer and it is simply not enough.

May they offer them a lighted path to eternal life leading away from the dark road to eternal destruction. May every Christian see the unsaved, not as simply wicked but terribly lost and in need of some really good news! May this book about the Book be used even in a small way to be a part of another's journey to our only Savior and Lord Jesus Christ. He is forever and ever our mediator and intercessor before the great and all powerful, ever glorious God, my Father. Amen and Amen.

Instructor's Notes

Conclusion to the Workbook

As we conclude this book, I would like to leave us with some final thoughts about our God of salvation and what His Son did on the cross for us. First, if you read these books and realized that you have never received Christ as Lord and Savior, then I would like to provide that opportunity. If you are ready to receive Him, you can pray this prayer:

Dear God,

> *I want to be a part of your Son's kingdom. I know that all I deserve is judgment for my sin. I am so sorry for what I have done. I believe Jesus is your Son. I know this because he resurrected from the dead. I believe that He died on the cross to pay the penalty for my sin. I believe that He is the only way to heaven. I welcome and receive Him into my life right now as Savior. I turn my life over to Him as Lord and Master. I want a love relationship with Jesus Christ. I thank you for the blessings you are bestowing on me right now. I am grateful for my entrance into heaven which was gained by the faith your Spirit gave me and not by any works. I will do my best to live for you and fulfill the purpose for which I have been created.*

If you prayed that prayer and meant it, then the Holy Spirit has entered you and you are now a child of God. You must find yourself a bible teaching church and begin your adventure. If you reject these truths, God will always be waiting even until the day of your death. Please be warned that once death comes, then comes judgment. In Hebrews 9:27, the author warns all, "In as much as it is appointed for men to die once, and after this, judgment." I leave you with the most well-known verse in the world. It is John 3:16, "For

God so loved the world, that he gave his one and only Son, that whoever believes in him should not perish, but have eternal life." I hope I will see you in heaven!

Second, if you are a believer, you must go out into the world and tell people about the gospel you have just studied. You now have the tools to make a full and clear gospel presentation. Go share the good news of Jesus with the world!

Conclusion to this Manual

In the book of Second Kings a story is recorded describing the reign of a king of Judah named Josiah. Due to Solomon's idolatry and his son Rehoboam's reckless decision-making in God's sovereign judgment, Israel split into two kingdoms. There was the kingdom of Judah which contained the two tribes of Judah and Benjamin and the kingdom of Israel which contained the ten other tribes. First and Second Kings tells the tale of this horrible split and the kings that reigned before Israel was destroyed by the Assyrians and Judah by the Babylonians. Most of the kings were wicked with only a few who were righteous.

One of the righteous ones reigned in Judah whose name was Josiah. He ascended the throne at the tender age of eight. Due to the constant idolatry of God's people over the years, the temple had fallen into disarray, was filled with idols, and was in desperate need of repair. At twenty-six, King Josiah ordered Hilkiah the high priest and Shaphan the scribe to oversee this repair by taking the money which had been deposited by the people in the house of the Lord and use it to clean up and repair the temple.

During this process, Hilkiah made an amazing discovery. In 2 Kings 22:8, the inspired author describes it in these words, "Then Hilkiah the high priest said to Shaphan the scribe, 'I have found the book of the law in the house of the LORD.' And Hilkiah gave the book to Shaphan who read it. Shaphan the scribe came to the king and brought back word to the king and said, 'Your servants have emptied out the money that was found in the house, and have delivered it into the hand of the workmen who have the oversight of the house of the LORD.' Moreover, Shaphan the scribe told the king saying, 'Hilkiah the priest has given me a book.' And

Shaphan read it in the presence of the king. When the king heard the words of the book of the law, he tore his clothes. Then the king commanded Hilkiah the priest, Ahikam the son of Shaphan, Achbor the son of Micaiah, Shaphan the scribe, and Asaiah the king's servant saying, 'Go, inquire of the LORD for me and the people and all Judah concerning the words of this book that has been found, for great is the wrath of the LORD that burns against us, because our fathers have not listened to the words of this book, to do according to all that is written concerning us.'"

Isn't that amazing? God's people had lost the Scriptures. The reading and study of the scriptures had become so unimportant to the lives of the Jewish people that had misplaced their "Bible" and found it in of all places the temple. And notice the result - he discovered that they were not following the ways of God but man's. Some may have even thought they had been following the Lord, but they were not because they were not reading and studying the Word.

Our greatest tool in the living of our Christian lives and serving the Lord as He desires is His Scriptures. The most powerful solutions to solving our problems, dealing with our temptations, and handling our distress are in the Bible. Yet, often times in bible studies, life groups, circle groups, or whenever Christians meet to study the Scriptures, very little of the Scriptures are taught and instead is replaced by the discussion of ideas and opinions that are often filled with human wisdom and even concepts contrary to God's truth. The Bible is often sprinkled in the group study books and questions and taken out of context and portraying even wrong assertions about God's truth. The purpose of my books is to bring the Bible back into the group study of His church. May this instructor's manual help you in this great endeavor.

AN INSTRUCTOR'S MANUAL

ABOUT THE AUTHOR

Dr. Donald Jones is currently a Christian Pastoral Counselor with thirty-eight years of experience in the fields of pastoral ministry, public education, and Christian counseling. He carries degrees and certificates from four major universities and from a variety of educational institutions. He has been a professor of Languages and Bible, a television commentator, and a featured speaker at a variety of events and seminars at churches, schools, and other organizations across the United States. He is a member in good standing of several secular and Christian professional organizations. Dr. Jones has been a published author since 1976. For further information view his website at www.donjonesphd.com.

www.ingramcontent.com/pod-product-compliance
Lightning Source LLC
Chambersburg PA
CBHW020329240426
43665CB00043B/94